FLEET BATTLE AND BLOCKADE

FLEET BATTLE AND BLOCKADE

The French Revolutionary War 1793–1797

Edited by Robert Gardiner

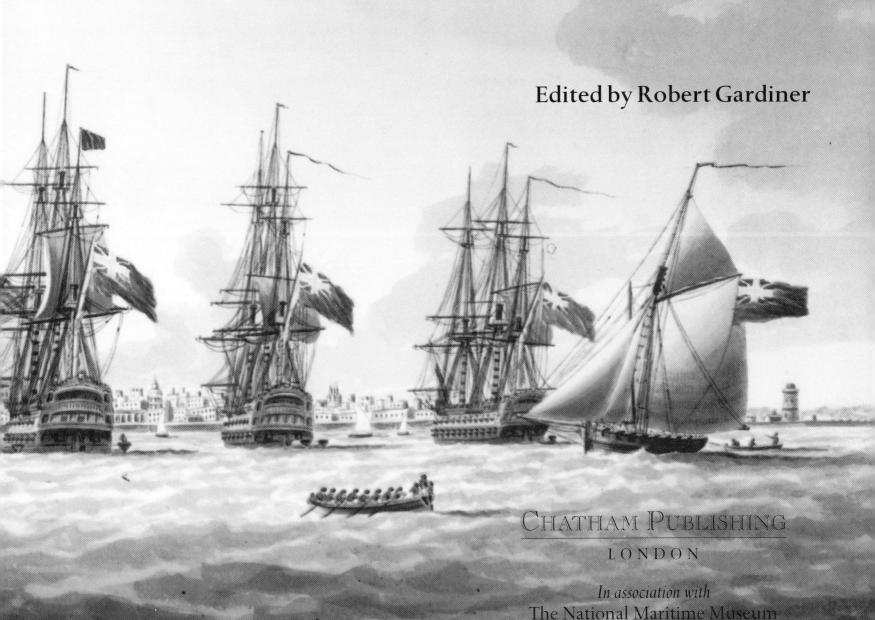

CHATHAM PUBLISHING
LONDON

In association with
The National Maritime Museum

Contributors

FRONTISPIECE
The meaning of close blockade: the Inshore Squadron, under
Nelson's command, off Cadiz in the summer of 1797, water-
colour by Thomas Buttersworth (1768-1842).
NMM neg 3841

Copyright © Chatham Publishing 1996

First published in Great Britain in 1996 by
Chatham Publishing,
1 & 2 Faulkner's Alley,
Cowcross St,
London EC1M 6DD

Chatham Publishing is an imprint of
Gerald Duckworth & Co Ltd

British Library Cataloguing in Publication Data
A catalogue record for this book is available from
the British Library

ISBN 1 86176 018 3

Designed and typeset by Tony Hart, Isle of Wight
Printed and bound in Great Britain by
Butler & Tanner Ltd, Frome

Nicholas Tracy
Introduction
Part I: Home Waters 1793-1795
Part II: War on Trade
Part III: Mediterranean Theatre 1793-1797
Part IV: Ireland and the Channel 1795-1797
Postscript

Stephen Chumbley
The Nootka Sound crisis 1789-1790
The Low Countries 1793
The West Indies 1793-1794
Capture of the Cape 1795
East Indies 1793-1796
The West Indies 1795-1797
The Corsican Campaign 1794
Santa Cruz de Tenerife
The Great Mutinies of 1797

Robert Gardiner
First shots of the naval war
Ships of the Royal Navy: the First Rate
The Glorious First of June: preliminary skirmishes
The Glorious First of June: the battle
A ship of the line in action
The Glorious First of June: aftermath
The Glorious First of June: the prizes
'Dangers of the sea': fire
The Channel Fleet 1794-1795
Bridport's action, 23 June 1795
The Channel frigate squadrons
Ships of the Royal Navy: the 18pdr frigate
Commerce warfare in the West Indies
The cruise of a frigate
Occupation of Toulon
Political tangles
The original Martello tower
Evacuation of Toulon
Ships of the Royal Navy: fireships
Ships of the Royal Navy: flush-decked ship sloops
The Mediterranean Fleet under Hotham
Britain withdraws from the Mediterranean
Battle of Cape St Vincent, 14 February 1797
Nelson's Patent Bridge
The naval officer: recruitment and advancement
Blockade of Cadiz
Close blockade
The Irish Guard
Inshore warfare in the Channel
The Black Legion invades Wales
'Dangers of the sea': grounding
A global war

David Lyon
French naval bases: Brest
French naval bases: Cherbourg
Droits de l'Homme, 13-14 January 1797
The North Sea Squadron
The battle of Camperdown, 11 October 1797
Camperdown: end of the battle

Julian Mannering
Notes on artists

Roger Morriss
London: commercial capital of the world
The naval officer: duties and privileges
The naval officer: life at sea
Portsmouth–key to the Channel

CONTENTS

Thematic pages in italic

PREFACE

THIS IS the second contribution to a new series begun with *Navies and the American Revolution,* and those who are familiar with the earlier volume will have to forgive me for repeating the rationale for the series.

Although the eighteenth century lacked the kind of mass, and instantaneous, media so familiar in the late twentieth, the earlier age was just as interested in news and current affairs. This was largely satisfied by the written word—at increasing chronological distance from the events themselves, newspapers, journals and books. But even in the 1700s, the written medium was not the only source of information. A sophisticated printselling industry evolved, producing relatively cheap, and sometimes tasteless images of a nature that even modern tabloids would eschew, purporting to depict recent happenings of public interest. However, among them were also to be found fine engravings based on the works of well known artists, including remarkably detailed maps and charts of land and sea engagements, which often stand up in point of accuracy to modern research.

In this fashion the public was provided with an image of the great occurrences of the time, and the 'Chatham Pictorial Histories' are intended to recreate this impression in the naval sphere, which for an island nation like Britain was a paramount concern right down to recent decades. Of course, besides the public prints, there were also more formal representations like the oil paintings commissioned by those involved, but by their very nature they are celebratory and, although often the result of the most meticulous research by the artist, they lack immediacy. They are also quite well known, and another of our concerns has been to seek out the less familiar, and in some cases the never previously published, so while we do use some finished paintings, we have preferred the artist's own sketchbooks where available; they reveal not only the lengths the painters went to get details correct, but often cover occurrences that are not otherwise represented, or where the art world has lost track of the finished work.

In the search for original and, if possible, eyewitness depictions, we have also dipped into some of the logs, journals and contemporary manuscripts. Naval officers, in particular, were encouraged to observe closely, and part of the training process involved making sketches of everything from coastal features to life on board. To a lesser extent, this was true of army officers, who were often fine mapmakers—especially those in the technical branches like the engineers and the artillery (today most people in Britain are unaware of why the best official mapping of the country is called the Ordnance Survey).

However, the series was inspired by the Prints and Drawings collection of the National Maritime Museum at Greenwich, on the outskirts of London. Reckoned to comprise 66,000 images, it is a surprisingly under-used resource, despite the fact that an ongoing copying programme has made three-quarters of it available on microfilm. While this forms the core of the series, we have also had recourse to the Admiralty Collection of ship draughts—itself running to about 100,000 plans—as well as some reference to the charts collection in the Navigation Department and logs and personal journals kept by the Manuscripts Department. This last is a very substantial holding with no easy mode of access to any illustrations it may contain, so although some work has been done in this area, it must be said that there is probably far more to discover if only time were available for the task.

The series is intended first and foremost to illustrate the great events of maritime history, and we have made little attempt to pass artistic judgement on any of the images, which were chosen for content rather than style. The pictures are grouped, as far as practical, to show how events were presented at the time. Since this is not primarily a work of art history, for the technical credits we have relied on the Maritime Museum's extant indexing, the product of a massive and long-running documentation programme by many hands with some inevitable inconsistencies, depending on the state of knowledge at the time each item was catalogued. We have reproduced what information there is, only correcting obviously wrong attributions and dates, and quoting the negative number or unique reference number of each illustration for anyone wishing to obtain copies of these from the museum or archive concerned.

Unlike *Navies and the American Revolution,* which was a stand-alone volume, *Fleet Battle and Blockade* is intended to form the first of five titles covering the whole of the period of the great French wars from 1793 to 1815, including America's 'Quasi-War' with France and the conflict with the Barbary states. The series runs chronologically, except that the War of 1812 fills a single volume of its own, and each otherwise covers its period completely. However, the thematic spreads are cumulative in their coverage, because we are keen to illustrate many general aspects of the weapons and warfare of the period which stand outside the chronological structure. Therefore, we devised a single programme of such topics and simply positioned each at an appropriate point in the series. The best example is provided by the many features on individual ship types and their roles, which will add up to a complete analysis of the function of the Navy's order of battle by the end of this five-volume set. Similarly, *Fleet Battle and Blockade* looks at the life of commissioned officers, while later volumes will do the same for warrant officers and seamen; and there will be ongoing picture essays on themes like the perils of the sea, and on individual ports and harbours. This, we believe, avoids predictability and gives every volume variety and additional interest.

Acknowledgements

My intellectual and emotional debts for this volume are much the same as for *Navies and the American Revolution* and I am happy to repeat my thanks.

The project would have been impossible without the co-operation of those at the National Maritime Museum's publications division, initially David Spence and latterly Pieter van der Merwe, who negotiated and set up a workable joint venture. I received generous and friendly advice from Clive Powell on logs and journals and from Brian Thynne on charts, while the staff of the library were endlessly patient with demands for myriads of photocopies and frequent requests to put right snarl-ups in the microfilm readers. Karen Peart organised the crucially important visit to the outstation where the original prints and drawings are stored, and Nick Booth was a tower of strength in hauling out and reshelving more than sixty boxes that I needed to investigate.

However, our greatest thanks must be reserved, as previously, for Chris Gray, Head of Picture Research, who organised and executed the massive programme of photography that we demanded within a very unreasonable timescale. He and David Taylor of the same division remained cool under considerable pressure, coping with whatever was asked of them, and smoothed the path of a vast number of prints through a photographic studio struggling to keep up with an avalanche of work.

Robert Gardiner
London, October 1996

INTRODUCTION

FRENCH intervention in the American Revolutionary War, which had ended in 1782, had been decisive in the achievement of American independence, but the French Treasury had been severely hurt by the expense of the war. The need to obtain national support for new taxes, and the intoxicating example of a people rallying to the cause of 'The Rights of Man', proved to be the catalysts of revolution in France. In May 1789, for the first time since 1614, the Estates General were summoned. The bourgeois 'Third Estate' forced the establishment of a National Assembly in which it could dominate the political process. This moderate constitutional development was rapidly eclipsed by revolutionary activity. In July the Paris mob stormed the Bastille prison, peasant risings during the summer began to drive the aristocracy into exile, in December Admiral d'Albert de Rions, commandant at the naval dockyard at Toulon, was imprisoned by the mob when he tried to deal with mutiny and in July 1790 Louis XVI was forced to agree to a liberal constitution. In June 1791 he attempted to go into exile himself but was stopped before he reached the frontier.

Under pressure from French *emigrés* to intervene in support of royal government and of Louis's Austrian wife Marie-Antoinette, Frederick William II of Prussia and Emperor Leopold II of Austria agreed that they would only do so with the unanimous consent of the powers. This, however, was seen in Paris as a threat. In February 1792 Prussia and Austria allied, and in response, the Assembly forced the King to declare war. During the summer of 1792 constitutional government broke down altogether, and was replaced by the Paris Commune and the extremist Jacobin clubs. In September war was declared against Sardinia, and a French army entered the territory of Savoy. A French squadron under Rear-Admiral Laurent-Jean-François Truguet landed soldiers at Nice, Montalban, Villefranche and Oneglia which was taken by assault.

Confident of an easy victory, Austria and Prussia began military operations against the debilitated French state. However, the weakness of French finances, and the disruption of the institutions of the state by emigration, was soon shown to be offset by revolutionary ardour. Early defeat was followed on 20 September 1792 by a victory over a Prussian army at Valmy in a heavy fog. Although a minor action, it was psychologically important in reviving French military morale.

In September 1792 the French monarchy was abolished, and in November the army, having pushed the Prussians back across the Rhine, occupied Brussels. The Scheldt, which had been closed to navigation for two centuries because it threatened Dutch commerce and the safety of the English south coast, was now opened. In the south, Savoy and Nice were annexed to France. In January 1793 Louis XVI was executed, and the British government under the leadership of William Pitt the younger expelled the French Ambassador, M. Chauvelin, as the representative of a regicide regime. In response, the French National Convention, successor to the Assembly, declared war against Britain, the Netherlands and Spain, and they, with Sardinia, allied with Prussia and Austria in what became known as 'The First Coalition'. In fact, the French had already commenced hostilities against Britain when on 2 January fire had been opened from the Brest batteries at the 16-gun brig *Childers*. Letters of Marque against Spanish shipping had also been issued prior to the declaration of war. The new French Republic had set out to conquer all the powers of Europe, and nearly succeeded.

The *Marine de la Républic Française* entered the war with a strong fleet constructed during the last years of the *ancien régime*, first under Charles-Eugène de La Croix, Marquis de Castries, who was appointed Minister of Marine in October 1780, and then by his successor César-Henri, Comte La Luzerne. According to William James, whose *Naval History of Great Britain 1793-*

1820 was first published in 1822, at the outbreak of war the French fleet possessed eighty-two ships of the line, including three 120-gun ships, five 100-gun ships, ten two-decker 80-gun ships, and sixty-four 74-gun ships. The Atlantic fleet was divided among three dockyards. At Brest was the largest squadron of thirty-nine ships of the line and thirty-four frigates. At Lorient were stationed ten 74-gun ships and six frigates, and at Rochefort another twelve 74-gun ships and the only 64-gun ship in the French Marine, with sixteen frigates. In the Mediterranean based at Toulon were two ships of 120 guns, three 80s, nineteen 74s, and twenty-two frigates.

This numerical strength, however, was a symptom of the underlying weakness of the French state. The ships had been built at a cost which precipitated revolution, not only by its pressure on the central treasury, but also because it became impossible to pay the wages of seamen and dockyard workers. This stimulated local revolt and mutiny in the dockyards. Insolvency was to persist into the war years and precluded the effective supply of ships with sound equipment and adequate provisions. Throughout the war, the fleet was forced to sail under-canvassed because of the weakness of its equipment, and shortage of supplies was to prove operationally disastrous.

The effect of the Revolution on naval discipline and leadership was even more debilitating. The French Marine's command under the *ancien régime* had been divided among the closed naval elite of the *Grand Corps* which provided most of the executive officers, the *Officiers Bleu* who in wartime were transferred from the merchant marine, and the *Officiers de la Plume* who handled the accounts. An inefficient system, efforts had been begun by Castries between 1781 and 1786 to strengthen the professional element in the fleet. These, however, were overtaken by the Revolution. The central concern of the Marine Committee of the Constituent Assembly was not fighting effi-

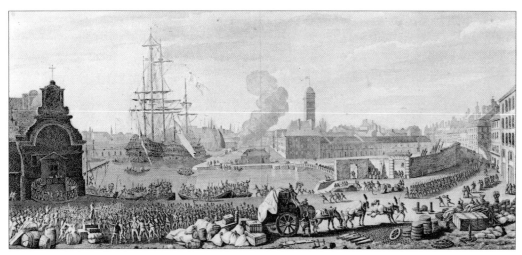

'Port de Brest. Insurrection des vaisseaux de Leopard et l'America en Septembre 1790', etching by Berthault from an original by Prieur. A contemporary French depiction of the Brest mutinies of 1790.   NMM ref PAD1498

ciency, but the need to ensure that the navy did not become an instrument of Royalist reaction. During the 1790 crisis over Spanish eviction of British traders from Nootka Sound on Vancouver Island the Constituent Assembly issued a new code of naval discipline, but when the fleet at Brest mutinied and were support by the municipal authorities, the Assembly agreed to review the provisions of the code. This marked the end of the efforts to reform the navy within the context of an effective Royal administration, and La Luzerne resigned the ministry.

The failure of central government to support the authority of the officer corps led to its disintegration. Officers sought leave, and failed to return, or deserted and went into exile. In 1790 only 40.5 per cent of the 212 officers given leave at Brest ever returned to their duty, and in 1791 only 18.5 per cent of 237 officers. The places of these experienced officers were taken by relatively junior officers or seamen, sometimes drawn from the administrative branch, or from the merchant marine, promoted to high command. The navy was all but paralysed by the assertion of popular sovereignty by the municipalities of Brest and Toulon and by the sailors. The commandant of the dockyard at Toulon, Joseph Marquis de Flotte, struggled to work within the concept of popular sovereignty, but in September 1792 he was dragged from his home and murdered by a Jacobin mob. When the revolutionary government turned to terror in 1793 and 1794 to re-establish authority, the guillotine further reduced the French officer corps. When in April 1794 Admiral d'Estaing, who was too loyal to emi-

grate and favoured moderate reform, was condemned to death for testifying in her defence at the trial of Marie Antoinette, he scornfully exclaimed: 'Send my head to the English: they will pay well for it.'

The army had also, figuratively but also quite literally, been decapitated, but new tactics were eventually developed to make use of the enthusiasm of men fighting for the new social order. The navy was not able to make a similar transformation. It took time for the new men to learn the technical skills of the naval profession, and there was less latitude for the development of new tactics to replace technical skill with *élan*. For that matter, men conscious of their technical limitations, and aware that vocal rabble-rousers, the *pistols*, had gained power over the professionals, showed little if any *élan*. Inevitably, awareness of technical inadequacy, and uncertainty about the social relationships within the navy, undermined morale. Even the professional corps of seamen-gunners was abolished as inconsistent with the revolutionary spirit. The use of army gunners crippled the fleet's armament. The breakdown of discipline, exacerbated by the collapse of the *inscription maritime* which had ensured a fair sharing of the burden of naval duty, extended from topmen who refused to go aloft to craftsmen who produced inferior cordage and sails.

The creative developments in ship design, signalling, and tactics which had occurred in the middle of the century, and had led to unparalleled success during the American Revolutionary War, found no sequel during the war against the 'First Coalition'. Du

Pavillion's system of tabular signals, which had been adopted by the fleet at the beginning of the American Revolutionary War, remained in use throughout the coming struggle. In one respect only was the French Marine more capable than had been that of the *ancien régime*: in 1792 lines of shutter telegraph stations had been constructed connecting the French dockyards with Paris. In clear weather, the naval ministry could pass simple messages to fleet commanders while they were in port or close off-shore in a matter of hours.

The Royal Navy, in contrast, was in good shape. The mobilisations of 1787 in support of William of Orange against the Patriot Party in the Netherlands, and that of the 1790 Nootka Sound crisis, had ensured that needed repairs were undertaken. William Pitt firmly supported Vice-Admiral Sir Charles Middleton, navy Comptroller from 1778 to 1790 and later a member of the Admiralty Board between 1794 and 1795, who built thirty-three new sail of the line. The appointments of Sir William Rule in 1784, and of Sir John Henslow in 1793 as surveyors, led to the building of larger warships than had been British practice. A 74-gun ship ordered in 1785, *Brunswick*, was 176ft long, the largest yet built in Britain. The Netherlands crisis had led to five ships being ordered in 1788, the largest of which was the 110-gun *Ville de Paris,* named after Admiral de Grasse's flagship which had been captured at the Battle of the Saintes. The 98-gun *Dreadnought* and 80-gun *Foudroyant* were each 3ft longer than earlier designs. *Mars* and *Centaur* were each built to *Brunswick*'s dimensions. Another 110-gun ship, *Hibernia*, was ordered in 1790. At the beginning of 1793 there were twenty-six ships of the line in commission, and another eighty-seven laid up 'in ordinary', or under repair. There were also another 191 ships in the fleet too small to take a place in the line of battle. A further twenty-eight ships and fifty-eight smaller vessels were on the list, but were too old for service except as harbour auxiliaries.

The defeats of the American Revolutionary War had stimulated reform. The use of a numerical signalling system, first introduced by Lord Howe on the North American station, had become general in the fleet, and was to be made the official system in 1799. In 1796 the British copied the French shutter telegraph, constructing two chains which joined Dover with London, and London with Portsmouth and Plymouth. Middleton had adopted the administrative plan in 1783 of reserving in the dockyards under each ship's name a large proportion of the imperishable stores needed for service. The result was that in material terms, mobilisation was able to take place faster than in any previous war. At the end of 1793 there were eighty-five ships of the line in commission, and 194 smaller vessels.

During the American War tremendous tactical advantage had been obtained by the extensive use of copper sheathing to stop the fouling of ships' bottoms, with a consequential increase in the effective manoeuvring speed of British fleets. A start had also been made in the introduction into the fleet of short, lighter, carronades which could fire a heavy shot to a range comparable to effective battle range for longer guns. By 1793 coppering was standard in all the major fleets, but the British had an advantage in the introduction of carronades. The standard in 1793 was for a first rate such as *Victory* to have four 32pdr carronades and six 18pdr carronades on her upper works, while 74-gun ships had two 12pdrs on their forecastles and four or six on the poop. Not every ship conformed to these standards, but by early 1796 carronades were being mounted in considerable numbers. Nine 50- and 54-gun ships purchased from the East India Company were armed with a tier of 32pdr carronades on the upper gun deck. Smaller carronades were also being issued for mounting on ships' launches for coastal assault and cutting-out expeditions.

Manning was always a problem, but Britain still had the mercantile resources to support the largest population of seamen in Europe, and the ability to recruit them for the navy, albeit by the rough methods of the press gang. In February and March 1793 a general port embargo was ordered so that no ship could sail until the navy was adequately supplied with men. The political divisions between senior officers which had played an important part in the defeats of the American War were at an end, quieted by the common cause against the Revolution, although in 1795 Middleton was to resign from the Board of Admiralty rather than comply with the First Lord's instruction

to appoint the comparatively junior Rear-Admiral Christian to command in the West Indies. The sympathy which existed between officers and seamen, however, was under stress due to the Revolution, and was to worsen as the fleet expanded to an unprecedented size. The numbers of landsmen in ships' companies increased, amongst whom many were Irishmen whose resentment at the life they found themselves in was strengthened by feelings of nationalism. The unsettling events in France provided an example which led to mutiny in the Mediterranean squadron in November 1794 when the crew of the 98-gun *Windsor Castle* demanded the removal of all their senior officers, including Rear-Admiral Linzee and the boatswain. Vice-Admiral Hotham complied in part, and pardoned the mutineers. In December 1794 the crew of *Culloden* of 74 guns was to mutiny, and barricade itself below decks. After a week of negotiations it surrendered, and five of the ringleaders were court martialled and hanged. Worse was to follow in the spring of 1797 when there was to be a general mutiny of the fleet in home waters.

Because of the numbers of ships in both fleets which were not really fit for sea, and because of the larger size of individual French warships, the discrepancy of force between the British and French battle-lines was not great. William James reckoned that the British line of 115 ships mounting 8718 guns could throw a

total broadside weight of 88,957lbs. Against that the French could in theory bring seventy-six ships with 6002 guns capable of throwing a total broadside weight of 73,957lbs.[1] The reality, however, was that deficiencies in French dockyards and in French discipline prevented the *Marine de la Republic Française* from bringing anything like that force into action.

When war was declared, Lord Chatham was at the Admiralty as First Lord. It was his task, and that of his Board, to put the navy into its war stations. As it had been when the French entered the American Revolutionary War, the first strategic requirements attended to were the convoy of trade, the reinforcement of the small squadron in the West Indies with seven ships of the line under Rear-Admiral Alan Gardner, and the maintenance in the Channel of a fleet able to prevent the enemy at Brest from acting offensively, and ready to send detachments to match any French deployment. To watch the Toulon fleet, a substantial British squadron sailed in four groups in the spring of 1793 to co-operate with the Spanish Admiral Don Juan de Langara based at Minorca. At the outbreak of war, Spain had a total of seventy-six ships of the line of which fifty-six were in commission, and 128 smaller vessels. Command of the British Mediterranean Squadron was given to Vice-Admiral Lord Hood who had acquired a strong reputation during the American war

'Blackwall . . . at the Launch of the Bombay Castle a 74 gun ship, Built at the Expence of the Honorable East India Company and presented by them to his Majesty', aquatint and etching by Robert Dodd (1748-1815) after his own original, published by J & J Boydell, London, 25 March 1789. This was one example of the strenuous efforts made by British naval administrators to rebuild the Royal Navy's strength in the years after the American War, in this case with the added bonus of not being paid for from the Navy's budget. This was a public relations exercise by the East India Company, which was being criticised at the time for exacerbating the Navy's timber shortages by building large Indiamen.   NMM Neg No 2707

1. William James, *Naval History of Great Britain*, London, 1826, Vol 1 p76.

1

The Nootka Sound crisis 1789-1790

THE GOOD condition of the fleet when war with France broke out in 1793 was partly attributable to a major mobilisation of the Royal Navy, occasioned by dispute between Britain and Spain over the seizure by a Spanish squadron of a British settlement and ships in Nootka Sound, Vancouver Island.

A trading post had been established at Nootka Sound in 1788 by the British East India Company to deal in furs for the China trade. A stockade was built and the British flag raised, and the traders built a 40-ton sloop, the *North-West America* (1), the first European ship built on the northwestern coast of Canada. However, since the Treaty of Tordesillas in 1494, the Spanish Crown had laid exclusive claim to the entire Pacific coast of the American continent, and in May 1789 the Viceroy of

2

3

Mexico sent two warships under a Captain Martinez to enforce this right. Four East India Company ships were seized, their crews complaining of rough treatment (2). Captain Colnett, of the *Argonaut*, claimed that his ship was taken by trickery and that Martinez, as was the standard Spanish practice in these situations, treated his captives little better than privateers.

On 11 February 1790, the Spanish envoy in London presented a demand that Spanish sovereignty in the Pacific be recognised and that the British government punish similar activities by its subjects in the future. This was of course totally unacceptable and on 30 April the Cabinet decided to demand redress for Captain Colnett and the others and assert the right of free trade in the Pacific Northwest. To this end, it was also agreed to fit out a naval squadron immediately to back up the claims. This was a large force, comprising twenty-nine ships of the line, nine frigates, two sloops, four cutters and two fire-ships, under the command of Admiral Lord Howe. This mobilisation was also notable for Howe's first issuing of his new system of numerical signals to his fleet, an important step forward in communications in the Royal Navy.

Although both Spain and France made some warlike noises, neither was in a position to oppose British naval power, and furthermore relations between the two old allies were strained because of the Revolution. On 28 October 1790 an agreement was reached whereby Spain would pay reparations for damages suffered, there would be joint rights of trade and settlement (3), and, most importantly, the Spanish abandoned their claims to exclusive rights to the northwestern coast of America. They even permitted freedom of navigation and fisheries in South American waters, although with a ten-mile exclusion zone off their possessions to maintain

their monopoly of trade with them.

This mobilisation (4), together with a second in 1791 owing to a dispute with Russia over Turkey, in which thirty-six ships of the line were fitted out under Vice-Admiral Lord Hood, meant that in 1793 the Royal Navy was in excellent condition and fully prepared to take advantage of the weaknesses of the French Marine.

---

1. 'The Launch of the North West America at Nootka Sound, Being the First vessel that was ever built in that part of the Globe', engraving by R Pollard from an original by C Metz, published by J Walter & Son, London, 16 August 1790.
NMM ref PAD6359

2. 'The Spanish Insult to the British Flag at Nootka Sound' engraved and published by Robert Dodd (1748-1815), London, 21 January 1791.
Beverley R Robinson Collection

3. 'View of Nootka Sound with the Spanish settlement, November 1792', unsigned, attributed to H Humphries.
Peabody Essex Museum, Salem MA neg 24067

4. A royal visit to a three-decker at Portsmouth, about 1790. This is probably part of the fleet mobilised during the Nootka crisis.
NMM ref PAH4084

4

Part I

HOME WATERS 1793–1795

COMMAND OF the British Channel Fleet was given to Admiral Lord Howe who was Britain's most experienced sailor. His interest in signals was but a part of his work on tactics. He sought, through giving his officers a useful degree of independence, to overcome the sterility which was so often the consequence of naval tactics which had become optimised for defensive rather than offensive purposes.

His judgment in operational strategy was more open to question, but was based on solid experience. He did not believe that it was good practice to maintain a close blockade of Brest, especially through the winter, because of the damage which it could be expected that the ships beating off-shore would suffer from the weather. The constant patrol of a close blockade honed seamanship skills to perfection and ensured that the fleet acquired a thorough knowledge of the enemy's home waters, and was demoralising to the enemy penned into its harbour. On the other hand, no close blockade could ever ensure that the enemy could not sail in the falling winds at the end of a gale during which it would have been necessary for the blockading fleet to seek sea room. If the British blockading force suffered damage in the gale and was driven into dockyard for repairs, the French, once out, would be free to pursue their operational goals. Howe, like most eighteenth century admirals, preferred to send frigate patrols to watch the enemy roads as closely as they could, while keeping the ships of the line in harbour. He chose to keep them as far up the Channel as Spithead, where they could most easily be supplied, but from that position he had difficulty reacting to the sailing of French squadrons.

At the beginning of 1793 the French Marine had twelve ships ready for sea at Brest and Lorient, three at Rochefort, and six at Toulon, and fifteen others fitting for sea. In March Vice-Admiral Morard de Galles was persuaded, against his judgment, to take a small squadron

of two 74-gun ships and the 110-gun *Le Républicain*, to sea in the Channel, but the crews proved to be both incapable and unwilling to go aloft when he encountered a severe gale. 'The vaunted ardour which is attributed to them,' he reported, 'consists uniquely in the words of "patriot" and "patriotism" which they repeat ceaselessly, and the acclamations of *"Vive la Nation"*, *"Vive la République"* when they are flattered. Nothing can make them attend to their duties.'[1] In May, after the outbreak of war, he nonetheless received orders to assemble the fleet in the exposed and dangerous waters south of Brittany to prevent the Royal Navy escorting supply ships to support the rebellion which had broken out in the Vendée. These were desperate times. On 23 August 1793, in response to the threat of invasion, a *levée en masse* was ordered of the entire male population of France between the ages of 18 and 25 capable of bearing arms. A few days later, at the invitation of the municipality of Toulon, the British Mediterranean Squadron occupied that port and landed a garrison. News quickly spread to the Brest fleet, and on 13 September the crews obliged their officers to return to port.

In Paris the period known as 'The Terror' had commenced on 2 June when the Convention was purged and parliamentary democracy was brought to an end by the Jacobins, who believed that only a strong revolutionary executive could meet the needs of war. The Committee of Public Safety, dominated by the puritanical figure of Maximilien Robespierre, sent *deputies en mission* through the countryside with powers of life and death to demand absolute obedience with the help of the guillotine. The Committee's expert on naval affairs, Jean-Bon Saint-André, was sent to Brest. 'They say we exercise arbitrary power,' he wrote, 'they accuse us of being despots: Despots! Us! hah! doubtless, if it is despotism which is necessary for the triumph of liberty, this despotism is political regeneration.'[2]

Morard de Galles was relieved of his command, which was given to Rear-Admiral Louis-Thomas, Comte de Villaret-Joyeuse, who was of noble birth but had shown his capacity to control his crew and was politically clean. With a firm ruthlessness characteristic of his Calvinist upbringing, Saint-André brought order to the fleet by issuing a new code of naval discipline along conservative lines and backed with the guillotine. The expression of popular sovereignty by the Brest municipality was even more ruthlessly suppressed.

Saint-André was not able to persuade the Committee of Public Safety that small raiding squadrons should be sent to sea as soon as possible to train ships' crews. With little comprehension of the requirements of naval training and morale, it wanted every ship carefully conserved so that they could be used to support an invasion of the British Isles. Economic collapse in France, however, produced by the revolutionary government's resort to unbacked paper money, the rapidly-depreciating *assignats*, and the failure of the 1793 grain harvest, forced the fleet to sea. On Christmas Day 1793, Rear-Admiral Vanstabel sailed from Brest with two sail of the line and three frigates to escort home from Hampton Roads in Virginia a large convoy of grain ships and the West Indies trade. On its outward voyage it was nearly brought to action with the entire Channel Fleet, which was cruising to the westward, but managed to get clear and complete its voyage to Virginia. It departed again from America on 11 April, and on the same date Rear-Admiral Nielly sailed from Brest with five ships of the line to meet it, and as it happened also to capture most of the British Newfoundland convoy. Finally, Rear-Admiral Villaret-Joyeuse sailed the Brest fleet to bring the convoy safely in. Deputy Saint-André accompanied the fleet to ensure by his

---

1. Quoted in William S Cormack, *Revolution and Political Conflict in the French Navy*, Cambridge, 1995, p219.

2. Ibid, p258.

presence, and by the threat that any captain who failed to carry out his orders would be guillotined, that neither disaffection nor incompetence should imperil the convoy.

The Channel Fleet sailed to try and intercept the convoy, but late on 28 May it ran into Villaret-Joyeuse to leeward of the convoy which was itself out of sight. The French were to windward of the British, in an irregular and reduplicated line abreast. The British were on the starboard tack in two columns, with a detached squadron of four of the line under Rear-Admiral Sir Thomas Pasley to windward. The French began to form an irregular line on the starboard tack. Howe responded by engaging the French rear with his advanced squadron. One of his tactical innovations had been conceived for the purpose of picking off the last ship in a fleeing enemy line by engaging it with each of his ships as they came up, and then circling away. In the rear of the French line was the one of four three-deckers in the French fleet, *Revolutionnaire* of 110 guns, which took a heavy beating and eventually struck to the British *Audacious* of 74 guns. Possession was not secured, however, and during the night she managed to get clear and get away to Brest. The badly-damaged *Audacious* withdrew to Portsmouth.

During this action Howe's advanced squadron had been able to work its way somewhat to windward of the French line, probably because Villaret-Joyeuse had other priorities. He later said that he had been threatened with the guillotine if the convoy were taken. In the circumstances, he proved remarkably effective. Rather than scramble to keep the windward position which in any case the poor sailing qualities of his fleet might have prevented, he concentrated on leading the British away from the track of the convoy.

The next day at 4am Howe ordered his fleet to form line of battle 'as most convenient' on the starboard tack. Villaret-Joyeuse was also on the starboard tack and to windward of the main British force. Howe decided to waste no time in forcing action and ordered his fleet to tack in succession starting from the van. This could have led it through the rear of the enemy line, and would have been very dangerous for the French, but Villaret-Joyeuse responded promptly by tacking his own van to come to the support of his rear. Considering

the disciplinary and training problems the French Marine were suffering from, this was a remarkably efficient operation.

Howe was not to be deflected from his purpose and he ordered his van to tack again, but his leading ships did not immediately respond and it was his own flagship, *Queen Charlotte*, which with two others cut through the French rear. The rest of the British fleet passed to leeward of the French rear and joined the flag.

By this time Howe had gained the windward position, and both fleets had suffered considerable damage from the heavy, if generally fairly long-range, cannonade. Villaret-Joyeuse wore his fleet to bring it back between the British and three of his disabled ships. During the next two days the fleets kept in touch with each other in a heavy fog, and by incredible good luck Neilly's squadron was able to join the French line.

Through the night of the 31st both squadrons took up a westerly course under a heavy press of canvas and then on the morning of 'The Glorious First of June', Howe dressed his line and bore down on the French in a larboard line of bearing. His tactical plan was to prevent them refusing close action by having all his ships steer to cut through the French line, and, having fired a raking broadside into each as it was passed, to engage them from the leeward. To do so, the fleet would have to make a dangerous approach nearly head-on, which Howe probably only risked because the French crews were known to be demoralised. The British captains were sufficiently uncertain about Howe's intentions that only seven of his ships managed to complete the manoeuvre, but Villaret-Joyeuse was not in fact seeking to avoid action. The melée action which followed was hard fought. The crew of the *Queen Charlotte* particularly distinguished themselves. The decisive factor probably was superior British gunnery. One French ship, *Vengeur*, was so severely damaged that it sank, and six were taken as prizes. Nothing like that scale of success outside of a chasing action had been seen since the battles of Barfleur and La Hogue in 1692.

Villaret-Joyeuse managed to reform his line to leeward to protect his damaged ships, and make off back to Brest. The convoy was got safely into Brest, and Villaret-Joyeuse kept his head.

The opportunity to strike a major blow against the revolutionary government in Paris,

such as it was, had been missed. Given the draconian measures being employed to keep the country at war, however, it is unlikely that hunger of itself would have brought the collapse of the revolution. Because the grain convoy reached port safely, its strategic importance can only be guessed at.

The French Marine had unquestionably suffered a grievous blow. Barère, the orator of the Committee of Public Safety, succeeded in obscuring the fact with lying rhetoric, but the reality could not be disguised from the navy itself. By the law of 22 Prairial (10 June 1794), juries were instructed to convict without hearing evidence or argument, and the rate of executions increased to 354 per month. Saint-André had to leave Brest to less effective men because of the need to reconstruct the Toulon fleet after the reoccupation of the port, and his own position became less secure when in July a coup (9 Thermidor) toppled Robespierre. The reign of terror continued into the autumn, but the nation was sickened by the violence and by October it was evident to the fleet at Brest that the guillotine no longer gave meaning to the code of discipline. For the navy, however, the coup was on the whole a positive thing. The Directory, which had taken the reigns of power, represented a bourgeois reaction to popular sovereignty to stabilise the French economy provided a framework within which the navy could be reconstructed along its traditional lines. Less fortunate was its neglect of the needs of the army, which converted it from a national force into a praetorian guard, was to lead to the caesarism which Robespierre had feared.

The dangers of sending ships of the line, especially First Rates, to sea in the middle of winter was confirmed late in December 1794, when the Brest fleet made a sortie intended to cover the departure of squadrons under Rear-Admiral Renaudin to the Mediterranean, another commanded by Rear-Admiral Kerguelen of six sail of the line and eight smaller warships with transports for 6000 soldiers to reinforce the French force at Isle de France (Mauritius), and a third intended to restore the authority of the French government in Saint-Domingue. The poverty of the Brest dockyard had made it impossible to fit the ships properly for sea, and most of them were only provisioned with two weeks' rations. These were contributing factors to the loss of five ships of the line in a severe storm. The incompetence of most of the officers was no less important. In the saner conditions after the overthrow of Robespierre, Villaret-Joyeuse felt able to express his criticisms freely.

The British Channel fleet itself had a close call in February 1795 when a south-eastern storm drove into its anchorage in Torbay. Nine ships of the line parted their cables, but were fortunate enough to bring to with another anchor before driving ashore or into other ships.

Howe, who was sixty-nine at the time of the Glorious First of June, had been so utterly exhausted by the five days of manoeuvre and battle that he collapsed at the end of the action. The victory had been less complete than it might have been because he was unable to keep the deck while Villaret-Joyeuse made off with five ships in tow. Howe spent part of the winter ashore, and soon after the Channel operations of February 1795 relinquished active command of the fleet, although remaining nominal commander-in-chief until 1797. He was succeeded by Admiral Lord Bridport, who himself was sixty-eight. At the Admiralty Lord Spencer had been appointed First Lord in December 1794. These new men continued the policy of distant blockade, and continued to favour Spithead for their fleet station despite the fact that it was too far to leeward.

One of the first tasks undertaken by the Royal Navy in home waters had been the support of the expeditionary force under the Duke of York, which was sent as part of an army under the Prince of Saxe-Coburg to assist the Dutch in resisting the advance of the French army. Against all odds, the French had prevailed, and in January 1795 they had entered Amsterdam. The Dutch fleet, frozen in at the Texel, was captured by cavalry galloping across the ice. When in May the new Batavian Republic declared war on Britain, fifteen ships of the line and thirty smaller ships were added to the forces controlled by the government in Paris.

With its base on the North Sea, the Dutch fleet presented a new strategic challenge to the Royal Navy. Vice-Admiral Duncan was given command of the station, and he used his small force operationally to maintain a close blockade of the Texel, while convoying the Baltic

trade. Pitt obtained the support of a Russian squadron under Vice-Admiral Peter Hanikoff, but it proved to be more of a liability than an asset.

The humiliation of Villaret-Joyeuse's winter sortie was not the end of the grim history of the Brest Fleet. In June 1795 Rear-Admiral Vence was sent with three ships of the line to provide protection for the traffic along the southern coast of Brittany. He fell in with Vice-Admiral the Honourable William Cornwallis with five ships, who gave chase. Vence abandoned his convoy, and ran for the shelter of Belle-Isle. He sent a message overland for support, and Villaret-Joyeuse was ordered to sea with nine of the line. Having collected Vence's squadron, on 16 June Villaret-Joyeuse met Cornwallis who had little choice but to flee. *Bellerophon* and *Brunswick* were sailing badly and by the next morning were in danger of capture. Cornwallis formed his squadron into loose line, which was sometimes reported to be a 'V' formation, with his flagship in the leading position. *Mars*, the last ship in the British line, came under heavy attack, but was saved when Cornwallis brought *Royal Sovereign* and *Triumph* around to engage the leading French ships with such a heavy fire that they sheered off. The frigate *Phaeton* played its part in the action from a position ahead of the British squadron by sending imaginary signals, which gave the impression that it was communicating with the main Channel Fleet just over the horizon. Villaret-Joyeuse felt impelled to abandon the action.

In his official report, Cornwallis remarked that

> it was the greatest pleasure I ever received to see the spirit manifested by the men, who, instead of being cast down at seeing 30 sail of the enemy's ships attacking our little squadron, were in the highest spirits imaginable. I do not mean the *Royal Sovereign* alone: the same spirit was shown in all the ships as they came near me; and although, circumstanced as we were, we had no great reason to complain of the conduct of the enemy, yet our men could not help repeatedly expressing their contempt of them.

A week later it was the British who enjoyed a numerical advantage, which was compounded

by the superior seamanship of the British fleet. Bridport with fourteen ships of the line, of which eight were three-deckers, was providing distant cover for a royalist landing on the Quiberon peninsula when he ran into Villaret-Joyeuse with a squadron of nine ships. In accordance with the current instructions, Villaret-Joyeuse shifted his flag to a frigate, and then set course for Isle de Groix off Lorient. His flight was hampered by the slow sailing of *Alexander*, which had been the reason for her capture from the British the previous year. She and *Redoutable* were put under tow, and he ordered his squadron to form line abreast on them, but his captains ignored the order. The next day when the British were coming into range he ordered the squadron to form line of bearing on *Alexander*, but only *Formidable* and *Tigre* obeyed. Those three ships became heavily engaged and were eventually taken. Doubting whether the remaining ships would put up any sort of fight, Villaret-Joyeuse took them into Lorient.

Bridport did not attempt to blockade them. Because of shortage of supplies, Villaret-Joyeuse sent most of the crews to Brest by land. When the coast was clear, the ships were sailed back to Brest three at a time with the ferry crew returning by road for the next lot, an indication of the shortage of skilled seamen in the French Marine. He made no effort to interfere with the Royalist invasion, but it defeated itself by its divided leadership, and by units of the army of the Republic commanded by the brilliant young General Lazare Hoche.

This was the nadir of the fortunes of the French Marine. Villaret-Joyeuse, complaining about the incompetence of his captains who had lobbied for their positions, and of many of his men, warned that 'patriotism alone cannot handle a ship'. The National Convention responded effectively. A new corps of gunners was established, and the entire officer corps was abolished. Many had to be reappointed, but the most incompetent were weeded out. When in October 1795 the Convention was dissolved, and the Directory assumed executive authority, an admiral of the old navy, Admiral Truguet, was appointed Minister of Marine. The task of rebuilding the French Marine forced it to avoid major encounters in 1796, and the wonder is that it was able to undertake serious operations at the end of the year.

First shots of the naval war

AS THE tension between revolutionary France and Britain increased, at the very end of 1792 the brig *Childers* was sent to reconnoitre Brest, the home of the main French Atlantic fleet. Although war was not declared by France until a month later, on 2 January 1793 the batteries of the Brest forts opened fire on the unwelcome intruder (1). If not seriously damaged, the brig was hit and brought home one of the cannonballs to present to the Admiralty as a sign of aggressive French intent. As such it is often regarded as the first shot in the long naval war that, with one short breathing space, lasted until 1815.

The Royal Navy's small ships were soon embarked on an almost unbroken run of single-ship victories. The first prize was the suitably named privateer *Sans Culotte* (celebrating the revolutionary mob who eschewed the garb of the gentry), taken on 13 March by the brig *Scourge* after a fierce three-hour struggle (2). However, the first frigate action was less satisfactory in its conclusion, since the *Venus* had to abandon her combat with the *Sémillante* (both 12pdr-armed and reasonably well-matched) at the point of victory when another French ship hove into view (3).

Success finally came on 18 June, when the ship which had rescued the *Sémillante*, the 12pdr frigate *Cléopâtre*, was brought to action by *Nymphe*, herself a French prize captured in the previous war and now commanded by

3

4

5

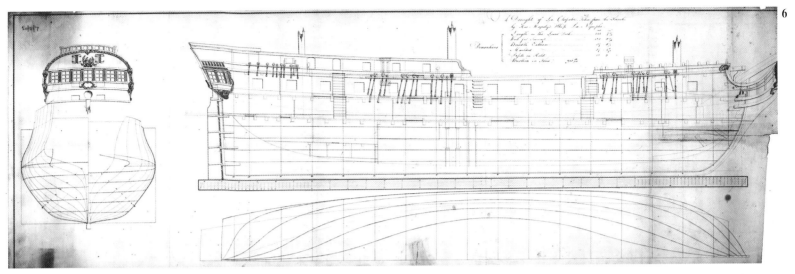

6

7

Edward Pellew (4), who was to become one of the greatest frigate captains of the war. The battle began with a curious exchange of old-world courtesies between the captains, cheering from both ships, and the nailing of a cap of liberty to the main truck of the French ship (just visible in (5)), before the serious business began. Close-range gunnery, a failed French attempt to board, followed by a British counter-attack, carried the *Cléopâtre* in 50 minutes. Because of her carronades, the British ship had slightly greater firepower, but more than offset by a French crew one-third larger. Casualties were high on both sides: 23 killed and 27 British wounded, compared with a total of 63 for the French. The prize was not badly damaged and was bought into British service as the *Oiseau* (6), since the Navy already had a *Cleopatra*.

As the first major naval victor of the war, Pellew could expect to be well rewarded, and indeed he received a knighthood after he was presented to the king. It rapidly became a popular subject for published prints, but they rarely let truth spoil a good story—Pellew did not lead the boarding action, and the hat-raising incident shown in (7) occurred before the ships opened fire; by this stage of the battle Captain Mullon was mortally wounded.

The value of enemy ships taken at sea was divided, on a sliding scale, between officers and crew, and prize money became a major incentive to keep a ship alert and efficient. They were also paid 'gun-and-head money' based on the size of crews of warships captured or destroyed, and in this illustrated scorecard (8) of *Phaeton*'s captures during 1793, the merchantmen are accorded values, but the warships and privateer are listed only by numbers of guns and men. *Phaeton*, commanded by Sir Andrew Snape Douglas, was a big 38-gun frigate and one of the crack Channel cruiser squadrons; she was already ten years old in 1793, but fought right through the war and was not sold until 1827.

1. 'The Batteries of Brest Harbour firing upon HM Brig Childers 1793', watercolour by Nicholas Pocock (1740-1821).
NMM ref PAH9032

2. 'HMS Scourge capturing the Sansculotte, 13 March 1793', oil painting by Lieutenant Thomas Yates (c1760-1796). The *Scourge* carried sixteen 6pdrs and 70 men to the privateer's eight 8pdrs, one 12pdr carronade, and 81 men.
NMM ref BHC0462

3. 'Action between HMS Venus and the Semillante, 27 May 1793', oil painting by Thomas Elliott (fl1790-1800). The 722-ton *Venus* fired a broadside of 222lb and carried 192 men, to her 940-ton opponent's 279lbs and 300 men.
NMM ref BHC0463

4. 'Sir Edward Pellew', stipple engraving by J Chapman, published London, 1 December 1801.
NMM ref PAD3458

5. 'To the Officers and Seamen of His Majesty's Frigate La Nymphe . . . taking Possession of the French Frigate La Cleopatre', coloured aquatint by Robert Dodd (1748-1815), published by the artist and Woodfall & Freeman, London,

undated. It shows the final stage of the action, after the mizzen was shot away and *Cléopâtre* had swung around.
NMM ref PAH7852

6. Sheer draught of *Cléopâtre*, as taken off after capture, 1793. Admiralty Collection.
NMM neg 6074

7. 'An exact Representation of the Boarding and taking the Cleopatre French Frigate by the La Nymphe Capt Sir Edward Pellew', engraving by J Pass from an original by Robert Dodd (1748-1815).
NMM ref PAD5436

8. 'HM 38 gun frigate Phaeton Captain Sir Andrew Snape Douglas. One year's captures. La Prompte 28 gun frigate—180 men. La Blanche corvette 22 guns. Le General Doumourier 22 guns 196 men 2,400,000 dollars: privateer Domen 16 guns 60 men: merchantman St Jago cargo worth £300,000', watercolour by Irwin Bevan; the painting is undated but the events relate to 1793.
NMM ref PAD9479

1

The Low Countries 1793

FOLLOWING THEIR declaration of war against the United Provinces on 1 February 1793, the French army under Dumouriez had advanced from Antwerp on the 16th, taking Breda on the 26th and reaching the Hollands Diep, besieging the fort of Willemstadt, which was situated on a small island some thirty miles from Hellevoetsluys, preliminary to making a crossing. This threat to Holland caused the British government to agree to the Stadtholder's previous request for military assistance, and on 1 March an initial force of

2

1. Dutch gunboats guarding the approaches to Dordrecht, 20 March 1793. Coloured etching by K F Bendorp from an original by M Schouman, published by W Holtrop.
NMM ref PAF4675

2. 'This Print representing the Relief of Williamstadt, in Holland by the British Forces under the command of His RH the Duke of York when besieg'd by the French Army . . . Feb 1793', coloured aquatint by Lewis from an original by J Chessell, published 4 October 1802.
NMM ref

3. 'Dumourier's Army driven from the Siege of Williamstadt by the Dutch Garrison, the English Gunboats and the Syren British frigate commanded by Captain Manley', etching by J Pass from an original by E Godefrey.
NMM ref PAD5428

4. 'Representation of taking and Seizing the French Stores and Garrison of Ostend by a Detachment from Admiral Macbride, March 30th 1793', engraving by J Pass from an original by Jean Baptiste Le Paon.
NMM ref PAD5429

5. 'Troops embarking near Greenwich', oil painting by William Anderson (1757-1837).
NMM ref BHC1805

2000 troops under the command of the Duke of York landed at Hellevoetsluys. Furthermore, Royal Navy crews were sent to man Dutch gunboats, of the type shown in (1), some of which flew British colours, and three of these vessels were instrumental in the first British success of the campaign, the relief of Willemstadt.

On the night of 15 March 1793, a detachment of the crew of HMS *Syren*, 32, lead by Lieutenant John Western, manned three gunboats for an attack on the French batteries besieging Willemstadt (2). Fog and calm conditions enabled the three boats to approach the positions unseen, and brought such an effective fire to bear that the French were forced to abandon their guns. The garrison of the fort took possession of these guns the following morning. Illustration (3) shows a rather dramatised version of the relief, with the *Syren* and gunboats in the background. Unfortunately, Lieutenant Western

was killed a week later whilst attacking another French position, the first British officer casualty of the war.

On 18 March the French army was defeated at Neerwinden by the Austrians under Prince Frederick of Saxe-Coburg, forcing them to abandon the Low Countries. Twelve days later, a squadron from Rear-Admiral John Macbride's command, comprising two frigates, a sloop and the floating battery *Redoubt*, which was armed with twenty large-calibre carronades, successfully co-operated with troops under General Sir Charles Grey in driving the French out of the ports of Ostend and Nieuport, capturing significant quantities of material (4). Ostend became the main port used by the British throughout the Flanders campaign, receiving troops shipped from England (5), until its evacuation in June 1794. Nieuport fell to the French on 16 July 1794, and its garrison, made up largely of French royalists, was massacred by the Republican army.

5

1

Ships of the Royal Navy: the First Rate

FIRST RATES, three-deckers carrying 100 guns or more, were the largest, most powerful and most costly ships to build, maintain and operate, and were probably the most complex industrial constructs of their day. Because they represented such substantial investments, First Rates were built with the greatest care and attention, always in the Royal Dockyards, and using the finest materials. Concern for longevity led to prolonged building times to achieve the most profound seasoning – ten years on the stocks was not unusual.

First Rates were rarely commissioned except in times of war and crisis, so their hulls were not subjected to the continuous stresses of long sea service. They were also maintained carefully while in Ordinary (reserve), and when necessary were treated to extensive repairs, amounting in some cases to major rebuilding. The aggregate effect of this was to endow First Rates with very long lives: as is well known, *Victory* had been afloat for forty years when she fought at Trafalgar, and *Britannia* was three years older. However, *Victory* had been in Dockyard hands for periods of around six months on four occasions between 1771 and 1788 and was substantially reconstructed between February 1800 and April 1803.

There were never many First Rates available, and because of lengthy building times, the substantial pro-

grammes of the 1790s were just bearing fruit when the war came to an end.

Year	No in Sea Service	No in Ordinary or Repairing*
1793	1	4
1796	6	0
1799	4	2
1801	4	2
1805	6	1
1808	4	2
1811	5	2
1814	7	0
1815	0	8

*All warships converted to other uses or in harbour service have been excluded; it lists only ships in active service or available for it.

At first sight it is surprising that the world's largest navy did not have the greatest numbers of First Rates, but in 1793 France could boast five of 110 guns and three even larger 118-gun ships; Spain in 1796 was even better off with ten 112-gun ships and the mighty *Santisima Trinidad*, a nominal four-decker of 136 guns and often regarded as the largest ship afloat, although displacing less than the French giants. These ships were not only larger – the

Commerce de Marseilles measured nearly 2750 tons—but the French ships in particular were more powerfully armed with lower deck 36pdrs (about 40lbs English).

By contrast, the newest ship in the British fleet in 1793 was the *Queen Charlotte* of 2286 tons, carrying thirty 32pdrs on the lower deck, thirty 24pdrs on the middle deck, thirty 12pdrs on the upper deck, plus four 12pdrs and fourteen 32pdr carronades on the forecastle and quarterdeck, and six 18pdr carronades on the poop (1). During the American War the cumbersome 42pdrs had been gradually replaced by the more practical 32s—only the old *Britannia* retained them by the 1790s, earning her the nickname 'Old Ironsides' long before it was applied to USS *Constitution*. The next major step forward was the introduction of the 110-gun class with the *Ville de Paris* (2), ordered in 1788, with thirty ports on each of the lowest two gundecks and thirty-two on the upper (where the calibre was also increased from 12s to 18pdrs); *Hibernia* of 1790 contrived two extra ports per gundeck, and reached 2500 tons. The *Caledonia* of 1794 was the first British 120-gun ship, which mounted thirty-two 32pdrs, thirty-four 24s, thirty-four 18s, and twenty 12s on the quarterdeck and forecastle. The last design of the war was the similar-sized *Nelson* class of identical armament (3, 4, 5). Smaller 100-gun ships came into service in the second half of the war, but there was a tendency to down-rate them to 98-gun Second Rates, the small three-decker being a British speciality with large numbers in the fleet.

In battle the First Rate formed a strongpoint in the line, and since they were almost always flagships inevitably attracted more than their fair share of enemy attention. If possible, three-deckers were opposed to their equivalents, so before the First of June action, for instance, Howe reorganised his line to take account of the French First Rates. French and Spanish admirals sometimes transferred to frigates, arguing that being outside the line gave them a better appreciation of the tactical development of the battle; but British admirals were expected to lead by example, metaphorically at least, although at Trafalgar *Victory* and *Royal Sovereign* led in a very literal sense. As with Howe's *Queen Charlotte* at the Glorious First of June, First Rates were usually in the thick of the action, and could mete out tremendous punishment, not just because of the weight of metal thrown but because of the concentrated firepower of three complete gundecks, which was regarded as a very real tactical and psychological advantage.

The First Rate could also survive very heavy damage—in the opening stages of Trafalgar *Royal Sovereign* was engaged single-handed with the enemy line for fifteen minutes before assistance arrived—and no British ship of this rate was lost to enemy action throughout the eigh-

2

teenth century. Equally, very few were taken from the enemy (although significantly more were destroyed in battle); the first was de Grasse's *Ville de Paris*, captured at the Saintes in 1782 and lost in a gale in the same year. In 1793 the British carried off the huge *Commerce de Marseilles* from Toulon, but she proved so weakly built that she never cruised. Similarly, of the two Spanish three-deckers taken at St Vincent only *San Josef* enjoyed an active career in the Royal Navy—the only prize First Rate to do so.

In terms of deployment, First Rates were almost exclusively reserved for the two main fleets, in the

3

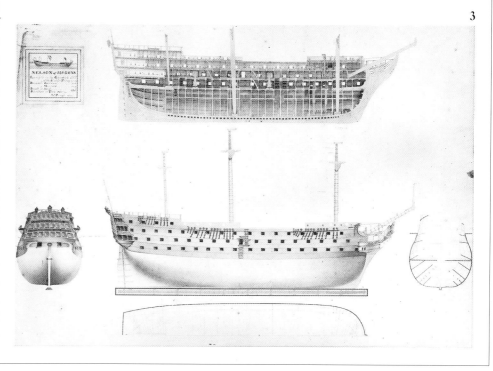

4

1. 'Review at Spithead, 1790, showing
Howe's Queen Charlotte', oil painting
by William Anderson (1757-1837).
NMM ref BHC2260

2. 'The Ship Ville de Paris under full
sail', oil painting by Thomas
Buttersworth (1768-1842).
NMM ref BHC2271

3. Pictorial plan of *Nelson*, 120 guns,
line and wash drawing signed 'Jas.
Pringle, 1811'.
NMM neg X22

4. Representation of the Launching of
the Nelson of 120 guns from His
Majesty's Royal Dock Yard Woolwich
the 4th July 1814 . . . to Charles
Cunningham Esqr, Commissioner of
His Majesty's Yards Deptford and
Woolwich', black and watercolour
pen and ink by James Pringle.
NMM ref PAH5250

5. 'The Howe of 120 Guns, Launched
in the Reign of Geo. III during the
Regency', anonymous engraving
from John Fincham's *A History of Naval
Architecture*, published London, 1851.
NMM ref PAD6112

Channel and Mediterranean, priority depending on the strategic situation. These ships were important assets that were jealously guarded: First Rates were unwieldy to handle, drew anything up to 27ft, and needed a major dockyard close at hand in case of anything but minor damage. During the war attitudes changed—under Lord Howe's regime they were not risked off the French coasts except in the summer months, whereas St Vincent took a more robust attitude to the blockade. However, it is worth pointing out the superior characteristics of the newer ships that supported this policy. *Queen Charlotte*'s lower ports had only 4½ft of freeboard and after the skirmish of 29 May 1794 her lower gundeck was full of water; *Caledonia*, in contrast, managed one foot more, and much of St Vincent's efforts as First Lord of the Admiralty were directed towards greater gunport freeboard for line-of-battle ships.

As an example of changing priorities, when Admiral Bruix's fleet escaped into the Mediterranean from Brest in 1799 three of the four First Rates in commission were sent south, leaving only the *Royal George* in the Channel. Conversely, in 1801 with the threat of imminent invasion from across the Channel, all four First Rates, including the newly commissioned *San Josef*, were at home—in fact, including the Second Rates, Cornwallis could call on fifteen three-deckers! Additions to the fleet thereafter were few: *Hibernia* in 1805 and *Caledonia* in 1809, and a couple of First Rates towards the end of the fighting in Europe. After Trafalgar, First Rates continued in commission in the main fleets, since Napoleon's powers of organisation made the threat of a revival in French naval power seem realistic to many in Britain, but the era of large-scale fleet engagements was over.

5

The Glorious First of June: preliminary skirmishes

FROM THE beginning of the war the Channel Fleet was under the command of Lord Howe (1), Britain's most distinguished admiral and an officer of advanced tactical ideas. Strategically, however, he was no advocate of the close blockade, used so productively in the Seven Years War and again by his successors later in this conflict, believing that it placed undue strains on officers and ships alike.

In the spring of 1794 his fleet put to sea in pursuit of an important French grain convoy from North America and finding the French fleet still in Brest on 5 May it stood out into the Atlantic to interpose itself between the convoy and what would become its covering force. Apart from the convoy's immediate escort, there was also a supporting squadron under Rear-Admiral Neilly, which had itself captured much of a British Newfoundland convoy and its sole escort, the frigate *Castor*. Howe's fleet retook some of these on the 21st which gave him information on the progress of his quarry, and a few days later he was assured of the proximity of the enemy when two French corvettes blundered into his fleet in

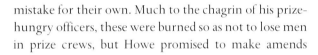

mistake for their own. Much to the chagrin of his prize-hungry officers, these were burned so as not to lose men in prize crews, but Howe promised to make amends

shortly. On 28 May his frigates spotted the enemy fleet, and he was given the chance to honour his promise.

The French fleet was commanded by Admiral Villaret-Joyeuse (2), a man who had been an ageing lieutenant shortly before the Revolution and his rapid elevation to rear-admiral, but he was a solid seaman who had learned his tactical trade under the great Suffren. He later claimed he was under orders to protect the convoy at all costs, on pain of the guillotine, and to keep him on the political straight and narrow the Convention sent him a 'political commissar' in the shape of Jean-Bon Saint-André—a man who seemed to have believed that revolutionary zeal was a substitute for seamanship and gunnery, which translated into an advocacy of boarding actions.

On 28 May the French fleet had the weather gage—it was up-wind of the British so it was difficult for them to get into action, and only Rear-Admiral Pasley's flying squadron of the fastest-sailing two-deckers could reach the rear of the French line. On his own initiative, Captain Vandongen of the huge three-decked *Révolutionnaire*, 110 guns—which as *Le Bretagne* had been d'Orvilliers flagship at another battle off Ushant sixteen years earlier—fell back and was set upon in succession by the 74s *Russell*, *Bellerophon*, *Leviathan*, *Thunderer* and *Audacious*. The French ship was badly damaged, and is supposed to have struck her colours, but a misunderstanding in the twilight between the equally crippled *Audacious* and the *Thunderer* allowed her to escape to Brest, escorted by the 74 *L'Audacieux*. The British *Audacious* was also sent home.

Battle was renewed on the 29th, with Howe attempting to break through the French line from his leeward position. The misbehaviour of his van ship, the 80-gun *Caesar*, spoiled his original plan, but he was able to get his flagship, the 100-gun *Queen Charlotte* (3), and *Bellerophon* and *Leviathan* through the rear of the line, cutting off

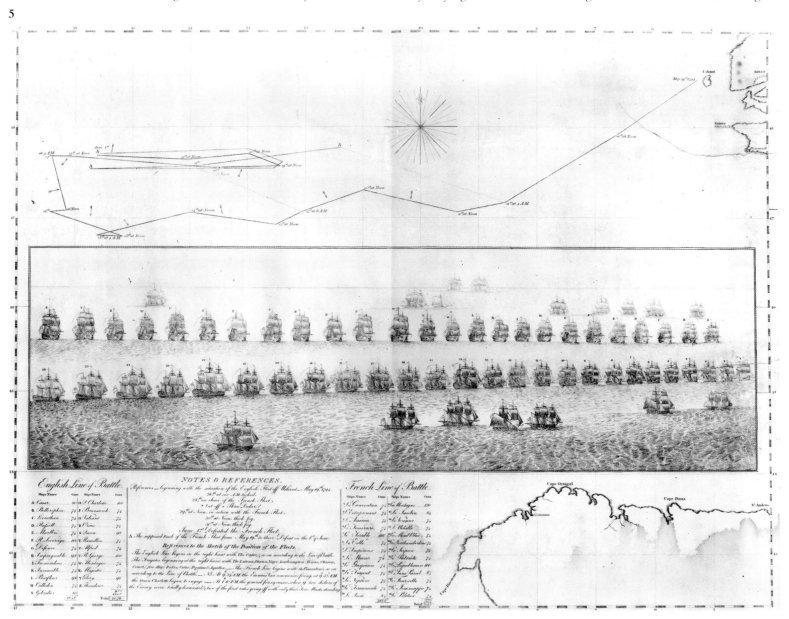

6

three ships. Villaret-Joyeuse put his fleet about, and came down to the rescue of his damaged ships, but at the expense of losing the weather gage (4). About a dozen British ships were seriously engaged, but although some were damaged, none needed dockyard attention; this was not the case in the French fleet, but those detached were replaced by the five ships of Neilly's squadron which were fortunate to find their main force on the following day (5).

As a footnote to the opening moves of the campaign, the *Castor*, 32, which had been captured by *Le Patriote* of Neilly's squadron, was retaken by the frigate *Carysfort*, 28 on the 29th in the Atlantic (6). Some of her original crew were prisoners on board; the remainder, including her captain, Thomas Troubridge, were to be unwilling witnesses of the ensuing fleet battle from on board the French *Sans Pareil*—although Troubridge was to have the satisfaction of striking her colours when she surrendered.

1. Admiral Lord Howe (1726-1799) on the deck of the *Queen Charlotte* during the battle of the Glorious First of June, detail from an oil painting by Mather Brown (1761-1831).
NMM ref BHC2740

2. Admiral Villaret-Joyeuse, French engraving by Forestier after an original by Ambroise Tardieu.
Chatham Collection

3. *Queen Charlotte* in 1800, detail from a coloured aquatint by John Chessell, published 20 April 1803.
NMM neg B256

4. 'To Admiral Earl Howe . . . This View of their gaining the wind of the Enemy's Fleet on the Evening of the 29th of May 1794 which led to their Splendid Victory on the 1st of June following', aquatint from an original by Robert Dodd (1748-1815), published by B B Evans, London, 25 January 1795.
NMM ref PAH7862

5. 'Mercator's chart shewing the Track of Earl Howe's Fleet in pursuit of the French National Fleet from the 19th of May . . . reached within random shot on the 1st of June 1794', brown etching from an original by James Bowen, published by Richard Livesay, Portsmouth, 1794.
NMM ref PAH7861

6. 'Capture of the Castor May 29th 1794', coloured aquatint engraved by Thomas Sutherland from an original by Thomas Whitcombe, published London, 1 June 1816.
NMM ref PAD5476

1

3

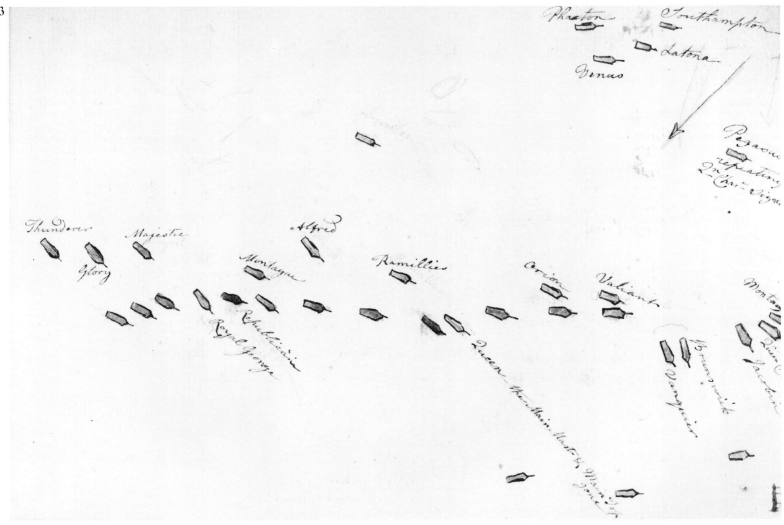

The Glorious First of June: the battle

THE SKIRMISHES of 28-29 May left the British fleet with the initiative. Holding the weather gage, Howe could attack whenever he thought best and the French would have to fight or run the risk of losing stragglers in a chase and, ultimately, the whole convoy. The next days were very foggy, but Howe kept in touch, while Villaret-Joyeuse slowly retired, giving his damaged vessels the opportunity to get away safely, leaving him twenty-six of the line or one more than Howe's fleet. The fog lifted in the middle of the 31st, but Howe held his hand. Captain Troubridge, prisoner aboard the *Sans Pareil*, suffered the mortification of hearing British nerve criticised, but Howe's decision to delay actually revealed his confidence—he was going to win a crushing victory, but needed a whole day to ensure it was complete.

After breakfast on 1 June, the line was carefully formed and signal No 34 was hoisted: '. . . having the wind of the enemy, the Admiral means to pass between the ships in the line for engaging them to leeward.' The fleet approached in a slanting line, called a line of bearing, intending each ship to break through the line and engage from the leeward side, bringing on a melee and preventing any damaged ships escaping. It was risky, since it meant a nearly end-on approach when the British would not be able to return effective fire, but Howe had seen the quality of French gunnery and discipline, and thought it a chance worth taking (1). Unfortunately, not all his captains either understood or

2

Van Division	Center Division	Rear Division
Main	*Mizen*	*Fore*
Cæsar *pasley*	Invincible *Bowyer*	Ramillies
Bellerophon	Barfleur	Bellona x
Leviathan	Theseus x	Alfred
Russel	Gibralter	R. George *Gell. Hood*
Malborough	Q. Charlotte *Lord Howe*	Montague
R. Sovereign	Brunswick	Majestic
Audacious	Valiant	Glory
Defence	Orion	Hector *Montague* x
Impregnable	Queen	Alexander x *Albon*
Tremendous	Ganges x	Thunderer
Culloden	Arrogant x	
Latona	Phaeton	Hebe x
Niger	Southampton	Pallas x
Venus	Pegasus	Comet
	Aquilon	Charon

4

5

between the French ship's stern and the *Jacobin*, which was to leeward and slightly overlapping. According to Codrington, who was a midshipman commanding a division of lower deck guns, the senior officers were so absorbed by this tricky manoeuvre that they forgot to order the batteries to open fire, which Codrington did on his own initiative, blasting both ships as the *Queen Charlotte* squeezed through. On board the frigate *Pegasus* was the marine artist Nicholas Pocock, a practical seaman in earlier life and one of the most meticulously accurate of his new profession. The frigate was detailed to repeat the flagship's signals, so Pocock was accorded the rare privilege of a grandstand view of the engagement, but from quite close in. His sketchbooks contain numerous details, including the ships identifying pendants (2), and a plan of positions at the height of the fighting (3).

Although the flagship received much of the attention in subsequent illustrations, the first ship through the French line was actually the *Defence*, which went into action under topgallants, to the admiration of the whole fleet. She was heavily engaged and totally dismasted, before the huge *Royal Sovereign* came to her rescue. *Defence*'s captain, James Gambier—nicknamed 'Dismal Jimmy' by the lower deck—was a leading evangelical, and his sombre manner made him the butt of jokes, even among his friends. Seeing the shattered state of *Defence* (4) as he sailed past, Captain Packenham of the *Invincible*

agreed, and in the event only *Queen Charlotte*, *Defence*, *Marlborough*, *Royal George*, *Queen* and *Brunswick* obeyed the signal as intended. Nevertheless, the French stood firm and Howe got the full-scale battle he sought.

As was fitting, *Queen Charlotte* made for the opposing flagship, the 120-gun *Montagne*, and forced her way

6

hailed: 'Jemmy, whom the Lord loveth He chasteneth!'

Much of the battle dissolved into almost single-ship engagements, none of which was fiercer fought or more widely celebrated than the duel of the *Brunswick* and *Vengeur* (5). Locked together by their anchors so closely that the *Brunswick* had to blast off her own gunport lids, the two ships pounded one another for about four hours —with the occasional intervention of other vessels— until the *Vengeur* struck her colours just after 2pm. She had been very badly hit between wind and water, and when the time came to secure the prizes she was found to be sinking. Boat crews from *Culloden* and *Alfred* approached to take off survivors, but the ship heeled over and went down rapidly.

The defence of the ship became a famous vehicle of republican propaganda, in which the ship was presented as sinking in action, *tricoleur* still flying, and the crew to a man refusing rescue, going down with the cry '*Vive la République*' on their lips. Many prints were produced supporting this fiction, even by reputable artist like Ozanne, (6) but in fact the captain, his son, and 150 of the crew were picked up. Wooden warship very rarely sank in action, and in truth *Vengeur* had put up a very fine resistance.

Her opponent, *Brunswick* (7), suffered the most severe casualties in the British fleet with 44 dead, including her captain, but by the end of the battle damage was widespread (8).

1

2

A ship of the line in action

ALTHOUGH A gun could be run out and fired in a moment, preparing a ship of the line for a fleet action was a more considered and time-consuming process. The area below decks was cluttered with all the paraphernalia of living, because a warship was a floating castle, equipped to support its garrison as well as for attack and defence. This was particularly true aft, where the officers enjoyed the privacy of cabins made up of canvas-covered timber frames enclosing their own furniture and a few personal effects. All this had to be carefully stowed out of the way—usually in the hold, but sometimes in the ship's boats, which might be streamed astern to lessen the risk of their being shot to splinters in battle.

As a safety measure, the galley fire was extinguished and no hot food would be available for the crew, however long the combat, so Howe's careful scheduling of breakfast before the First of June battle was a considerate gesture—one of many actions that built him the reputation of 'the seaman's friend'. A contemporary watercolour (1) shows the lower gundeck of the *Bellerophon* with guns run out, but the effect of 250 men crowding around the guns is completely lost. The guns, like the vast majority of the British fleet's main armament, were 32pdrs—guns firing solid shot of 32 pounds nominal weight—which were 9ft 6in long and weighing a little less than 3 tons, plus the heavy wooden carriages. They required a crew of ten or twelve, but on the assumption that only one broadside would be in action at once, the ship's complement only allowed the full number to half the guns; if both sides were engaged, then the gun crews were divided, each also manning the gun opposite. A trained crew in the Royal Navy was reckoned to fire three rounds every five minutes, but this could not be maintained for long. The usual tactic of the British, once battle was joined, was to pound the hull of the enemy ship, to dismount guns and disable their crews, and this would usually induce surrender before the ship was ready to sink—indeed the loss of a ship like the *Vengeur* was a very rare event, since they were very strongly built and not liable to much damage below the waterline.

Behind their wooden walls, the lower gundecks were relatively protected—especially as the French were renowned for firing high to disable rigging—but in battle they were still hell on earth. Midshipman Dillon commanded part of the *Defence*'s main battery at First of June, and points out some of the dangers:

The lower deck was at times so completely filled with smoke that we could scarcely distinguish each other,

3

and the guns were so heated that, when fired, they nearly kicked the upper deck beams. The metal became so hot that fearing some accident, we reduced the quantity of powder, allowing also more time to elapse between the loading and firing of them.

At his quarter he had fourteen killed or wounded, but he was lucky not to be stationed on the upper or quarterdeck—which he described as 'dreadfully shattered'—where additional hazards were small-arms fire (on which the French placed heavy emphasis), and spars, blocks and other top-hamper falling from aloft. Officers were expected to stand in exposed positions with the greatest *sang froid* encouraging the men by example (2).

An additional hazard was the prospect of boarding, another tactic in favour with the French. They generally carried larger crews, often took infantry to sea, and were encouraged to believe themselves superior in this regard. Before First of June Saint-André exhorted the French fleet to 'disdain skilful evolution' and 'try those boarding actions in which the Frenchman was always a conqueror, and thus astonish Europe with new prodigies of valour'. A boarding action was a desperate hand-to-hand affair, in which firearms were less use than a long boarding pike, a cutlass or even a hatchet (much used to cut through rigging as well as the opposition). The discipline under fire of marines or soldiers made them very valuable in these circumstances (3), and the captain of the *Audacious* singled out the men of the 69th

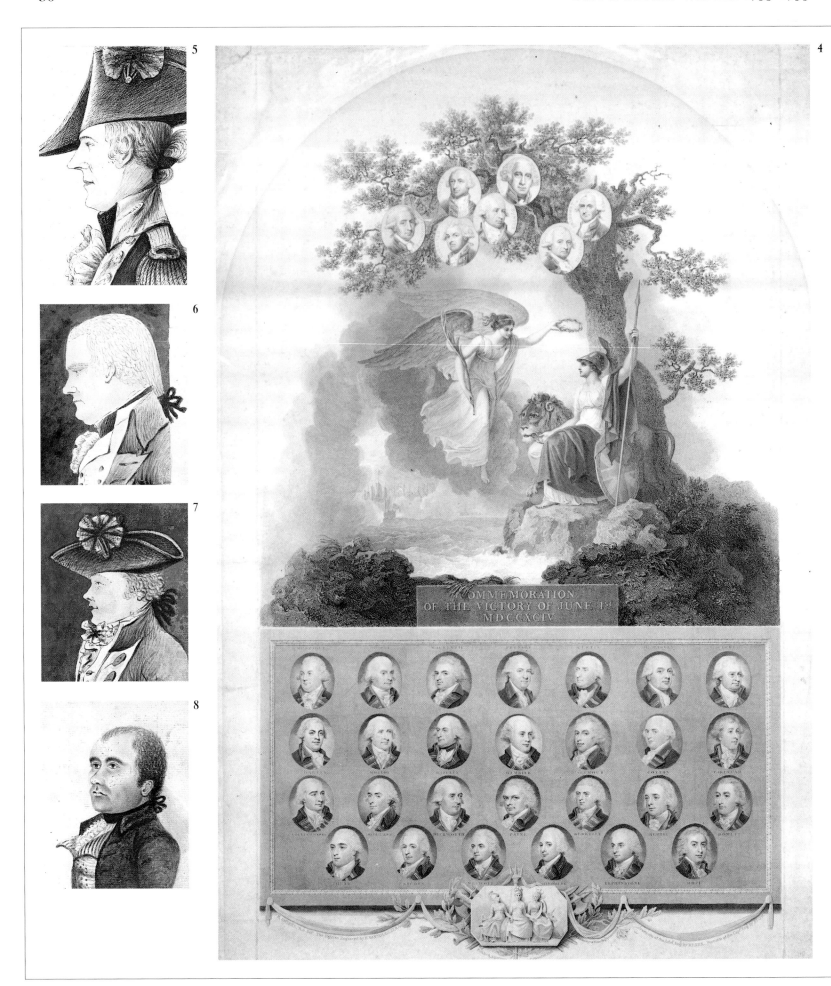

Regiment (serving in lieu of Royal Marines) for special praise for repelling two boarding attempts during the First of June.

Although gunfire was not shared between officers and men in the same proportion as prize money (as the old sailors' prayer would have it), yet there was often a heavy toll among the officers. Two admirals had legs shot off and another was seriously wounded, while the captains of the *Brunswick*, *Queen* and *Montagu* were killed or mortally wounded at the First of June. They had their official commemoration in the hall of fame (4), but more junior officers were often ignored. However, there is an anonymous sketchbook, apparently by a naval officer, that contains a number of portraits of officers engaged at the First of June. They are unsophisticated but apparently from life and some of the titling—'The great Frederick L: *Queen*', for example (5)—suggest familiarity. The *Queen*, with 23 killed and over 50 wounded, was one of the most severely handled during Howe's actions, and fittingly the portfolio contains portraits of some of these otherwise unsung heroes: Mitchell, the master, killed on 29 May (6), and Dawes, the second lieutenant, who died of wounds received on the 1st (7). As well as commissioned officers, the collection also includes Marine officers, a chaplain, and the purser of the *Queen Charlotte*, a Mr Marsh (8).

For those wounded in action, the horrors of the cockpit awaited them (9). Ashore, surgery was crude, with few instruments and minimal anaesthetic and antiseptics, the province of barber-surgeons rather than trained physicians (the reason why surgeons are still called 'Mr' rather than 'Dr'); at sea, it was the same, with the added complication of makeshift arrangements, a pitching and rolling 'surgery', and some hideous wounds for which there were no civilian equivalents. The surgeons and their assistants—called 'loblolly boys'—often worked for days after major battles, Dillon, for example, crediting *Defence*'s assistant surgeon with working twenty-two hours out of twenty-four; but even their best was inadequate. One problem was the insistence on treating patients on a first-come, first-served basis—even Nelson waited his turn—rather than prioritising attention, as is modern surgical practice. As a result, many saveable casualties died from bleeding while hopeless cases took up the surgeon's time.

In medical terms, the Channel Fleet was fortunate in the presence of a hospital ship—another example of Howe's concern for the welfare of his men, although the ship was singularly inauspicious in her name, *Charon* (in Greek mythology the boatman who carried the souls of the dead into the underworld). In attendance was Dr Thomas Trotter (10), the Physician of the Fleet and an expert on seamen's diseases, in particular, scurvy. However, the ship was neither a surgery nor a recovery ward for serious wounds, but was used to isolate cases of infectious diseases which shipboard life was prone to. After the battle, a number of sick prisoners were sent to the ship, the French fleet having more than its fair share of diseases like typhus, and even smallpox, on board, attributed by the scandalised British to the dirty and damp conditions between decks. Hospital ships accompanying fleets were not entirely new, but, possibly due to Howe's influence, they were to become more common during the war.

10

1. 'Gundeck of HMS Bellerophon', watercolour by H Hodgson, no date. *NMM ref PAD6115*

2. 'Shipboard scene of men firing cannons', anonymous graphite drawing, *c*1820. *NMM ref PAD8487*

3. 'Shipboard scene of fighting on deck', anonymous graphite drawing, *c*1820. *NMM ref PAD8485*

4. 'Commemoration of the Victory of June 1st MDCCXCIV (with 34 cameo portraits of admirals and captains)', engraving and etching by F Bartolozzi, John Landseer, Thomas Ryder and James Stowe, from an original by Sir Robert Smirke, published by R Bowyer, London. *NMM ref PAH5661*

5. 'Sketched Portrait of the Great Frederick L of the Queen', anonymous black and watercolour pen and ink. This may be Lawrie, the 6th Lieutenant who was wounded in the engagement, but his christian name was not Frederick, so 'the Great Frederick' may be a nickname. *NMM ref PAH4941*

6. 'Sketched portrait of Mitchell, master of the Queen killed in the battle of the 1st June [*sic*]', anonymous watercolour. Actually killed 29 May. *NMM ref PAH4927*

7. 'Sketched portrait of Dawes of the Queen killed in the battle of the 1st June', anonymous watercolour. *NMM ref PAH4926*

8. 'Sketched portrait of Marsh, Purser of the Queen Charlotte ca. 1794', anonymous blue and grey wash. *NMM ref PAH4888*

9. 'Scene below decks showing man having leg amputated', anonymous graphite drawing, *c*1820. *NMM ref PAD8484*

10. 'Thos. Trotter M.D. Physician to the Grand Fleet', stipple engraving by Daniel Orme Jnr from an original by Daniel Orme, published 1 May 1796. *NMM ref PAD3448*

9

1

The Glorious First of June: aftermath

ALL THE British line had suffered casualties—the official total was 287 killed and 811 wounded, counting the 28-29 May actions—but the French may have suffered as many as 3500 in total, with much the same number made prisoner. Damage to British ships, however, was more localised. Among the most heavily engaged was the *Queen*, 98, which had also suffered on the 29th. She was partially dismasted on the 'Glorious First', and having drifted to leeward at one point found herself facing eleven of the enemy, who were forced to give her rapid and accurate gunfire a wide berth (1). Her casualties were higher than any British ship except the *Brunswick*, but she reached home without external assistance. Another badly damaged three-decker was the 100-gun *Royal George*, which needed assistance after the battle from the frigate *Southampton* (2). She sent

2

over some spare spars which were used to set up a jury foremast.

As the battle drifted to an end during the afternoon, the sea was covered with disabled if not dismasted ships. William Dillon, a midshipman in the *Defence*, counted eighteen British ships with topgallants still across (*ie* not significantly damaged aloft), but there were twelve dismasted French ships in sight, the only British vessels in the same state being *Defence* herself and the *Marlborough*. Despite the fact that French frigates were actively employed recovering some of their dismasted battleships, no order to renew the battle was given; Howe was exhausted and retired to bed, leaving the clearing up to Sir Roger Curtis, the Captain of the Fleet. In the end six prizes were secured, and a seventh sank.

Any disquiet among more active officers was lost in the triumphant return of the victorious fleet to Portsmouth. No matter that the French grain convoy—the principal strategic target—had reached port safely, a morale-boosting victory had been won. Six prizes formed the largest haul of any eighteenth-century sea battle to date, and the King himself came to Portsmouth to greet the victors—an honour never before bestowed (nor ever again). On the quarterdeck of the *Queen Charlotte* the King presented Howe with a magnificent diamond-hilted sword (3), and there followed days of celebration (4). Already an earl, Howe refused any elevation in the peerage, but there were honours for the divisional admirals and a gold medal was struck and presented to officers who were considered to have distinguished themselves. There was some grumbling from those omitted—notably Collingwood, who later refused

3

his St Vincent medal until he received one for First of June—but the only really sour note was the whispering campaign against Molloy of the *Caesar*, who on both 29 May and 1 June had not done his utmost to follow orders. He eventually requested a court-martial a year later, which sentenced him to be dismissed his ship—but too late to dim the public glory of the battle.

4

1. 'Queen 1st June 1794 at noon', grey wash drawing by Robert Cleveley (1747-1809), dated 1794.
NMM ref PAH3968

2. 'The Situation of His Majesty's Ships Royal George . . . and the Marlborough . . . on the Close of the Action of the 1st of June 1794', aquatint published by Thomas Whitewood, 1 July 1796.
NMM neg A7129

3. 'George III presenting a sword to Earl Howe (1726-1799) on board HMS Queen Charlotte, 26 June 1794', oil painting by Henry Perronet Briggs (1792-1844).
NMM ref BHC0476

4. 'George III's Jubilee Review, 25 Oct 1809', watercolour by William Farrington. Although the occasion is different, this gives a colourful representation of how the celebrations during the royal visit would have appeared.
NMM ref PAD5926

1

The Glorious First of June: the prizes

HE SHIPS captured on 1 June made a fine sight
(1) as they were brought into Spithead under
their jury rigs, and once they were laid up in
Portsmouth harbour they became the object of considerable attention from the public in general and artists in
particular—see, for example, de Loutherbourg's sketch-

2

es recently published in Nicholas Tracy's *Nelson's Battles*—
and there were a number of prints published.

The ships were:

Sans Pareil, 80 guns, 2342 tons, launched at Brest in 1793
(2)

Le Juste, 80 guns, 2143 tons, launched at Brest in 1784 (3)

L'América, 74 guns, 1884 tons, launched at Brest in 1788
(3)

L'Achille, 74 guns, 1818 tons, launched at Brest in 1778

Le Northumberland, 1827 tons, launched at Brest in 1779 (4)

L'Impétueux, 74 guns, 1879 tons, launched in 1787 probably
at Brest (4)

As was common practice in the Royal Navy, they were
carefully surveyed—the above figures are calculated
tonnages by the British method—and plans taken off.
Apart from their trophy value, they were of very mixed
utility to their captors. In later years, as a prisoner of the
British, Villaret-Joyeuse dismissed the prizes as 'half a
dozen rotten old hulks', but he was not entirely fair.
L'Achille and *Le Northumberland* (named after a British ship
captured in 1744) were judged not worthy of repair—
there was a strong belief in the royal dockyards that
French ships were too lightly built to withstand the
higher proportion of sea-time required of them in

British service, which meant that they could expect only short active lives (incidentally, it was also believed that Toulon-built ships, where there was access to excellent Adriatic oak, had far greater longevity than those built on the Atlantic coast). Nor was service possible in the case of *L'Impétueux*, which accidentally caught fire on 24 August and burned to the waterline.

The others, however, gave some return to their new masters. *L'América*, according to William Dillon, was surprisingly valuable, having topsides studded with silver dollars, which had been fired into her during the battle by the *Leviathan*, a ship which had acquired some mysterious tins during Hood's occupation of Toulon; they were thought to be canister shot, but actually represented a nobleman's fortune, deposited in the dockyard for safekeeping! On a more serious note, *L'América*, renamed *Impétueux* to replace the ship lost by fire, was not broken up until 1813; *Le Juste* was employed until 1802; and *Sans Pareil*, the most serviceable acquisition, was a popular command for some fifteen years before being reduced to a sheer hulk. However, the ships also had a further use, as models for the hull lines of new ships. Rate for rate, French ships were usually larger than their British equivalents, which gave them the potential advantages of carrying their guns higher and, with a greater waterline length, making them faster. Copying the lines of prizes was a method of circumventing resistance to growth in ship-size within the Navy's administration

3

and dockyards, and was much used in the 1790s. *L'Impétueux*'s lines formed the basis of a class of two ships ordered in 1795 (confusingly named the *Northumberland* class after another First of June prize), while the *Sans Pareil* performed the same function for a new ship as late as 1840. The ships were built to British construction standards and were not crude copies as is so often claimed.

4

1. 'To the Right Honorable John Pitt, Earl of Chatham . . . This representation of the British Fleet . . . Bringing into Spithead the Six French Ships captured on the First of June 1794', aquatint engraved by Birnie and Robert Pollard from an original by Thomas Luny (1759-1837), published by John Jefferys, London. *NMM neg C647*

2. 'French Ship Sans Pareil 3rd Rate, 80 Guns captured at First of June', watercolour attributed to Dominic Serres (c1761-1804), c1800. *NMM ref C837*

3. 'Le Juste and Le America [sic] both captured and added 1 June 1794', aquatint engraved by J Wells after an original by R Livesay, published by R Livesay and J Norman, no date. *NMM neg no 1353*

4. 'Impetueux and Northumberland', coloured aquatint engraved by J Wells after an original by R Livesay, published by R Livesay. *NMM ref PAD8700*

1

'Dangers of the sea': fire

DURING THE whole of the period 1793-1815 the Royal Navy's losses of ships from accidental and natural causes exceeded the figure for enemy action in a ratio of ten to one. In the Naval Prayer these are defined as 'the dangers of the sea' and the 'violence of the enemy', and of the former probably the most feared —although not statistically the most likely—was fire, and the concomitant possibility of explosion. One of the First of June prizes, *L'Impétueux,* accidentally caught fire and was lost before seeing British service.

Wooden ships, crammed with combustible materials like rope, canvas, tar, not to mention gunpowder, were bonfires waiting to be lit—and since ships were illuminated by tallow candles and oil lamps, and food cooked on open galley ranges, potential sources of ignition were all around them. In action, red-hot shot was greatly feared because it might lodge in inaccessible timbers and the fire take hold before it could be located; in practice, however, the difficulties of heating and loading hot shot at sea, although it was tried by the Revolutionary French navy, tended to confine it to coastal batteries. The answer, whether in action or not, lay with prevention rather than cure, and tight discipline surrounded anything to do with naked flame.

The numbers of British warships so lost was not great — eight ships of the line and two smaller between 1793 and 1815—but it afflicted large and important ships out of all proportion, possibly because the bigger the ship the more dark recesses where fire might take hold. The most significant loss during the period covered by this book was the Second Rate *Boyne* of 98 guns, at the time the flagship of that great disciplinarian Sir John Jervis, which caught fire while laying at anchor at Spithead on 1 May 1795. The rest of the fleet sent boats very quickly and all but eleven of her large crew were saved (1), before the ship's loaded guns began to go off, causing casualties and damage all around. Finally the magazine exploded (2), witnessed and graphically described by Captain Brenton:

> The afternoon was perfectly calm and the sky clear: the flames which darted from her in a perpendicular column of great height were terminated by an opaque cloud like a round cap, while the air was filled with fragments of the wreck in every direction, and the stump of the foremast was seen far above the smoke descending into the water.

The cause of the fire was never determined, but one exotic theory was that smouldering cartridges from Marines exercising with muskets on the poop were blown into the admiral's cabin which set alight to his papers.

2

Sudden explosion was less common than one induced by a fire at large, but it did happen. On 22 September 1796, while completing repairs in Plymouth dockyard, the frigate *Amphion* simply blew up (3). She was due to sail the following day and was filled with relatives as well as the crew: some 300 of the 312 on board did not survive, but the captain, Israel Pellew, had a miraculous escape when he was blown through the stern cabin windows, while a visiting captain he was entertaining was killed.

3

1. 'View of His Majesty's Ship Boyne of 98 Guns, on Fire by Accident at Spithead, May 1795', aquatint engraved by J W Edy from an original by Captain T M Waller, published by T Whitwood Jnr, London, 1 July 1797. *NMM ref PAH0753*

2. 'Explosion from His Majesty's Ship Boyne after having burnt to the Water's Edge, and grounded on the Horse Shoal near South Sea Castle', aquatint engraved by J W Edy from an original by Captain T M Waller, published by T Whitwood Jnr, London, 1 July 1797. *NMM ref PAH0752*

3. 'Dreadful Explosion of the Amphion Frigate' anonymous coloured aquatint. *NMM ref PAD5505*

1

The Channel Fleet 1794-1795

THE POLICY of distant blockade—which earned Howe the nickname of 'Lord Torbay' after the fleet's habitual anchorage—allowed small French squadrons to evade or brush aside the watching frigates, and so exposed convoys to attack by forces far stronger than their escorts were ever intended to fend off. One

2

such squadron of five 74s, three frigates and a brig, under the energetic Rear-Admiral Neilly, on the lookout for homeward-bound convoys in November 1794, encountered the British 74s *Canada* and *Alexander* on the 6th returning from convoying the Mediterranean trade to a safe latitude.

The British ships separated and the former escaped, but *Alexander* was a sluggish sailer and was soon overhauled. For two hours she fought off attacks by three of the 74s in succession, until damage to her rigging made escape impossible, and Captain Richard Bligh struck his colours to save further loss of life beyond the 40 killed and wounded already sustained (1). The harsh treatment of the captured crew was the first indication to the British that the era of eighteenth-century civilities was over, and a grim foretaste of the ideological hatreds to come. The capture of a British 74 was a rare event during these wars—only five were lost, four of which were recaptured, compared with eighty-seven French ships of the same rate taken or destroyed by the British. However, the one-sided appearance of the conflict was not apparent in 1794, and what has been called the Royal Navy's 'habit of victory' was not yet established.

Despite the victory of First of June, the Channel Fleet at this time was neither as efficient nor as well motivated as it was to become. The crew of the *Culloden* (2), a ship whose First of June performance was far from glorious, mutinied in December, claiming the ship was unfit for

3

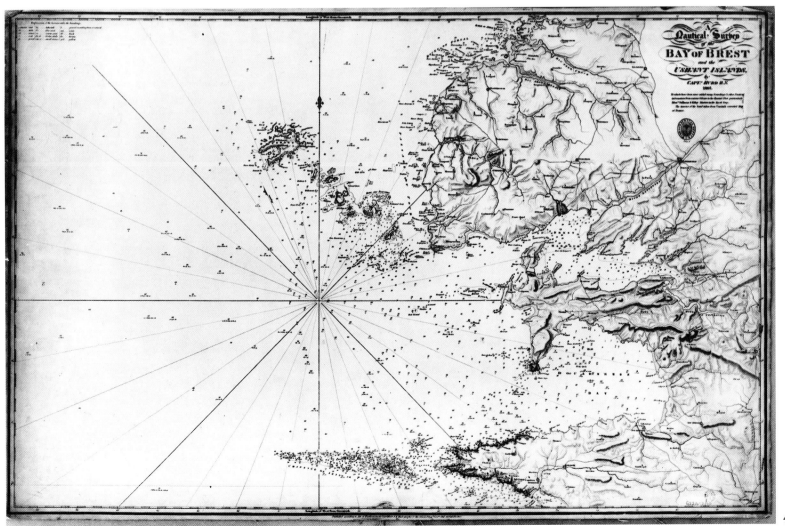

4

6

sea. Admirals Bridport, Cornwallis and Colpoys could not persuade the men to return to duty, but Thomas Pakenham, a popular captain and Irishman like many of the mutineers, did the trick. However, when they surrendered, ten were tried and eight hanged, which the men regarded as a breach of promise, and apparently never forgot. This incident had sinister portents for the future: notes from the mutineers were signed 'a delegate', a word which alarmed the authorities with its overtones of revolutionary committees and one which would surface again with greater menace in 1797. During the Great Mutiny, 'Remember the *Culloden*' became a rallying cry against all those who favoured negotiation.

Despite these travails, the main task of monitoring the activities of the Brest fleet went on. One of the arguments against the close blockade was the constant risk attending a rock-strewn bay that was a lee shore in prevailing winds; it placed almost unbearable stress on ships and men alike (3). The port itself was too far inland to allow observation from the sea, but ships riding in the inner roads could be seen through the narrow channel known as *Le Goulet*, and fleets ready for sea often lay at anchor in Bertheaume Bay to the north or Camaret to the south (4). To make worthwhile reconnaissance required a ship to get in very close, and one of the most audacious was Sir Sidney Smith's incursion in the frigate *Diamond* on 3 January 1795. He possessed a fluent command of French and under the *tricoleur* took his ship right up to the entrance to *Le Goulet* and even spoke to a number of French ships without arousing their suspicions.

This achievement simply underlined the difficulty of blockading Brest. When on station, the British fleet usually cruised off Ushant to give them a safe amount of sea-room, but they needed frigates inside the bay to spot emerging French ships. The frigates could be easily driven off by adverse weather or superior force, whereupon there were a number of exit routes open to a seagoing squadron—the *Passage du Four* to the northwest and the *Passage du Raz* to the southwest being the main ones. In short, it was never possible to prevent the escape of small squadrons in all circumstances, and British detachments were at risk when this happened. One of the most famous of such incidents was the fighting retreat forced on Vice-Admiral Cornwallis's squadron when it encountered a large part of the French fleet on 16 June 1795. His flagship, the 100-gun *Royal Sovereign*, was forced to go to the assistance of one of his four 74s, the *Mars*, which was heavily pressed by advanced units of a fleet comprising one 120-gun ship, eleven 74s, and eleven frigates. After a long chase the French were mislead by one of Cornwallis's frigates, the *Phaeton*, making signals to an imaginary fleet, which when coupled with Cornwallis's confident counter-attack persuaded them that help was at hand. They broke off an action in which all five British ships should have been taken, and 'Cornwallis's Retreat' became as famous as many of the Royal Navy's real victories (5). Cornwallis (6) was well-practiced in the art of withdrawal under fire, having carried out almost a dress-rehearsal against de Ternay in the West Indies in June 1780.

5

Bridport's action, 23 June 1795

3

FOLLOWING ITS failure to capture Cornwallis's squadron, the French fleet under Villaret-Joyeuse found the roles reversed a week later when it ran into the Channel Fleet of two 100-gun First Rates, six 98s, six two-deckers and some frigates. Commanded by Lord Bridport while Howe was recuperating ashore, it was providing cover for the landing of an *emigré* French royalist army in Quiberon Bay escorted by a small squadron under Commodore Warren.

Outnumbered, the French retired, and Bridport sent a flying squadron of *Sans Pareil* (the 80-gun ship captured at First of June), and the 74s *Orion, Colossus, Irresistible, Valiant* and *Russell* in pursuit, but soon ordered the whole fleet in general chase. A day-long hunt developed, but it was

4

5

not until the early hours of the following day, 23 June, that the rear of the French line was seriously engaged (2). Rearmost was the *Alexandre*, no better a sailer now than when captured from the British as the *Alexander* the previous year; she was recaptured along with the *Formidable* and *Tigre*, two new 74s that were added to the Royal Navy, the former as the *Belleisle* (supposedly under the impression that the battle had been fought off that island rather than Isle de Groix).

Much of the damage had been wrought by the flying squadron's *Sans Pareil* and *Irresistible*, plus the surprisingly fleet-footed *Queen Charlotte* (3), although owing her prominence to skilful handling rather than sheer speed. When Bridport's flagship, the *Royal George*, came up about 8am (4), she surprisingly signalled the leading ships to discontinue the action when at least a further handful of French ships were within the fleet's grasp (5). It was a victory, but of a partial kind that would be unsatisfactory within a few years: Jervis and, above all, Nelson would not settle for anything less than annihilating the enemy.

1. 'View of Lord Bridport's action off L'Orient 1795', aquatint published by Bunny & Co, London, 1 April 1799.
NMM ref PAG7059

2. 'Lord Bridport's Action off Port L'Orient June 23rd 1795', coloured aquatint engraved by J Bailey from an original by Thomas Whitcombe (c1752-1824), published 1 May 1816.
NMM ref PAD5492

3. 'An Exact Representation of the Capture of Three Ships of the Line, and Total defeat of the French Fleet, by a Squadron under Command of Admiral Lord Bridport, on the 23 of June 1795', engraving by J Pass from an original by E Godefroy, published 1 October 1795.
NMM ref PAD5494

4. 'Lord Bridport's Action off L'Orient at the Close of the Action in the Centre is seen the Royal George Continuing the Chase the Tigre having Struck her Colours & Bore up appears to the Left on the Right is Formidable & Alexander . . . The Isle de Groix with Port Louis & L'Orient in Distance on the Right', watercolour of the eighteenth century British school.
NMM ref PAD8507

5. 'View of the Close of the Action between the British and French Fleets, off Port L'Orient on the 23rd of June 1795', aquatint engraved by Robert Dodd (1748-1815) from an original by Captain Alexander Becher RN, published by the engraver 12 June 1812.
NMM neg 867

1

2

3

The Channel frigate squadrons

IRRESPECTIVE OF whether the French Brest fleet was subject to close or distant blockade, there was always the possibility of frigates and smaller craft putting to sea from lesser ports, not to mention the usual swarm of privateers. The normal level of convoy escort could cope with the smaller ships, but for the Admiralty, the perceived danger was of squadrons of powerful frigates cruising against trade, and indeed in the early years of the war the French dispatched several raiding groups of this nature.

The British response was to form what were in effect hunting squadrons, composed of the most powerful

4

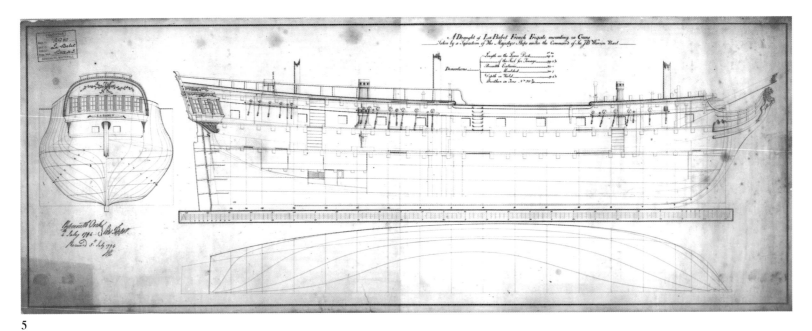

5

frigates and the most competent captains. As a stream of new 18pdr-armed ships came into service in the 1790s, they were assigned to these squadrons, which at one time or another included many of the officers who were to become the Royal Navy's best-known frigate captains – Sir John Borlase Warren of the *Flora*, 36; Sir Edward Pellew of the *Arethusa*, 38; Sidney Smith of *Diamond*, 38; Sir Edmund Nagle of the *Artois*, 38; Sir Andrew Snape Douglas of the *Phaeton*, 38; Sir Richard Strachan of the *Concorde*, 36; and Richard Goodwin Keats of the *Galatea*, 32, to name but a few. In 1796 the Channel cruisers comprised three 24pdr, seventeen 18pdr and only five 12pdr

ships, the cream of the British frigate force. The number of prizes, both privateers and national cruisers, taken by these squadrons in the early war years is a tribute to their effectiveness.

One of the first to make a name for himself was Sir James Saumarez, knighted for capture of the *Réunion* by the *Crescent* on 20 October 1793. This, one of the first victories of the war, was hard-fought, and became a popular subject for the print industry, among the most detailed being those by Robert Dodd (1, 2). Saumarez, a Guernseyman by birth, was given command of a small squadron operating off the Channel Islands, and in a

6

7

smart little defensive action in June 1794 demonstrated his tactical skill against a far superior French force. He was in company with the *Druid*, 32 and the *Eurydice*, one of the notoriously slow-sailing small post ships of 24 guns (3). Being reluctant to sacrifice her, Saumarez's two ships fought off two big cut-down 74s (called *rasées* by the French), two 36-gun frigates and a brig, plus some small craft. Once the *Eurydice* was safely away, the two British ships made for Guernsey, but so closely pursued that Saumarez had to change course and run down the line of the French squadron to further distract their

attention (4). He then took his ship into Guernsey Road through a rock-strewn channel never previously used by a large warship.

The French *rasées* constituted a particular worry, and the British responded by cutting down three fast-sailing 64s, the *Indefatigable*, *Anson* and *Magnanime*, all of which had 24pdr main batteries, but the French also built limited numbers of very large frigates with 24pdrs. In theory there was nothing in the Royal Navy to match them, but the practical answer seemed to be the frigate squadron. The most successful of these in the first years

8

9

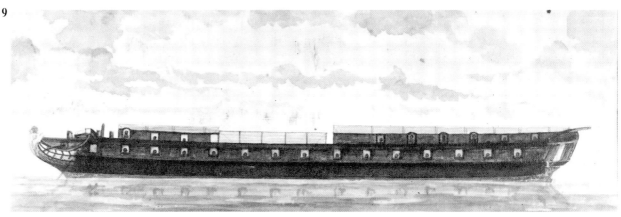

1. 'His Majesty's Ship Crescent attacking the French Frigate La Reunion . . . on the 20th October 1793', aquatint and etching, published by Robert Dodd, London, 20 January 1794.
NMM ref PAH7844

2. 'The Submission of the French Frigate La Reunion to His Majesty's Frigate Crescent', aquatint and etching, published by Robert Dodd, London, 20 January 1794.
NMM ref PAH7845

3. 'Sir James Saumarez in the Crescent and Capt. Ellison in Druid engaging a French Squadron of superior force, to cover the escape of the Eurydice Capt. Cole, June 8th 1794', aquatint engraved by William Westall, published by Richard Bentley, 1838.
NMM ref PAD5477

4. 'Captain Ellison's Action off Guernsey with an Enemy's Squadron', aquatint engraved by Richards from an original by John Theophilus Lee, published by Joyce Gold, London, 31 March 1808.
NMM ref PAD5478

5. Sheer draught of *Babet* taken off after capture. Admiralty Collection.
NMM neg 2980-45

6. 'Capture of La Pomone, L'Engageante & La Babet April 23rd 1794', coloured aquatint engraved by Thomas Sutherland from an original by Thomas Whitcombe, 1 July 1816.
NMM ref PAD5471

7. 'View of Falmouth & Sir John Borlase Warren's Prizes entering the Harbour', aquatint engraved by Thomas Medland from an original by Nicholas Pocock, published by Bunny & Gold, 1 July 1816.
NMM ref PAD5470

8. Model of the *Revolutionnaire* as captured 1799, apparently contemporary.
NMM neg 9874

9. 'Revolutionnaire 1799', anonymous watercolour.
NMM ref PAF5793

10. *Flora* and *Arethusa* driving ashore two French corvettes, watercolour attributed to Joseph Gear (1768-1853). Although undated, it almost certainly represents the action with the *Espion* and *Alert*, 7 August 1794.
Peabody Essex Museum, Salem MA neg 15300

of war was that commanded by Sir John Borlase Warren, and he was destined to take the first French 24pdr ship to fall into British hands, in a well-handled squadron action on 23 April 1794. With the 18pdr frigates *Flora*, *Arethusa* and *Melampus*, and the 12pdr-armed *Concorde* and *Nymphe*, he fought and captured the *Pomone* (with a main battery of twenty-six 24pdrs), the 12pdr *Engageante* and the 20-gun *Babet* (5); only the *Résolue*, 36 escaped (6). Along with other prizes taken on Warren's cruise, the squadron made a fine sight as it came into Falmouth harbour (7). At nearly 160ft length on the gundeck and 1239 tons the *Pomone* was a particularly valuable prize, and the British laid down a ship on her lines called the *Endymion* whose excellent sailing qualities made her a favourite for over thirty years.

The 24pdr ships were few in number, but France also experimented with very large 18pdr-armed frigates. These rarely had the opportunity to prove themselves, so close was the British control of the Channel and its approaches. The brand-new *Révolutionnaire* of 1148 tons, for example, was barely a week out of Le Havre when on 21 October she ran into a squadron comprising *Arethusa*, *Artois*, *Diamond* and *Galatea*; *Artois* was the best sailer and got into action first, but the French ship only surrendered as the other frigates came up. She was another very large frigate, and caused considerable interest in the Royal Navy. Besides the lines being taken off in the time-honoured fashion, a fine model survives (one of the very few models of a named French prize in the official Admiralty style, (8) and there is also a naïve watercolour of the ship as captured (9). Years later in 1802 a frigate was ordered to her lines, but the keel was moved from one yard to another and the *Forte*, as she was named, was not launched until 1814, by which time her size was not unusual.

Warren's squadron operated close in to the French coast, so that even small warships were denied freedom of movement. One example was the pursuit of a small detachment of a frigate and two corvettes in August 1794, the latter being chased ashore and boarded right under the defending batteries in Audierne Bay, just outside Brest, by the *Flora* and *Arethusa* (10).

Ships of the Royal Navy: the 18pdr frigate

1

THE FRIGATE as understood at this period was defined as a ship with a single gundeck, quarterdeck and forecastle, but with a complete, unarmed lower deck (appropriately termed the 'berth deck' in the US Navy, since it accommodated the crew). This lower deck was important because it gave frigates much greater freeboard for their single main battery—often 7ft or more in British ships—which meant that they could use their guns in all weathers, unlike two-deckers which might have to close the lower deck ports in stormy conditions. The most famous scenario of this kind was the *Indefatigable*'s harrying to destruction the French 74 *Droits de l'Homme* during a January gale in 1797.

To use a modern analogy, the heavy cruiser of the 1790s was a frigate of between 32 and 40 guns armed with 18pdrs on the main deck. They had been introduced by the British in 1778, at a time during the American War when the Royal Navy's traditional numerical superiority was under threat, in an attempt to counter larger numbers with more individual firepower. The resulting *Minerva* class 38s, with main batteries of twenty-eight guns, and the 36s of the *Flora* and *Perseverance* classes, with

1. A stern view of a frigate, showing rigging, including studding sails. Anonymous grey pen and ink and wash drawing. Although the ship is unidentified, it may be said to represent the general appearance of the main run of frigates of the 1790s. *NMM ref PAF5789*

2

2. 'Frégate Anglaise en panne', Plate 29 from *Collection des Toutes les Especes de Batiments* drawn and engraved by J J Baugean, 3rd edition, Paris, 1826. Although unidentified, the ship's disposition of gunports marks her out as a 36, and most probably one of the numerous *Apollo* class. *NMM ref PAD7405*

3. 'The *Pomone*, Captain Robert Barrie RN', coloured lithograph by T G Dutton (c1819-1891) after an original by G F St John, published by Day & Sons, London, no date. The ship was the second of the standard *Leda* class and an exact sister of Philip Broke's famous *Shannon*, having been built in the same yard in the previous year, 1805. *NMM neg 5666*

4. A pictorial plan of *Lively* at ⅛th of an inch to the foot scale; one of a pair with the 120-gun *Nelson*. The drawing depicts the latest and largest standard class of 38 by the closing years of the Napoleonic War. *NMM neg X1976*

5. '*Bacchante* off Deptford 1811', an anonymous watercolour. One of the last of the *Lively* class, the ship was only launched in November 1811, so must depict the ship fitting out. *NMM ref PAH0785*

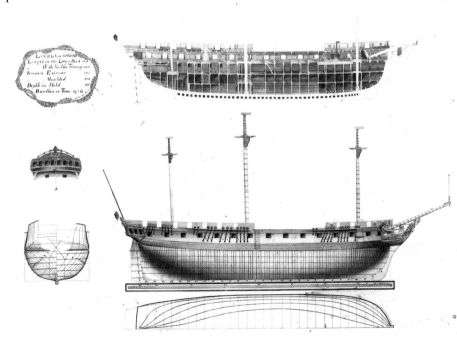

two less, were very powerful cruisers and for some years they had no equivalent in the navies of the main naval powers, a superiority enhanced by the addition of carronades to the 9pdr long guns on their upperworks. However, like so many British ships, they were found to be too small for their batteries, and as a result when new classes of 36s and 38s were ordered in the 1790s (1) there was a move towards increasing the space between the guns. At the time there was also a wider concern that French ships seemed faster under sail, and this was considered to be a result of the relatively short hull favoured by British designers for strength and manoeuvrability. Therefore, the ships tended to get proportionately longer, but Lord Spencer's administration promoted significantly larger ships (as it was simultaneously doing with ships of the line).

For frigates the new policy manifested itself in a rapid increase in absolute size, frequent design changes, with many 'one-off' and experimental hull forms, and a shift in proportions towards longer and shallower hulls. French designs became the focus of concerted attention for the first time since the 1760s, and a number of prizes were 'copied'—although their structure and layout followed British practice, which required far more robust and better-appointed ships suitable for very long range cruising. Armament was considerably augmented at the same time by the gradual adoption of 32pdr carronades for the upperworks, leaving only two or four 9pdr chase guns, giving a total of forty-six to a nominal 38-gun frigate. As part of the drive towards bigger frigates, two vessels (*Acasta* and *Lavinia*) were ordered with thirty 18pdrs and rated as 40-gun ships, but later designs preferred the greater space allowed by twenty-eight gunports and a pair of bridle ports for occasional use with chase guns.

The new heavy frigates were a high priority in the 1790s and their numbers increased rapidly from both new construction and numerous prizes:

Year	No in Sea Service	No in Ordinary or Repairing
1793	11	6
1795	36	0
1797	45	2
1799	46	4
1801	68	1
1804	57	7
1808	76	15
1812	98	9
1814	103	11

Such was the speed of change under Spencer that no standard 38 or 36 had emerged by the time St Vincent

took over as First Lord in February 1801. The new administration, believing the Peace of Amiens would last, dedicated itself to retrenchment and dockyard reform. What few orders were placed followed St Vincent's stated belief that ships had become unnecessarily large, and reverted to older and smaller designs, including a return to the original 36-gun 18pdr of 1778.

Although the 1790s had established the 36 and 38 as the current norm for frigates, there were a few smaller 18pdr ships rated as 32s. The early 800-ton ships were an attempt to build a minimal 18pdr ship and the rapid leap to 900 tons pointed to their inadequacy. The main difference from 36s was the quarterdeck and forecastle armament of 6pdrs and 24pdr carronades, giving the nominal 32 a total of 40 guns.

The nature of the conflict changed after Trafalgar, particularly once the introduction of the Continental System and the economic blockade made it a war of attrition. Numbers became even more important, while after a decade or more of almost uninterrupted success against all comers technical improvement in ship design seemed less of an issue. As a result, frigate building was confined to large numbers of standard designs—as with the 'Surveyors' class' 74s or the *Cruizer* class brigs. However, for frigates the designs were well-proven and all dated from the 1790s: the chosen 36 was the *Apollo* (2), the medium 150ft 38 the *Leda* (3), and the large 154ft 38 the *Lively* (4, 5). The *Leda* was based on the French *Hébé*, captured as far back as 1782, but still employed as a hull form by the French Navy so not outclassed; the other two were designs by Sir William Rule and were fine all-round ships. These were the only frigates ordered between 1806 and the outbreak of the War of 1812. Even then, although larger 24pdr ships were designed, the existing classes continued to be built. In fact, a fir-built 'austerity' variant of the *Apollo* called the *Scamander* class and a fir-built of version the *Leda* formed the backbone of the war emergency programme.

Part II

WAR ON TRADE

VILLARET-JOYEUSE'S gallant defence of the grain convoy at the battle of 'The Glorious First of June' put an end to the British attempt to starve France into submission. Experience in earlier wars had made it apparent that the difficulties involved in stopping the flow of supplies to France were generally too great to be overcome. Only where it was possible to focus blockade effort on a cargo such as the heavy timbers, tar and hemp from the Baltic, which were used in shipbuilding and maintenance, and which had to be carried by sea to a few clearly identified destinations, was a tight blockade operationally practicable. The typical commercial blockade of the eighteenth century was a relatively open *guerre de course* intended as much to enrich the captors as to undermine the credit of the French government. These operations obtained their results through their cumulative effects. Most effective were those directed at reducing the flow of trade goods from the West Indies which, when re-exported to European markets, accounted in 1787 for 34.7 per cent of French export trade.

The total contribution of West Indian commerce to the French economy was probably 20 per cent, and it was at least as important that it employed 25 per cent of French mercantile tonnage, and 20 per cent of seamen registered for the *Inscription Maritime*. These proportions made the French West Indian trade a major consideration in the competition for naval power. In reply to a question put by a Commons committee in 1790, Admiral Lord Rodney said he was 'fully convinced that had it not been for the French West Indian commerce, that nation could not have been in a condition to dispute with Great Britain the empire of the ocean in the last war.'[1] The Chairman of the Committee on Colonies in the French National Assembly, Barnave, declared much the same thing that same year, that 'almost all our navigation at this time is the direct or indirect result of the possession of our colonies. From that I conclude that if we abandoned them we would lose

the means to form and occupy during peace the number of seamen necessary to sustain our naval forces in war.'[2]

The possibility of disrupting the French war effort by injuring French trade, however, was less important than was the profit which might be made by British interests, and which could help pay the expense of Britain's war effort. Britain's West Indian commerce contributed 10 per cent of her larger trading economy, and British investment in the West Indies generated 7 per cent to 10 per cent of Britain's annual income. Capture of Saint-Domingue, for instance, could more than compensate Britain for the loss of the American colonies.

In the mid-eighteenth century, advanced economic theorists in Britain had began to call in question the entire mercantilist system. In 1776 Adam Smith published *The Wealth of Nations* which attacked the idea that states should seek to monopolise wealth. Only wealthy states, he argued, had the capacity to be good markets. The growing awareness of the value of free trade, however, did not immediately lead to an end of the great mercantilist trade war. In 1786

William Eden negotiated a lower level of tariffs with France which encouraged trade, but French manufacturers objected that freer trade benefited the more advanced British industry, and the Eden tariffs became one of the grievances in the French Revolution. The wars of the French Revolution and Empire were fought with unswerving mercantilist purpose, and with mercantilist means. French strategy was as much mercantilist as was that of Britain, although the French had more reason to hope that Britain could be driven out of the war through attacks on its trade.

Hope that Britain could be driven to seek peace by undermining her mercantile prosperity had been fed by grave doubts felt in the most respectable banking quarters about the stability of the British economy. To a Frenchman, that economy seemed to be fundamentally unsound because it lacked the strong agricultural base which France enjoyed. The British national debt, which in 1775 had been £124 million, was £230 million in 1793. At the time of the Peace of Amiens in 1802 it was to be no less than £507 million, which was only £80

'Shipping Sugar, Antigua', coloured lithograph engraved by Thomas Goldsworth Dutton from an original by W S Andrews, printed by Day & Sons. Sugar was one of the crops that made the West Indies central to the economies of the European powers and ensured that it became a major theatre of fighting in any war. NMM ref PAH2989

million less than it was to be in 1914. It appeared to be inevitable that a campaign against British trade would lead to the failure of Britain's international credit. No less an authority than Adam Smith had drawn attention to the vulnerability of Britain through trade war by demonstrating that it had been exports of manufactured goods, not of bullion, which paid for the Seven Years War.

In contrast to France and Britain, Spain was a relatively easy target for naval action against trade. Spanish credit depended upon the flow of silver from the mines of Peru, and the annual Spanish treasure convoys were always an important object of war. However, the fact that the naval officers who succeeded in capturing a Spanish treasure ship could become immensely wealthy may have been more important than any other strategic rationale in ensuring that naval resources were devoted to that purpose.

Squadron action against French convoys from the Indies, privateer attacks on individual merchant ships, and combined operations to seize control of the islands where the sugar crops were grown, were all part of the navy's action against French trade. The French islands at the outbreak of war were in a state of turmoil because of the revolution, with its promise of *liberté* and *égalité*, which with differing interpretations were demanded by the poor whites, mulattos and black slaves. The need to arrest the spread of these dangerous doctrines in order to preserve intact the economies of the British islands, as well as the hope to acquire valuable new colonies, had made operations in the West Indies a priority at the outbreak of war. Vice-Admiral Laforey, who commanded the small British squadron at Barbados, carried a force of soldiers under Major-General Cuyler to recapture the island of Tobago which had been lost to the French in the American War. The fort at Scarborough was carried by storm, and the island capitulated. Rear-Admiral Gardner, who had been hurried out to the West Indies with seven of the line and two regiments of foot under Major Bruce, was less successful in an effort to bring Martinique to declare for the royalists. They were forced to evacuate the royalist insurgents who would certainly have been put to death. The commander of the Jamaica station, Commodore John Ford, was luckier when he

responded to the requests from French colonists in Saint-Domingue for protection from the republicans. The mulattos had revolted, and commissioners from the National Assembly, hoping to strengthen their hand against the forces of colonial independence, had proclaimed the emancipation of the black slaves at the end of August 1793. Dreadful cruelties were committed by the warring factions, and the *Grandes Blancs*, the leading white planters, welcomed the British as protectors. One of the best harbours in the islands, St Nicholas Mole, protected from the sea by a strongly-sited battery, was thus closed to enemy privateers. In Newfoundland waters, the French fishery island of St Pierre was captured by a small force out of Halifax.

The British did not reinforce their establishment in the West Indies until the spring of 1794 when Vice-Admiral Sir John Jervis and Lieutenant-General Sir Charles Grey were sent to capture Martinique, St Lucia, and Guadeloupe. Martinique was taken in March 1794 after a successful combined operation in which sailors moved heavy guns up prodigious heights to bring fire on enemy positions. St Lucia resisted briefly but its defences were taken by storm and the island capitulated on 4 April. On 12 April the post at Fleur d'Epée on Guadeloupe was stormed by soldiers and seamen who had to climb a steep hill under fire and charge the walls with pike and bayonet. The other posts on Guadaloupe capitulated without further resistance.

The decision was then made to send the soldiers not required for garrisoning the captured islands, reinforced by four regiments from Ireland which had arrived at the end of the season, to secure the position on Saint-Domingue which had begun to deteriorate after the initial, but incomplete, success. This proved less fortunate, perhaps because Grey and Jervis were so interested in plunder that they directed operations against Port-au-Prince, where merchant shipping had taken refuge, rather than the militarily more important post of Cap Françoise on the north coast or the republican strongholds at Les Cayes and Jacmel on the south coast. The plundering throughout the captured islands was so comprehensive that the French colonists began to reconsider their hostility to the French republic.

The absence of a large part of the British

force in Saint-Domingue had disastrous consequences when a small force of two frigates and transports, which had been able to get out of Brest because of Howe's decision to keep the Channel Fleet at Spithead, arrived at Guadaloupe. By the time Jervis and Grey learned of the development, the French had recovered Point-à-Pitre and moved their ships into harbour behind the guns of the batteries. They were able to depend on local support, of which Commissioner Victor Hugues made certain by carrying the Reign of Terror to the colony. The decimation of the British army by yellow fever eventually forced it to evacuate the island on 10 December 1794. When Hugues had secured his reconquest, Paris sent out reinforcements with which he recaptured St Lucia, and stirred up revolt throughout the other British-held islands.

British cruisers attacked French commerce, and employed 'the Rule of War of 1756' to justify the seizure and condemnation of neutral American ships carrying cargoes for the French, which French navigation regulations would not have permitted them to carry in peacetime. It was legally impossible, however, to stop Americans carrying French cargoes to American ports and then reloading them into American ships bound for neutral European harbours, or to intercept Americans trading between neutral ports, but Jervis's captains transgressed on these distinctions to such an extent that the United States embargoed the shipment of provisions to the British islands, and Grey had to deploy troops to meet an expected American act of war. When the Admiralty courts in the islands refused to condemn half of the captures, Grey and Jervis established new, more compliant, but unauthorised courts.

Unlike all earlier wars in the eighteenth century, with the exception of the end of the War of the Austrian Succession, the British government forbade the provision of insurance by the British market to enemy ship owners. The Traitorous Correspondence Act was

---

1. Great Britain, House of Commons, *Sessional Papers*, 'Reports and Papers 1790. Slave Trade,' 177, 183. See: Michael Duffy, *Soldiers, Sugar, and Seapower. The British Expeditions to the West Indies and the War against Revolutionary France*, Oxford: Clarendon Press, 1987, pp5-33.

2. *Procès-verbal de l'Assemblé National*, xiv (Paris, 1790) no. 223, 9-11.

far from being an obvious measure, because traditionally British mercantilist objectives had been furthered by forcing the enemy to pay exorbitant war risk premiums, but generally it was obeyed. The revolution had changed the nature of the public attitude to war, vastly increasing the stakes.

French efforts to protect their trade had begun soon after the outbreak of war, when a small French squadron of three ships of the line had sailed under Rear-Admiral Sercey to the West Indies, where it joined another ship which had sailed out previously. Because of the threat to the French islands, the usual convoy to France was diverted to Virginia, where in the spring of 1794 it joined the grain convoy to Brest. Sercey's squadron had returned to Brest late in 1793.

In strategic terms, the injury which was done to French re-export business by the cruisers, and by the island campaigns, was cancelled out by the French Treasury which exacted levies on the countries conquered by French armies. The retention by their commanding generals of the specie they seized, and its use to relieve the suffering of the soldiers, helped to turn the national army into an instrument which the generals could use to establish their political power. Edmund Burke's prediction was to prove correct, that the war would be 'long and dangerous,…the most dangerous we were ever engaged in.'

In the East Indies fighting had commenced as early as November 1791. Cornwallis, then a commodore, used force to stop and search a French frigate believed to be carrying supplies to Tipu Sahib. Tipu, the Sultan of Mysore, was carrying on the policy of his father, Hyder Ali, in violent opposition to the British East India Company. News of the declaration of war in 1793 reached the British at Calcutta promptly because Mr Baldwin, consul at Alexandria, sent a message overland. French posts in India were immediately occupied. That at Pondicherry, which was the only real fortress in French India, was subjected to a heavy bombardment at the end of July, and capitulated.

A small squadron under Commodore Peter Rainier sailed from home waters for Madras to protect British trade. To ensure that the French were not able to use the leverage provided by Dutch colonial assets in Africa and Asia, Pitt decided to send squadrons under Sir George

Elphinstone, Lord Keith, and Commodore Blankett to land troops under General James Craig at Cape Town. The settlement was occupied in June 1795 with little resistance, and was used as a base for blockade of the French post at Isle de France (Mauritius), but Rainier did not have enough force to contain the aggressive efforts of the French. In August 1795, however, he was able to seize the Dutch post at Trincomalee, which was the only safe harbour in the Bay of Bengal. The same month another force under Captain Newcome captured Malacca on the southwest coast of the Malayan peninsula, and in early 1796 Rainier occupied Amboyna in the Moluccas, and Banda, from the Dutch. These conquests ensured that Britain would retain control of the trade from Asia, although they could not prevent privateers out of Isle de France raiding British shipping. A strong squadron was stationed at Cape Town to prevent any French effort at reconquest.

In response to the French recapture of Guadeloupe, in late 1795 a force of eight ships of the line under Rear-Admiral Christian, with 137 transports and support vessels carrying 16,000 soldiers under General Abercrombie, was ordered to sail from Portsmouth to the West Indies. In total, 30,818 soldiers, virtually half of the active British army, was sent out to the West Indies between December 1795 and March 1796. Christian's convoy encountered a severe Channel storm and was forced to return to Portsmouth. A second attempt to sail in December was similarly prevented, and it was not until April and May 1796 that the force was to reach the islands. It was thereby condemned to go on service in the rainy season.

The wastage of British manpower in the islands due to disease was so great that 40,000 died and a like number were left unfit for service. No provision had been made to move the soldiers to a healthier climate during the sickly season, and planter opposition to copying the French use of black soldiers held back that development until 1797, when the government was reduced to purchasing the cargoes of slave ships in order to fill the ranks. As an offensive measure, the island campaign was hardly cost-effective.

General Abercrombie and Rear-Admiral Christian overcame stiff resistance to recapture St Lucia, and the revolts in St Vincent and Grenada were suppressed. The Dutch colonies

were also occupied without resistance. When it became possible for them to turn their attention to Saint-Domingue however, their forces were so reduced that it was impossible to achieve anything. In any event, the revolution and war had so profoundly affected the plantation economy that possession of Saint-Domingue could have done little to improve Britain's financial position. The ceding of Santo Domingo by Spain to France in June 1795, as part of the peace settlement by which Spain left the First Coalition, widened the scope of the island conflict but added nothing to Britain's advantage. Although St Nicholas Mole was held until 1798, its hinterland was difficult to defend. The enfranchised blacks and mulattos found a leader in Toussaint l'Ouverture who proved himself a military genius.

The warfare in the Windward and Leeward islands did serve to prevent any serious attempt by the French to act offensively against Jamaica, although a revolt amongst the Maroons had to be suppressed at great expense.

Guadeloupe remained a threat to British commerce in the islands, but the entry of Spain into the war on the side of France in 1796 diverted attention to the easier prospect of seizing her possessions. Spanish privateers were no less of a threat than were those of France, so the capture of Spanish islands served a defensive as well as a mercantilist purpose. In February 1797 General Abercrombie received the surrender of Trinidad with little resistance, and three Spanish ships of the line were destroyed by their own crews in the harbour. They mustered little more than half of their proper complement, and had been quite unable to force their way out of harbour. An attempt on Puerto Rico, on the other hand, showed that that island was too strongly held to be similarly taken.

French squadron attacks on British shipping had only got under way when the difficulties of equipping the battlefleet needed to guard against invasion had been met. Political attention was focused on the question of Britain's vulnerability to blockade of food supplies in 1795, when there was a poor harvest that reduced yields by 20-25 per cent. However, Britain weathered that crisis. French resources were not well suited for an attempt to deny Britain access to supplies, and in fact that was never the focus of French strategy. In October

1795 Rear-Admiral Joseph de Richery, with three ships of the line and six frigates, which had with great difficulty been fitted out at Toulon, attacked a Smyrna convoy. *Censeur* of 74 guns, which had been captured from the French in the Mediterranean in March, was re-taken, and thirty of the sixty-three merchant-men were captured. Rather than continuing across the Atlantic as planned, he retired into Cadiz with his prizes and spent the rest of the winter finding buyers for them. Eighteen ships were taken out of the Jamaica convoy by a squadron of French frigates, forty prizes were taken off the Madeiras, and during the summer of 1796 Richery at last proceeded on his mission. He repeated Neilly's 1794 success, and destroyed over 100 fishing vessels from the Newfoundland fleet, and burned fishing stations along the Newfoundland coast.

The weakness of the French battlefleet encouraged a return to Marshal Vauban's early eighteenth century operational strategy of exploiting the predatory instincts and skills of the French maritime community to conduct a *guerre de course* against British shipping. The commerce raiding of the French Marine was seconded by the efforts of French privateers. Their number never reached that which had been seen in the wars of the early eighteenth century, however, and in the early years of the Revolutionary War the *guerre de course* was motivated primarily by the need to obtain badly needed trade goods for the domestic market, especially cargoes of food. From the British perspective, the depredations of the small luggers in the Channel working out of Boulogne, Calais, Dunkirk and ports in the Netherlands were especially dangerous.

The abolition of the *assignats* in 1796, which enabled merchants to return to an undepreciated metallic currency, restored enough confidence that there was an increase in the number of privateers fitted out. The French islands in the West Indies, and from 1796 the Spanish islands, became nests of privateers. In Guadeloupe, Commissioner Hughes all but abandoned his efforts to recover French colonies because his attentions were diverted to the profits he could make as a privateer. Indian Ocean trade came under attack from privateers based on Isle de France (Mauritius). The most successful was Robert Surcouf who early in 1796 took up a position off the Hooghli river

'*View of Bridgetown and part of Carlisle Bay in the Island of Barbadoes*', watercolour by Edward Pelham Brenton. This illustration by a serving naval officer – who also became a historian of the war – shows the main assembly point for the rich convoys whose protection was such an important function of the naval forces in the region. NMM ref PAF8416

and even used a captured pilot brig to tempt his prey within range. In 1797 British commerce was to suffer its worst losses.

The Royal Navy convoyed overseas trade, and trade to the Baltic. In 1792 there had been 1495 clearances from British ports on the long-distance trades, all of which required convoy except for a relatively few fast ships which sailed as independents: 878 clearances were issued for voyages to southern Europe, and 3101 to northern European ports. There were at the outbreak of war about 5500 British ships in foreign trade, and these made on average about one and a half return voyages to southern European ports each year, two to Baltic and Scandinavian ports, and three or four a year to the Netherlands. To protect ships sailing independently on coastal voyages, cruisers were deployed to attack French privateers. It was notoriously difficult to find the privateersmen, however, who were more familiar with the British coast than were the sort of unenterprising junior officers who tended to be put in command of small craft. The fact that the Channel Fleet did not maintain a close blockade of Brest during the early years of the war reduced the difficulty for French privateersmen in getting their prizes safely home. Some recaptures were made, however, by British privateersmen earning 'prize salvage' from shipowners.

Abercrombie's failure to secure Saint-Domingue had put an end to the ability of Pitt's administration to finance the war on credit. Government stocks were being offered for sale at 48 per cent of par. Lord Malmsbury was twice sent to negotiate peace with France, but the Directory sent him away because Britain's position appeared to be so desperate that France

need make no concessions for peace. The writing appeared to be on the wall when in 1797 the Bank Restricting Act released the Bank of England from its obligation to redeem paper currency. The mutinies in the Channel and North Sea appeared to be the final blow, although the Channel Fleet mutineers made it clear that they would sail if it was necessary to do so to escort home a convoy. To Frenchmen, the evils of paper currency were all too obvious. Precarious credit, and blockade of a narrow range of manufactures, were expected to put many of Britain's 'over-specialised' labour out of work, and thus lead to revolution.

In fact, Pitt was able to weather the storm by the introduction of income tax which raised national revenue adequate to pay for the war, provided liabilities in the West Indies were abandoned. Lieutenant-General John Simcoe conduced a brilliant campaign in Saint-Domingue in early 1797, but the government had already decided that the island should be evacuated. Carefully playing off the hostile factions against each other, the island was handed over to Toussaint and his army of former slaves. The privateer war had diverted some naval resources to trade protection, and there was dislocation of commercial patterns. British shipowners and insurers, however, retained their capacity to make compensations for marine war risk. The losses of ships to privateers throughout the war probably did not exceed 2½ per cent of the volume of trade. The British Treasury strengthened as the war progressed and was able to subsidise the military efforts of each successive coalition formed by Pitt, and later by Addington, to confront first the Revolution, and then Napoleon's Empire.

The West Indies 1793-1794

THE WAR in the West Indies began with the recapture of the island of Tobago from the French in April 1793. The commander of the Barbados station, Vice-Admiral Sir John Laforey, sailed from Bridgetown on 12 April with his flagship *Trusty*, 50, the 18-gun sloop *Nautilus*, the armed schooner *Hind* and the merchant ship *Hero*, carrying 470 troops under the command of Major-General Cuyler, arriving in Great Courland Bay, Tobago on the 14th. The troops were landed that night and the fort at Scarborough, held by Lieutenant-Colonel Monteil, the commandant of the island, and approximately 200 men, was ordered to sur-

3

render. This being refused, the British troops stormed the fort at 1am on 15 April, with minimal casualties to themselves (1). As was common in assaults on fortifications, particularly at night, the soldiers of the 9th and 60th regiments attacked with the bayonet alone, to prevent the assault breaking down as men stopped to return the defenders' fire.

A later attempt by Laforey's successor at Barbados, Rear-Admiral Gardner, to take Martinique was a failure. The decision of the French Assembly in 1791 to grant citizenship to the slaves on the French West Indian islands had provoked a state of virtual civil war on many of them, with French colonists declaring for the royalist cause and seeking British help and protection. Gardner arrived with his squadron at Martinique on 14 June 1793, accompanied by a French 74, the *Calypso* and the frigate *Ferme* which had declared for the royalists, and landed 1100 British troops and some 800 royalists, intending to march overland and attack the French forts at St Pierre on the 18th. However, the royalist contingent accidentally fired upon one another during the approach, and fell back to the landing site, forcing the British troops to

do likewise, as they now believed themselves outnumbered by the Republican defenders. By the 21st the whole force had re-embarked, and as many of the Royalist inhabitants of the island as possible were evacuated to spare them from reprisals.

In September, Commodore John Ford's Jamaica squadron, which comprised only his flagship *Europa*, 50, a few 12pdr frigates and some smaller vessels, achieved far greater success at Saint-Domingue. Having been approached by a representative of royalist sympathisers at Jérémie offering terms for the town's capitulation to the British, Ford's squadron arrived on 19 September and was warmly welcomed by the inhabitants of the town. Hearing that the republicans intended to take the fine harbour of St Nicholas Mole (2), Ford proceeded there on the 21st to forestall this. The town, with its strong defences, agreed to the same terms as Jérémie, its inhabitants fearful of the reprisals the republicans and the liberated slaves would take. By the end of the year, other areas of the island had likewise surrendered to the British.

The arrival of Vice-Admiral Sir John Jervis on the

4

Barbados station at the end of January 1794 ushered in a highly active campaign against French possessions in the West Indies. On 2 February 1794, a squadron consisting of Jervis's flagship *Boyne*, 98, two 74s, two 64s, eight frigates, four sloops and the bomb vessel *Vesuvius*, sailed from Bridgetown carrying 7000 soldiers under Lieutenant-General Sir Charles Grey for an attack upon Martinique, arriving off the island three days later.

Landing were made in three locations, to prevent the defenders concentrating their forces, and by 16 March the whole island except for Forts Bourbon and Royal had fallen to the British. Throughout this campaign, sailors from the squadron were highly active on shore, principally in the establishment and manning of batteries of guns and mortars for the attack on the French fortifications, where their ability to get guns into positions thought inaccessible both by the enemy and their military colleagues caused great astonishment. They also took part in the assaults on the various French positions on the island, storming them with boarding pikes and pistols (3).

On 17 March the batteries established by the navy opened fire on the French forts defending the town of Fort Royal, and an attempt was made by the boats of the squadron to cut out the French frigate *Bienvenue*, moored in the harbour. The ship was taken, despite heavy fire from the shore, but could not be sailed out of the harbour and had to be abandoned. However, the success of this attack decided the British to make an immediate attack upon Fort Royal (4), combining a seaborne assault against the town and its principal fortification, Fort Louis, with a land attack against Fort Bourbon. This plan was put into action on 20 March. Illustration (5) shows the boats of the squadron carrying troops with scaling ladders against the town itself. In the lead boats are men from the three battalions of grenadiers in Grey's force. Nearly half of Grey's army was made up of grenadier and light infantry companies taken from their regiments and formed into elite battalions, giving the British a considerable qualitative advantage on land. The landing is being directly supported by fire from the warships, including high-angle mortar fire either from the bomb vessel *Vesuvius* or the batteries established ashore. Meanwhile, Fort Louis was taken by the bold action of Captain Faulknor of the sloop *Zebra*, 14, who brought his small ship right up alongside the fort and then led his ship's company over the side and took it by storm (6, 7). The capture of the fort caused the French governor in Fort Bourbon, General Rochambeau, to ask for terms, and on 22 March the fort capitulated. The capture of Martinique was followed by a similarly-conducted assault on the island of St Lucia, by a detachment of the forces which had taken Fort Royal, which lasted only four days, the French garrison surrendering on 4 April 1794, with no fatalities on the British side.

The next objective was Guadeloupe, where the squadron arrived on 11 April, making landings immediately. The strong fortified position of Fleur d'Epée was

5

6. 'N. E. View of Fort Louis in the Island of Martinique, 5 Feb–22 Mar 1794', coloured aquatint engraved by Samuel Alken, published by the Reverend C Willyams after his own original, 1 August 1796. *NMM ref PAG8922*

7. 'S.W. View of Forts Bourbon and Louis in the Island of Martinique, 5 Feb–22 Mar 1794', coloured aquatint engraved by Samuel Alken, published by the Reverend C Willyams after his own original, 1 August 1796. *NMM ref PAG8924*

8. 'View of the Bay and Town of St Pierre (Martinique)', coloured aquatint engraved by Samuel Alken, published by the Reverend C Willyams after his own original, 1 August 1796. *NMM ref PAH3023*

9. 'View and Plan of French occupied Guadeloupe', anonymous black and watercolour pen and ink. *NMM ref PAH5035*

6

stormed the next day by a mixed force of soldiers and seamen, the naval contingent under the command of Captain Faulknor of the *Zebra*. The rest of the island, including the nearby islands of the Saintes and all other dependencies of Guadeloupe, were surrendered to the British on 20 April 1794. However, on 3 June a French squadron of nine ships arrived and landed troops commanded by Victor Hugues, taking the British very much by surprise. Although many French settlers had initially welcomed British rule, they had been alienated by the eagerness with which the British commanders pursued prize money, threatening to confiscate all property on those islands which had offered resistance and laying claim to all the French shipping in the harbours they had captured. The inhabitants of St Lucia paid an estimated £150,000 in lieu of confiscation of their property, and it was rumoured that the British were to demand £250,000 from Martinique (8). The republican army was able to recapture Fleur d'Epée and the other posts on the island (9).

Jervis had returned to the island in force once the arrival of the French became known, landing a relief force on 22 June. Fighting was indecisive, with the British army badly weakened by sickness, and following a costly failed attack on the town of Pointe á Pitre, British forces were evacuated from Grande Terre on 3 July. Basse-Terre likewise fell to the French in October, although many of the British troops were successfully evacuated. The garrison of St Lucia had also been taken off in the armed storeship *Experiment* on 19 June, having suffered greatly both from disease and the enemy.

Following the surrender of St Nicholas Mole on the southern side of Saint-Domingue in 1793, Commodore Ford of the Jamaica station had offered terms to the French garrison of Port au Prince in February 1794, which were refused. A campaign was launched against the fortifications around the town on 31 May, and on 2 June the important position of Fort Brissoton was taken by assault, and two days later Port au Prince surrendered, leaving the British in control of several principal strongpoints on the island, although many areas were still under French control.

7

8

9

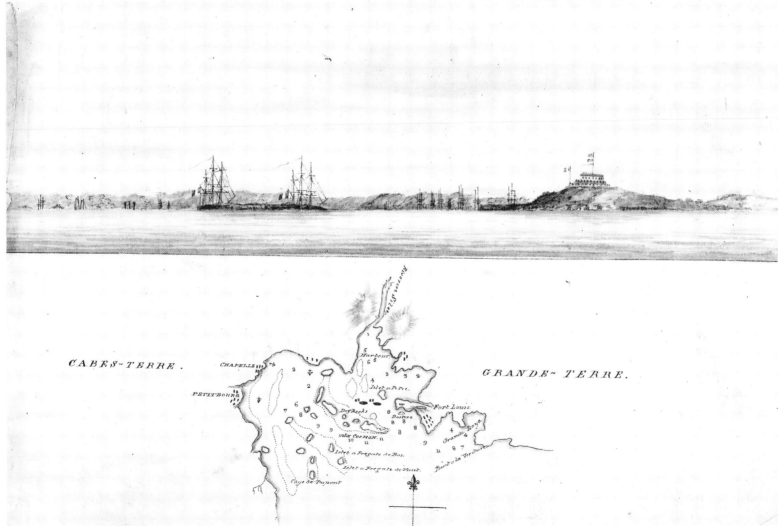

CABES-TERRE. CHAPELLE GRANDE-TERRE.

PETITBOURG Fort Louis

1

1. 'The Antilope Packet beating off Le Atalante a French Privateer in the West Indies 2 Dec 1794', coloured aquatint engraved by William Elmes after his own original, published by John Fairburn, 1 February 1797. *NMM ref PAD5481*

2. 'The La Raison of 24 guns, Captn Beresford, beating off a French Frigate, of 44 guns, near Halifax 25 Aug 1796', aquatint engraved by William Elmes after his own original, published by John Fairburn, 1 February 1797. *NMM ref PAD5504*

3. 'A King's Brig in Chase of a Privateer', aquatint engraved by William Elmes after his own original. *NMM ref PAD6124*

4. 'The Lapwing Captn Barton, capturing a French Frigate, and sinking a brig, in the West Indies 25 Nov 1796', coloured aquatint engraved by William Elmes after his own original, published by John Fairburn, 21 August 1797. *NMM ref PAD5512*

Commerce warfare in the West Indies

THE WEALTH of the West Indies made it a favoured hunting ground for French privateers, which were helped by the maze of tiny islands and narrow passages where large warships could penetrate only at great risk to themselves. The average size of West Indian privateers was quite small and the Royal Navy was always hard put to provide enough small cruisers to combat them. The West Indies merchants were also well organised politically and could lobby for additional protection if they felt especially threatened.

However, this powerful caucus was also a potential source of patronage to indigent artists and printsellers. One such partnership, between William Elmes and John Fairburn, seems to have specialised in West Indian actions, although not to the exclusion of other waters. Elmes employed a crude but vigorous style that made him highly distinctive. His forte seems to have been very small scale actions, some of which—like the packet *Antelope*'s repulse of the privateer *Atalante* (1)—would not merit a mention in most modern histories, but was doubtless of importance to local commerce. It was, in fact, a very gallant action, and was celebrated by better artists than Elmes.

Since his principal concern was drama rather than accuracy, he was quite happy to exaggerate the relative sizes of combatants. The August 1796 encounter between the *Raison* and the *Vengeance* is a case in point (2). Admittedly, the British Sixth Rate measured only 472 tons to her opponent's 1180, but their relative lengths were about 110ft to 160ft, rather than the 2:1 the artist

2

presents. However, a ship with 9pdrs fighting off one of the largest 18pdr frigates in the French navy was indeed a David-and-Goliath contest, so doubtless the artist felt justified.

Much of the Navy's commerce protection force was made up of brigs, both the larger 16- to 18-gun vessels rated as sloops (entrusted to a Commander), and the smaller gunbrigs (commanded by Lieutenants). During the course of the war they were to become the most numerous type on the Navy List, and although some were involved in notable actions, for the majority life was a mundane round of patrols, with the occasional excitement of a chase (3).

Because warship development, in the eighteenth century as in the twentieth, involved growth, the smallest ships of each rate tended to be the oldest. Small frigates like the 28s, effectively obsolescent by the 1790s, were often sent to the West Indies where they might be useful against French corvettes and the larger privateers. One of Elmes's better compositions is inspired by one of these, the *Lapwing*, 28, which captured the *Décius*, 20, and drove the *Vaillante*, 10, ashore in November 1796 (4).

3

4

1

Capture of the Cape 1795

2

THE FRENCH victory in the Netherlands and the formation of the Batavian Republic as a satellite state of France made it vital for the British to secure the Dutch colony of the Cape of Good Hope (1), so as to safeguard communications with the East Indies. Consequently, an expedition was sent from England, under the command of Vice-Admiral Sir George Keith Elphinstone (2), comprising *Monarch, Victorious* and *Arrogant*, all 74s, the 64-gun ships *America* and *Stately*, and the sloops *Echo* and *Rattlesnake*, both of 16 guns. A detachment of troops from the 78th Regiment of Foot, commanded by Major-General Craig, was also embarked.

The squadron arrived in Simon's Bay, Cape of Good Hope, in early July, and the Dutch governor, General Sluysken, was requested to place the colony under British protection. This was refused, and Sluysken evacuated the population of Simonstown, intending to burn the town, but a mixed force of soldiers and marines landed and took possession of the place before this could be done. The Dutch had taken up positions on heights blocking the way to Capetown, and on 7 August the British advanced against them. Elphinstone had landed a detachment of 1000 sailors, bringing the land forces up to some 1800 men, and had improvised a gunboat and

armed the squadron's boats with carronades to give support to the attack. The Dutch positions were brought under fire from the sea by *America, Stately* and the two sloops, driving the defenders out well before the troops under Craig reached the place, which was finally occupied that afternoon. A Dutch counter-attack on the following day was beaten off, the seamen on shore playing the major part and being praised by Major-General Craig, who likened their performance to that of regular infantry.

On 3 September 1795, the Dutch were about to make a general attack on the British camp, when the arrival of fourteen East Indiamen bringing reinforcements to Craig caused them to call off their offensive. With these new forces, the British decided to move immediately on Capetown, the troops beginning their march on the 14th, whilst the *America*, the two sloops and an East Indiaman sailed to Table Bay (3) as a diversion. At this, the Dutch commander asked for terms, and the colony surrendered on 15 September 1795. Two Dutch East India Company vessels, the *Castor* and the armed brig *Star*, fell into British hands at Capetown, the latter being commissioned into the Royal Navy as the *Hope*.

In February 1796 a small Dutch squadron (4) under

3

Rear-Admiral Englebertus Lucas slipped through the British blockade of the Texel with the intention of recapturing the Cape, and arrived in Saldanha Bay, fifty miles north of Simon's Bay on 3 August. Elphinstone's squadron, now numbering two 74s, five 64s, a 50, two frigates and four sloops, sailed to intercept them. Outnumbered and outgunned, having two 66-gun ships, a 54, four frigates and a sloop, all with under-strength crews, Lucas surrendered without a shot being fired. The Cape remained in British hands until it was returned to the Dutch under the Treaty of Amiens in 1802.

1. 'The Cape of Good Hope. La Cap de bonne Esperance', engraving from an original by Jan Van Ryne, published by Robert Sayer, London, 1754.
NMM ref PAD1919

2. 'Admiral Lord George Keith Elphinstone (1746-1823), 1st Viscount Keith', oil painting by William Owen.
NMM ref BHC2815

3. 'View from the anchorage in Table Bay, Cape of Good Hope. A squadron of ships beating into the bay', watercolour by Lieutenant William Innes Pocock (1783-1836).
NMM ref PAF0076

4. A Dutch Frigate from two angles, shown flying the flag of the Batavian Republic, anonymous watercolour.
NMM ref PAD5485

4

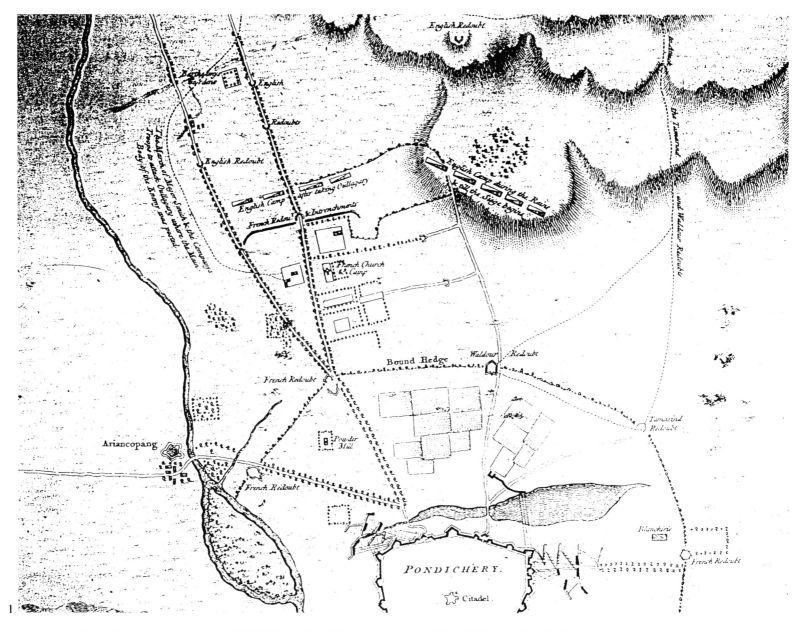

1. 'Pondicherry 15 Jan 1761',
anonymous etching, 1761.
NMM ref PAD5291

2. 'Marine Francais. La Prudente et La
Cybelle (de 36 et de 40) . . . Contre le
Diomede et la Centurion . . . 22
Decembre 1794', coloured lithograph
engraved by Jean Baptiste and Henri
Durand-Breger after their own
original, published by Jeannin and the
Anaglyphic Company, 15 August
1844.
NMM ref PAG8932

3. 'View of the waterfront of
Colombo', anonymous graphite
drawing.
NMM ref PAH2698

4. 'Distant View of Trincomale
Ceylon', coloured aquatint published
by Samuel Daniell after his own
original, 1 March 1807.
NMM ref PA10224

3

East Indies 1793-1796

ALERTED TO the outbreak of war with France by the British consul in Alexandria in June 1793, British forces in India immediately moved against the French possessions there. The naval commander at Madras was Commodore The Hon William Cornwallis, with the *Crown* of 64 guns and a few frigates and sloops based at or near Calcutta. The majority of the French factories in India fell without resistance, except for the major fortress of Pondicherry (1). The illustration shows the previous siege in 1761, but the defences were reported to be in as good a condition in 1793 as they had been in the Seven Years War, and a formal siege was begun on 1 August, lasting until the 23rd of that month, during which time Cornwallis in the *Minerva*, 38, drove off a small French squadron attempting to get supplies into the town. By the end of 1793, almost all the French possessions in the Indian Ocean had fallen, save for the important exception of Isle de France (Mauritius), where French ships continued to pose a threat to British trade. On 22 October 1794, the British *Centurion*, 50, and *Diomede*, 44, engaged a French squadron off Mauritius, comprising the *Cybèle* of 40 guns, the *Prudente* of 36 guns, *Jean Bart*, 20, and *Courier*, 14 which had sailed to engage the British squadron (2). *Centurion* was badly damaged thanks to the inactivity of the *Diomede*, whose commander, Captain Matthew Smith, was consequently court-martialled and dismissed from the service. The French ships all returned to Mauritius, which remained in French hands until 1810.

In May 1794 a convoy under Commodore Peter Rainier sailed from England with reinforcements for the Madras station, arriving in November after a non-stop voyage, without losing a ship. In June 1795, having been promoted to Rear-Admiral, he began operations against the Dutch possessions in the Indian Ocean. By the end of July all the posts in Ceylon (3) had surrendered, Trincomalee, the major fort (4), having done so on the 26th. A separate squadron had secured Malacca at the same time.

Although the campaign in the East Indies was minor from the point of view of actual fighting, the economic value of the French and Dutch possessions was more important, not least to those responsible for their capture. When Rainier's squadron took the Moluccan islands from the Dutch in February 1796, the five captains present were reported to have each received £15,000 in prize money, an astronomical sum in those days. By 1796 the British were in overall control of the Indian Ocean.

4

1

London—commercial capital of the world

2

LONDON WAS both capital city and principal port of Great Britain and her empire. It had developed at the lowest convenient bridging point of the River Thames over fifty miles from the sea, and in 1775 its population was growing at a rate that matched that of Britain as a whole. In 1700 it had housed about 575,000 people. By 1750 this figure had risen to 675,000 and by 1801, the year of the first national census, its inhabitants had increased to 900,000. At the beginning of the eighteenth century, the old city walls enclosed about a third of this population; a hundred years later they enclosed less than one-sixth. Urbanisation on the south bank was limited before 1750 by the existence of only one bridge, London Bridge; but that year Westminster Bridge was built, and Blackfriars Bridge in 1769.

The new suburbs were occupied not just by immi-

grants from rural southern England, shedding population with economies and innovations in agriculture, but by Scots, Welsh, Irish, Germans, Dutchmen, Frenchmen (especially Huguenots), and Jews, especially from eastern Europe. There was also an increasing number of negroes and Indian lascar seamen, respectively brought back through the slave trade with east Africa and by the East India Company which was always shorthanded on the return voyage from the east. The main thrust of expansion was east along the banks of the Thames to absorb the riverside villages of Wapping and Shadwell on the north bank and Rotherhithe on the south (1). Here the new inhabitants mainly served the river. The only wet docks along these banks were the Brunswick Dock at Blackwall used by the East India Company, and the Greenland Dock at Rotherhithe, dug between 1696 and 1700, and used by the South Sea Company's whalers. Otherwise shipping had to unload their cargoes at twenty Legal Quays, where imports were assessed for customs duty, and twenty-one Suffrance Wharfs, mainly on the southern bank of the river. These wharves were mainly below London Bridge, which blocked upward passage of ships ascending the Thames, so that ships moored predominately in that reach of the river just below the bridge and called the Pool of London (2).

Here ships moored raft-fashion from either bank, with a narrow channel in the middle, their masts forming what seemed a solid forest. Here, after the American War, a survey of the shipping claimed that between May and October each year there were over 400 West Indiamen of 200-500 tons, mainly importing sugar; nearly the same number of timber ships from the Baltic, many discharging their cargoes directly into the river and taking up twelve times their own mooring space; over 300 colliers, discharging coal into barges; and about 50 East Indiamen, most moored below Deptford. In addition there were smaller coasters, and over 3000 barges, lighters, hoys and punts.

Population, shipping and trade brought industry and commerce. Many trades met the luxury consumption demands of the wealthy as well as the basic needs of the middle and lower orders, but the greatest proportion—employing perhaps a quarter of the population—depended on the port. These trades included ship-, boat- and barge-building; and in the 1720s Daniel Defoe noted thirty-three yards for refitting, repairing and building merchant ships. Subsidiary industries like cooperages, breweries, distilleries, sugar-refining also flourished. Many others manufactured for export, especially to the North American colonies, but also to northern, nearby and southern Europe (3). By 1700 London handled no less than 80 per cent of England's imports, 69 per cent of her exports, and 86 per cent of her re-exports; and to convey this trade London owners possessed more than the combined shipping tonnage of the rest of the nation: about 140,000 tons, as opposed to 103,000 tons owned in other ports.

Moreover, London's trade and shipping grew during the eighteenth century. In 1700 its foreign imports were worth £4.8 million; £5.5 million in 1750; and £12.3 million by 1790. London's exports over the same period rose from £5.4 million to £10.7 million. London-owned ship-

3

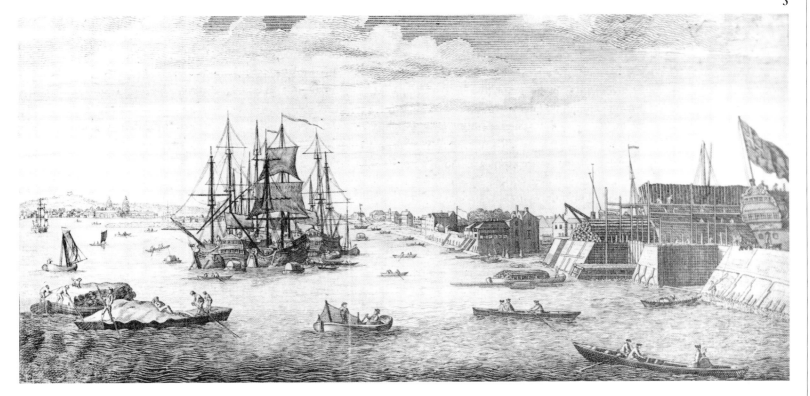

1. 'The Cities of London and Westminster accurately copied from the table of the Camera Obscura in the Royal Observatory at Greenwich', etching by Tomlinson from an original by Pugh, published by Sherwood, Neely and Jones, 1 March 1809.
NMM ref PAH2187

2. 'The South East Prospect of London From the Tower to London Bridge 1746', coloured engraving and etching by John Bowles from an original by Maurer, published by J Bowles & Son, London, 25 March 1746.
NMM ref PAH2186

3. 'A view of Blackwall and Dock Yard, looking towards Greenwich', etching published by Carington Bowles, London, 2 March 1773.
NMM ref PAD1393

4. 'The Custom House', anonymous etching.
NMM ref PAD1405

ping engaged in foreign trade rose from 157,000 tons in 1705, to 235,000 in 1751, and to 620,000 tons in 1794.

Managing this trade and shipping were the great sixteenth and seventeenth century merchant companies: the East India, South Sea, Africa, Russia, Levant and Hudson Bay companies. During the eighteenth century these great companies were being gradually outgrown by the vast number of independent merchants like those trading to the West Indies, who formed their own looser organisations. All benefited from the existence of trading centres like the Royal Exchange, founded in 1566, and by the development of London's financial market.

Insurance was originally undertaken by merchants meeting brokers and underwriters on the floor of the Royal Exchange or at nearby coffee houses. Insurance companies like the London Assurance, the Westminster, the Hand-in-Hand, and the Sun Fire Office, had all came into existence by 1720; numerous others by 1791, included the Phoenix, Union, Equitable and Amicable. The need for shipping information to calculate risks prompted the owner of Lloyd's coffee house to produce a specialist news sheet. This in 1734 became the still-extant *Lloyd's List*. A record of the opinions of surveyors who examined the hulls and assessed the seaworthiness of ships was also established in 1764 and was known as *Lloyd's Register*. Lloyd's insurance company subsequently came to dominate all others in the field of marine insurance.

London's goldsmith bankers had been the mainstay of the government in the mid-seventeenth century.

However small private banking companies like Child's, Stone's, Hoare's, and Martin's were all in existence by the end of the century, above thirty-five separate private banking concerns by 1760, with fifty-six by 1789. By then these banks were extending their services outside London, acting as agents both for individual clients and for country banks, of which there were 150 by 1776 and 280 by 1790. Operations became more fluid after the foundation of a central clearing house in Lombard Street in 1775.

These private banks were already under the central influence of the Bank of England, founded by a group of London merchants in 1694. This bank's main functions were to issue notes and to discount Exchequer and Navy bills issued by the government's Treasury. It also acted as the guardian of the Consolidated Fund and other balances deposited by the government; and of the reserves accumulated by the London and country bankers. These deposits permitted the Bank of England to lend at interest, and to discount commercial bills on behalf of British and overseas merchants.

Such was the capital accumulated by the Bank of England in the late eighteenth century, and such was the strength and stability of the London financial market, that investors in government stocks and bonds were attracted from other European countries, including France, Holland and Switzerland. Loans too were made on an international scale, some indeed to foreign nationals with whom Britain went to war. For London by 1793 had become the financial capital of Europe.

4

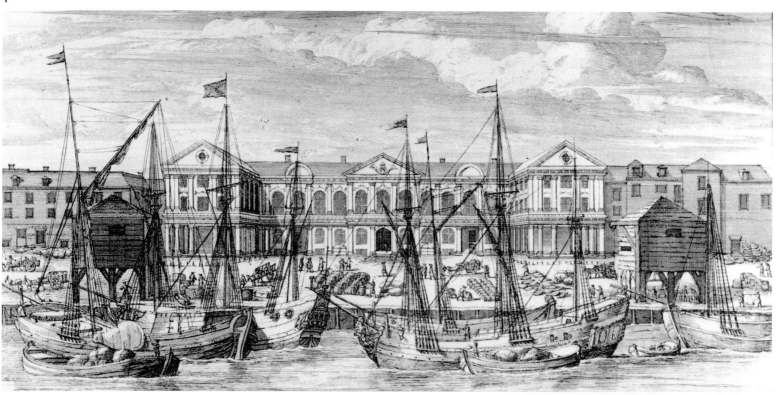

The West Indies 1795-1797

THROUGHOUT 1795 and 1796 fighting continued between British forces on West Indian islands and the French and their supporters among the local populations. In early January 1795 the British frigate *Blanche* of 32 guns, commanded by Captain Robert Faulknor, was operating off Guadeloupe, which had been retaken by the French the previous year. Faulknor found the 36-gun French frigate *Pique* in the harbour of Point à Pitre, and after a few days of indecisive manoeuvring, succeeded in luring the French ship out from under the cover of the shore batteries by taking a captured American schooner in tow and setting sail for Dominica on the evening of 4 January. When the *Pique* was seen to be pursuing, the *Blanche* cut the schooner free and turned to attack her.

The ships were closely engaged, broadside to broadside, for two and a half hours until, at 2.30am on the 5th, the *Blanche* surged ahead of the *Pique* in an attempt to turn and rake her bows. But at that moment her main and mizzen masts fell and the *Pique* collided with her (1). Whilst trying to lash the two ships together, Captain Faulknor was killed by a sharpshooter (2). A second attempt was successful, and the *Blanche* effectively took the *Pique* in tow. But fire from French sharpshooters and the ship's deck guns continued, to which the *Blanche* could make little effective reply, as she lacked any stern gunports. These were, however, rapidly improvised by

3

4

5

simply firing two 12pdrs through the stern-frame. Fire from these guns brought down the *Pique*'s main mast (3) and at 5.15am the ship surrendered, having lost all her masts. Out of a crew of 279 men, the *Pique* had lost 76 killed and 110 wounded. The *Blanche*, on the other hand, lost only 8 killed and 21 wounded. This wide disparity in casualties was to increasingly become the norm in such engagements as the war continued. The *Pique* was towed to the Saintes, and later commissioned into the Royal Navy.

The French made numerous attempts to reinforce their islands, and on 10 October 1795 the British frigate *Mermaid* of 32 guns captured the French *Brutus* of 10 guns (4), and four days later the 18-gun *Républicaine*, intercepting troops on their way to Grenada.

On 9 December 1795 a large convoy of transports, accompanied by seven warships commanded by Rear-Admiral Sir Hugh Cloberry Christian, had set sail for the West Indies to recapture the islands lost the previous year, but bad weather drove the fleet back to Spithead (5), where it was forced to remain until 20 March 1796, not arriving at Barbados until 21 April. The first task undertaken was the recapture of St Lucia, an attack which proceeded along standard lines, and French forces capitulated on 24 May. The expedition then moved on to take St Vincent, which fell on 11 June, and Grenada which surrendered a few days later.

Campaigning on Saint-Domingue continued with an attack on the French positions at Léogane (6), a combined operation between ships from the Jamaica station and troops marching overland from Port au Prince under the command of Major-General Forbes. A landing was made on 21 March 1796, but the place proved stronger than expected and following heavy damage to the masts and rigging of *Leviathan*, 74, and *Africa*, 64, by the guns on shore, the attack was abandoned. Despite the strength of British forces in the West Indies, and the blockade of the French ports in European waters, the French were still able to send two squadrons in early 1796 with reinforcements for their garrisons on Saint-Domingue, both of which delivered their cargoes and returned safely to France.

An attempt by the French to land troops on the island of Anguilla in November 1796 was frustrated by the frigate *Lapwing*, 28, commanded by Captain Richard Bowen (7). His arrival on 26 November caused the immediate re-embarkation of the French forces aboard the *Décius*, 20, and *Vaillante*, 10. *Décius* was captured by *Lapwing* after an hour's fighting, and *Vaillante* was destroyed by the frigate's guns after running ashore.

In February 1797, a squadron under the command of Rear-Admiral Henry Harvey, carrying troops under Lieutenant-General Sir Ralph Abercromby, sailed from Martinique to attack the Spanish island of Trinidad, where on 16 February they discovered four Spanish ships of the line, the *San Vincente* of 80 guns, the three 74s

6. 'Vue de La Rade de Leogane, Isle St Dominique' engraving and etching by Nicolas Ponce from an original by N Ozanne, 1795.
NMM ref PAH3000

7. 'Capture of Le Desius Novr 25th 1796. Captured French Decius (20) and drove the Vaillante (20) ashore at Anguilla. Next Day Lapwing was chased and Barton was Compelled to Burn Her', coloured aquatint engraved by Thomas Sutherland from an original by Thomas Whitcombe, published for J Jenkin's *Naval Achievements*, 1 September 1816.
NMM ref PAD5513

8. 'The capture of Trinidad, 17 February 1797', oil painting by Nicholas Pocock, 1800.
NMM ref BHC0494

9. Sheer draught of *San Damaso* as captured, dated Portsmouth Dockyard 29 March 1798. Admiralty Collection.
NMM neg 928

8

Gallardo, Arrogante and *San Damaso*, and the 34-gun frigate *Santa Cecilia*, in Shaggaramus Bay, defended by a battery mounting twenty guns and two mortars. Given the apparent strength of the enemy, Hervey sent his transports to find a berth some distance away, and anchored his four ships of the line in gun range of the Spanish ships and batteries, preparing to attack them the next day. But on the night of the 16th the Spanish set fire to their ships (8), only the *San Damaso* surviving to be taken by the British (9), since they had less than half the number of men available needed to man them. Troops took possession of the battery, and on the 17th a landing was made near Port of Spain, which surrendered peacefully and the next day the whole island capitulated. The squadron then moved on to attack Puerto Rico, arriving there on 17 April, but San Juan was found to be well-fortified and actively defended by gunboats, and the attempt was abandoned on 30 April.

9

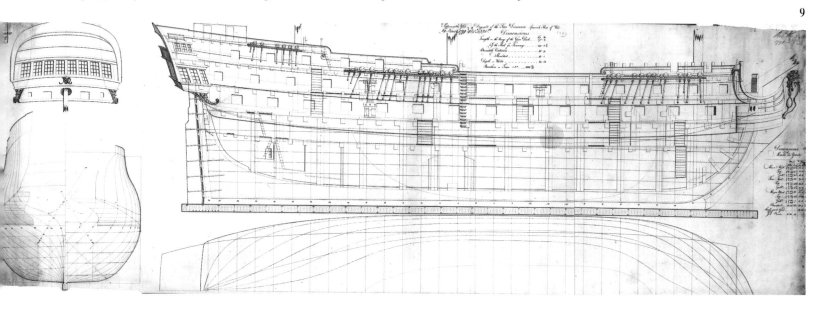

The cruise of a frigate

AMONG THE many sketchbooks at Greenwich which appear to be the work of serving officers is one by a Lieutenant Edward Bamfylde Eagles of the Royal Marines. Although he seems to have served after the Napoleonic Wars, his sketchbook depicts scenes of warfare against the French which can only refer to that period. Whether or not he had personal experience of these events, they amount to a lively representation of the kind of everyday incidents that are rarely the subject of more formal art. The books themselves have no sense of sequence, but it is possible to arrange the drawings to form a fictional, but in many ways typical, cruise of a frigate in wartime.

The story begins with the ship lying at anchor, boat streamed astern, in light airs—perfect weather to loose the 'small sails' (staysails and other fore-and-aft canvas) to dry. If this were truly a postwar ship, one would expect gaff-headed spencers between the masts, rather than staysails, which tended to be replaced after 1815 (1). With the wind getting up, the frigate decides to shift her berth, setting fore and mizzen topsails; the boat is probably carrying out a kedge anchor (2).

Having received orders to sail, the ship flies the Blue Peter from the fore truck, and with topsails backing and filling, weighs anchor; the cable is 'up and down' and the crew preparing to fish and cat the anchor are visible on the forecastle (3). In this case, the harbour was Portsmouth and the frigate leaves in fine style, under all plain sail to skysails (4). First duty on patrol is to check the identity of all vessels encountered, and having been challenged by the frigate, this British merchant brig responds with her number, a two-flag signal from the foremast (5); even today, some people describe intro-

4

ducing themselves as 'making my number'. Many of a
frigate's duties are similarly humdrum, but none is so
frustrating as convoy escorting. Seen here bringing a
convoy out of St John, Newfoundland (6), the officers of
the frigate will have been driven mad by their wayward
charges long before they reach the other side of the
Atlantic. Relations between the merchant service and
the Royal Navy have always been ambiguous, and many
a merchant skipper chafed under the discipline of convoy – the logs of ships on escort duty are replete with
references to firing shots across the bows of their charges
to bring them into line, literally as well as figuratively.

However, the appeal of a frigate to both officers and
men was the chance for independent action and the
consequent prospect of prize money. It is surprising how
often during the course of the Napoleonic War that
frigates of comparable force met in single combat, but as
the war went on the British were increasingly compelled
to force action on a reluctant enemy: here (7) it involves
a chase in heavy weather carrying all plain sail, which is
only resolved by the French frigate losing her main topmast. Having struck her colours in token of surrender
the chase heaves to (8); a small prize crew will then be
put on board to sail the ship to a friendly port, so the victor removes part of the complement of the defeated
ship to reduce the chance of the prisoners rising and
retaking the ship (9) .

For the victorious frigate, her greatest moment of
glory comes as she leads her prize into harbour, with the
Union flag over the French tricolour (10). Similar scenes
were enacted hundreds of times during the war, but for
those involved it never lost its savour.

5

6

7

8

9

1-10. Black pen and ink drawings from a sketchbook by Lieutenant Edward Bamfylde Eagles, dated to *c*1840 but clearly depicting events, real or imaginary, of the Napoleonic War.

1. 'Light airs and clear. Small sails loos'd to dry'.
NMM ref PAF2618

2. 'Moderate Breezes, Frigate shifting her Berth'.
NMM ref PAF2604

3. 'Blue Peter up, getting under weigh'.
NMM ref PAF2665

4. 'Frigate leaving Portsmouth Harbour'.
NMM ref PAF2631

5. 'Brig showing her number to the ship under the land'.
NMM ref PAF2634

6. 'Outside view of St John's Newfoundland. Frigate coming out with a Convoy'.
NMM ref PAF2613

7. 'The Enemy's Main Topmast going over the side'.
NMM ref PAF2582

8. 'The Chase just struck'.
NMM ref PAF2598

9. 'Taking the Prisoners out of the Prize'.
NMM ref PAF2668

10. 'Frigate going into Harbour with her Prize under Jury Masts'.
NMM ref PAF2637

10

Part III

MEDITERRANEAN THEATRE
1793-1797

THE ROYAL Navy squadron which had been assembled in the Mediterranean in the spring of 1793 under the command of Vice-Admiral Lord Hood was made up of two First Rates of 100-guns, *Victory* and *Britannia*, three 98s, twelve 74s and four 64s. Facing them at Toulon under the temporary command of Rear-Admiral the Comte de Trogoff were seventeen ships of the line ready for sea, including the 120-gun *Commerce de Marseilles*. Another four were refitting, and nine repairing. Co-operating with the British fleet was a Spanish squadron operating out of Minorca under the command of Admiral Langara. The prospect of an Hispano-British fleet engaging the French Toulon fleet, however, was short-lived.

The Jacobins had obtained control of the Toulon municipality in November 1790, but the excesses throughout France following the execution of the king led to their overthrow in Toulon in July 1793. When the government in Paris sent an army to restore its control in Provence, the Toulonese, out of desperation, invited Hood to occupy the port. He stipulated that they must make a declaration in support of the the Dauphin. The crews of the French fleet were at first determined to resist the British, but in the end large numbers of them deserted so as to avoid a civil war with the people of Toulon.

Hood landed two regiments of British infantry and 200 marines, and a Spanish army was rushed across the frontier to provide its landward defence. Captain Horatio Nelson, in command of *Agamemnon* 64, and Sir William Hamilton the British Minister at the Court of Naples, persuaded King Ferdinand to send another by sea. Small contingents were also sent by the Piedmontese and the Sardinians. Command of the troops was given to the Spanish Rear-Admiral Don Federico Gravina. The French fleet moved into the inner harbour and landed its gunpowder. About 5000 of their crews were put onboard four disarmed and

unserviceable 74s, and sailed under passport to the Atlantic ports before the arrival of the army of the Republic under General Carteau and General Lapoype. On their arrival at Brest and Rochefort, the sailors found that were regarded as deserters for not having defended their ships.

Nelson had acquired a poor opinion of Spanish naval manpower when he visited Cadiz on his way to the Mediterranean, which is not surprising considering that the Spanish mercantile marine was so small that only about 10 per cent of the muster role of Spanish warships could be filled with experienced seamen. More surprisingly, the Spanish army proved to be no more capable. Professional and national jealousies impeded the defence. When Gravina was wounded, a Spanish lieutenant-general, Valdez, asserted his own claim to be placed in command of all the allied troops. To support him, Langara moved his three-decker flagship into a position broadside on to *Victory* with two other three-deckers on her bow and quarter. Hood, however, resisted this attempted intimidation.

After winning a desperate fight for control of the high ground overlooking Toulon harbour, the French army used its artillery, under the command of the young General Napoleon Bonaparte, to overcome the fire from *Princess Royal*, 98, a Spanish 74, and two floating batteries. On 14 December the defences on the landward side were driven in. Toulon was taken, thousands of the leading citizens being guillotined.

Before Toulon was evacuated, British and Spanish incendiary parties commanded by Sir Sidney Smith were sent to destroy the arsenal and the ships in the harbour, but he was unable to burn more than ten of the Toulon fleet. Langara later admitted that he had ensured the Spanish contingent did not play its part, because he did not want Britain to acquire too disproportionate a naval strength. Hood, however, was able to get fifteen French ships out of

Toulon before the fall. This number included the *Commerce de Marseilles* of 120 guns and *Pompée* of 74, both of which were found to be exceptional ships, although the *Commerce* proved to be too structurally weak for service in the British fleet. She was converted into a store ship, but was strained so badly during the storm which forced Rear-Admiral Christian to put back from his relief of the West Indies in November 1795 that her enormous cargo was unloaded and she never put out of harbour again. Hood also took with him an *Ingénieur de Marine*, Jean Louis Barrallier, who was to be appointed Assistant Surveyor of the Navy in 1796. In that office he was able to bring French scientific study of ship design to the service of the Navy Board, but the opinion of British shipwrights was that he was so absorbed in theory that he was inefficient.

Soon after the Mediterranean Squadron was driven from Toulon, Captain Samuel Hood returned from a cruise in the frigate *Juno* late at night and brought her right into the inner harbour, where she took the ground. A kedge anchor was put out, and succeeded in hauling her clear, but when the port authorities came out to the ship it gradually dawned on the ship's company that they were prisoners of war. The wind just made possible a course for the harbour entrance, however, so the French officials were disarmed and hustled below. Through a cross-fire from the batteries around the outer harbour, *Juno* was taken back out to sea.

A less happy conclusion occurred when *Ardent*, 64, was on a patrol. She did not return and a large piece of her quarterdeck was discovered floating in the sea, making all too clear that she had blown up, killing all hands.

While still in occupation of Toulon, Hood had sent a small squadron made up of three ships and two frigates under Commodore Robert Linzee to attempt to persuade the French garrisons on Corsica to declare for the royalists. He did not have any success in that, but he did succeed in gaining possession for a short time of a round gun tower near Cape Mortella guarding San Fiorenzo Bay. The design was so greatly admired that it became the basis for similar defensive works along the south coast of England, and guarding colonial harbours. Corsica had only been incorporated into France in 1768 in the teeth of strong local opposition led by General Paoli, who again sought British assistance to establish an independent government. When the fleet was forced to leave Toulon, Hood moved to Hyères Bay on the Riviera, but when on 24 January 1794 officers he had sent to communicate with Paoli returned with encouraging reports, it was decided to return to San Fiorenzo Bay.

The tower at Mortella had to be retaken, and its three guns beat off the bombardment made by *Juno* and *Fortitude*, damaging the latter considerably. It was only when guns established ashore employed red-hot shot to set the bass-wood backing for the parapet alight that the garrison asked for terms. A redoubt at Fornelli was then attacked by a battery of 18pdrs hauled by the sailors straight up the side of a cliff. With the anchorage secure, Hood moved on to lay siege to Bastia, using only sailors and marines, and with Paoli's irregulars in support. It capitulated 21 May, and a

Corsican Corte voted to separate from France and accept a British viceroy, Sir Gilbert Elliott. On 10 August Calvi was taken after another difficult siege during which Nelson received the wound which cost him the sight of his right eye.

Control of the Mediterranean was vital to the efforts of the Austrians, Spaniards, and Neapolitans to co-ordinate their military efforts against the French revolutionaries. The remaining ships of the Toulon fleet were as short of supplies as were those at Brest, and as poorly manned, but Jeanbon Saint-Andre energetically set to work restoring order. Rear-Admiral Pierre Martin was put in command with orders to clear the way for a military force to reconquer Corsica, but he felt entirely inadequate to the task: it had been only two years since he had received his commission as lieutenant. When Saint-André returned to Paris, however, Deputy Letourneur was left to stiffen Martin's resolve. Command was divided between them. The opportunity to destroy this incapable force, however, was twice

missed by the Mediterranean squadron.

Hood was succeeded in command of the British squadron in the Mediterranean by Vice-Admiral William Hotham, who proved to be unsuited to the task of command-in-chief. He ran into the Toulon squadron in March 1795 when on both sides together over a thousand men were killed or wounded in a passing action, and again in July. Both times he failed to make the most of his advantage, being glad enough to make no major mistake.

This relative failure was to be an important contributing factor to the defeat of the Austrian army on the Riviera. Nelson had been detached on 4 July with a small squadron consisting of his *Agamemnon*, a small frigate, a sloop and a cutter, to attack French shipping to the westward of Genoa. He had some little success, and was sent back again with more force in August, and was in action in the Gulf of Genoa again the following March, but, with the threat from Toulon unresolved, Hotham could not detach enough of his ships to stop French traffic altogether.

Spanish fleet in Leghorn Roads to receive the Infante 29 April 1794. Engraving by G Bougean, 1797. During the few years in which the Spanish operated alongside the British, their allies formed no great opinion of the level of Spanish training and skill (the French had harboured a similar view during the previous war) and this was to be confirmed at the Battle of Cape St Vincent after the Spanish changed sides. NMM ref PAI0060

The only bright side from the British point of view was the spirited part played by Nelson in attacking an 80-gun ship, *Ça Ira* during the March encounter. He was forced by *Ça Ira*'s effective use of stern chasers to open fire earlier than he wished, but thereafter he kept *Agamemnon* weaving across the stern of his enemy so that he could repeatedly rake her, and suffer no damage himself.

At a quarter before eleven A.M., being within one hundred yards of the *Ça Ira*'s stern, I ordered the helm to be put a-starboard, and the driver and after-sails to be braced up and shivered, and as the Ship fell off, gave her our whole broadside, each gun double-shotted. Scarcely a shot appeared to miss. The instant all were fired, braced up our after-yards, put the helm a-port, and stood after her again. This manoeuvre we practiced till one P.M., never allowing the *Ça Ira* to get a single gun from either side to fire on us.[1]

The poor seamanship, poor gunnery, and generally poor equipment of the French fleet told, and eventually Nelson was on hand to take possession of the prize. The *Censeur* had also struck, to be retaken in October when Rear-Admiral Richery attacked the Smyrna convoy, but against that had to be set the capture of *Berwick* of 74 guns by the French before the action. She had been dismasted and was struggling under jury rig to rejoin the Mediterranean squadron when she was caught. The losses on both sides became even when the *Illustrious*, 74 guns, ran ashore after breaking her tow following the battle.

In the June encounter, Martin had had no choice but to flee from superior numbers and vastly more capable officers. His last five ships became engaged by the leading British units, and one of them, *Alcide* of 74 guns, was set on fire and blew up. Hotham, however, recalled his fleet just as they were getting in amongst the enemy.

The arrival of Admiral Sir John Jervis to take command in December 1795 produced a dramatic change in the efficiency of the Mediterranean squadron. His standards of discipline and drill, his care for the health of his men, his own obedience to duty, and his honesty, were unparalleled. Toulon was to be closely blockaded for 150 days the following summer. Nevertheless, he could not arrest the progress of French arms because its own leadership had been transformed.

Napoleon had been arrested when Maximilien Robespierre fell from power, because he had been employed by his brother Augustin as military planner for the Army of Italy, but he was saved from the guillotine by Deputy Saliceti who was a fellow Corsican. Still under a shadow, he was in Paris when in October 1795 he secured his position by turning his guns on the Paris mob which reactionaries were trying to use against the corrupt bourgeois Directory to force a return to constitutional government. Napoleon's 'whiff of grapeshot' put an end to its political power. As a reward, he was appointed in March 1796 to command the Army of Italy, to which he brought a new spirit.

A starving rabble were inspired with confidence in its ability and with the hope for plunder. Nice was captured, the Austrian army was defeated at Millesimo on 13 April 1796, and the Piedmontese at Mondovi on 22 April. Having studied the failure of Maréchal de Maillebois's 1745-46 campaign on the Riviera, when a British squadron cut the supply route along the Corniche road, Napoleon combined the use of coastal batteries to protect the road, and parallel supply routes through the mountains, to ensure that his conquest of northern Italy

Vue de Bastia Isle de Corse', black and gouache pen and ink by Zacherie Felix Doumet, c1794. The short-lived capture of Corsica inspired a number of illustrations of the island itself as well as the events of the campaign. NMM ref PAH8378

would not be thwarted. King Victor Amadeus was forced to conclude a separate peace with France, Nice and Savoy being ceded to the French Republic. Napoleon then pursued the Austrians and defeated them at Lodi on 10 May. He entered Milan on 15 May 1796 and the King of Naples, the Pope and the Dukes of Parma and Modena paid heavy prices for a truce.

A break from the operations in support of the Austrian army occurred in March 1796 when Vice-Admiral Waldegrave had to be detached from the Mediterranean Squadron and sent with *Barfleur*, 98 guns, and four 74s to Tunis where *Nemesis*, a 28-gun British frigate, had been taken as a French prize. Under the guns of the force, sailors in the ships' launches cut her out, and also took one of her captors, a ship-corvette called the *Sardine*.

In May 1796 Napoleon moved south from Milan, laid siege to Mantua, and forced the Duke of Tuscany to make peace. French soldiers entered the port of Leghorn on 25 June, closing it to the British Mediterranean squadron, and cutting them off from their principal source of supply. Corsica itself was threatened. Jervis maintained a close blockade of Leghorn, based on Porto Ferrajo in Elba which Nelson, whom Jervis had appointed a commodore, occupied in July. He succeeded in keeping Napoleon from passing soldiers to Corsica until mid-October, but the situation was precarious.

In July 1795 Spain had been forced to conclude peace with France, and in August 1796, by the Treaty of San Ildefonso, the imbecile Charles IV was committed to war against Britain and Portugal. This was finally precipitated in October after Pitt sanctioned an ill-conceived attempt to seize the homecoming Spanish treasure ships. The Spanish fleet, although woefully badly manned, was large enough to make the danger of it cooperating with the Toulon fleet a serious threat to Jervis's command. Worse, the Queen of Naples, Maria Carolina, warned that a plan had been developed to use the combined naval strength of France, Spain and the Netherlands to make possible the invasion of the British Isles.

Admiral Langara sailed from Cadiz with nineteen sail of the line and ten frigates, brushing aside Rear-Admiral Man's division which Jervis had posted to watch Cadiz, and passed into the Mediterranean. Langara collected the seven ships at Cartagena and cruised as far as Cape Corso. He did not attack the British lying in San Fiorenzo Bay, but proceeded to Toulon, where the combined Franco-Spanish fleet, totalling thirty-eight ships of the line, heavily outnumbered the Mediterranean squadron which had lost a third of its strength when Man fled precipitantly back to the Channel.

The threat in home waters, and the impossible odds against Jervis in the Mediterranean, necessitated a change of operational focus for the Mediterranean squadron from the Gulf of Lyons to Cadiz. It was also known that francophile Corsicans were preparing to rise against the British. Orders were sent from London to evacuate Corsica, but on 19 October, before they could be carried out, General Casalti managed to get the first part of the French invasion force out of Leghorn. A small division of soldiers were landed, and reached Bastia two days later with a large body of Corsican supporters. As a Briton who was present in Bastia remarked: 'when they found that the English intended to evacuate the island,' the Corsicans 'naturally and necessarily sent to make their peace with the French.'[2] The British garrison and viceroy were withdrawn from Corsica, and taken to Elba.

Jervis sailed to Gibraltar, and there, in a heavy gale, *Courageux* was wrecked and four other ships were damaged. Four others were grounded in the Tagus, where Jervis had gone to provide the Portuguese with moral support, and two others were damaged after he sailed to take up his station at Cape St Vincent. This reduced his force to ten ships of the line, but the Admiralty was able to reinforce him with another five under Rear-Admiral Sir William Parker when winter weather put an end to any immediate threat to Ireland.

Without British naval support, Naples had no choice but to seek peace with France, and in April 1797 Austria came to terms. Napoleon then occupied Venice, which was ceded to Austria as part of the Treaty of Campo Formio in October.

Nelson had been sent back in a frigate from Gibraltar to withdraw the garrison at Elba, and at the end of January 1797 he steered for the rendezvous off Cape St Vincent. West of Gibraltar, in the dark, he sailed right through the Spanish fleet which had sailed from Cartagena to escort home an immensely valuable convoy of four ships laded with mercury for refining silver from the mines of Peru. He reported to Jervis in the morning, rehoisted his flag in *Captain* of 74 guns, and was on hand to take a dramatic and important part in the action which took place on St Valentine's Day.

When the fleet, now commanded by Admiral Don José de Cordova, appeared out of the mist the next morning, it greatly outnumbered the British. It was in poor order, however, and there was a wide gap between the convoy with its close escort and the twenty or twenty-one ships of the main force. Jervis had kept his squadron in close formation during the night, in a double column, but he now ordered it to 'form the line of battle ahead and astern as most convenient' to prevent delays while slower ships tried to reach their proper position in the formal order of battle, and signalled: 'The admiral means to pass through the enemy's line.' His purpose was to give the Spaniards no time to reform their line. Cordova, however, took the chance and, in order to retain the weather gage, ordered his fleet to form line 'as convenient' on the larboard tack. In foggy weather, this movement, which required captains with badly-manned ships to tack while forming up, only completed Spanish disorganisation.

Jervis had once declared, 'Lord Hawke when he ran out of the line [at the Battle of Toulon] and took the *Poder* sickened me of tactics.' His consummate qualities as an admiral, however, included a strong grasp of tactical possibilities. When he had taken over command of the Mediterranean squadron he had issued an additional instruction to the standing Fighting Instructions which indicated that, in the event of the enemy succeeding in gaining the weather gage, the fleet was to decrease sail, form into a strong body, and force through the enemy line from leeward. It was then to tack and engage those enemy ships cut off from their centre and rear, and to prevent their reuniting. Meanwhile, the British centre and rear would engage the enemy centre and rear, doing

---

1. 'Transactions on Board His Majesty's Ship *Agamemnon*, and of the Fleet, as seen and known by Captain Nelson', Sir Nicholas Harry Nicolas, *Dispatches and Letters of Vice-Admiral Lord Viscount Nelson*, 7 vols, London, 1846, Vol 2 pp10-15.

2. James, Vol 1 p447.

everything possible to prevent them from reuniting with their van. This proved to be a remarkable anticipation of what actually happened off Cape St Vincent. This idea may have owed something to the work of John Clerk of Eldin who had published the first part of his *An Essay on Naval Tactics* in 1790. The full edition was not to be published until 1797, but the manuscript had previously been circulated amongst 'his friends'. Clerk had written that if a large fleet advancing in thick weather in an irregular line abreast with the wind abeam should run into a smaller fleet coming the other way in rough line ahead, the admiral of the latter could hardly do better than proceed on his course to split the larger fleet.

Captain Cuthbert Collingwood, who commanded the *Excellent*, wrote that

> The truth is, we did not proceed on any system of tacticks. In the beginning we were formed very close and pushed at them without knowing, through the thickness of the haze, with what part of the line we could fall in. When they were divided, & the lesser part driven to leeward, the Admiral wisely abandoned them, made the signal to tack, and afterwards stuck to the larger division of the fleet, which was to windward, and could not be joined by their lee division in a short time. After this we had neither order nor signals, for the Admiral was so satisfied with the impetuosity of the attack made by the ships ahead of him that he let us alone.[3]

Collingwood, however, was confusing manoeuvre with tactics. Jervis's intention was to disorganise the Spaniards by the immediacy of the attack, and to make most use of his own fleet's seamanship and gunnery.

The action which followed makes it evident that Jervis's discipline and training had created a highly effective force. Captain Thomas Troubridge in *Culloden* led the line which opened fire in passing the disordered Spanish fleet. Jervis then signalled it to tack so as to come on the same course when overwhelming fire could be brought against the Spanish rear. So familiar was Troubridge with Jervis's intentions that he had his acknowledgment at the masthead, stopped and ready, before the signal was made to tack. He brought his ship around

on the instant, and engaged the Spanish line with his port guns.

Cordova responded by ordering his fleet to tack. There was some danger that the Spanish van would be able to join the convoy escort passing across the British rear. To forestall this, Nelson wore the *Captain* out of line, passed back through it, and attacked the Spanish van. This, placed his ship in extreme danger, confronted by seven Spanish ships, three of which were of 100 guns, and a fourth the only four-decker in the world, the 130-gun *Santisima Trinidad*. Jervis immediately signalled Collingwood, last in the line, to leave his station and tack into Nelson's wake to provide support, and soon Nelson was also supported by the British van coming down along the Spanish line. St Vincent's flag captain, Sir Robert Calder, later remarked that Nelson's breaking the line was unauthorised, to which Jervis responded: 'It certainly was so…and if ever you commit such a breach of your orders, I will forgive you also.'[4] Had the Spanish fleet been as well-trained and manned as was the British, Nelson's action would have been suicidal. But as it was, his prompt response to a tactical requirement was a nicely judged stroke.

Only four Spanish ships were captured, but the evident capacity of Jervis's command, and his victory against such apparent odds, discouraged the Franco-Spanish forces at Brest from seeking action in the Channel. The British public regained its confidence, and the ministry was saved from political defeat. Jervis was elevated to the peerage as Earl St Vincent, as much for the training he had given his command as for his victory. Nelson, whose promotion to Rear-Admiral was already confirmed, was at his request made a Knight of the Bath. Cordova was dismissed from the Spanish navy, and forbidden to appear at court.

The mutinies at Spithead and the Nore in April and May tested St Vincent's capacity as a commander to the limit. The news travelled fast, by letters and by the deployment of ships to join the Mediterranean squadron. His response was to keep up his unremitting attention to the welfare of the men, and to visit any manifestation of insubordination with court-martial and prompt execution. The introduction of lemon juice into the sailors' diet for the first time and despite the expense proved to be of fundamental importance. Scurvy, the curse

of blockading squadrons, was eliminated. British society was spared the horrors of revolution by isolating and outwitting sailors attempting to alter their condition.

St Vincent knew that the boredom of unremitting blockade was too dangerous for him to permit. Nelson was put in command of the inshore squadron watching Cadiz and he distinguished himself in a night boat action. Three times his coxswain saved his life, once interposing his hand to ward off a sword blow aimed at Nelson. His motive for a flag officer risking his life in this way was to support St. Vincent's disciplinary efforts with a demonstrable willingness to share his men's hardships and dangers. Nelson was a man who always led from the front, and his men responded accordingly. On 11 July he wrote home 'Our Mutinies are I hope stopped here, the Admiral having made some severe examples, but they were absolutely necessary.'[5] His own part had also been important.

As a reward, St Vincent gave Nelson command of a detachment sent a few weeks later to capture Spanish merchant shipping in the harbour of Santa Cruz de Tenerife. His determination that all odds must be overcome led him to persevere even when it was discovered that the Spanish garrison and island militia were far more capable than had been anticipated. He later wrote that he 'never expected to return.'[6] He burnt all the letters from his wife before going ashore from *Theseus*. The operation was a disaster. The defenders included thousands of militia, their morale high and their arms effective. Troubridge tried to bluff the Spaniards into surrender by threatening to burn the town, but in the end was only able to negotiate an honourable withdrawal after promising to cease to attack the Canaries. Nelson lost his right arm, and almost lost his life.

3. To Carlyle, 3 June 1797, Edward Hughes, ed, *The Private Correspondence of Admiral Lord Collingwood*, Navy Records Society, Vol 98, London, 1957, 42 p83.

4. J S Tucker, *Memoirs of Admiral the Rt Hon the Earl of St Vincent*, 2 vols, London, 1844, p262n.

5. Nelson to his wife, 11 July 1797, George P B Naish, *Nelson's Letters to His Wife and other Documents 1785-1831*, Navy Records Society, 1958, No 192 p330.

6. 24 July 1794, Anne Fremantle, *The Wynne Diaries 1789-1820*, Oxford: Oxford University Press, 1982, p278; and Nelson to Sir Andrew Hamond, 8 September 1797, Naish, *Nelson's Letters to His Wife*, p280.

The naval officer: duties and privileges

IN THE latter half of the eighteenth century there were three types of naval officer serving at sea in the Royal Navy: commissioned, warrant and petty officers.

The commissioned officers held authority from the Crown and received their commissions from the Board of Admiralty. They included admirals, captains and lieutenants. Admirals were divided into three squadrons, dating from the mid-seventeenth century, which wore either a red, a white or a blue ensign. Within these squadrons, the admirals were divided by seniority into the most senior, full admirals, and their subordinate vice-admirals and rear-admirals. Some captains, termed Commodores, were ordered to hoist a broad pendant as a distinguishing flag and assume command of small squadrons of ships themselves commanded by other captains; they exercised most of the authority of an admiral but held only temporary commissions. In the same way, some senior lieutenants were temporarily commissioned to command particular ships as commanders. They assumed the authority of a captain and, with this experience, were usually appointed to their own ship. Ships bearing commissioned captains were known as post ships; they ranged from Sixth Rates to First Rates; and their commanders were known as post captains.

Warrant officers were so-called because they were appointed by a board warrant rather than a commission. They included the master and surgeon who received their warrants from the Navy Board; the purser, carpenter and boatswain who received theirs from the Board of Admiralty; and the gunner who received his from the Board of Ordnance.

Petty officers also received a warrant but were initially appointed by a ship's captain. They included the surgeon's mates, armourer, cook, master-at-arms, sailmaker, chaplain and schoolmaster.

Distinct from the warrant and petty officers, because they were regarded as potential sea-officers, were midshipmen and master's mates, who might be drawn from the most socially elevated families in the land (1). Like the commissioned officers, they were permitted the all-important distinction from other ranks of being permitted to walk the quarterdeck—the after end of the ship was generally regarded as 'officer country' (2), and remained so in British warships until well into this cen-

1

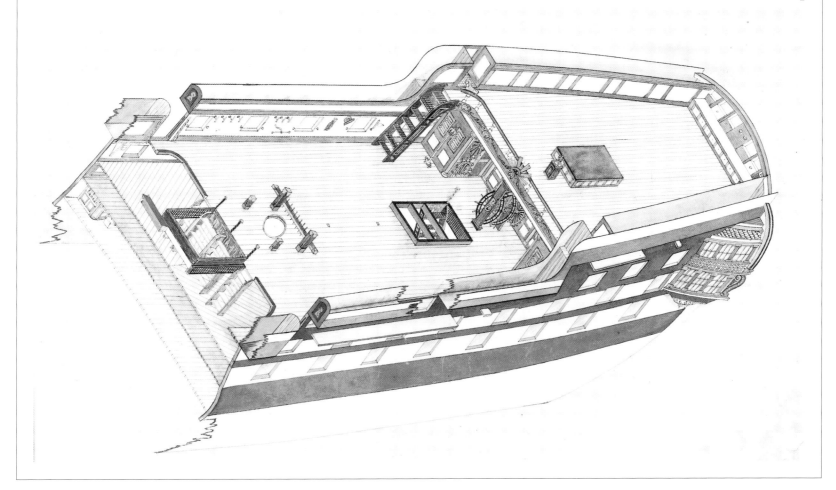

2

3

tury; there were rigid rules about access and a quarter-deck etiquette reflecting the hierarchy of the officers. Both midshipmen and master's mates were generally appointed by the captain to assist the lieutenants and other officers carry out their duties in managing the ship. The number of Midshipmen varied in proportion to the size of the ship: twenty-four to a First Rate, eighteen to a Second Rate, twelve to a Third Rate and so on. Usually aged thirteen on entry, though they could be younger, their own purpose was to learn the skills and knowledge of a sea officer. After two years, at the age of about fifteen, if sufficiently skilled in navigation and seamanship, they might obtain promotion to the situation of a master's mate, a position in which they were given charge of boats or sailing prizes into port. At the age of nineteen, if they had six years experience at sea, they became eligible to take an examination, upon passing which they could receive a commission as a lieutenant. However, most ships held numerous older midshipmen who had been unable to pass their examination. Master's mates had often passed their examination but had not yet received an Admiralty commission as a lieutenant.

Midshipmen, like admirals, commanders, and lieutenants, received an established uniform in 1748 (3). These, with their side-arms, separated them from the common seamen who frequently wore slops—the standard style of dress issued to a purser for sale (by deduc-

tion from their wages) to seamen—but had no formally designated uniform until the mid-nineteenth century. Admirals and captains often dressed their own boats' crews in distinguishing hats and jackets (4), but this was a point of individual prestige, depending on the wealth and conceit of the officer, rather than standard procedure. The more flamboyant also spent money on the appearance of their ship, and its boats were particular objects of display (5).

A lieutenant was one of several in any rated ship: a First Rate had ten or more. These lieutenants managed a ship on behalf of the captain; indeed, the first, most senior, lieutenant deputised for the captain in his absence, and all had authority to place any subordinate under arrest. Each took their turn in commanding watches, when they were expected always to be on deck, checking the sailing trim and navigation of the ship, keeping account of the men then under their particular command, and sending master's mates or midshipmen around the ship to check the conduct of the seamen off watch and to detect any source of fire or other danger to the welfare of the vessel and her company. In action, each had a particular role as deputised by the captain, some to assist him on the quarterdeck, others to supervise sections of the crew on the gundecks or aloft. A specific part of their duty was to keep a journal or log of their ship's progress and of incidents on board which, with certificates of service, had to be passed at the

4

5

Admiralty before they were permitted their pay. However, from the beginnings of their careers they were taught to observe and note, and even as midshipmen they would usually have kept semi-official journals, which they filled with navigational, astronomical and meterological observations, and information on any of the sciences pertaining to their profession. An important aspect of this was the encouragement to draw, which might manifest itself in practical objects like pilotage sketches (6), but often developed into more artistically sophisticated work, some of which survives and forms an excellent first-hand impression of the Navy of the sailing era.

Captains were given responsibility for larger ships as they obtained experience in smaller ones. Their burden was comprehensive, a captain being answerable for any questionable conduct in action, in navigation, in his ship's equipment, in the management of his subordinates, and, through them, in the behaviour of his crew. From the time of the receipt of his commission, he was expected never to sleep out of his ship until that commission was ended. Being responsible for the appropriate punishment of transgressors of ship regulations, including the Articles of War, he was expected himself to act as a model of moral virtue. He was responsible for the proper surveying and receipt of the designated quota of stores, and for obtaining as nearly as possible his complement of crew. Through his officers, he had to exercise and train this crew to engage enemies in battle, as well as to cope with adverse conditions of weather and

navigation. During all such eventualities, he had to provide leadership, and set an example of courage and resolution.

For it was upon his captains that an admiral depended in arranging and fighting his fleet. The latter oversaw everything for which a captain was responsible, temporarily appointing his officers, or arranging and discharging courts martial as they became necessary. But above all he was accountable for the achievement of the purposes for which his fleet was equipped and set out. Military engagement was the most likely possibility and he had to practise his ships in tacking, going about, sailing line abreast, and forming a line of battle composed of ships in the order he had decided was the most balanced and specific for the tactical object in mind. Whether anchoring or sailing, he had to have considered all dangers, and ensured at all times he was equipped with all possible information from scouting frigates of the whereabouts of the enemy. His ability to draw up clear instructions to his captains was vital, as was a capability to impose his will on them, arranging councils of war as necessary, entering into diplomatic negotiations, or offering advice to the King's ministers. It was ultimately upon the capability of the Admiral that the effectiveness of a fleet at sea relied. For a Royal Navy admiral, whose decisions might determine the safety of the country, the responsibility was awesome: not surprisingly, at the end of major battles the stress reduced many commanders to a state of collapse, and is probably the reason why many a partial victory was not followed up.

1. 'William IV 1765-1837 . . . As midshipman on board Prince George 1782', stipple engraving after an original by Benjamin West. *NMM ref PAD3482*

2. 'Diagram and section of the well and poop decks of HMS Canopus', anonymous black and watercolour pen and ink, no date. *NMM ref PAH0758*

3. 'Unknown gentleman wearing officers uniform of 1795-1812. One of four painted at Malta. Shows captain's undress coat, epaulettes, cocked hat, white waistcoat, white pantaloons, black hessian boots, sword, sword belt, white stock and yellow gloves', anonymous watercolour, no date. *NMM ref PAD3111*

4. 'Sketch of Andromeda's barge crew', anonymous grey wash, no date. The particularly splendid headgear may date from the period when the frigate was commanded by Prince William Henry (later King William IV). *NMM ref PAH4899*

5. 'A naval barge with eight oarsmen', grey wash by Nicholas Pocock (1740-1821), no date. *NMM ref PAD8876*

6. 'The Land from Point . . . to the Town of . . . near Belle Isle in the Bay of Biscay Sketched on board HMS Ramilles by R F Hawkins August 1st 1793. *NMM ref PAD8520*

6

2

Occupation of Toulon

1

THE MEDITERRANEAN command, traditionally second only to the Channel, was entrusted to Vice-Admiral Viscount Hood, himself second only in distinction to Lord Howe among Britain's active naval officers (1). During the American war, he regarded himself as unfortunate to be so often second-in-command to the second-rate, and was fond of telling others how an action could have been fought better. Given this shortcoming, he was to do remarkably well in a position which required co-operation not only with army officers and politicians, but also with difficult allies and quasi-enemies.

When his fleet of twenty-one ships of the line went out to the Mediterranean it had no clear plan beyond defend-

ing British trade, and relieving the pressure that French republican armies were putting on the Sardinians, but it was known that there was serious opposition to the extremes of Jacobinism in parts of the south of France, and the possibility of capturing Toulon, Marseilles or Corsica was mooted. Frightened by the merciless advance of local republican forces, the authorities of Toulon opened negotiations with Hood, and the British fleet was invited to enter the port, the political fiction being that it was held in trust for the restored French monarchy, and the white Bourbon flag was raised. The British insisted that the French fleet be disarmed and the forts turned over to their control, and after a few days of internal struggle the royalists emerged victorious. On 28 August, with the newly arrived Spanish fleet of seventeen in attendance, the British entered Toulon. It was an amazing coup: as Nelson said, '... that the strongest place in Europe, and 22 sail-of-the-line should be given up without firing a shot. It is not to be credited.'

It was a very well-equipped arsenal with two large basins within the defences—the Old Port to the east (2) and the New Port alongside it to the west (3). Beyond this was the Inner Road (or *Petit Rade*), but it was shallow and could not provide safe anchorage for much of the fleet, but was protected by two arms that were defended by the Aiguillette and Balaguier forts to the south (4), and the *Grosse Tour* to the north. A fleet ready for sea normally lay in the Outer Road (or *Grand Rade*), but it was not entirely safe from the levanter winds common on that coast. This contemporary view (5) shows its northern shore from Cape Brun to the *Grosse Tour*, with a fleet lying in the Inner Road.

To take Toulon was one thing, but to keep it was another. The principal difficulty was that the town and anchorages were surrounded by high ground (6), and to protect the fleet involved defending a perimeter of fifteen miles. Hood had a few troops employed in lieu of marines, but nothing like the numbers needed, and his appeals to the mutually jealous allies produced few more and often of poor quality. The French royalists were mistrusted, and there were still many Jacobin supporters in the town, and so many in the fleet that in September Hood sent four old disarmed French 74s to the Atlantic ports with the disaffected seamen to avoid the danger of a 'fifth column'. There were great calls on the seamen of the fleet, and they were magnificently led while ashore by Captain Elphinstone (later Lord Keith). Problems abounded, not least the difficulty of mooring the three-deckers in the shallow Inner Road where they could be used for effective counter-battery fire.

Sir Sidney Smith's own map (7) makes the topography clear. The republican attack was concentrated to the west, especially after Bonaparte arrived in September to superintend the artillery, and there were soon batteries on the shore of the Inner Road, but he was thwarted in his attempt to take the heights above the village of La Seyne. The heights to the north of the city were also captured, but instantly retaken in a spectacularly efficient counter-attack, but as republican victories in the surrounding areas freed troops for the siege, Toulon's position became ever more precarious. By November the allies could muster about 12,000 effective troops, made up of a rag-bag of Spanish, Neapolitan, British, Piedmontese (Sardinians) and French royalists, and Hood was so short of seamen that he was forced to hire 1500 from the Grand Master of the Knights of Malta.

4

7

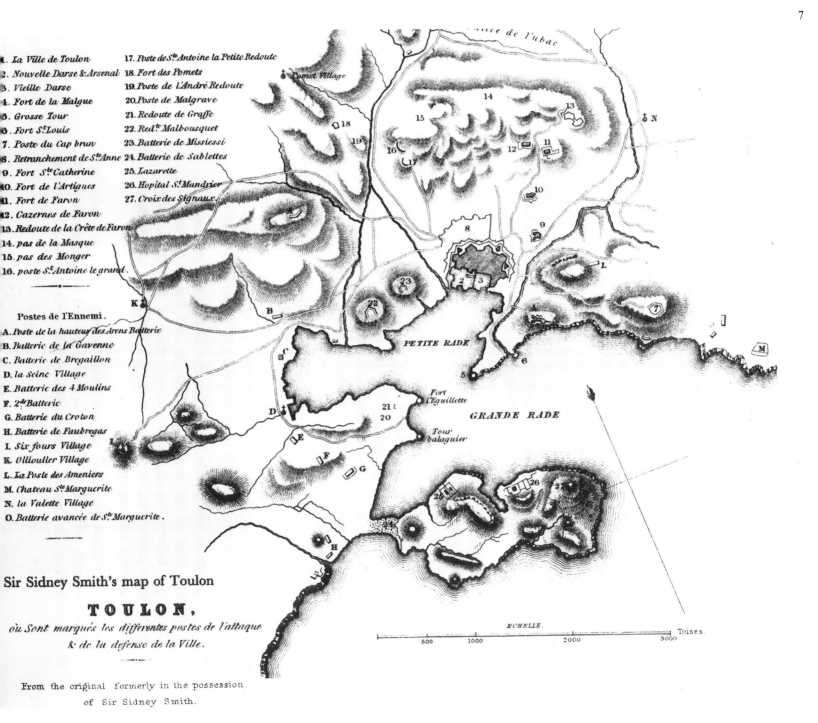

1. La Ville de Toulon
2. Nouvelle Darse & Arsenal
3. Vieille Darse
4. Fort de la Malgue
5. Grosse Tour
6. Fort St. Louis
7. Poste du Cap brun
8. Retranchement de Ste Anne
9. Fort Ste Catherine
10. Fort de l'Artigues
11. Fort de Faron
12. Cazernes de Faron
13. Redoute de la Crête de Faron
14. pas de la Masque
15. pas des Monger
16. poste St Antoine le grand

17. Poste de St Antoine la Petite Redoute
18. Fort des Pomets
19. Poste de l'André Redoute
20. Poste de Malgrave
21. Redoute de Graffe
22. Redte Malbousquet
23. Batterie de Missiessi
24. Batterie de Sablettes
25. Lazarette
26. Hopital St Mandrier
27. Croix des Signaux

Postes de l'Ennemi.

A. Poste de la hauteur des Arens Batterie
B. Batterie de la Gavenne
C. Batterie de Bregaillon
D. la Seine Village
E. Batterie des 4 Moulins
F. 2de Batterie
G. Batterie du Croton
H. Batterie de Faubregas
I. Six fours Village
K. Olliouller Village
L. La Poste des Ameniers
M. Chateau Ste Marguerite
N. la Valette Village
O. Batterie avancée de Ste Marguerite.

Sir Sidney Smith's map of Toulon

TOULON,
*où sont marqués les différentes postes de l'attaque
& de la défense de la Ville.*

From the original formerly in the possession
of Sir Sidney Smith.

PETITE RADE

GRANDE RADE

Fort l'Eguillette

Tour balaguier

ECHELLE.
500   1000   2000   3000   Toises.

2

Political tangles

THE DEFENCE of Toulon was potentially compromised by the many other duties that fell to Hood's fleet—indeed, only the five three-deckers spent much time in the port. These duties were complicated by the tangled politics of the region: the south of France itself was riven by factions ranging from one end of the political spectrum to the other, and these shockwaves rippled out to the numerous small nominally

1

neutral states of northern Italy. Corsica, which had been French for no more than a generation, added a further dimension, when patriots rose against the republican garrisons and appealed to the British for aid. In September 1793 Commodore Linzee was sent with a small squadron to co-operate with the insurgents, but they never appeared, and after a rapid success over the soon-to-be-famous tower at Mortella, suffered a more bruising encounter with the fort at Fornelli in San Fiorenzo bay (1). The damaged squadron was withdrawn, having achieved nothing.

Many of the Italian ports on which the British fleet depended for supplies had pro-revolutionary factions and most were actively involved in shipping foodstuffs to the republican armies operating in war-ravaged southern France. One of the most important was Genoa, which was regarded as too pro-French in its stance. The British had complained of the provocative behaviour of a French frigate and two armed tartans, but receiving no redress, decided to cut them out. Two 74s

3

and a brig, led by Captain Robert Mann of the *Bedford*, made short work of the opposition, and brought out the *Modeste* and the tartans. Militarily efficient, but politically inept, the incident was made the subject of republican French propaganda about the 'massacre' of the crews (2) –even though casualties were very light–but relations were broken off, and one very damaging long-term consequence was that the 5000 seasoned troops offered by Austria for the defence of Toulon could not embark from Genoa, and in the event never arrived at all. However, another frigate, the *Impérieuse*, was cut out at La Spezia, and Leghorn (as Livorno was known to the British) was more successfully coerced, the Grand Duke of Tuscany stopping supplies to the French.

To Hood's way of thinking, malign French influence stretched to the other side of the Mediterranean, where it was necessary to send an expedition to remind the Bey of Tunis where his best interests lay. Traditionally, Britain had been very tolerant of the Barbary states, since they were a source of water and victuals for the Royal Navy when the European shore might be very hostile, but Hood was intent on stopping the French supply convoys from Tunis, and ordered Linzee's refitted squadron to undertake the task. As a reinforcement, he was sent the 64-gun *Agamemnon*, but with the luck of her captain, Horatio Nelson, she ran into four French frigates returning from convoy duty to Tunis, and in a running battle gave the *Melpomène* a pounding before damage to her own tophamper forced the *Agamemnon* to break off the action (3). *Melpomène* limped into Calvi, where she was captured the following August, after a siege where the ubiquitous Nelson again played a major part (4). The mission to Tunis, dismissed by Nelson as 'a damn palaver', was a complete failure.

1. 'St Fiorenzo in the Island of Corsica, drawn on the spot by Captn Percy Fraser RN 1794', coloured aquatint engraved by Francis Jukes, no date.
NMM ref PAH2313

2. 'Massacre de l'equipage de la Modeste dans le Port de Genes par les Anglais le 5 Octobre 1793, ou 13 Vendemiaire An 2 de la Republique', engraving by Berthault after an original by Nicolas Ozanne, no date.
NMM ref PAD5441

3. 'The Agamemnon engaging four French Frigates', watercolour by Nicholas Pocock (1740-1821), 1810.
NMM ref PAF5873

4. Draught of *Melpomene* as captured. Admiralty Collection.
NMM neg 1649

4

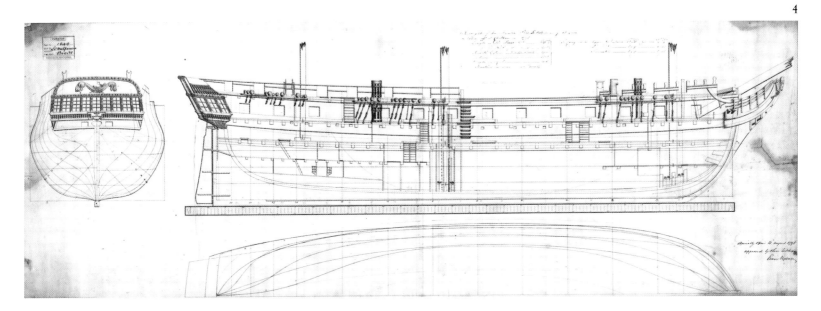

The original Martello tower

MORTELLA TOWER.

A *Middle Story*
B *Second Story*
C *Entrance door*
D *Counter scarp*
E *Gallery*
F *Embrasures for 2 Guns*
G *Cistern*
H *Ditch or entrenchment or bastion*

WHEN THE British attacked a simple gun tower on Cape Mortella during their campaign against Corsica in February 1794, they could not have guessed at the impact it would have on defence policy over the next fifteen years. Although its gun crew had fled the previous year when faced with the frigate *Lowestoffe*, this time it was better supplied, and beat off a determined attack by the 74-gun *Fortitude*, causing serious damage from red-hot shot and over 60 casualties. It eventually capitulated to shoreside bombardment, but a garrison of thirty-three men fighting a 6pdr and two 18pdrs had proved itself a serious obstacle. Both the army and the navy were impressed.

A somewhat crude but detailed drawing was made of the tower by an army engineer (1, 2, 3), and Admiral Jervis forwarded a model to the Admiralty, noting, 'I hope to see such works erected…on every part of the Coast likely for an enemy to make a descent on.' Other officers present on Corsica during the campaign included George Elphinstone (later Lord Keith), David Dundas, Abraham D'Aubant, Thomas Nepean and John Moore, all of whom were to have some influence on the development of British coastal gun towers. These were not uncommon in the Mediterranean, and the British themselves built somewhat similar towers on Minorca, when the island was commanded by Sir Charles Stuart (another Corsica veteran), while Lord Keith had some erected to defend the anchorage of Simonstown after he captured the Cape from the Dutch in 1795.

However, the tower entered the national consciousness when the Defence Committee of 1804, faced with the serious threat of French invasion, proposed a line of over a hundred towers along the south and east coasts, based on the tower at Mortella. However, the name became garbled in transit, and they became known as Martello towers. As is so often the case, the danger was

1

3

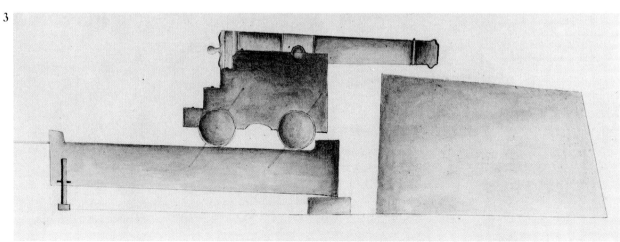

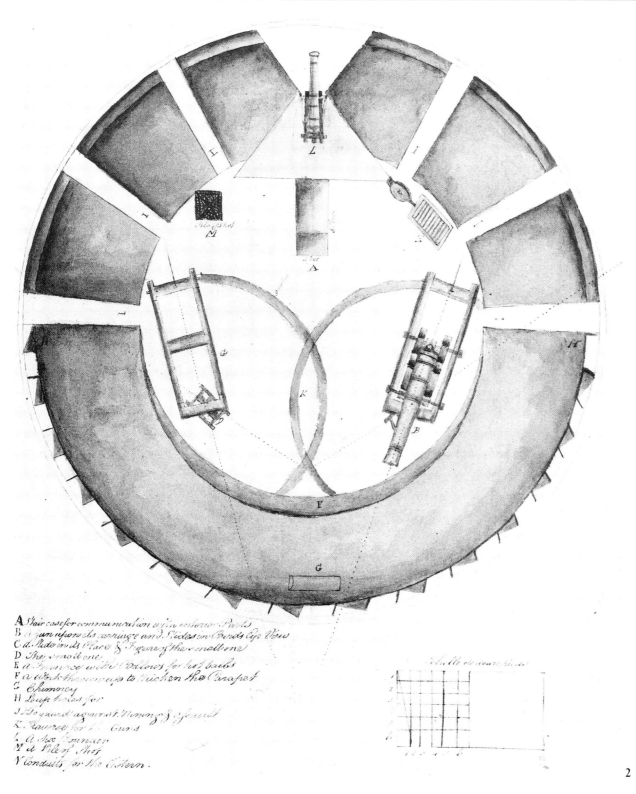

A Stair case for communication with interior Ports
B A gun upon its carriage and S[l]ides in Birds Eye View
C d. [*illegible*] in its Place & Figure of the small one
D The small one.
E a Furnace with Bellows for hot balls
F a Work thrown up to thicken the Parapet
G Chimney
H Loup holes for
J [*illegible*] against Storming & Assault
K Traverse for Guns
L a Six Pounder
M d 13 ? Shot
N Conduits for the Cistern.

2

over by the time the programme was complete, but some saw service in later wars and many still survive. The British design was rather different—aptly decribed as looking like an upturned flower-pot—being more squat and often having an elliptical cross-section that made the walls thicker on the seaward side where the threat was greater, but they seem to have been directly inspired by an incident in an otherwise fruitless campaign.

1. 'Mortella Tower, Corsica (elevation). First illustration in Plan of Mortella Tower, St Fiorenzo Bay, Corsica 1794', watercolour by C F D, 1794. *NMM ref PAD1621*

2. 'Inside view of Mortella Tower (plan). Second illustration in Plan of Mortella Tower, St Fiorenzo Bay, Corsica 1794', watercolour by C F D, 1794. *NMM ref PAD1622*

3. 'A cannon at Mortella Tower. Third illustration in Plan of Mortella Tower, St Fiorenzo Bay, Corsica 1794', watercolour by C F D, 1794. *NMM ref PAD1623*

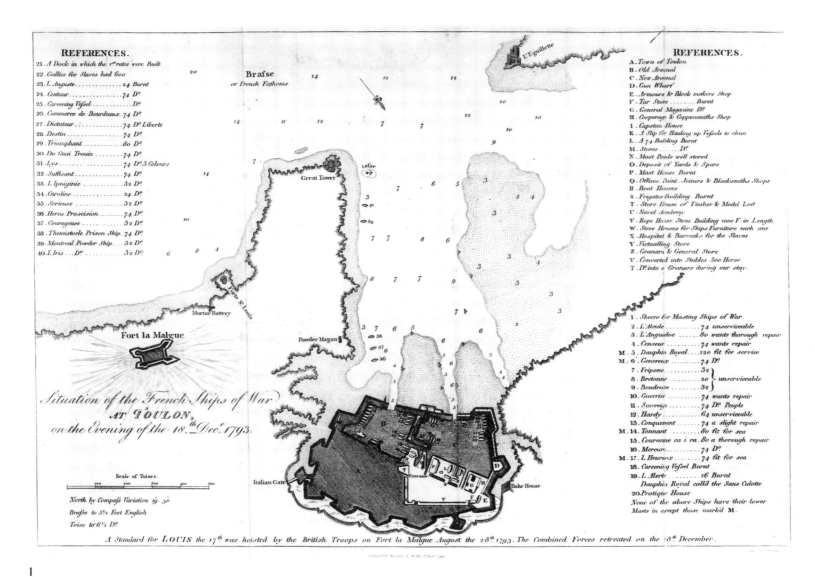

REFERENCES.

21. A Dock in which the 1st rates were Built
22. Gallies for Slaves had 600
23. L. Auguste .... 24 Burnt
24. Centaur .... 74 D°
25. Careening Vessel .... D°
26. Commerce de Bourdeaux . 74 D°
27. Dictateur .... 74 D° Liberte
28. Destin .... 74 D°
29. Triomphant .... 80 D°
30. Du Guai Trouin .... 74 D°
31. Lys .... 74 D° 3 Colours
32. Suffisant .... 74 D°
33. L. Ipnignie .... 32 D°
34. Caroline .... 24 D°
35. Serieuse .... 32 D°
36. Heros Proscision .... 74 D°
37. Courageuse .... 32 D°
38. Themistocle Prison Ship . 74 D°
39. Montreal Powder Ship .. 32 D°
40. L Iris .... D° .... 32 D°

Brasse or French Fathoms

Great Tower

Tour St. Louis

Mortar Battery

Fort la Malgue

*Situation of the French Ships of War
AT TOULON,
on the Evening of the 18th Dec.r 1793.*

Scale of Toises.

North by Compass Variation 19. 30'
Brasse to 5½ Feet English
Toise to 6½ D°

Powder Magan

Italian Gate

Bake House

L'Eguillette

REFERENCES.

A. Town of Toulon
B. Old Arsenal
C. New Arsenal
D. Gun Wharf
E. Armours & Block makers Shop
F. Tar Store .... Burnt
G. General Magazine D°
H. Cooperage & Coppersmiths Shop
I. Capstan House
K. A Slip for Hauling up Vessels to clean
L. A 74 Building Burnt
M. Stores .... D°
N. Mast Ponds well stored
O. Deposit of Yards & Spars
P. Mast House Burnt
Q. Offices, Paint, Joiners & Blacksmiths Shops
R. Boat Houses
S. Frigates Building Burnt
T. Store House of Timber & Model Loft
U. Naval Academy
V. Rope House Stone Building 1000 F. in Length
W. Store Houses for Ships Furniture each one
X. Hospital & Barracks for the Slaves
Y. Victualling Store
Z. Granars & General Store
V. Converted into Stables 500 Horse
T. D° into 6 Granars during our stay.

1. Sheers for Masting Ships of War
2. L'Alcide .... 74 unserviceable
3. L'Anguedoc .... 80 wants thorough repair
4. Censeur .... 74 wants repair
M. 5. Dauphin Royal .. 120 fit for service
M. 6. Genereux .... 74 D°
7. Friponne 32
8. Bretonne .... 20 } unserviceable
9. Boudeuse 32
10. Guerrie .... 74 wants repair
11. Sovereign .... 74 D° Peuple
12. Hardy .... 64 unserviceable
13. Conquerant .... 74 a slight repair
M. 14. Tonnant .... 80 fit for sea
15. Couronne ca i ra . 80 a thorough repair
16. Mercure .... 74 D°
M. 17. L Heureux .... 74 fit for sea
18. Careening Vessel Burnt
19. L Alerte .... 16 Burnt
Dauphin Royal call'd the Sans Culotte
20. Pratique House
None of the above Ships have their lower
Masts in except those mark'd M.

A Standard for LOUIS the 17th was hoisted by the British Troops on Fort la Malgue August the 28th 1793. The Combined Forces retreated on the 18th December.

1

2

Evacuation of Toulon

AS 1793 drew to a close, the position of Toulon's defenders deteriorated rapidly. Ever since the fall of Lyons in October, republican reinforcements had arrived in ever larger numbers, while a misunderstanding of the situation by the British government led them to remove some of Hood's precious few British regulars. The end came on 17 December when Bonaparte finally managed to capture Fort Mulgrave on the heights above La Seyne and a separate force took Mount Faron to the north of the city. A rapidly convened conference among the allies agreed that evacuation was the only course open, and it was decided to burn as much of the dockyard and the demilitarised French fleet as possible. Sir Sidney Smith, who had recently arrived in his own small sloop from the Levant, volunteered to organise the conflagration, in concert with a Spanish party under Don Pedro Cotiella.

This remarkable drawing (1) shows the exact position of all the ships on the night of the evacuation. With a few disreputable exceptions—the Neapolitans are said to have broken and fled without orders—the troops fought an effective rearguard action, and most were taken off by boats from the shoreline near Fort la Malgue, but there were also many royalist refugees to consider, and the chaos must have resembled Dunkirk in 1940. There were only six of Hood's ships in port, and of these the damaged *Courageux* had to be warped out without a rudder.

3

In the meantime Sir Sidney set about the ships and installations in the basins, lashing the properly primed fireship *Vulcan* across a trot of ships. He was under fire, and threatened by 600 galley slaves who provided the dockyard's heavy labour force, but in the end nine ships of the line, three frigates and three corvettes were destroyed; others were damaged but not fatally (2, 3). The buildings were less successfully fired, and since the Spanish are often accused of dereliction of duty, it is worth noting Smith's own report:

4

1. 'Situation of the French Ships of War at Toulon on the Evening of the 18th Decr. 1793', etching published by Bunny & Gold, London, 1 August 1799.
NMM ref PAH7846

2. 'A exact Representation of burning the Arsenal & blowing up the French Ships of War in the Harbour of Toulon 18 Dec 1793', etching by J Pass after an original by Crystal, published 1 July 1794.
NMM ref PAD5444

3. 'Burning the Ships of war at Toulon', anonymous engraving, no date.
NMM ref PAD5445

4. 'To the Rt Honble Lord Hood . . . employ'd in the defence of Toulon . . . the conflagration effected there on the night of the 18th Decr 1793 under orders . . . of Sir Sidney Smith', aquatint and etching by Archibald Robertson after his own original, published 28 April 1794.
NMM ref PAH7847

5

they, as well as ourselves, were in a manner thunderstruck by the explosion of some thousand barrels of powder on board the *Iris* frigate, lying in the inner road without [outside] us, and which had been injudiciously set on fire by the Spanish boats, in going off, instead of being sunk as ordered; the concussion of the air, and the shower of falling timber ignited, were such as nearly to have destroyed the whole of us. Lieutenant Patey of the *Terrible*, with his whole boat's crew, nearly perished; the boat was blown to pieces, but the men picked up alive. The *Union* gun-boat, which was nearest to the *Iris*, suffered considerably, Mr Young being killed, with three men, and the vessel shaken to pieces. . . . I had given it in charge to the Spanish officers, to fire the ships in the basin before the town, but they returned and reported that various obstacles had prevented their entering; we attempted it together, as soon as we had completed the business in the arsenal, but were repulsed in our attempt to cut the boom, by repeated volleys of musketry from the flag-ships and the wall of the *Batterie Royale* . . .

. . . The guns of the fire-ship going off on both sides, as they heated, in the direction that was given them, towards those quarters from whence we were most apprehensive of the enemy forcing their way in upon us, checked their career; their shouts and republican songs, which we could hear distinctly, continued till

The explosion of the *Iris* is depicted in all its gruesome drama in this illustration (4), with the other powder ship, the *Montreal*, being fired in the distance by a Spanish lateen rigged gunboat. The republicans are firing from L'Aiguillette, and two-decker nearest the Great Tower is the *Themistocle*, a prison ship whose inmates were freed by Sidney Smith before she was burned. Although anonymous, this watercolour (5) and its accompanying key (6)

6

1 Windsor Castle Barge   2 Victory's Boat   3 Spanish Barge   4 Swallow arm'd Tender   5 Hero 74   6 Themistocle 74   7 Powder Frigate   8 Frigate that had been exchang'd by the Sardinians for the Alceste   9 Old Corvette   10 Arsenal with 8 sail of the line &c on fire afloat as well as several parts on shore   11 Old Arsenal   12 Town of Toulon   13 Part of the Heights of Pharon — 14 Malbosquet throwing shells   15 Grand Tour abandon'd   16 Fort Balaguier firing — 17 Fort Equilette firing — 18 Neapolitan Fortified Hill   19 Spanish Fortified Hill   20 Fort Mulgrave on les Hauteur des grasses

show a remarkable knowledge of the events, although the timescale is somewhat truncated.

The British brought off fifteen ships, and once a few had been transferred to the allies, they retained three large frigates, *Perle, Arethuse* and *Topaze*, two 74s, *Puissant* (which never cruised) and *Pompée*, and the huge 120-gun *Commerce de Marseilles* (7). This ship was over 20 feet longer, and over 600 tons more burthensome, than the *Victory*, and was regarded as a fine sailing ship. However, in confined waters she was a menace, at full load drawing nearly 30 feet—the same as a Second World War battleship—and was so weakly built that she was converted to a gigantic storeship. With over 1100 men and their equipment, plus 500 crew, the ship attempted to sail with Christian's ill-fated convoy to the West Indies in November 1795; after a short but nightmarish voyage, she was forced back into Spithead and never put to sea again, becoming a prison hulk the following year.

The last act of the black farce of Toulon occurred in January 1794, when on the 11th the frigate *Juno*, with some of Hood's levies from Malta, sailed into a darkened inner harbour. A French boarding party attempted to persuade them to go further up the harbour, but the ship was actually aground, and by the time she had hauled herself off, the tricolour cockades of the boarders had been noticed; they were bundled below, and *Juno* fought her way past the batteries and safely out to sea (8).

7

8

Ships of the Royal Navy: fireships

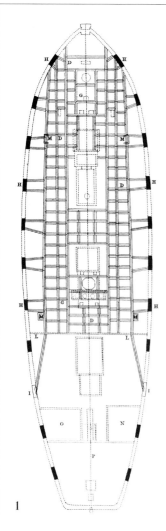

1

A S A TACTIC, the release of a burning vessel to drift down with the wind or tide on the enemy is probably as old as naval warfare itself, but it reached its apogee of success in the wars of the latter half of the seventeenth century. Very large fleets, lacking manouevrability and tactical sophistication, fighting in restricted waters, made for situations which the fireship could exploit.

Any merchant ship or superannuated warship could do the job if filled with combustibles, but fireships became more sophisticated as time went on. Ingenious developments included methods of making the fire spread quickly, like grating decks and air funnels to create draught; downward-hinged gunports that would not fall closed when the fire burned through the port tackle; cofferdams below deck to prevent the masts catching fire and coming down prematurely; grappling irons on the yardarms to make it difficult for the target to free itself; and elaborate fusing systems and a large sallyport to allow the crew to escape at the last moment. This made the quick conversion of existing vessels more difficult, and late seventeenth-century navies tended to build specialist fireships, which could cruise as sloops until they were needed (1). This may seem like an expensive solution, since the ship was built to be 'expended' (the official term), but it might be seen as a forerunner of a modern guided missile—also expensive, but cost-effective if it destroys a far more valuable target.

The building of dedicated fireships died out in the Royal Navy at the end of the War of Spanish Succession in 1713, but was revived during the American Revolutionary War. In 1779 a combined Franco-Spanish fleet had dominated the Channel, and for most of the rest of the war Britain was on the strategic defensive at sea. In these circumstances fireships might prove an 'equaliser', and two of the leading tactical innovators of the time, Howe and Kempenfelt, were strong advocates of their aggressive employment. However, Kempenfelt pointed out to the Comptroller, Sir Charles Middleton (later the Lord Barham of the Trafalgar campaign), that one reason for earlier lack of success with fireships was that they were slow sailers, so any new ones needed to be fast enough to keep up with a fleet. This was the origin of the *Tisiphone* class of the 1780s, which were modelled on the lines of a highly regarded French prize of the 1740s (2).

Byam Martin, who commanded the name ship in the Mediterranean in 1793, confirms that they were considered fast-sailing ships. He could perhaps count himself lucky that he was not called upon to use his fireship in earnest, since two of her class-mates in Lord Hood's fleet were so employed at the evacuation of Toulon: *Vulcan* was 'expended' in the time-honoured fashion to set fire to a line of French battleships, but *Conflagration*, under repair and immovable, had to be burnt to avoid capture. Howe, as would be expected of a fireship partisan, had a number of these ships during his command of the Channel Fleet, although their presence was disguised by their cruising rating as sloops. There were no opportunities—and indeed no need—for deploying fireships in fleet actions, but they became an important part of British attempts to destroy various enemy squadrons trapped by an ever more effective blockade. The only other purpose-built fireship expended, the *Comet*, was sent into Dunkirk Roads with three converted sloops in July 1800 in an attempt to destroy four large frigates: the fireships set fire to nothing, but in the confusion the *Desirée* was cut out by the sloop *Dart*.

An increasing preoccupation for the Royal Navy from

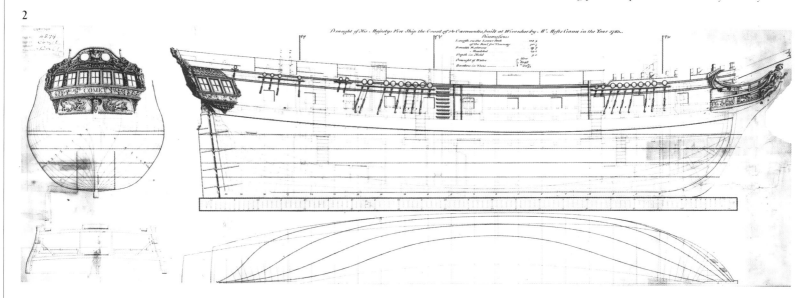

2

3

1. The fire room of a fireship showing the elaborate system of wooden troughs carrying the fuses, which are led through the protective bulkhead L to the sallyport, I, where the train is lit as the crew escapes. H represents gunports for draught which were blown open by charges placed behind them, and had downward-hinged ports so that they would not close when the fire burnt through the port ropes.
From Falconer's Universal Dictionary of the Marine, *1815 edition*

2. As fitted draught of *Comet*, 1783, one of the few fireships of this era employed for her intended purpose. Admiralty Collection.
NMM neg 8229

3. 'Action between HMS Phosphorus and the French privateer L'Elize 14 August 1806', watercolour by Irwin Bevan, no date. In external appearance, the 'fire brig' was indistinguishable from any other small merchant vessel.
NMM ref PAD9481

4. Sheer draught for *Comet*, dated 10 October 1805, one of the 'repeat *Tisiphone*' class. Admiralty Collection.
NMM neg 6868

the mid-1790s was the assembly of would-be invasion craft across the Channel. Fireships might well be useful during an attempted crossing, but conceivably might also be employed against the shipping inside its harbours and anchorages if the opportunity presented itself. With this kind of operation in mind a number of smaller, shallower draught, merchant ships were converted as 'fire vessels' (3), but no opportunity had presented itself by the peace of Amiens and they were all paid off.

Unfortunately the peace lasted little more than a year, and the war took up where it had left off, with an invasion threat even more serious than that of 1801. Six fireships modified from the *Tisiphone* design (4) were laid down (although in the event all saw out the war as sloops), but as a short-term measure more of the small fire vessels were taken up.

The last—and probably most infamous—set-piece use of fireships was Gambier's attack on the French squadron embayed in Basque Roads in 1809. Lord Cochrane led the attack, which included all the latest weaponry: cutters firing rockets, numerous fire vessels, a bomb, and three explosion vessels. The action became notorious because the initial success was not followed up, and provoked a very damaging public argument between Cochrane and Gambier. Leaving aside the rhetoric, it is worth noting that fireships and explosion vessels were rarely dangerous in themselves, but created panic that could be exploited by conventional forces.

4

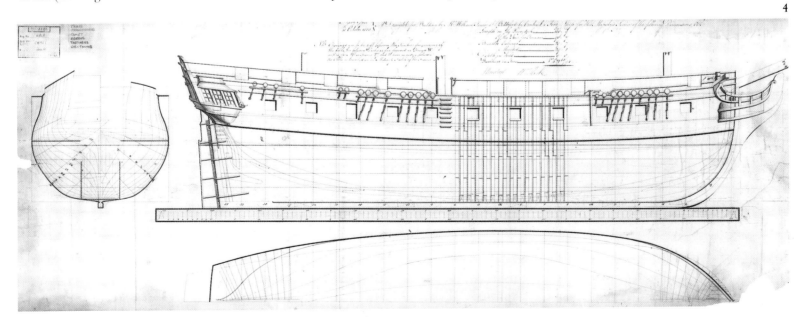

1

The Corsican campaign 1794

San Fiorenzo

After the fall of Toulon, Lord Hood moved the Mediterranean Fleet to Hyères Bay, east of Toulon, but, hearing that the republican troops on Corsica were short of supplies, he decided to make that island his base of operations. He had already opened communications with the Corsican leader General Pasquale de Paoli, who sought the removal of the French from the island and British support. Several ships were detached from the fleet to prevent the French being resupplied, one being the *Agamemnon*, 64, commanded by Captain Horatio Nelson. On 21 January 1794, a landing party from the *Agamemnon* destroyed a flour mill near the port of San Fiorenzo as part of this campaign of raiding against coastal traffic and defences.

    Hood sailed from Hyères on 24 January, but a storm drove the fleet away from its destination of San Fiorenzo

Bay and it was forced to take shelter in Porto Ferrajo on Elba. From here, a squadron consisting of three 74s, *Alcide* (the flagship of Commodore Linzee), *Egmont* and *Fortitude*, and the 32-gun frigates *Lowestoffe* and *Juno*, with transports carrying troops under Major-General Dundas, sailed for Mortella Bay on Corsica, arriving on 7 February. The next day the tower at Mortella was attacked from both land and sea, but the small fort was so well defended that after two and one half hours the *Fortitude* and *Juno* were forced to break off their bombardment and withdraw out of range, the *Fortitude* having suffered sixty-two casualties and been set on fire. The tower surrendered the next day, having come under fire from guns landed from the ships (1) and its wooden breastwork set alight. The British then moved on to attack the Convention Redoubt, the main defence of San Fiorenzo itself, armed with twenty-one heavy guns, which after a two-day bombardment was stormed on 18 February.

2

The French fell back into San Fiorenzo (2), where they set fire to the frigate *Fortunée* and allowed the *Minerve*, 38, to sink as a result of damage she had taken from the British bombardment, and then retreated to Bastia. The town was occupied the same evening, and a few days later the *Minerve* was raised, being commissioned into the Royal Navy as the *San Fiorenzo* (3), there already being a ship named *Minerve* in service.

Bastia

The campaign continued with the British laying siege to the French garrison at Bastia (4, 5, 6). This was largely a naval affair, as Major-General Dundas felt unable to proceed after the fall of San Fiorenzo until reinforcements had arrived from Gibraltar. Hood, on the other

hand, was eager to press on, and cruised with his squadron off Bastia until 5 March 1794 (7), when he returned to San Fiorenzo. Finding Dundas still unwilling to move without the 2000 new troops he was expecting, Hood decided to use the forces he had to hand, and sailed again for Bastia, landing there on 4 April. The landing force consisted of only 1248 men (although Corsican troops co-operated with them), with the seamen being commanded by Captain Nelson of the *Agamemnon*, whose own ship's company were very active in landing guns for the siege and manning the batteries established ashore.

By 11 April the preparations for the siege were complete, and Hood demanded the town's surrender, but the French governor General Lacombe Saint-Michel refused, resulting in a hard-fought siege of thirty-seven

3

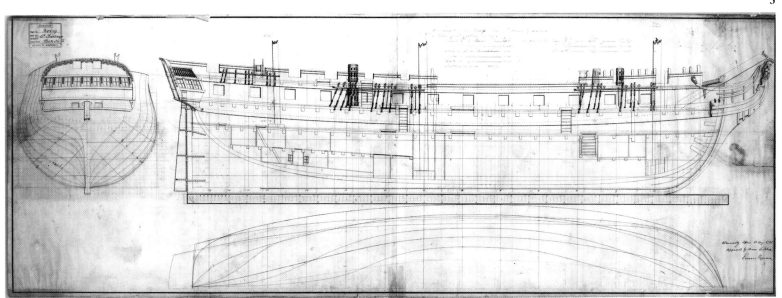

4

days, costing the British nineteen killed and thirty-seven wounded. The map (8) shows the British siege-lines. On 21 May, with provisions almost exhausted, the town surrendered, and two days later British troops marched through the gates. There had been some bad feeling between the navy and the army during these operations, and Nelson expressing frustration at the unwillingness of the army commanders to detach troops for the siege. As a result of the fall of Bastia, General Paoli formally transferred Corsica's allegiance from France to Great Britain on 19 June.

Calvi

The British then moved to attack Calvi on the north-western coast of the island, a stronger place than Bastia, defended by three forts. Again Nelson was put in charge of the naval forces involved, and Lieutenant-General The Hon. Charles Stuart commanded the troops. The squadron arrived off Calvi on 18 July 1794, but bad weather hampered the landing operations, a storm forcing the ships to stand out to sea on 22 June to avoid being wrecked, and it took some time to get the guns and supplies necessary for the siege ashore. Calvi held out for fifty-one days, the besiegers suffering badly in the heat of the Corsican summer, Nelson reporting at one point that half his force was sick. It was here, on 10 July, that Nelson received the injury that cost him the sight of his right eye (9), when he was hit in the face by stones and fragments from a shell bursting against the battery he was inspecting. Nine days later Fort Muzello, the main defence of the town, fell, and the British were thus able

5

6

7

1. 'Blue Jackets Landing Artillery and Ammunition on Corsica', anonymous grey and watercolour pen and ink, c1794.
NMM ref PAH2355

2. 'View of the town of San Fiorenzo', anonymous watercolour.
NMM ref PAH2349

3. Sheer draught of *Minerve*, as captured. Admiralty Collection
NMM neg 2069

4. 'Bastia in the Island of Corsica, drawn on the Spot by Captn Percy Fraser RN 1794', coloured aquatint engraved by Francis Jukes.
NMM ref PAH2314

5. 'A Southern View of Bastia in the Island of Corsica from on Board His Majesty's Ship Victory during the Siege of that Town in May 1794', watercolour by Ralph Willett Miller, 1794.
NMM ref PAH2324

6. 'Vue de Bastia en Corse', anonymous graphite drawing, c1795.
NMM ref PAH2325

7. 'A View of Bastia', showing Admiral Hood's squadron offshore in 1794, aquatint engraved by Thomas Medland from an original by Nicholas Pocock, published by Bunny and Gold, 1 July 1799.
NMM ref PAD5982

8. 'Siege de Bastia Par les Anglais et les Corses Rebelles en 1794', etching by Adam from an original by Fachot.
NMM ref PAD5469

9. 'Loss of His Eye Before Calvi', etching by William Henry Worthington from an original by William Bromley, published by Robert Bowyer, 1 March 1808.
NMM ref PAD5479

8

SIEGE DE BASTIA PAR LES ANGLAIS ET LES CORSES REBELLES EN 1794.   Pl. VII.

9

to bring their guns to bear upon Calvi itself. The French commander negotiated a twenty-five day truce, promising to surrender if he had not received reinforcements after that time, a ploy to exploit the sickness rife amongst the besiegers, but the siege held and on 10 August Calvi surrendered. Two French frigates were taken in the harbour, the 40-gun *Melpomène*, which was taken into the Royal Navy as a 38, and the 32-gun *Mignonne*, which was considered too small and unserviceable to be useful and was later burned at Porto Ferrajo. After the siege, Nelson was worried that, as at Bastia, he would not receive full credit for the part he had played from the army, a symptom of the continued friction between the two services in this campaign. He wrote: 'What degree of credit may be given to my services I cannot say. . . They hate us sailors; we are too active for them. We accomplish our business sooner than they like.' Corsica was held by the British until November 1796.

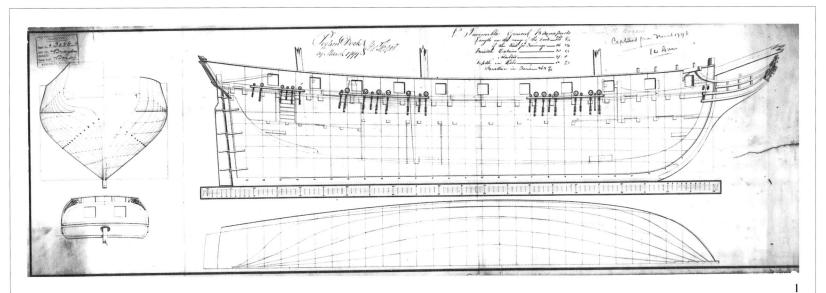

1

Ships of the Royal Navy: flush-decked ship sloops

IN NAVAL parlance, the word 'sloop' had a number of meanings, ranging from a single-masted rig to a rating—in effect, any vessel in the charge of an officer with the rank of Master and Commander (or Commander for short). Such ships were usually small cruisers, below the 20-gun post ships in size, but the rating also applied to vessels like a bomb or fireship when cruising, or even a ship of the line when armed *en flute* as a troopship or storeship.

The ancestry of the sloop of war can be traced back to the small craft—often little more than large boats—that accompanied sixteenth- and seventeenth-century fleets. In the eighteenth century, sloops grew in size and developed more ship-like characteristics, at the same time assuming more independent cruising roles. They were originally two-masted, but in the 1750s became ship rigged and in most respects small frigates, armed with

fourteen or sixteen 6pdrs, although a few larger vessels carried eighteen. They proved more seaworthy, more habitable, longer-ranged and better armed than the old two-masted type, and the ship rig must have conferred some advantages in battle—three masts would have made them less vulnerable to damage aloft than two. But the one quality the new-style sloops did not possess was speed, and from the late 1770s the sloop category began to include faster and more weatherly brigs.

Quarterdecked ship sloops could be easily overtaken by far more powerful frigates and a number were captured under these circumstances: *Alert* and *Hound* in 1794, *Peterel* in 1798, *Cyane* and *Ranger* in 1805, and *Favourite* in 1806. Moreover, their sluggish sailing could result in the loss of other ships, like the *Africaine* in the Indian Ocean in 1810, surrendered because the British commodore could not assemble his force in time to prevent

2

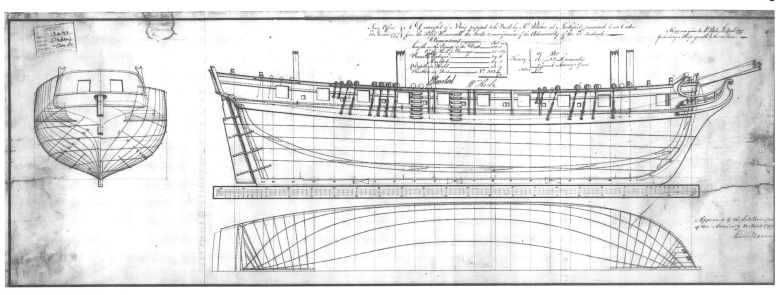

3

it, largely due to the slow progress of the *Otter*.

As a result it was rare for any ship sloop of the traditional type to be employed by the main fleets, and certainly not in frontline roles. They were not weatherly enough for the Channel blockade, and were not fast enough or powerful enough to act as scouts for the battlefleet. When attached to fleet commands, they were usually to be found detailed to convoy merchantmen within that command's jurisdiction. It is perhaps indicative of the official view of the quarterdecked ships that they tended to retain their long 6pdrs on the main deck, where the larger brigs were quickly converted to 32pdr carronades: the ship sloops seem to have been regarded as the smallest viable independent cruiser (for which a mixed armament was more useful), and patrol and convoy work, especially on more distant stations, was their usual lot for most of the war.

Almost all the sloops attached to the Channel Fleet in the early years of the war were brigs. However, a new type of flush-decked vessel was developed in the 1790s, initially entirely acquired by capture (1) but from 1797 purpose-built as well. These latter were essentially brig hull designs given three-masted rigs (2), whereas most of the French prizes were more ship-like, but lacking substantial upperworks were more weatherly and usually faster. The Channel Fleet's *Scourge* was of this design, while the 500-ton *Bonne Citoyenne* was a particular favour-

ite; she proved a very effective scout for the Mediterranean Fleet leading up to the battle of St Vincent, and in most respects was a good substitute for a frigate (3). As the Admiralty searched for new sources of supply, the shipbuilders of Bermuda offered their services, and in 1797 the first of a class of very sharp-hulled ship sloops were launched, using local cedar timber. Again, they were rather brig-like in their open flush deck, but a bow with a full set of headrails and false quarter galleries gave them the appearance of larger warships (4).

In this light it is instructive to look at the relative development of the two types of ship rigged sloops of war in the Royal Navy of this period.

Quarterdecked ship sloops

Year	No in Sea Service	No in Ordinary or Repairing
1794	32	1
1797	43	2
1799	38	0
1801	34	0
1804	19	2
1808	49	3
1810	54	2
1812	50	1
1814	43	1

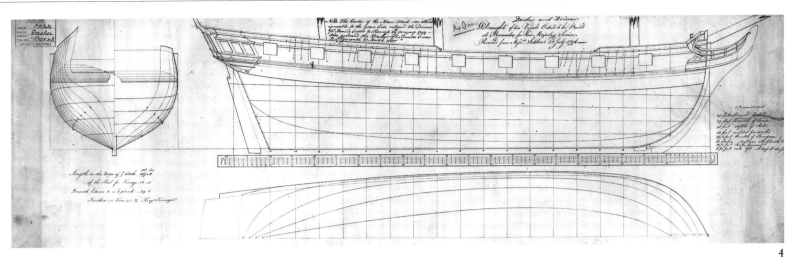

4

Flush-decked ship sloops

Year	No in Sea Service	No in Ordinary or Repairing
1794	0	0
1797	10	0
1799	23	0
1801	22	3
1804	37	0
1808	27	7
1810	19	2
1812	12	1
1814	9	1

The flush-decked ships grew in numbers in the French Revolutionary War just as the quarterdecked ships declined, reflecting the fleet concerns of the period, and the willingness of the Spencer Admiralty to back innovation in ship design (only one quarterdecked type was ordered after 1795). With sloops, as with so many other classes, a regression began with the St Vincent administration; the 1802 programme included fourteen quarterdecked ships to a design of 1795, and succeeding admiralties built even more. This period was obsessed with the threat of invasion, and the good defensive qualities of the quarterdecked sloop may have seemed a better bet in the circumstances; certainly new building declined with the post-Trafalgar change in priorities. The flush-decked sloop also staged a small recovery later, thanks to the victories of the big American ship sloops in the War of 1812 forcing the construction of similar ships, for which the British reverted to the hull form of the highly regarded *Bonne Cityonne* (5).

1. Sheer draught of the *Brazen*, ex French privateer *Invincible General Bonaparte*, as taken off at Portsmouth Dockyard, 19 March 1799. Admiralty Collection. *NMM neg 3088-46*

2. Sheer draught of the *Osprey*, 21 March 1797, showing both the original brig rig, and the revised three-masted arrangement. Admiralty Collection. *NMM neg 3477-50*

3. 'Constantinople. North view, taken from the Artillery Quay (called Tophana) with H.B.M.'s ships Le Tigre and La Bonne Citoyenne under the command of Sir Sidney Smith', coloured aquatint engraved by J Jeakes after an original by John Thomas Serres, published by Edward Orme, 1 August 1805. *NMM neg B7136*

4. Sheer draught of the *Dasher*, as received from the builders, 22 July 1796. Admiralty Collection. *NMM neg 3224*

5. Sheer draught of the *Hermes* class sloops of 1810; those built as a response to the big American ship sloops in 1812 were slightly reduced versions, but with two extra gunports. Admiralty Collection. *NMM neg 2926*

5

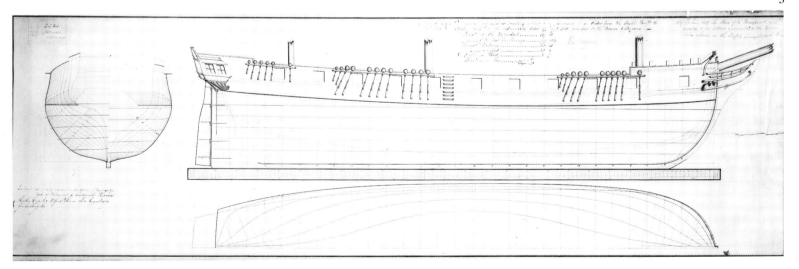

The Mediterranean Fleet under Hotham

2

LORD HOOD'S last service in the Mediterranean was to chase a French squadron that had escaped the Toulon holocaust into Gourjean Bay in June 1794. They were blockaded, but eventually escaped into their home port during a gale a few months later. Hood sailed for home in the *Victory* in November, turning over command to Vice-Admiral Hotham.

By early in 1795 the French had repaired enough of the Toulon damage to send a sizeable squadron to sea, and in February the 120-gun *Sans Culotte* (more famous to history under her later name of *L'Orient*), led three 80s, eleven 74s and half a dozen frigates on a mission to reconquer Corsica. British intelligence was very good, and Hotham's fleet—four three-deckers, seven 74s and two 64s—caught sight of them off Genoa on 13 March. The French had enjoyed a small victory a week earlier in capturing the jury-rigged *Berwick*, 74 which was strug-

gling to join the rest of the fleet at Leghorn, but showed no intention of taking on the whole Mediterranean Fleet. Hotham signalled 'general chase' and in their precipitate retreat the *Ça Ira* of 80 guns collided with another 80, the *Victoire*. The former lost her topmasts and was audaciously attacked by the frigate *Inconstant*, Captain Fremantle, but in an equally daring counter, with the British vanguard approaching, the French *Vestale* coolly took the stricken two-decker in tow.

First up was Nelson's *Agamemnon*, which skilfully tacked under the bigger ship's stern for three hours (1), by which time *Bedford* and *Edgar* were in action with the rear of the French line, including the giant *Sans Culotte*, but they were all recalled by the admiral. The pursuit was renewed at first light and *Ça Ira* was duly captured, along with *Censeur*, 74 which had taken over the tow from the gallant *Vestale* (2). The French made an attempt to rescue the prizes, but were thwarted by light winds, although *Illustrious* and *Courageux* were damaged. As in a number of these early fleet battles, the French fired red-hot shot, but to no great effect.

The day was yet young, and Nelson told his wife,

I went on board Admiral Hotham as soon as our firing grew slack in the Van, and the *Ça Ira* and *Censeur* had struck, to propose him leaving our two crippled ships, the two Prizes, and four frigates to themselves, and to pursue the enemy; but he, much cooler than myself, said 'We must be contented, we have done very well.' Now, had we taken ten sail, and allowed an eleventh to escape when it had been possible to have got at her, I would never have called it well done: we should have had such a day, as I believe the annals of England never produced.

Hood had received much the same response from Rodney after the Saintes in 1782, and it is interesting to speculate what Hood would have done in Hotham's place.

Having received a powerful reinforcement of nine of the line, including the famous *Victory*, in June Hotham sent the frigates *Dido*, 28 and *Lowestoffe*, 32 to investigate a report that the French fleet was at sea. By coincidence, the French frigates *Minerve*, 40 and *Artémise*, 36 had been sent on a similar mission, and the resulting action between the pairs of cruisers demonstrated the growing divide between British and French fighting skills. Although the smaller ship, the 9pdr-armed *Dido* as the senior officer's command chose to tackle the 18pdr-armed *Minerve*, at 1100 tons nearly twice the size of the British ship (3). Some support was supplied by the 12pdr *Lowestoffe* during the battle, but when *Minerve* surrendered it was the *Dido* which had done most of the damage. *Artémise* took little part in the action and fled when *Lowestoffe* was ordered in pursuit. *Minerve* became a favourite command in the Royal Navy, and carried Nelson's broad pendant during one famous clash with Spanish frigates in 1796.

Whatever his shortcomings, Hotham recognised Nelson's suitability for detached service, and in the following months the *Agamemnon*, with frigates and small craft in attendance, was often in action along French-held coastal territories. His squadron was chased by the

3

French fleet in July, but escaped to warn Hotham, who eventually brought them to one of his partial actions that so frustrated Nelson—on the 13th off Hyères he captured the *Alcide*, 74, but shortly after she struck, this prize caught fire and blew up, taking with her nearly half of her 615-man complement.

Nelson was more successful with his next detachment, in support of the Austrian campaign along the Gulf of Genoa, when he raided shipping in Alassio and Languelia Bays (4). He cut out a French corvette and a gunbrig, two galleys and five merchant ships, and destroyed two others, before his force escaped without loss.

4

1

Britain withdraws from the Mediterranean

UNDETERRED BY the minor defeats inflicted upon it by Hotham, the Toulon fleet sent very effective squadrons to sea on commerce-destroying missions under Richery and Ganteaume in the autumn of 1795. In November Hotham struck his flag and was replaced the following month by Sir John Jervis, a harsh disciplinarian but an effective and inspiring leader. Unfortunately for Britain, in March 1796 the French 'Army of Italy' was turned over to an even more effective young general, Napoleon Bonaparte, who began the phenomenal campaign that made him a household name throughout Europe.

For the Royal Navy, the first major blow was the French capture of Leghorn on 30 June (1), because this neutral port was a much-used rendezvous and a source of stores and victuals. One of the British ships in the harbour when French troops arrived was the frigate *Blanche*, whose complement included the American sailor-of-fortune Jacob Nagle, who left a description of a typical display of naval *sang froid*—followed with almost comic-book speed by a reversal of policy:

Early in the morning the French began to fire at us, but the guns from the batteries could not reach us by 15 or 20 yards though their guns was chock'd so that they could not recoil . . . we lay still and washed our

2

3

decks down as usual in the morning. At 8 o'clock we piped to breakfast. During this time, finding they could not reach us, they got a long gun from a tower on the S.W. side of the town and brought it to the nearest battery to us and began to open upon us. The very first shot went over us a quarter of a mile.

Immediately the hands were turned up to weigh anchor, got under way, and began to beat out, having a head wind from the westward. Our vessel being light, we fell to leeward and having to stretch along shore past all the batteries, they kept a continual fire upon us and we returning the salute till we were out of reach of their guns, which was not less than two hours.

After Leghorn the next French target was likely to be Elba, another possession of the Grand Duchy of Tuscany, which would provide an ideal springboard for the French recapture of Corsica. The British moved quickly and on 10 July Nelson's squadron occupied the heavily defended fortress town of Porto Ferrajo with the agreement of the local authorities (2, 3).

The British position in the Mediterranean worsened throughout the year, as one by one Britain's allies were

4

5

forced to sue for peace by French land victories. Spain's attitude hardened, and as a French squadron sheltered in Cadiz in August (4), an alliance with France was signed at San Ildefonso. This became a declaration of war in October, which raised the old spectre of Franco-Spanish domination of the Channel, as in 1779, followed by an invasion of Britain herself. The Mediterranean Fleet had to be positioned where it could rapidly reinforce the Channel, so the decision to withdraw from the Middle Sea was taken. This meant abandoning Corsica, and Nelson withdrew the garrison of Bastia in October and in November Jervis's fleet sailed from San Fiorenzo for Gibraltar, and eventually Lisbon. At this point there was not a single British battleship inside the Straits of

Gibraltar—even Nelson had to hoist his broad pendant in a frigate to evacuate the last British outpost, on Elba, in December.

While operating alongside the Spanish as allies, the British had formed a low opinion of their fighting efficiency, even if they never lacked bravery. This was confirmed on 13 October in the first clash between the new enemies, when after a battle of about an hour and a half the frigate *Mahonesa* surrendered to James Richard Bowen's *Terpsichore*, 32; Bowen had only four wounded, but Spanish casualties were around thirty dead and a similar number wounded (5). The prize was a fine big ship (921 tons), but was so badly knocked about in the action that she was never commissioned for British service (6).

6

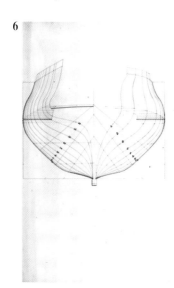

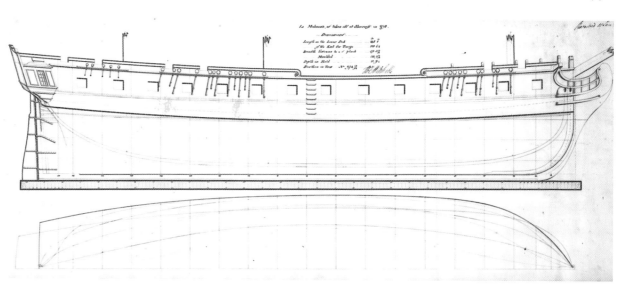

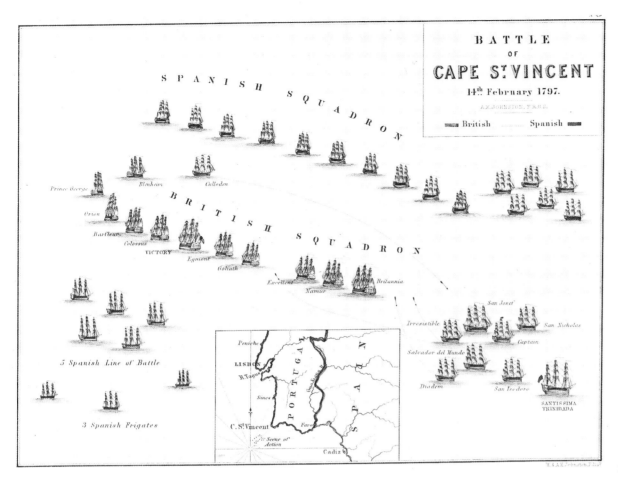

Battle of Cape St Vincent, 14 February 1797

AFTER ITS strategic withdrawal from the Mediterranean, the British fleet under Sir John Jervis (1) was based in the Tagus below Lisbon, where a sequence of accidents reduced its numbers to ten of the line, but a reinforcement of five from the Channel Fleet arrived early in 1797 and the combined fleet then included six powerful three-deckers. On 13 February Nelson's *Minerve*, having successfully evacuated Sir Gilbert Elliot, late Viceroy of Corsica, arrived with the news of sighting the Spanish fleet—indeed, the frigate had been vigorously chased by two 74s. Commanded by Admiral Cordóba, the Spanish force comprised seven three-deckers, two 80s and eighteen 74s, plus a dozen frigates.

Jervis, who once said 'men, not ships, win battles', was undaunted. He put to sea immediately, and on the morning of the 14th the Spaniards were sighted off Cape St Vincent heading for Cadiz in two loose groups. His view of the strategic situation was put simply and starkly to his captains—'a victory is very essential to England at this moment'—and he formed a single line of battle and steered for the gap in the opposing formation, by

this time reduced to a total of twenty-five of the line. Through the early morning mist the Spanish took the British force to be no more than nine of the line, but as light winds cleared away the fog they saw their mistake and their danger.

The leeward squadron was actually the close escort for a small but highly valuable convoy carrying mercury for the all-important refining of silver, and Cordóba took his main body of seventeen ships downwind to close the gap. The better-disciplined British reached it first and a distant cannonade began as the fleets passed, and the British van then tacked in succession, led by the *Culloden*, to pass up the starboard, lee side of the enemy line, which closed the range and allowed the British line to keep in touch (2). One of the strengths of the Spanish fleet was its concentration of three-deckers, including six of 112 guns (3), each more powerful than the *Victory*, Jervis's flagship. At this point in the battle, one of these from the leeward group made an attempt to drive past the *Victory* to rejoin the main body. The incident is recorded in the usual laconic official style in the ship's log:

3

4

5

1. 'Admiral John Jervis (1735-1823), 1st Earl of St Vincent', oil painting after the style of John Hoppner (1758-1810). *NMM ref BHC3002*

2. 'Battle of Cape St Vincent 14th February 1797', coloured etching by W Johnston after an original by A K Johnston, published by William Blackwood & Sons, no date. *NMM ref PAH6270*

3. 'Vais [seau] Espagnol de 100 Canons, a la Cape', coloured engraving by Gaetano Canali after an original by Emeric, published 1794. *NMM ref PAH9399*

4. 'HMS Victory raking the Salvador del Mundo at the battle of Cape St Vincent, 14 February 1797', oil painting by Thomas Luny (1759-1837). *NMM ref BHC0484*

5. 'Historia de la Marina reale Espanola. La Funestra Battalla del Cabo de San Vicente . . . Santisima Trinidad', coloured lithograph engraved by Augusto de Belvedere and De Martinez y Ca., no date. *NMM neg no B9302*

6. 'Lord St Vincent's Victory, Feby 14th 1797', etching by Francesco Ambrosi after an original by William Wilkins, no date. *NMM ref PAF4683*

½ past [12], a Spanish Vice-Admiral attempted to pass ahead of the *Victory*. The *Culloden* and *Blenheim* on the larboard tack and passing to windward of our line . . . The Spanish Vice-Admiral forced to tack close under the *Victory*'s lee. Raked her both ahead and astern, he appeared to be in great confusion [and] bore up, as did six other of the enemy's ships.

This moment was caught very accurately by Thomas Luny's painting (4), except that at the time it was believed the opposing ship was the *Salvador del Mundo*; in fact, it was the flagship of Vice-Admiral Moreno, the *Principe de Asturias*, that received the double raking.

One by one, the British ships tacked, but the head of the Spanish line was far to the northeast of them, threatening to pass around the stern of the British formation and join up with the lee squadron. At this point Nelson, last but two in the British line, dramatically intervened: wearing his 74-gun *Captain* out of line, he recrossed the line ahead of *Excellent* (which then followed his manoeuvre) and steered across the van of the Spanish line, heading directly for the fleet flagship, the 136-gun *Santísima Trinidad*. This ship inspired awe, and not a few legends—a four-decker and the largest ship in the world—believed at the time and perpetuated by later historians. In fact, she was only a 'four-decker' by dint of a reconstruction shortly before St Vincent in which the

forecastle and quarterdeck were joined and armed with an extra eight 8pdrs a side; she was also comfortably exceeded in dimensions and tonnage by the latest French 120-gun ships. Nevertheless, she was a very potent vessel and instantly recognisable, and although three other three-deckers were close by, she became the *Captain*'s target (5). The battle of manoeuvre was over and the contest of gunnery was about to begin (6).

6

1

Nelson's Patent Bridge

1. 'The battle of Cape St Vincent, 14
February 1797', oil painting in the
style of Nicholas Pocock (1740-1821).
A sophisticated painting with the
main details right, but the style of
painting the British ship suggests
postwar execution.
NMM ref BHC0491

2. 'St Vincent. Nelson boarding the
San Nicolas 14th February 1797',
watercolour by Thomas Buttersworth
(1768-1842) dated 1797. Relative
positions of the ships is not correct;
Captain is too far forward.
NMM neg no 7155

3. 'Commodore Nelson boarding the
San Nicholas of 80 and the San Josef of
112 14th Febry 1797', watercolour by
Captain Ralph Willett Miller, no date.
Crude but most interesting because
based on a drawing by Nelson's own
flag captain.
NMM ref PAG8949

4. 'Nelson boarding the San Nicolas
and the San Josef', watercolour by
Nicholas Pocock (1740-1821), no date.
San Josef seems to have fore-reached
too much.
NMM neg no A3423

ABOARD THE frigate *Lively* at St Vincent was Colonel John Drinkwater, a member of Elliot's staff from Corsica and the historian of the great siege of Gibraltar during the American War. Both men had begged Jervis to be allowed to sail with the fleet for the imminent battle, and he had obliged. Drinkwater therefore became an eye-witness, but, being on one of the frigates, at sufficient distance to appreciate the larger manouevres, and he later published the best contemporary account of the battle. Although he talked to many of those involved and collated reams of notes, he was particularly struck by Nelson, who came on board shortly after the fighting stopped and regaled him with the typically Nelsonic combination of charm and ego-

2

tism. Drinkwater's popular narrative was therefore responsible for fostering the idea that Nelson had, in effect, won the battle for Jervis.

Captain's dramatic intervention in the battle was certainly the most popular aspect of the battle with artists, and particularly the moment when the British ship crashed into the 84-gun *San Nicolas* which in turn collided with the 112-gun *San Josef* (1-4). The episode is best told in Nelson's own words:

The *Excellent* [Captain Collingwood] ranged up with every sail set, and hauling up his mainsail just astern, passed within ten feet of the *San Nicolas*, giving her a most awful and tremendous fire. The *San Nicolas* luffing up, the *San Josef* fell on board her, and the *Excellent* passing on for the *Santísima Trinidad*, the *Captain* resumed her situation abreast of them, close alongside.

At this time, the *Captain* having lost her fore topmast, not a sail, shroud, or rope standing, the wheel shot away, and incapable of further service in the line or in chase, I directed Captain Miller to put the helm a-starboard, and calling for the boarders, ordered them to board.

The soldiers of the 69th Regiment, with an alacrity which will ever do them credit, with Lieutenant Pierson, of the same regiment, were amongst the foremost on this service. The first man who jumped into the enemy mizen chains was Captain Berry, late my First Lieutenant. . . . He was supported from our spritsail yard, which hooked into the mizen rigging. A soldier of the 69th Regiment having broke the upper quarter-gallery window, jumped in, followed by myself and others as fast as possible. I found the cabin doors fastened, and the Spanish officers fired their pistols at us through the windows, but having broke open the doors, the soldiers fired, and the Spanish Brigadier (Commodore, with a distinguishing pendant) fell as retreating to the quarterdeck . . . Having pushed on to the quarterdeck, I found Captain Berry in possession of the poop, and the Spanish ensign hauling down. I passed with my people and Lieutenant Pierson on to the larboard gangway to the forecastle, where I met two or three Spanish officer prisoners to my seamen, and they delivered me their swords [5].

At this moment a fire of pistols or muskets opened from the admiral's stern gallery of the *San Josef*; I directed the soldiers to fire into her stern, and, calling to Captain Miller [his flag captain], ordered him to send more men into the *San Nicolas*, and directed my people to board the First Rate, which was done in an instant, Captain Berry assisting me into the main

3

chains. At this moment, a Spanish officer looked over from the quarterdeck rail and said they surrendered [6]; from this most welcome intelligence it was not long before I was on the quarterdeck, when the Spanish captain, with a bow, presented me his sword, and said the admiral was dying of his wounds below. I asked him, on his honour, if the ship were surrendered? he declared she was; on which I gave him my hand, and desired him to call his officers and ship's company, and tell them of it—which he did; and on the quarterdeck of a Spanish First Rate, extravagant as the story may seem, did I receive the swords of the vanquished Spaniards; which, as I received, I gave to William Fearney, one of my bargemen, who put them with the greatest sang-froid under his arm [7].

4

5

6

To capture two ships in succession in a such a fashion was unique in the Royal Navy's long and illustrious history, and the exploit was soon known in the fleet as 'Nelson's Patent Bridge for Boarding First Rates'.

Needless to say, there were others who saw their efforts diminished by Nelson's capture of the limelight, if not all the prizes. Some argued that _Culloden_ was already coming up with the leading Spanish group, when _Captain_ arrived in such an operatic, and unauthorised, fashion, while others felt that Nelson had actually taken _their_ prizes. In truth, the whole fleet fought very well, but it suited Britain to elevate Nelson's achievement to the level of the extraordinary—it boosted public morale at a dark time, and was another step on the ladder towards establishing the Royal Navy's aura of invincibility in the minds of its enemies.

Given the odds, the final haul of prizes—the 112-gun _Salvador del Mundo_ and _San Josef_, the 84-gun _San Nicolas_ and the 74-gun _San Isidro_—was extraordinary, but before

7

7. 'Commodore Nelson receiving the Sword of the Spanish Admiral', engraving published by J & J Cundee, 1813. Although crude, it shows all the main features.
NMM ref PAD7691

8. 'San Nicolas 84 guns', watercolour by William Innes Pocock, no date but presumably 1797.
NMM ref PAF0603

9. 'The San Isidro 74 Guns', watercolour by William Innes Pocock, no date but presumably 1797.
NMM ref PAF0604

8

Jervis could get them home he had to ward off a threatened rescue attempt by Cordóba's undamaged ships, but they did not press home the attack. The prizes were splendid trophies—especially the three-deckers, which were only rarely captured in battle—but they were not much of an addition to the strength of the Royal Navy. The two-deckers were rather old, the *San Nicolas* (8) built at Cartagena in 1769 and the *San Isidro* (9) a year earlier at Ferrol; they were portrayed on their voyage to the Tagus, battle-scarred and under jury rig, by Lieutenant William Innes Pocock, son of the famous Nicholas, but he lacked his father's talent as a marine artist. As a stopgap measure they were all retained with the British fleet until October, but after they returned to Britain for survey, none was found suitable for sea service. Spanish ships had a reputation for heavy sailing—at least partly based on experience with the 80-gun *Gibraltar* captured in the previous war—but the *San Josef* was refitted in 1801, probably as a quick replacement for the *Queen Charlotte* which had caught fire and blown up the previous year. Fittingly, she was earmarked as Nelson's flagship, but this appointment was overtaken by events.

Following the battle, the honours were generous for the victors, Jervis henceforth being known as the Earl of St Vincent; two junior admirals were made baronets, and Nelson became a Knight of the Bath. Conversely, Cordóba and his second in command were cashiered and stripped of titles, and half a dozen Spanish captains dismissed or reprimanded.

9

The naval officer: recruitment and advancement

TOWARDS THE end of the war that stern disciplinarian Admiral St Vincent, reflecting on changes in the Navy, expressed strong reservations to the King about what might be called the gentrification of the officer corps. There had always been a few aristocrats in the service, but as the Navy became more successful, and as its standing in the country rose, more and more young gentlemen sought to make a career at sea. The experience of having a son in the Navy became a common one for many families—some of Jane Austen's few overt references to the war she lived through occur in *Persuasion*; the naval officers might be drawn from life since she had two brothers who became prominent in the service. In this common experience the caricaturist Cruickshank found a ready market, and in a popular series published after the war, he satirised the process of turning callow youths into naval officers.

His hero is Master William Blockhead, shipping as a Midshipman aboard HMS *Hellfire* and destined for the West Indies (1). He is seen in childish mood (a new Mid was often some way short of his teens when first going to sea) chasing his sister with the dirk that marked his rank, as a sword would do when he became more senior. His mother weeps, as mothers always do, at the prospect of losing him, while his father surveys with obvious dis-

taste the mountain of bills for the various requirements of a young naval gentleman. These items, scattered about his sea-chest, include luxuries like preserved meats and cherry brandy, but since the ship is off to the dangerous West Indies there are also medicines and 'rags for wounds'.

5

6

7

It is clearly a well-to-do household, and Blockhead's first sight of the licensed bedlam of the Midshipmen's berth is a shock (2). The boisterous cheek-by-jowl existence, the noisy merriment, and lack of privacy is evident, although if he had been educated at an English public school and not by private tutor he would hardly have noticed the difference. The artist even manages to convey something of the smell of the place, with the hatch to the noisome hold open. His introduction to his duties is no more encouraging, keeping the middle watch in cold, rainy conditions (3), but the inevitable youthful clashes with authority bring even less pleasant retribution (4). Sending malefactors to the masthead for long periods was a common punishment for even minor misdemeanors, and since the caption says he is 'enjoying the fresh air for the 304th time', he is frequently in trouble. The accompanying dialogue, the cause of his punishment, will be recognisable to any schoolchild who has ever faced the unreasonable and arbitrary exercise of adult power:

Lieutenant:	Pray Mr B, did you call the Master?
B:	No, Sir. I *thought* . . .
Lieutenant:	You thought Sir! How dare you *think* Have you marked the Board?
B:	No, Sir. I didn't think . . .
Lieutenant:	Didn't think; why *didn't you think* Sir!!! Up to the Masthead directly . . .

Midshipmen were officers in the making, and were given nominal authority over far older and more expe-

rienced seamen from early in their careers. In ships of the line they might command a part of a gun deck, and a boarding action could find them in the thick of hand-to-hand fighting. They had to grow up quickly, and as the caption suggests, Blockhead has already reached Soldier in Shakespeare's Seven Ages of Man, 'seeking the bubble reputation, even in the cannon's mouth' (5). In fact, a midshipman could not seek more, since his promotion depended on passing an examination, for which (in theory at least) he could not be entered until he was at least nineteen years of age and had six years of certified sea-time. It was an ordeal, but once successfully negotiated it brought with it, after 1812 at least, a splendid epaulette to set off the new uniform and a dress sword (6).

However, further promotion, and even an appointment, thereafter depended on 'interest'—who one knew or who the family might be connected to. Calling at the Admiralty in person was the last resort, and its waiting room (7) was the graveyard of many an ambition. This lively conclusion to the series depicts a very mixed collection of officers, civilians and even a seaman, through which the proud new Lieutenant Blockhead struts. One man, perhaps a half-pay officer, spells out 'DAMNA . . .' in dust on the floor, and an ominous piece of graffitti on the wall declares:

In sore affliction, tried by God's commands
Of patience, Job, the great example stands
But in these days, a trial more severe
Had been Job's lot, if God had sent him here.

1-7. Coloured aquatints engraved by George Cruickshank, published by Thomas McLean, 1 August 1835.

1. 'Midshipman Blockhead. Fitting out Mastr. Willm Blockhead HM Ship Hellfire West India Station'. *NMM ref PAD4721*

2. 'Master B finding things not exactly what he expected'. *NMM ref PAD4722*

3. 'Master B on the Middle watch, cold blows the wind & the rain's coming on'. *NMM ref PAD4723*

4. 'Mr B mastheaded or enjoying the fresh air for the 304th time'. *NMM ref PAD4724*

5. 'Mr B seeking the bubble reputation'. *NMM ref PAD4725*

6. 'Mr B Promoted to Lieut. & first putting on his uniform'. *NMM ref PAD4727*

7. 'Waiting room at the Admiralty (no misnomer)'. *NMM ref PAD4726*

1

Blockade of Cadiz

FOLLOWING ITS smashing victory over the Spaniards off St Vincent, Jervis took the fleet back to the Tagus, where the most damaged vessels, including the *Victory*, were dispatched home and the remainder refitted. Reinforcements included the brand-new *Ville de Paris*, the first 110-gun ship in the Royal Navy and named after de Grasse's flagship captured at the Saintes in 1782. With middle and upper deck batteries of 24pdrs and 18s, she was more than a match for the Spanish 112-gun ships with their 18pdrs and 12s, although not quite as large as the *San Josef*. She became the flagship of the newly ennobled Admiral St Vincent, and led the fleet of twenty-one of the line to sea on 31 March 1797 to blockade Cadiz (1).

The sheltered Bay of Cadiz (2) still contained twenty-six ships of the line, now under the command of Mazzeredo, and the British fleet trailed its coat off the port for six weeks, but could not draw them out (3). On

19 May St Vincent established a close blockade, anchoring off the town in a crescent formation (4), with an Advanced or Inshore Squadron under Nelson right in the mouth of the harbour (5). However, there was also what a military man might call a 'forlorn hope', in the shape of the frigate *Blanche* whose crew still included Jacob Nagle, last noticed off Leghorn, and he left a record of his ship's thankless and forgotten duty:

Jervis's fleet lay at an anchor outside, then Nelson with a squadron of seven sail of the line lay inside of them, and we were stationed within the whole, laying off and on from one shore to the other, all hands at quarters during the night with the hatches laid over that no one was allowed to go below, and let us stand on the one tack or the other, we would have a shot or shell flying over us during the night. The reason was to keep the gunboats off from annoying the line of battle ships. The gunboats would come out and lay off and keep firing at the ships laying at their anchors, but when we were inside we could cut them off, but the batteries on either shore could fire at us. We remained on this station about a fortnight, then we were relieved . . .

Having failed to shame the Spanish fleet into action, St Vincent resolved to bombard the town, which seemed likely to provoke some defensive moves. Nelson, now a rear-admiral, was given the task and on the night of 3 July the bomb vessel *Thunder* with gunboats and the boats of the fleet stood in towards the tower of San Sebastian. The Spanish countered with gunboats and other small craft and Nelson was involved in a savage hand-to-hand fight with the boat of the Spanish commander, Don Miguel Tyrason, as recounted by one of the sailors present (see the next section for illustration):

John Sykes was close to Nelson on his left hand, and he seemed more concerned for the Admiral's life than his own: he hardly ever struck a blow but to save his gallant officer. Twice he parried blows that must have been fatal to Nelson. . . . It was cut, thrust, fire, and no load again—we had no time for that. The Spaniards fought like devils, and seemed resolved to win from the Admiral the laurels of his former victory; they appeared to know him, and directed their particular attack towards the officers.

Twice had Sykes saved him; and now he saw a blow descending which would have severed the head of Nelson . . . but Sykes saved him—he interposed his own hand! We all saw it . . . and we gave in revenge one cheer and one tremendous rally. Eighteen of the Spaniards were killed, and we boarded and carried her; there not being one man left on board who was not either dead or wounded.

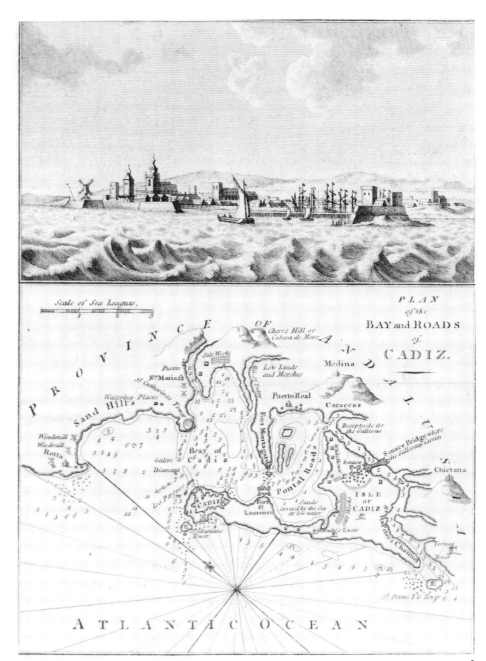

2

3

4

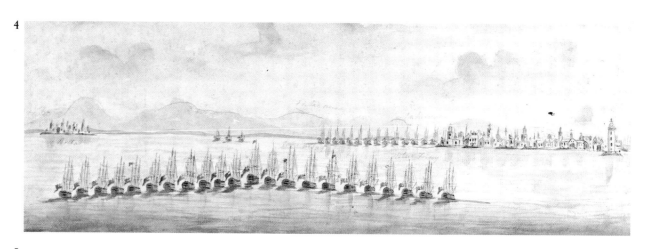

5

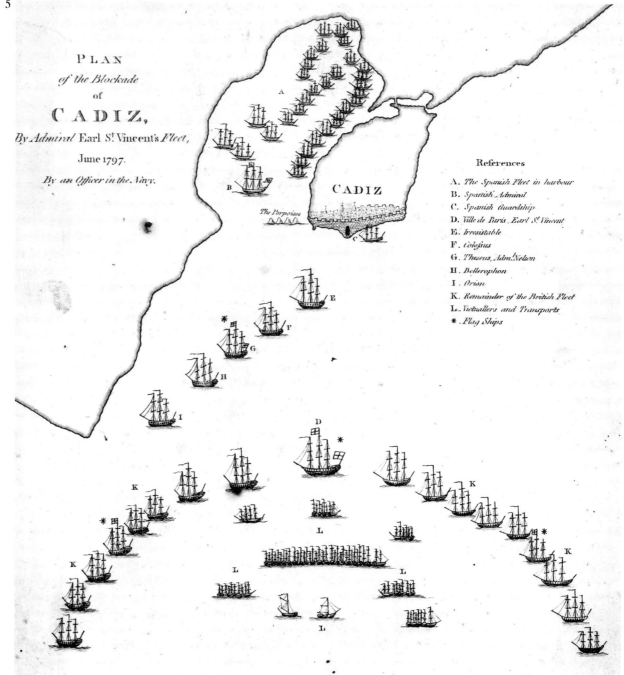

1. 'Earl St Vincent leaving Lisbon in the Ville de Paris 31 March 1797', grey wash by Thomas Buttersworth (1768-1842).
NMM ref PAH9502

2. 'View of Cadiz in Spain from the West. European Magazine. Plan of the Bay and Roads of Cadiz', engraving by J Cary, published by I Fielding, 1 January 1783.
NMM ref PAD1662

3. 'The inshore blockading squadron at Cadiz, July 1797', oil painting by Thomas Buttersworth (1768-1842).
NMM ref BHC0499

4. 'A View of the Blockade off Cadiz by the British Fleet under the Command of the Right Honble Earl St Vincent', anonymous watercolour, no date.
NMM ref PAF4685

5. 'Plan of the Blockade of Cadiz, by Admiral Earl St Vincent's Fleet June 1797. By an Officer in the Navy', engraving, no date.
NMM ref PAD5519

6. 'Blockade of the Port of Cadiz August 1797 by the Fleet under the Command of Adm. Sir John Jervis—with the Advanced Squadron', watercolour by Thomas Buttersworth (1768-1842).
Peabody Essex Museum, Salem MA neg 15121

7. 'Representation of the advanced Squadron under the command of Rear-Admiral Lord Nelson during the Blockade of Cadiz exhibiting a View of the Harbour and Fortifications taken from the Original Drawing by T Buttersworth now in his Lordship's Possession', published by T Williamson, London, 1 July 1802.
NMM ref PAG7151

6

Besides the commandant's launch, the British captured two mortar boats, but the bombardment was a failure, as was a more powerful attack with three bombs two days later. The frustrated Nelson was dispatched on the even more disastrous Santa Cruz expedition later in the month.

Meanwhile the blockade went on. That the events of this period are so well illustrated is largely due to Thomas Buttersworth, who was serving as a seaman in the fleet and must have observed at first hand the incidents he illustrates—his depictions of the Advanced Squadron, for example, both as original watercolours (6) and as prints (7).

St Vincent withdrew the main fleet to the Tagus in the autumn, but a squadron of observation was kept cruising off Cadiz during the winter.

7

Santa Cruz de Tenerife

URING THE blockade of Cadiz, rumours reached Earl St Vincent that a Spanish treasure ship, the *Principe de Asturias*, carrying £7 million in gold from Manila, had taken shelter in Santa Cruz de Tenerife in the Canary Islands. The loss of this bullion would be a crippling blow to Spanish finances, an important boost for the British exchequer, and, not least, a fabulously rich prize for the admirals and captains responsible for its capture.

On 15 July 1797 a squadron commanded by Rear-Admiral Nelson sailed for Tenerife (1). It comprised Nelson's flagship *Theseus*, the *Culloden* and *Zealous*, all 74s, the *Leander*, 50, the frigates *Seahorse, Emerald* and *Terpsichore*, the cutter *Fox* and a mortar boat. The ships arrived off Tenerife on the 20th, but bad weather and contrary currents prevented an immediate landing and the element of surprise was lost. The island turned out to be far more strongly defended than expected, and a landing on the 22nd was abandoned without loss when the heights above the town of Santa Cruz were found to be too strongly held to be taken.

However, Nelson did not give up, and on 24 July attempted another attack, this time against the defences of the harbour entrance, with the *Fox* and a number of the other ships' boats, Nelson himself in command. It was far from usual for a rear-admiral to participate directly in small boat actions, but it was Nelson's practice to lead from the front, as at St Vincent and later at Cadiz when he was involved in a battle with a Spanish launch, (2) where one of his sailors had saved his life three times in vicious hand-to-hand fighting. But this time he was not to be so lucky. The attack was met by heavy fire, the *Fox* being sunk by three direct hits. The boats managed to reach the mole head, but Nelson was hit in the right elbow as he stepped out of his boat (3), fell back into it and was carried back to the *Theseus*, where his arm had to be amputated.

Meanwhile, the battery at the mole head had been taken and its guns spiked, but almost the entire attacking force was then either killed or wounded by fire from the citadel and the houses nearby. Among those killed was Captain Richard Bowen (4) of the *Terpsichore*, who had distinguished himself after the battle of Cape St Vincent by pursuing and engaging the famous 136-gun *Santísima Trinidad* in his 32-gun frigate, only breaking off when other Spanish ships appeared. Other boats had managed to put their men ashore elsewhere, but the surf was so high that many had had to put back, and the men who were landed had their ammunition ruined by water. By dawn there were some 340 sailors and marines ashore, under the command of Captain Thomas Troubridge of the *Culloden*, facing a reported 8000 Spaniards. Amazingly, Troubridge was able to negotiate a withdrawal, the Spanish governor, Don Antonio Guttierrez, permitting the British to re-embark, even providing them with boats and rations, in return for a promise of no further attacks on any of the Canary Islands.

The expedition had been very costly. The British had lost 141 men killed, 95 of these drowned when the *Fox* was sunk, and 105 wounded. By comparison, only seventy-three men had been killed aboard British ships at the battle of Cape St Vincent. Nelson had been lucky to escape with his life.

1. 'View of Santa Cruz', coloured aquatint engraved by T Medland from an original by W Alexander, published by Messrs Cadell and Davies, 4 June 1806. *NMM ref PAD1949*

2. 'Nelson in conflict with a Spanish Launch, July 1797', oil painting by Richard Westall, 1806. *NMM ref BHC2908*

3. Nelson wounded at Tenerife, 24 July 1797', oil painting by Richard Westall, 1806. *NMM ref BHC0498*

4. 'Captain Richard Bowen 1761-1797', stipple engraving by H R Cook, published by J Gold, 31 May 1810. *NMM ref PAD3035*

3

4

Part IV

IRELAND AND THE CHANNEL 1795–1797

BY THE Treaty of Basel in April 1795 Prussia had made peace with France. With the end of fighting on the mainland, French military planning could concentrate on plans against the Britain Isles. The combined naval forces of France, Spain and the Netherlands, if they could find the means to co-operate well together and overcome the training and supply problems of the French, and the manpower shortages of the Spaniards, would be a formidable force in the Channel. Unlike the Duc de Vergennes, who had refused to contemplate the large-scale invasion of England during the American War because he feared the reverberations throughout Europe such a marked change in the balance of power would cause, the revolutionary government had nothing to lose by invading the British Isles. The need to counter the danger of invasion was to to be a major factor in British defence planning until in 1805 that option was decisively closed for the enemy. The events of 1796 and 1797, however, were to show how inadequate the naval resources of France, even when allied to Spain and the Netherlands, were for the task.

The stimulus for invasion of Ireland came from the United Irishmen, led by Lord Edward Fitzgerald. After a preliminary sounding of the ground in Paris, he and Arthur O'Connor met General Hoche at Basel to discuss a plan. Hoche and Admiral Truguet were in close agreement on the value of an operation to undermine Britain's position by outflanking her in Ireland, and in October 1796 Villaret-Joyeuse was ordered to fit out the Brest fleet to land a French army under General Hoche at Bantry Bay. Discipline had been restored in the fleet, but the dockyards were still desperately short of supplies, and the men lacked the training and experience to inspire confidence.

Villaret-Joyeuse said so, and was replaced by Admiral Morard de Galles.

The Irish nationalist Wolfe Tone had developed the plan of operations with Hoche, and now accompanied the expedition. It was intended that the Brest fleet should avoid naval action. The army was to be landed at Bantry Bay in southwest Ireland, and it was to make a quick movement to Cork where the Royal Navy victualling stores would have been easily taken. There was next to no British military force ashore in Ireland.

De Galles was able to sail his fleet of seventeen ships of the line, and nineteen light craft with seven transports and a powder ship, from Brest without opposition because Vice-Admiral Colpoys was not on station, but he lost a ship, *Séduisant*, 74, which ran on a rock. Indeed, it was the inadequacy of French seamanship, and the fact that the ships were supplied for only a few weeks, which was to defeat the expedition. The frigate *Fraternité*, aboard which were the admiral and General Hoche, became separated from the rest of the squadron, which made its way under Admiral Bouvet but missed its proper landfall and spent days beating against gale-force easterlies into Bantry Bay. The fleeting opportunities which occurred to put the army ashore were missed by General Grouchy acting in the absence of Hoche, and the continued easterly wind and shortage of supplies made it unhealthy to remain long in the Bay when Bridport could be expected to appear with the Channel Fleet.

In fact, however, the operational inadequacy of Spithead as the base for Channel Fleet operations was made abundantly clear by the difficulty Bridport experienced in getting to the westward when ordered to sea by the Admiralty. His own indolence was a contributing factor, and he also had bad luck when several of his ships collided on leaving the anchorage. He did not even get far enough down Channel to meet de Galles on his way back to Brest.

A straggler from the fleet, *Droits de l'Homme*, was engaged in heavy weather by Captain Sir Edward Pellew with two frigates, the 44-gun *Indefatigable* and the 36-gun *Amazon*. The high sea, and the fact that *Droits de l'Homme* had lost her fore and main topmasts which prevented her putting up sails to steady her roll, made it impossible for her to use her lower deck guns. *Indefatigable* was armed with long 24pdr guns on the lower deck, and 42pdr carronades on the upper, so she was a formidable opponent.

> During the whole of this long engagement, [wrote William James] the sea ran so high, that the people on the main decks of the frigates were up to their middles in water. So violent, too, was the motion of the ships, that some of the *Indefatigable*'s guns broke their breechings four times; some drew their ring-bolts from the side, and many of the guns, owing to the water having beaten into them, were obliged to be drawn immediately after loading.[1]

In the murk, navigation became inexact. When land was sighted close under their lees all three ships broke off their fight to claw themselves clear, but only *Indefatigable* saved herself from the rocks in Audierne Bay.

Part of the Toulon fleet under Vice-Admiral Villeneuve had followed Jervis out of the Mediterranean, passed him at Gibraltar during the gale which had caused him such heavy losses, and safely reached Brest. At the end of June 1797 there were nineteen fully armed ship of the line at Brest, and many armed *en flûte* for use as transports. These were to co-operate with the movement of the Dutch fleet to escort an invasion force from the Texel to England. However, the Battle of Cape St Vincent had discouraged the combined Franco-Spanish fleet seeking action in the Channel. A political convulsion in Paris which temporarily eclipsed the power of the Directory brought the dismissal of Admiral

---

1. Jemes, Vol 2, p20.

2. I bid, p32.

Truguet from the naval ministry. He was replaced by M. Pléville-de-Peley who was inexperienced with naval affairs but was able to execute the instruction to disarm the Brest fleet and sell some of the frigates. The Directory recovered its power in September and ordered the rearming of the fleet at Brest, but it was to take all winter before it was again in a condition for sea.

The threat from the small navy of the Netherlands became critical when on 15 April 1797 the seamen and marines at Spithead refused to sail until their grievances about pay, victuals, and treatment of sick and wounded were met. 'The spirit of mutiny,' wrote William James, 'had taken deep root in the breasts of the seamen, and, from the apparent organisation of the plan, seemed to be the result of far more reflection, than the wayward mind of a jack-tar is usually given credit for.'[2] Against this well-organised collective action the government was powerless, and to his credit Spencer did not compound the problem by attempting the use of force. Instead, Parliament rushed through a bill on 10 May agreeing to the seamen's demands, and the King signed a pardon for all the sailors involved. About half of the officers whom the seaman had sent ashore were relieved of their duty. The popular Lord Howe was called out of retirement to meet the seamen's delegates and respond to their demands. The affair ended in a mood of rejoicing and the fleet went to sea.

A more violent sequel broke out at the Nore on 15 May and spread to the North Sea squadron at Yarmouth. Vice-Admiral Adam Duncan kept control of his own flagship, *Venerable,* and regained control of *Adamant* when he intervened personally and held at arm's length overboard the only sailor who dared contest his authority, but the rest of the ships sailed to join the mutineers at the Nore.

Spencer found it impossible to negotiate with these delegates, and their leader Richard Parker, because they did not have clearly defined objectives, and were too emotional. Even the seamen at Spithead expressed their concern about the events at the Nore. The mutineers stopped merchant shipping entering or leaving the Thames in the hope of forcing the government's hand.

Eventually the supply of victuals to the fleet was cut off, the forts at Tilbury, Gravesend and Sheerness were prepared to fire red-hot shot, and the buoyage in the estuary was removed to deter attempts to take the ships to the Texel. Gradually the ships' companies turned against their leaders, fights broke out, and finally one by one the ships sailed away to surrender. Parker and twenty-eight delegates were hanged, and others were flogged round the fleet.

Duncan had kept up the blockade of the Texel with his flagship and *Adamant*, anchoring in the mouth of the harbour when the wind blew from the east so that the Dutch could sail. False signals were made to suggest that the main force was just across the horizon. Soon he was reinforced by six ships from the Channel Fleet under Sir Roger Curtis, and the Russian squadron put in an appearance. Finally the chastened mutineers returned to their duty.

In July the army was embarked on the Dutch transports, but as Wolfe Tone recorded dismally in his journal, the wind was steadily foul for departure. The invasion plan was abandoned when Hoche died, but Admiral de Winter was nonetheless ordered to seek action at sea. The opportunity occurred in October when Duncan was in Yarmouth. The battle which followed, known as the battle of Camperdown, was exceptionally hard-fought. The stubborn courage of the Dutch was a marked contrast to the performance of the

French Marine since the revolution. The Dutch, however, were at a disadvantage because their ships were small, and because the armament of the British ships included carronades which increased the weight of shot that could be fired.

De Winter took a position close to the shoals. To prevent him slipping to leeward into such shallow water that the deeper-draught British ships could not follow, Duncan sought to break through the Dutch line and engage from the leeward. He attacked in two divisions which concentrated on the Dutch van and rear, and his captains managed to break through in several places. His approach tactics exposed his leading ships to fire they could not immediately return, but when the ships in the rear of the columns came to the support of the leaders their superior gunnery carried the day. The former mutineers, who greatly respected their admiral, showed no reluctance to fight and die for their King and country. Unlike actions with the French and Spaniards, who sought to immobilise their enemy by firing into their rigging, the Dutch and British both concentrated on firing into the enemy gun decks, and at the waterline, to destroy their fighting capability.

At the end of 1797 the Directory again took up the idea of invading Britain, and General Bonaparte, back from Italy was put in command of the Army of England. He surveyed the embarkation ports and ordered the construction of troop-carrying gunboats, but his advice to Paris was that invasion was impossible without command of the sea. Rather than persevere in a campaign which was likely to be the end of his career, if not to cost him his life, he suggested that he be sent with an army, first to conquer Egypt, and then from that base to cooperate with Tipu Sultan in India. His modest goal was the conquest of Asia.

1

Close blockade

BECAUSE THE Channel Fleet was not permanently on station off Ushant, the close blockade of
Brest was entrusted to detached squadrons of
ships of the line (1) and frigates, although even this
degree of attention was neither consistently nor rigor-
ously applied. While major movements of the French
fleet might not escape attention for long, it was less difficult for small divisions of the battlefleet, and especially
frigate squadrons, to slip out undetected.

In April 1795 a squadron of five of the line and three

2

frigates under Rear-Admiral Sir John Colpoys discovered and chased three French frigates. These split up, leaving the 32-gun *Astraea* to pursue and bring to action the 36-gun *Gloire* on the evening of the 12th. They were well matched 12pdr-armed ships, although without any carronades the British ship had a lower broadside weight of fire, and as usual high-trajectory French fire damaged the top-hamper of her opponent (which lost all her topmasts), whereas the British fired into the hull, causing about 40 casualties before *Gloire* struck her colours (2). One of the other frigates, *Gentille*, was taken by the 74-gun *Hannibal* the following morning.

The independent Channel cruiser squadrons were also active in hunting down frigates that escaped the watch off the ports. By 1796 they contained some very powerful ships that under Sir Edward Pellew, for example, consisting of the cut-down 64 (or *rasée*) *Indefatigable*, a 24pdr-armed ship rated at 44 guns, the 44-gun two-decker *Argo*, the big, ex-French *Revolutionnaire*, 38, and the 36-gun *Amazon* and *Concorde*. In April they pursued and captured the *Unité*, 36 guns, and no sooner was the prize dispatched than another strange sail was sighted and the squadron set all sail in pursuit. The stranger was very fast, but Pellew had insisted that *Indefatigable* retain her full-sized spars when cut down a deck and this powerful rig gave her an advantage over her consorts. After a 15-hour chase covering 168 miles, she brought to action the French 40-gun frigate *Virginie*; the ensuing battle lasted nearly two hours and although heavily outgunned the French ship only surrendered when *Amazon* joined *Indefatigable* (3).

By this stage in the war the Channel was a dangerous

3

cruising ground for French commerce raiders, and neither mid-winter darkness nor bad weather offered any respite, as the *Nereide* discovered in December 1797. She was pursued all of the 27th and into the night by the *Phoebe*, 36 and in a somewhat confused battle in the darkness forced the French ship to surrender. One of Whitcombe's more dramatic compositions (4) shows the *Phoebe* charging past her quarry, who has tacked without the British ship noticing. It proved another engagement where ships of nominal force—36 guns—were actually heavily mismatched, the British 18pdr-armed frigate having a significant advantage in firepower over her 12pdr opponent, reflected in the French casualties which were six times those of the *Phoebe*.

4

1. 'A Squadron standing along a coast under Easy Sail, A Cutter under the Stern of the Commodore for Orders', engraving produced and published by Robert Dodd, London, 21 February 1793.
NMM neg B3858

2. 'Capture of La Gloire April 10th 1795', coloured aquatint engraved by Thomas Sutherland after an original by Thomas Whitcombe (c1752-1824), 1 June 1816.
NMM ref PAD5488

3. 'The Indefatigable of 44 Guns Capt. Sr Edward Pellew engaging and capturing La Virginie of 44 Guns', coloured engraving, published by C Sheppard, 1 June 1797. This is both crude and inaccurate as a depiction of the battle—the ships went into action carrying more canvas and they never seem to have passed on opposite tacks —but the *Indefatigable* is correctly shown as having the stern gallery on the level of the quarterdeck, a legacy of her origins as a 64-gun two-decker.
NMM ref PAD5498

4. 'Capture of La Nereide Decr 21st 1797', coloured aquatint engraved by Thomas Sutherland after an original by Thomas Whitcombe, 1 May 1816.
NMM ref PAD5533

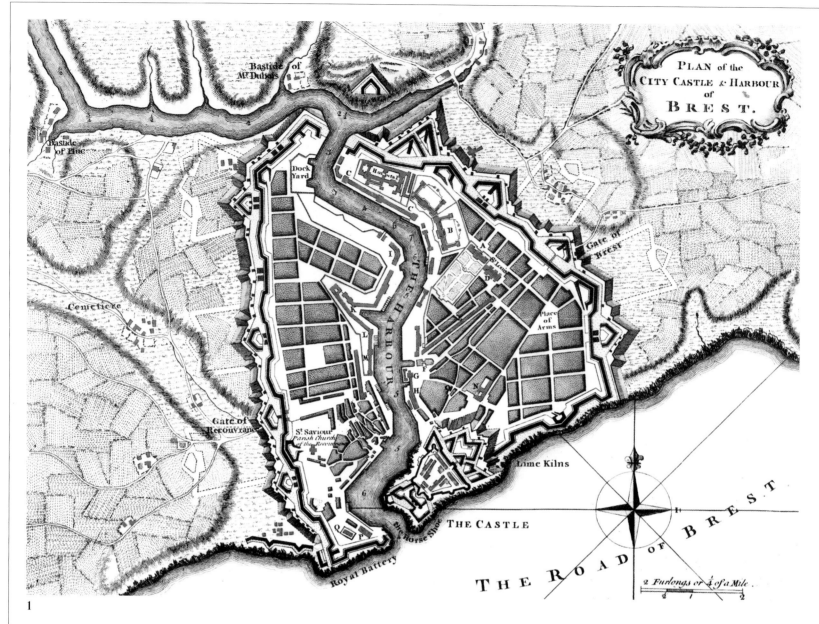

1

French naval bases: Brest

BREST HAD been France's major Atlantic base since the time of Louis XIV, with a dockyard set up by Colbert and fortifications by Vauban (1). A century later it was to be Revolutionary France's main base against Britain. The dockyard installations (2, 3) were set on the banks of the little river Penfeld, with the massive bulk of the castle overshadowing its mouth (4).

Outside the river mouth lay an enormous area of sheltered water—the *Rade de Brest* (Brest roads)—which led out to sea through the narrow gap of the *Goulet* (literally the Gullet). This gap was both a great advantage, as it was narrow enough to be commanded by batteries on both sides and therefore any enemy could be prevented from coming into the *Rade* and threatening Brest itself, but also it was a major disadvantage as the prevail-

ing westerly wind blew directly into it, and made access to the open sea difficult, particularly in the face of a blockading fleet, and there were severe navigational difficulties in using the passages immediately outside, especially in bad visibility or by night when trying to obtain surprise.

The ironbound coast of western Brittany tested to the utmost the skill of the British ships charged with the close blockade of the French Brest fleet. Illustration (5) shows the view from a blockading ship penetrating as close to the *Goulet* as was possible without risking total destruction. However, usually only the inshore squadron was actually off Brest, the rest of the blockading fleet being out to sea or in reasonably well-sheltered bays, knowing that the French would find it very difficult to

2

get out through the *Goulet* without adequate warning being given to catch them. An onshore gale might make it necessary for the blockading fleet to run for the shelter of Torbay, but would equally pin the French in port, and any change in the wind would bring the blockading fleet back, just as it would help the French emerge.

Geography imposed other problems on Brest. At the extreme western end of the comparatively barren Breton peninsula, its land communications with the rest of France were poor, and local supplies quite inadequate to support such a major base. The obvious supply route was by sea, and was strangled by the same blockad-

ing squadron that kept an eye on the Brest fleet. Napoleon initiated plans for a canal from Nantes to Brest which would bypass the blockade, but it was completed far too late to be of assistance in his wars.

From the very start of the Revolution in 1789 there was conflict in and around Brest with mutinies by parts of the Army garrison and (in 1790) by the fleet as well. The fleet was still in a state of indiscipline shading into outbreaks of actual mutiny in 1793. By this year Brest had become an island of republicanism in a Brittany almost entirely given over to counter-revolution. Troops from the port gained a narrow victory over local

3

4

1. 'Plan of the City Castle & Harbour of Brest', etching by T Jefferys, 1761. *NMM ref PAD1500*

2-4. Etchings of the Port of Brest by Yves Maire Le Gouaz after originals by Nicolas Marie Ozanne, 1776.

2. 'Le Port de Brest. Vu de la cale de construction atenant au Bureau general. Reduit de las Collection des Ports de France dessines pour le Roi en 1776. Par le Sr. Ozanne Ingenieur de la Marine Pensionnaire de sa Majeste', *NMM ref PAD1502*

3. 'Le Port de Brest. Vu du Chenal devant le nouveau quai aux canons. Reduit de las Collection des Ports de France dessines pour le Roi en 1776. Par le Sr. Ozanne Ingenieur de la Marine Pensionnaire de sa Majeste'. *NMM ref PAD1503*

4. 'Le Port de Brest. Vu du Magazin des vivres en face de la Chaine. Reduit de las Collection des Ports de France dessines pour le Roi en 1776. Par le Sr. Ozanne Ingenieur de la Marine Pensionnaire de sa Majeste'. *NMM ref PAD1504*

5. 'View of Brest Harbour', aquatint engraved by Robert Pollard after an original by Nicholas Pocock (1740-1821), published by Burney & Co, 1 February 1799. *NMM ref PAD1505*

royalists, but for some time Brest was even more isolated than usual. Famine and epidemics ravaged the population, and, whilst the escape of the French grain convoy from America in 1794 may not have saved the country, it probably did rescue Brest from starvation. In the circumstances the fact that the fleet at Brest managed to achieve anything at all is more surprising than that it did not do well. Its difficulties were added to by the fact that in 1792 much of its reserves of timber and naval stores were moved to Toulon in anticipation of a war restricted to the Mediterranean, and were lost there a year later.

The British blockade of Brest was fairly effective in strangling the port; and, though it had been the chief centre for naval shipbuilding for Atlantic France in the eighteenth century, during the last decade of the Napoleonic wars most new major warships were building at Antwerp, Cherbourg, or in the Mediterranean.

5

1

The Irish Guard

I N THE allocation of big frigates, the Irish squadron based at Cork and commanded during this period by Vice-Admiral Kingsmill, was probably second only in priority to the Channel Fleet. Not only did it have the Atlantic coast of Ireland to patrol and the shipping in the Western approaches to defend, but Ireland itself was a frequent target for invasion. Apart from Kingsmill's near-stationary flagship, ships of the line could not be spared permanently to guard against this eventuality and so large frigates were the next best thing—they possessed sufficient seakeeping for boisterous Atlantic conditions, and were weatherly enough to claw off the

2

3

many lee shores of the command's cruising grounds. Kingsmill's frigates proved active and successful, and were almost the only ships in a position to oppose Hoche's abortive Bantry expedition in the winter of 1796-7, the British battle squadrons being completely wrong-footed.

June 1796 proved a particularly successful month for the Irish Guard. On the 8th the 18pdr 32-gun *Unicorn* and 12pdr 36-gun *Santa Margarita* sighted part of a French cruiser squadron that had escaped from Brest a few days earlier; having lost touch with the *Proserpine* it now comprised the 36-gun frigates *Tribune* and *Tamise*, and the corvette *Légère*, 18. The French squadron formed a bow and quarter line, but as the British frigates came into range, the *Légère* hauled up to windward and passed asern at long range (far right in '1'). The struggle soon dissolved into two separate single-ship engagements,

the *Santa Margarita*, a prize from the Spanish, taking on the *Tamise*, the ex-British *Thames* captured by the French in 1793. There was little difference in firepower between the ships, but after a fierce 20-minute exchange *Tamise* surrendered and was returned to her original ownership. As a tribute to the efficiency of Captain Byam Martin's ship, she lost only 2 dead and 3 wounded to the enemy's 32 killed and 19 wounded. *Santa Margarita*, an active cruiser under Martin's command, had been the subject of a sketch by Nicholas Pocock while lying in the Cove of Cork earlier in the year (2).

The other fight was not so quickly ended; in fact, *Unicorn* was involved in a running battle, covering over 200 miles before, with the onset of night, the wind dropped and the British ship carrying every fair-weather sail was able to creep up on the *Tribune*'s weather quarter, stealing her wind. This moment is the subject of one of

Pocock's most dramatic renderings of single-ship engagements (3), with the British ship lit from within by the fire of her first broadside and the chaotic mass of flapping canvas silhouetted against the sky. The *Tribune* was well handled by her *émigré* American captain, but not well fought, and when she struck her colours, with 37 dead and 18 wounded, she had not inflicted a single casualty on her, admittedly more powerful, opponent.

A few days later another of Kingsmill's cruisers was in action, and the target was the missing frigate from the same French squadron, *Proserpine*, 40. She was chased and captured after a similarly one-sided action by the 18pdr-armed *Dryad* (4). Even the *Légère* was snapped up on 22 June by the frigates *Apollo* and *Doris* so all the units of this French raiding group had been eliminated in a matter of days.

1. 'To Captain Thomas Byam Martin This Print representing the Engaging and Taking La Tamise French Frigate, by His Majesty's Frigate Santa Margaritta', aquatint engraved by Robert Pollard after an original by Nicholas Pocock (1740-1821), published by the artist 4 June 1796. *NMM neg no C626*

2. 'His Majesty's Ship Santa Margarita J. B. Martin Esq. Commander as she appeared on the morning of 14th Jany 1796 at the Cove of Cork. J. C. From a sketch by Mr Pocock June 1811', grey wash. *NMM ref PAD8650*

3. 'To Captain Sir Thomas Williams, This Print representing The Capture of the French Frigate La Tribune by His Majesty's Ship The Unicorn on the 8th June 1796', aquatint engraved by Francis Chesham after an original by Nicholas Pocock (1740-1821), published by the artist 14 August 1797. *NMM neg no B3226*

4. 'Capture of La Prosperine, June 13th 1796', coloured aquatint engraved by J Jeakes after an original by Thomas Whitcombe, published 1 May 1816. *NMM ref PAD5501*

4

1

The naval officer: life at sea

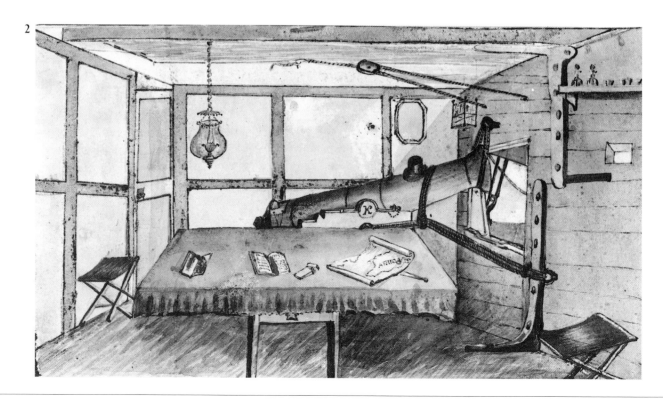

2

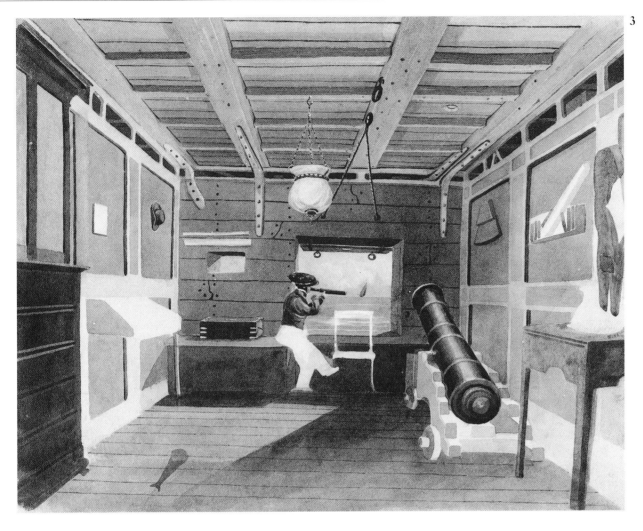

3

FOR THE younger sons of gentlemen, life at sea in the Royal Navy was no less arduous than that of the ordinary seamen and, relative to the comforts in which they had invariably been raised, a great deal more uncomfortable. A career at sea for a young man nevertheless often had more to attract him than the alternative professions: the church, the army, medicine or trade. The attraction of escape to an adult world exploring foreign ports, with all the temptations they offered, was the poorer man's version of the nobility's grand tour. Moreover it held out the prospect, where patronage was available, of a career that in some cases led to distinction and even affluence. For, although wage payment was always in arrears, the proportion of prize money shared among officers—one quarter between the commissioned and warrant officers—ensured each of them a significant proportion that in a few cases amounted to small fortunes.

The young gentlemen who succumbed to these attractions would find, however, that sea life had a great deal more to endure than, in their original enthusiasm, they had foreseen. So much depended on patronage: initial entry and, even having proved courage and ability,

being recommended and obtaining appointments. Employment was likely in wartime, but even in the eighteenth century, peace prevailed for just as many years as wars lasted. There were therefore long periods of waiting and writing for appointments, which equally

4

balanced the activity afloat. Even there, calculations show that ships of war spent as long in port as cruising at sea. And, even at sea, an officers' life in a small ship, where much fell to one officer, was very different from that in larger ships of the line, where duties were more specialised.

For young officers a berth in a ship of the line, with the prospect of notice and promotion, was more attractive to those wishing to rise in the service. In these large vessels, the working of the ship, changes of watch, cleaning of decks, meal times, taking navigational sights at noon, occasional punishments and weekly divine service, when there was a chaplain or taken by the captain, who also read the Articles of War, all formed a framework within which sea officers pursued their existence. A large part of their time was spent in supervising sections of the crew to which they were allotted on a divisional system in which midshipmen assisted lieutenants in supervising sub-sections. At sea gun drill ensured seamen were trained for action, while in port they were invariably occupied in repairing, painting, mending or shifting equipment and stores.

Sea life was essentially communal for the lower ranks (1), but in larger ships a berth of their own was provided for the senior lieutenants (2) and warrant officers where they could occasionally gain moments of privacy, to read and write. Their officially required production of a daily journal always involved them some of the time in calculating positions—note the sextant case on the bulkhead of the master's cabin in (3)—and recording events. Otherwise they enjoyed games of backgammon (4), cards, even fishing. Some admirals enjoyed music and had musicians among their crews for regular soirees. Other musical officers who played instruments had to avoid unpopularity with watch-keeping messmates trying to sleep. But their playing complemented the dancing and singing of crewmen and introduced a cultivated

element to the atmosphere of a ship primarily concerned with working at sea. Even literary endeavours were not unknown—indeed, Captain Edward Thompson was a nationally recognised poet.

Among officers, for much of the time socially isolated together, meal times provided a focus of their communal life. Officers dined in the wardroom (5). The wealth of the participants determined quality of diet and accessories like wine; just to take a place at this table demanded income sufficient to dress appropriately and pay the wardroom bills. Boorish drunken behaviour was on the decline by the late eighteenth century, while honour—the mark of a gentleman—self-discipline and sociably pleasing conduct were points of recommendation, while skill at conversation was a quality increasingly prized. Those meals with the captain present, or when invited in turn to the admiral's table, were high points in an officer's life. For a captain himself, living in the god-like isolation of the great cabin (6), such socialising was often the only relief from the proverbial loneliness of command.

For an officer with permission, the ability to leave the ship and enjoy days or longer on shore in port provided relief and access to wives, families or other society. In the Mediterranean some took the opportunity, for example, to visit sights of classical antiquity. In England there were theatres and concert rooms. However, in port some captains brought their own women on board, and tolerated the wives of a few warrant or petty officers sailing and berthing with the crew. Childbirth on board was not uncommon, while the presence of children as well as animals created something of a domestic environment.

The smaller vessels—frigates, brigs, sloops and gun vessels—were more usually detached on services distant from the main fleet, which offered greater variety of tasks and movement between coasts. Officers on such vessels had less space and fewer companions, which

5

6

reduced the variety of social activities and increased crowding. In bad weather officers as well as seamen became wet and cold, as much from water leaking through decks as from working on watch (7). Winters at sea, poorly prepared food, blockade or routine convoying, with little prospect of immediate relief or patronage could be demoralising. An important role of senior officers was accordingly the maintenance of morale among their juniors as much as in the crew. For it was upon these subordinates that the reputations of sea officers were built.

1. 'Life on the ocean: midshipman's berth in a British frigate at sea', oil painting by Augustus Earle (*fl*1806-1838).
NMM ref BHC1118

2. 'Study of accommodation in a vessel. 3rd Officer's Mess Room Wexford 1809. 10. 11', watercolour by Charles Copland 1809. This is actually an East Indiaman but gives a good impression of the cramped space, often containing a gun, and the partitions of canvas stretched over a wooden frame, all of which had to be taken down when clearing for action.
NMM ref PAF2387

3. 'Master's cabin 1825', watercolour attributed to the Reverend Thomas Streatfield. Although the details are accurate, the proportions are woefully wrong, appearing to give far more space (and particularly more headroom) than was ever the case.
NMM ref PAD8627

4. 'Sketch of Thomson and Harris playing backgammon on board Andromeda', anonymous black & wash, grey pen & ink sketch probably by a naval officer, no date, but about 1790.
NMM ref PAH4903

5. Officers at dinner in the wardroom. From a sketchbook of Edward Pelham Brenton, 1801-2.
NMM ref PAF8407

6. 'Interior of a ship's cabin ca. 1819', anonymous watercolour of the nineteenth- century British school, 1820.
NMM ref PAD5857

7. Midshipman at the wheel learning to steer the ship. Anonymous watercolour, undated.
NMM ref 4886

7

1

Inshore warfare in the Channel

2

WARFARE IN the Channel was a matter of overlapping layers of defence. The main fleet was usually retained in Torbay or Spithead, with the occasional cruise off Ushant, the closer blockade being maintained by detached squadrons and frigates. However, there was a more advanced element that took the war right up to the enemy's high-water line. France could be greatly inconvenienced by interference with her coasting trade, or *cabotage*, since the road and canal network of the western departments was not well developed. The British became adept at daring boat attacks—'cutting-out' expeditions they were called—and many a small vessel was surprised, boarded and carried from harbours and anchorages (1). The prospect of a descent on any small port increased the sense of insecurity and drew off troops for coast-defence duties that might have been more dangerously employed elsewhere. An urgency was added to British actions from 1795-96 with the threat of invasion, and many of the small craft assembled in the French Channel ports for a possible landing became a higher priority target.

These inshore squadrons were usually commanded by frigate captains, and none was more active than Sir Sidney Smith (2). The exploits of his *Diamond*, 38, including the audacious reconnaissance of Brest, added to a reputation already established by burning part of the French fleet at Toulon. Even frigates drew too much water for many of these activities, and the square rig of conventional ships did not make them sufficiently handy. As a result, much of the burden

Published 30th April, 1806, by J. Gold, 103, Shoe Lane, Fleet Street.

3

4

5

fell on cutters and luggers, many of which were hired or purchased rather than purpose-built by the navy. One of the best known was the lugger *Aristocrat*, which had fought an epic action lasting eighteen hours off the Channel Islands in July 1795, when she had finally escaped from the French flotilla of nine ships that had surrounded her (3). Along with the brig *Liberty*, she volunteered to join Sidney Smith's squadron in a typical attack on Herqui in March of the following year, where a 16-gun corvette, and her convoy of four brigs, two sloops and one armed lugger were burnt and destroyed. As he said in his report, 'I was much pleased by the conduct of Lieutenant Gosset in the hired lugger.'

These actions often involved landings and attacks on shore batteries and were very high-risk ventures. Sidney Smith's luck ran out the following month when a night attack on a lugger off Le Havre went horribly wrong. The official account, printed in the Annual Register for 1796, set out the details (4):

> Advice was received at the Admiralty, brought by Lieutenant Crisp of the cutter *Telemachus*, of the capture of the enterprising Sir Sidney Smith, commander of HMS *Diamond*, on the coast of France, having on the 18th instant, boarded and taken a lugger privateer belonging to the enemy, in Havre de Grace har-

bour, by the boats of his squadron, then on a reconnoitring expedition; and the tide making strong into the harbour, she was driven above the French forts, which the next morning, the 19th, discovering, at break of day, the lugger in tow by a string of English boats, immediately made the signal of alarm, which collected together several gun-boats and other armed vessels, that attacked the lugger and British boats, when, after an obstinate resistance of two hours, Sir Sidney had the mortification of being obliged to surrender himself prisoner of war, with about sixteen of his people, and three officers with him in the lugger.

In these circumstances, the shallow draught gunboats, with their single or paired big guns and the manoeuvrability endowed by their sweeps (large oars), were particularly effective (5). The Annual Register continued:

> The *Diamond* frigate is safe, but could afford her commander no assistance, there not being a breath of wind during the whole of this unfortunate transaction.... When the officers on board the *Diamond* heard of the disaster which had befallen their gallant commander, they sent a flag of truce into Havre, to discover whether he was wounded, and entreating that

he might be treated with kindness. The governor returned for answer that Sir Sidney was well, and that he should be treated with the utmost humanity and attention.

However, the authorities did not honour the governor's promises. Sir Sidney should have been exchanged quickly with a French officer of similar rank, as was the standard custom of the day, but his incendiary activities at Toulon had earned him the special animosity of the French government and he was consigned to the notorious Temple prison in Paris. His eventual escape and return to service in May 1798 only added to his public reputation.

However active the British inshore flotillas, it was impossible to bottle up permanently every small French harbour, and privateers continued to pose a significant threat to British commerce. Most captures of merchantmen were too mundane to attract artists, but the French were obviously proud of the capture of the cutter *Swan* by the *Unité* in January 1797 (6). *Swan* was not a naval vessel but may have been a revenue cutter.

1. The cutting out of a French brig, possibly la *Chevrette*. Black and wash, grey pen and ink sketch by P J de Loutherbourg, undated.
NMM ref PAH8407

2. 'Sir William Sidney Smith 1764-1840', stipple engraving after an original by Daniel Orme, no date.
NMM ref PAD3504

3. 'The Aristocrat armed Lugger engaging a French Flotilla, consisting of nine sail. Captain Wilkins got away from 9 French vessels after a running fight of 18 hours 15 July 1795', aquatint engraved by Hall after an original by John Thomas Serres, published by Joyce Gold, 30 April 1806.
NMM ref PAD5497

4. 'His Majesty's frigate the Diamond . . . off Cape La Heve . . . to cut out a French lugger named Le Vengeur . . . 18 April 1796 . . . was boarded . . . but the cable cut by one of the prisoners . . . swept . . . into the River Seine . . . surrender', coloured aquatint engraved by J Jeakes after an original by J Boxer and J T Serres, published by Edward Orme, September 1803.
NMM ref PAH7892

5. 'A French Gun Boat', engraving by J Tomlinson after an original by J Flight, published by J Stratford, 24 November 1804.
NMM ref PAD5500

6. 'Combat du Corsaire Francais L'Unite contre le cutter Anglais Le Swan (Janvier 1797)', lithograph engraved by Ferdinand Victor Perrot and Roger et Cie, after an original by Perrot, no date.
NMM ref PAD5516

6

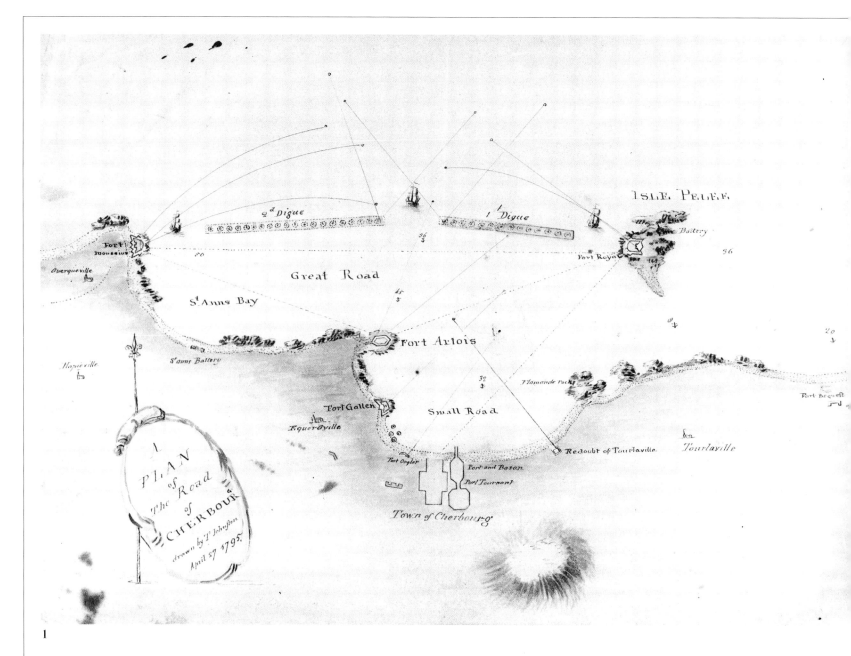

1

French naval bases: Cherbourg

IN ANY war with Britain France was badly handicapped by having no natural large, sheltered, anchorages or good deepwater ports on her Channel coast to compare with Falmouth, Plymouth and Torbay, and, particularly, the shelter provided by the Isle of Wight and Portsmouth harbour. The French channel ports were on river mouths, difficult of access, cramped and usually unsuited to larger vessels. Ports like Saint Malo, Le Havre and Dieppe were fine for merchantmen, privateers and even frigate squadrons, but were unsuitable for even one or two ships of the line, let alone fleets of these vessels. Projects for constructing an artificial haven opposite the English coast were raised from time to time and these usually involved the port of

Cherbourg, situated at the top of the Cotentin peninsula. During the reign of Louis XIV the great French engineer Vauban had made plans which did not get very far, his half-complete fortifications being demolished for fear that the British would land and occupy the Cotentin.

A century later, in 1776, just before France joined in the American War of Independence in support of the North American colonists, work was begun on modernising and enlarging the port. This was masterminded by Captain de la Bretonnière and involved the construction of a couple of basins (the 'Port Tornant' of the 1795 map (1)). This was followed by an ambitious attempt to form a protected anchorage by sinking a series of enormous cones (2), made of wood and filled with stones, to form a protective breakwater between the west end of St. Anne's Bay to Pelée Island. These were to be in two lines (*1st Digue* and *2nd Digue* in (1)). These massive and extremely expensive constructions were meant to serve as forts as well as a sea defence, and had they been successful would have provided a large and secure anchorage. Louis XVI made an unprecedented trip to see the sinking of one of the cones, an event marred by a fatal accident. The whole project was, in any case, doomed. The cones began to disintegrate as soon as they were emplaced, and, by the time of the summoning of the Estates General in 1789 it had become obvious that they were not working.

During the Revolutionary War, Cherbourg was a base for privateers, and had some importance as a centre of shipbuilding, particularly for invasion barges. Napoleon began a programme of port improvement, which included the construction of a mole, but the work was far from complete at his downfall and was not finished until 1853, in the reign of his nephew Napoleon III. However the large basin capable of holding a fleet of line of battle ships was ready by 1813, when Cherbourg was formally opened as a naval port, and Cherbourg had for some time been noted for building frigates, and as a base for that type of vessel.

---

1. 'A Plan of the Road of Cherbourg', watercolour by Thomas Johnston, 27 April 1795.
NMM ref PAD1488

2. 'View of a Cone Constructed in the Year 1785 being conducted to its place in the Road of Cherbourg, in order to be sunk', engraving by Thomas Pratten, published by John Sewell, 1 April 1794.
NMM ref PAD1489

2

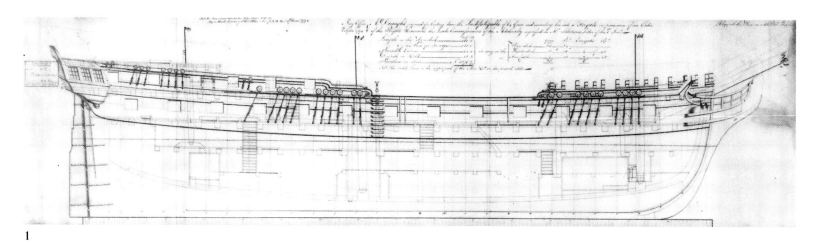

1

Droits de l'Homme, 13-14 January 1797

SIR EDWARD Pellew was perhaps the most successful British frigate captain of the early years of the war, and in the heavy frigate *Indefatigable* he had a command worthy of him. She had been built as a 64-gun line of battle ship and then cut down to a 38-gun frigate (1). As a result both her main armament (24pdr guns) and her construction were much heavier than a standard frigate of nominally the same number of guns – or a 36-gun ship such as her consort, the *Amazon*, both of which had 18pdr guns as their main armament. The two ships together formed a powerful fighting force, but not one, in ordinary circumstances, which could have successfully taken on a 74-gun line of battle ship, though that is what they successfully did in one of the most dramatic actions of the war.

At the end of 1796 a French expedition intended to land in Ireland escaped from Brest under cover of darkness, but in considerable disorder – a disorder which was worsened by Pellew's intervention with the *Indefatigable*, firing false signals and assisting in the scattering of the French fleet. This dispersal ensured that no landing took place, as the frigate carrying both the land and sea commanders failed to rejoin the majority of the force which contrived to gather off the Irish coast before being dispersed again by a storm. Meanwhile Pellew was returning to his watch off Brest, accompanied by the *Amazon*. Early in the afternoon of 13 January 1797 with 'the wind ... blowing hard, with thick hazey weather ...' he sighted a French warship some 50 leagues off Ushant and immediately steered to cut her off. This was the *Droits de*

2

l'Homme, a 74-gun ship, with over 700 soldiers aboard, returning from the Irish coast. She was an experimental vessel, without a poop and longer and lower than usual. As the British ships approached she became further handicapped by carrying away both fore and main topmasts, which made her roll heavily. It seems that, partly because of this and her design, and because she was heavily laden with soldiers and military supplies, that she could not use her heaviest guns on the lower deck. These were too close to the water to open the gun ports safely. When this was tried she nearly sank. This meant that the French ship was now only capable of firing a broadside of roughly the same power as the *Indefatigable* by herself, though the massed musket fire of the troops made her more dangerous at close quarters. As night fell Pellew's ship caught up (2), ranged up alongside, and then, after her enemy had nearly succeeded in ramming and boarding her, surged ahead. The *Amazon* then came up into action (3). Through the night the two frigates, stationing themselves on either bow of the 74 and yawing to fire broadsides, harried the French ship, which would occasionally herself yaw to reply. By about 4am the *Droits de L'Homme* was virtually out of ammunition and almost unrigged, with her opponents not in a much better state: 'The sea was high, the People on the main Deck were up to their middles in water, some Guns broke their Breechings four times over . . . All our masts were much wounded, the Maintopmast completely unrigg'd and sav'd only by uncommon alacrity . . .'

Breakers were sighted, and Pellew, thinking he was in the Bay of Brest, turned north. He was, in fact, in the next bay south, Audierne Bay, and was saved by his

Breton Royalist pilot shouting 'Non, non mon Capitaine, the oder way'. As the *Indefatigable* managed to claw her way off the lee shore she sighted her opponent, aground on a shoal (4). Pellew escaped by the skin of his teeth, and consummate seamanship, but *Amazon* was less lucky. She went aground, though nearly all of her crew escaped to land and captivity. The major tragedy was the fate of the French ship they had harried to her doom. She had already lost some 103 dead and 150 wounded, and it took four days for the weather to moderate enough for help to reach the wreck. The total loss was perhaps in the region of 1000 troops and crew.

1. Sheer plan of *Indefatigable*. The dotted line shows the original outline of her upperworks before she was cut down to a frigate in 1795.
NMM neg 6199

2. 'Destruction of the Droits de l'Homme, 14 January 1797', oil painting by Ebenezer Colls (fl1852-1854), no date.
NMM ref BHC0482

3. 'Destruction of the Droits de l'Homme', anonymous oil painting of the nineteenth-century British school, no date.
NMM ref BHC0483

4. 'Destruction of Le Droits de l'Homme . . . Frigates in Hodierne Bay near Brest, with the Indefatigable . . . throwing up rockets . . . 13 Jan 1797', coloured aquatint engraved by Robert Dodd after his own original, published by I Brydon, February 1798.
NMM ref PAG7155

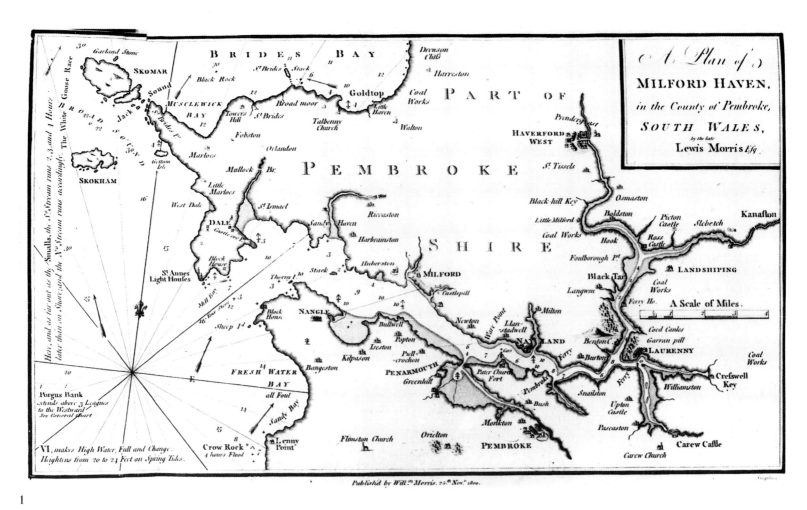

A Plan of MILFORD HAVEN, in the County of Pembroke, SOUTH WALES, *by the late* Lewis Morris *Esq.*

Publish'd by Will.ᵐ Morris, 25.ᵗʰ Nov.ᵣ 1800.

1

The Black Legion invades Wales

MOST BRITONS believe that their islands have not been invaded since the Norman Conquest in 1066, but although none has forced an unwilling change of government on the population, since then there have been forty-two successful military landings. None, however, was as bizarre as the last: a force of 1800 galley slaves and convicts, rejoicing under the name of the Black Legion, commanded by a revolutionary American, were put ashore in February 1797 in the extreme west of Wales and surrendered without a fight.

Originally conceived as a diversion during the landings in Ireland, the plan was to land and burn Bristol (or hold it to ransom), the country's second port and one with virtually no fixed defences. Like the main invasion it was confounded by the weather. The whole force was embarked in the big new frigates *Résistance* and *Vengeance*, the corvette *Constance* and a lugger, but even these weatherly vessels could not beat up the Bristol Channel in the face of an easterly gale, and eventually the 'troops' were put ashore at Fishguard. There was little of strategic value in the area, except perhaps the shipbuilding around Milford Haven (1), and it is difficult to find any

logic in their final choice of target. Despite the fervour of a few Jacobin officers, the jailbirds had no stomach for a fight, and soon surrendered to the local militia, led by Lord Cawdor, and were marched off to prison in Haverfordwest. A persistent legend in Wales holds that a number of inquisitive local women, in the traditional garb of red cloak and tall black hat, lined the cliff, and were mistaken for regular soldiers by the Black Legion, which convinced them of the folly of resisting.

While the incursion was another embarrassment for the Royal Navy, the French frigates did not reach port unmolested. When in sight of Brest, two of Bridport's frigates, the 18pdr-armed *San Fiorenzo* and the 12pdr *Nymphe*, intercepted *Résistance* and *Constance*; a running fight of half an hour ended with the capture of both. The frigate, at 1180 tons, was one of the biggest and newest ships of her type, an experimental vessel with a unusual hull form (3). She was renamed *Fisgard*, the usual contemporary spelling of the invasion port, and made a considerable name for herself under the active command of Thomas Byam Martin. *Constance* was similarly purchased as a 22-gun Sixth Rate post ship.

2

1. 'A Plan of Milford Haven in the County of Pembroke, South Wales, by the late Lewis Morris Esq.', published by William Morris, 25 November 1800. *NMM neg A129*

2. 'The capture of the Resistance and Constance by HMS San Fiorenzo and Nymphe, 9 March 1797', oil painting by Nicholas Pocock (1740-1821), no date. *NMM ref BHC0495*

3. Sheer draught of *Résistance*, as captured. Admiralty Collection. *NMM neg 1917*

3

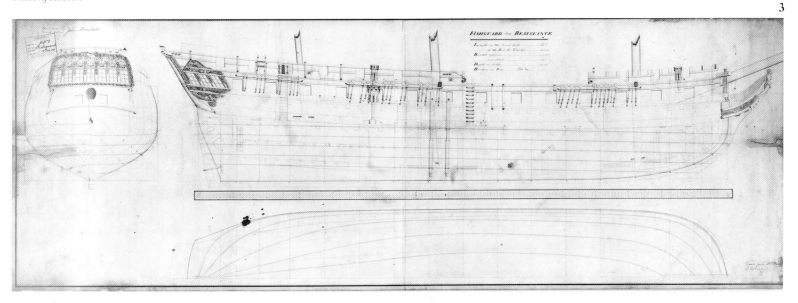

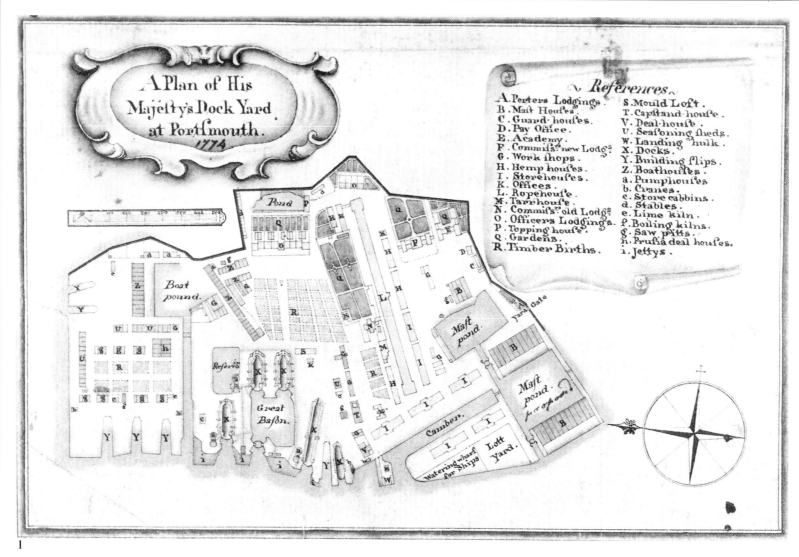

1

Portsmouth – key to the Channel

ETWEEN 1793 and 1815 Portsmouth was the Royal Navy's principal naval base and Spithead the main anchorage of the Channel Fleet and departure point for many of the fleets and convoys despatched all over the world. Sheltered from southwesterly winds by the Isle of Wight, Spithead had long been an assembly point for expeditions. In a stretch of water over three miles by eight miles, fleets and a multitude of transports and storeships could assemble without danger of collision, their main departure route southwest around the point of St Helens on the eastern point of the island, but in the event of emergency westward through the Solent and into the English Channel past the Needles. However, in the 1790s, with the policy of distant blockade of Brest, it was too far to the westward for an ideal base for the main fleet, and Torbay was often used as the fleet's preferred anchorage.

With such a capacious and convenient anchorage, Portsmouth had been a storage and distribution point

for naval expeditions since the twelfth century. A dock was ordered to be dug at Portsmouth by Richard I as early as 1194, and a wall to enclose the excavation was ordered by King John in 1212. However, it was not until 1495-96 that the dockyard took shape when King Henry VII acquired more land along the eastern side of Portsmouth Harbour within which was constructed the first reinforced dry dock to be built in England, and new building slips. The *Mary Rose* was laid down at Portsmouth in 1509 and it was from there that the fleet set out to drive off the French fleet in 1546 when the *Mary Rose* sank in sight of the land off Portsea.

Portsmouth dockyard was little used after 1560 and during the early seventeenth century, when the Spanish Netherlands and Holland harboured the nearest enemies. Then the dockyards along the Rivers Thames and Medway had greater strategic value. However, as France became increasingly powerful, Spithead and the dockyard at Portsmouth became more important. There was a need for a base from which warships could defend the south coast and western approaches, especially when easterly winds confined ships in the Thames estuary and River Medway. Stores were also needed further west, at a harbour of refuge for ships returning hard pressed from the Atlantic. Oak timber was readily available close by in the New Forest, and the route from London to Portsmouth relatively direct. During the years of the Commonwealth after 1650 new docks and building slips were created, and after the Restoration in 1660 a commissioner's house and a rope house. Further facilities were created after 1698 and the yard was pre-eminent among the six home dockyards by 1739 (1).

Fire, rather than a wartime enemy, was the main danger at this time. In 1760 a fire totally destroyed two large hemphouses containing hemp, tar, oil and other stores connected with rope-making. Another even more damaging fire occurred in the ropehouse in 1770, causing damage valued at £149,000; and a third fire in 1776, allegedly ignited by a thief sympathetic to the American cause, known as John the Painter. The fires resulted in a rearrangement of storage for all inflammable material, and new storehouses for hemp were erected away from the rope houses (2).

Ironically, as the eighteenth century proceeded and ships became larger, the harbour itself became a problem for the fleet refitting and repairing in time of war at Spithead. Ships had to come into harbour to receive new masts at the sheerhulk or to be taken into dock for work on their hulls. Yet a bar of shallow water stretched across the mouth of the harbour, providing only 14ft of water at low tide, with another 12ft to 15ft in spring tides (3). Ships of the line accordingly had to remove their guns and reduce their draught outside the harbour before entering and even then had to ride in on high tides, the reverse procedure happening as they were taken out.

This was not always easy as eddies ran across the harbour mouth on both sides of the bar. Yet the removal of ships outside the harbour was generally imperative for, as the fleet became larger, the small amount of deep water within the harbour became inconveniently crowded (4).

For by the time of the American War the harbour was also the location of a naval victualling yard, gunpowder stores and ordnance wharves. Victualling premises—a bakery, slaughterhouse, meat store and storehouse—were scattered in various places around the town of Portsmouth. But a good supply of fresh water had permitted the Victualling Board to establish a brewery on the western, Gosport, side of the harbour, opposite the dockyard, which also included a large cooperage. North of the victualling yard, also on the western side of the harbour, was the gunpowder magazine managed by the Board of Ordnance. The magazine, enclosed within walls of immense thickness, was laid out in 1773 and had capacity for around 4500 barrels of powder. Known as Priddy's Hard, the magazine was complemented by gun wharves storing actual ordnance close to the harbour mouth, just south of the dockyard.

Also on the Gosport side of Portsmouth Harbour, but facing Spithead, was Haslar Naval Hospital. Ordered to be built in 1745 as an alternative to the more expensive method of contracting sick seamen out to private houses and public hospitals, Haslar was completed in 1761 and was the largest purpose-built medical establishment then in existence. Initially designed for 1500 patients, the design was enlarged to 1800 in 1754, and the hospital actually housed 2100 patients in 1779. A survey in 1780 revealed it had 84 general medical and surgical wards, including isolation wards for consumption, fever and smallpox. Haslar Hospital has remained the main centre of medicine in the Royal Navy.

1. 'A plan of His Majesty's Dock Yard at Portsmouth 1774', anonymous coloured etching, published post-1785.
NMM ref PAD1077

2. Model of Portsmouth Dockyard.
NMM neg D539D

3. Chart of Portsmouth 1785.
NMM neg 2533

4. 'Le Port de Portsmouth Vu du cote de l'Est. Reduit de la Collection des Ports d'Angleterre dessines par Milton et graves par Suntache l'annee 1788', etching by Antoine Suntache after an original by Thomas Milton, 1788.
NMM ref PAD1056

2

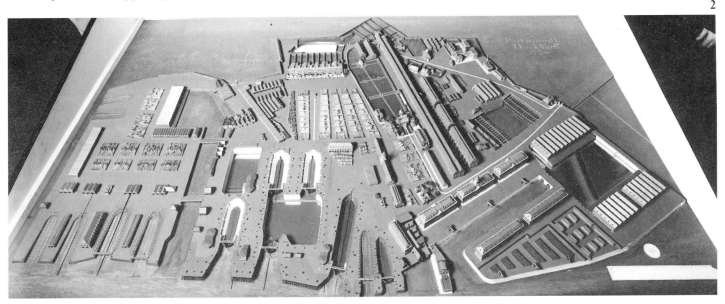

3

4

1

The Great Mutinies of 1797

AT THE outbreak of war in 1793, there had officially been 45,000 seamen and marines in service in the Royal Navy, but by 1797 this had increased to 120,000. By this time, the Navy had had to resort to any means necessary to obtain men. The Quota Acts of 1795 obliged counties to provide set numbers ('quotas') of men, and naturally judges and magistrates took the opportunity to hand over beggars, minor offenders and other social nuisances to the fleet, which resulted in the Navy receiving large numbers of untrained and unruly landsmen on board their ships. Coupled with the bad conditions aboard these ships, the low level of wages, which for many were years in arrears, poor rations and the almost complete lack of shore leave (unsurprising in a fleet manned in part by pressed men and criminals, where desertion was rife), unrest was inevitable, particularly at a time of social and political turmoil following the French Revolution.

Although there had been mutinies aboard individual ships in previous years, 1797 saw a series of organised 'strikes' aboard the ships of the Channel Fleet at its vari-

ous anchorages. On 15 April 1797 the men of Lord Bridport's fleet at Spithead refused to put to sea, each ship's company appointing delegates to speak for them and on 17 April submitted a list of their grievances. The fleet flagship *Queen Charlotte* was the headquarters of the mutineers. They wanted an increase in pay to reflect the increased cost of living, better quality rations in fair measures, better treatment for the sick and wounded, and shore leave to visit their families. As seamen's wages had last been set in 1653, there was considerable justice in their demands, and within the week a pay rise had been given and a pardon issued to all mutineers. However, the failure of the Admiralty to meet the seamen's demands regarding rations caused the crew of the *London* to continue their resistance to orders at St Helen's in early May, and shots were fired, five seamen being killed. The mutiny spread to other ships, but Lord Howe, who was highly respected by the men, came to negotiate with them and on 16 May the fleet put to sea as ordered. At the end of the mutiny, there was a celebration at Portsmouth, with the ships' crews saluting Lord Howe

3

1. 'A View of the Queen Charlotte
Man of War, of 100 guns, laying at
Spithead , wherein the Ship's
Company is represented Manning the
Yards, in order to Salute the Admiral
coming aboard', aquatint published
by John Fairburn, London, 24
December 1796.
NMM ref PAF7981

2. 'The Delegates in Council or
Beggars on Horseback', by
Cruickshank, published by J W Forest,
London, 9 June 1797.
NMM ref PAF3899

3. 'Parker the Delegate, Sketch'd by a
Naval Officer', coloured etching
published by W Holland, London,
June 1797.
NMM ref PAD3033

4. 'Richard Parker, President of the
Committee of Delegates, tendering
the List of Grievances to Vice-Admiral
Buckner, on board the Sandwich at
the Nore', mezzotint published by G
Thompson and I Evans, London, 3
July 1797.
NMM ref PAG6424

5. 'View of the Telegraph erected on
the Admiralty Office Charing Cross in
Feby 1796, By an Officer on Duty',
published by S W Fores, London, 26
March 1796.
NMM ref PAH2206

6. 'Escape of HMS Clyde from the
Nore Mutiny', oil painting by William
Joy (1803-1866), no date.
NMM ref BHC0496

7. 'HMS Clyde arriving at Sheerness
after the Nore Mutiny, 30 May 1797',
oil painting by William Joy (1803-
1866), no date.
NMM ref BHC0497

2   The DELEGATES in COUNCIL or BEGGARS on HORSEBACK.

4

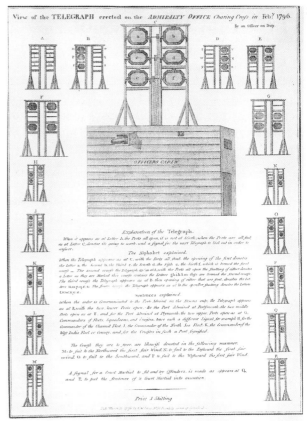

5

6

by manning the yards as he was rowed through the fleet, as shown in this earlier picture of the fleet flagship (1).

The Spithead mutiny appears to have been entirely concerned with the men's complaints about their conditions of service, and their petition stressed their loyalty to their country, despite the government's fears of radical agitation in the fleet. However, the next outbreak was not only more serious and more violent, but also believed to be more influenced by radicalism, as the cartoon by Cruickshank shows (2), with the opposition leader Charles James Fox and the French under the table leading the simple seamen astray. On 20 May, the ships at the Nore elected delegates to present grievances very similar to those which had been largely settled at Spithead, and elected one Richard Parker as their overall leader. Parker (3) was a man of some education—in fact, a naval officer disrated for disobedience—who was trusted by the men and chosen to present their demands to Vice-Admiral Buckner (4), the local commander.

By the end of the month all the ships save Admiral Duncan's flagship *Venerable* had joined the mutiny, leaving him to maintain the blockade of the Texel with this single ship of the line. Duncan was a powerful man and had retained control of his flagship by holding the one sailor who had defied his authority over the side of the ship and threatening to let go unless he returned to duty. The situation escalated dangerously when the mutineers moved their ships to blockade the Thames, but the government began to set up batteries on shore and move other ships to threaten the mutineers. Throughout the crisis, the Admiralty in London kept in constant touch with the Nore by means of the chain of shutter telegraph stations which linked the major fleet anchorages to London (5). Fearing reprisals, ships' companies began to desert the 'strike', the first being the *Clyde*, 38, which slipped away into Sheerness on the night of 30 May (6, 7). By 13 June all the ships had surrendered, without any concessions being gained from the Admiralty. In the aftermath, Parker and thirty-five others were hanged, with many more being flogged or imprisoned. The Nore Mutiny had come at a time of great danger to Great Britain, but her enemies had failed to exploit the situation quickly enough, although they were well informed of developments.

There were numerous outbreaks of mutiny aboard single ships in later years, but nothing to equal these mass uprisings. The harshness of the punishments for mutiny, however, continued to show the Admiralty's fear of disobedience amongst its crews.

7

1

'Dangers of the sea': grounding

THE ROYAL Navy expected to be able to take its ships anywhere there was water to float them, but this last consideration often posed a problem. With little more than sounding rods and lead-lines for tools, marine surveying was at best an inexact science, with the charting of coastal waters very variable in the quality of printed information available. Furthermore, states—and particularly navies—regarded charts as restricted if not secret documents, and it was not until the next century that the Admiralty's hydrographic office made the Navy's greatest contribution to maritime history by not only systematically charting the world's waters but also releasing the charts to the world's mariners irrespective of nationality or creed.

The power of the wind was also uncertain, and currents and tides similarly unstudied, so even the most experienced seaman might find himself putting a ship aground from time to time. Depending on conditions this need not cause major damage, and unlike a modern steel ship the full facilities of a dockyard were not always

2

3

necessary. In fact, a wooden warship was remarkably self-sufficient and could repair all but the most serious damage itself. These points are demonstrated by a series of watercolours showing the grounding and subsequent refloating and repair of the frigate *Thetis* in the winter of 1795-96 off the American coast, an incident of no great significance in itself but typical of the ingenuity and self-reliance of the service.

Thetis, 38, was on the North America station, probably patrolling the American coast to prevent supplies of food reaching France, when she ran aground off Currituck Inlet, North Carolina a few days before Christmas 1794. The first view shows the ship with anchors carried out astern to warp herself off (1). Two of her boats in the foreground are sounding, using lead-lines to discover the surrounding depth of water, and her consort, the 32-gun *Cleopatra*, is standing by. Having got the ship off a week later, with topmasts struck she is towed by *Cleopatra* into the Chesapeake, attended by *Thisbe*, 28 and *Lynx* sloop (also of the squadron) and the pilot schooner *Sally* of Norfolk, Virginia (2).

The next view (3) shows the squadron riding out bad weather in Lynhaven Bay, just inside the entrance to the Chesapeake, before the *Thetis* can be moved up to Gosport to be hove down and the underwater damage inspected and repaired (4). Gosport had minimal facilities at this time and the repairs were effected by the ship's crew, taking over a month. The ship cannot have suffered badly from her ordeal, since she was in service until 1814.

4

1-4. A series of watercolour originals by George Tobin, dated 1795, which have the feel of first-hand experience.

1. 'No.1. Thetis on shore near Currituck Inlet, North Carolina Dec 23rd 1794 . . . Cleopatra at anchor near her, Thisbe and Lynx answering private signals'.
NMM ref PAG9750

2. 'No.2. Dec 31st 1794, The Cleopatra towing the Thetis towards the Chesapeake, Lynx and Thisbe attending . . . A Virginian pilot boat the Sally of Norfolk in the foreground'.
NMM ref PAG9751

3. 'No.3. January 2nd 1795, Thetis, Cleopatra and Thisbe at anchor in Lynhaven Bay at the mouth of the Chesapeake'
NMM ref PAG9752

4. 'No.4. Thetis Feby 1795 - Repairing at Gosport in Virginia'. Another pilot schooner, the *Hamilton* of Norfolk, sails in.
NMM ref PAG9753

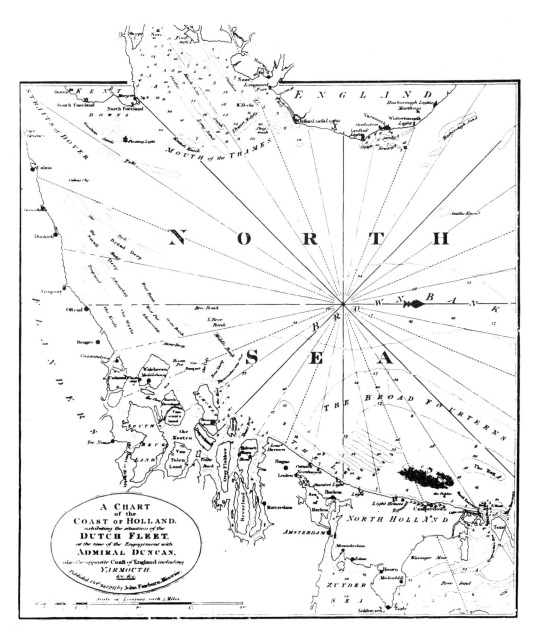

A CHART of the COAST of HOLLAND, exhibiting the situation of the DUTCH FLEET, at the time of the Engagement with ADMIRAL DUNCAN, also the opposite Coast of England including YARMOUTH. &c &c.

Published Oct 24 1797 by John Fairburn, London.

Scale of Leagues each 3 Miles.

2

From the London-Gazette Extraordinary, October 16, 1797

Venerable, off the Coast of Holland, October 13, 1797.

IN the Morning of the 11th, I got Sight of the Enemy, forming in a Line on the Larboard Tack to receive us, the Wind at North West. As we approached near, I made the Signal for the Squadron to shorten Sail, in order to connect them. Soon after, I saw the Land between CAMPERDOWN and EGMONT, about Nine Miles to Leeward of the Enemy; and, finding there was no Time to be lost in making the Attack, I made the Signal to bear up, break the Enemy's Line, and engage them to Leeward, each Ship her Opponent; by which I got between them and the Land. The Action commenced about Forty Minutes past Twelve, and lasted near Two Hours and a Half; when I observed all the Masts of the Vice Admiral's Ship to go by the Board: She was, however, defended for some Time in a most gallant Manner; but, being overpowered by Numbers, her Colours were struck, and Admiral De Winter was soon brought on-board the Venerable. On looking around me, I observed the Ship bearing the Vice-Admiral's Flag was also dismasted, and had surrendered to Vice-Admiral Onslow, and that many others had struck. They were in Nine Fathoms Water, and not farther than Five Miles from the Land. One of the Enemy's Ships caught Fire in the Action, but was extinguished, and she is One of the Ships in our Possession. The Squadron has lost a Number of Men, but in no Proportion to that of the Enemy. The Two Dutch Admiral Ships had no less than Two Hundred and Fifty Men killed and wounded in each Ship.

Signed, ADAM DUNCAN.

LIST OF SHIPS TAKEN.

Vryheid,	Adm. De Winter,	74 Guns, 550 Men.		Alkmaar,	Capt. Kraft,	56 Guns, 350 Men.
Jupiter,	Vice Ad. Reyntjes,	74	550	Delft,	Capt. Verdoorn,	56	375
Gelykheid,	Capt. Ruysen,	68	450	Munnikendam,	Capt. Lancaster,	44	270
Haarlem,	Capt. Wiggers,	68	450	Ambuscade,	Capt.-Lieut. Huys,	32	270
Adm. Devries,	Capt. Zegers,	68	450				
Wassenaer,	Capt. Holland,	64	450	N. B. Another Line-of-Battle Ship reported to be		
Hercules,	Capt. Van Ryfoort,	64	450	taken, Name unknown.		

Disposition of the British Squadron, in the Order of Battle, October 11, 1797.

LARBOARD, or LEE DIVISION.			STARBOARD, or WEATHER DIVISION.		
Rd Onslow, Esq. Vice-Admiral of the Red, Commander.			Adam Duncan, Esq. Admiral of the Blue, and Commander-in-Chief, &c. &c. &c.		
	Guns.Men.				
1 Russel, Henry Trollope, Capt.	74	590		Brought over, 552	
2 Director, William Bligh, Capt.	64	491	9 Triumph, William Henry Essington, Capt.	74	
3 Montagu, John Knight, Capt.	74	590	10 Venerable, Ad. Duncan, W.G.Fairfax, Capt.	74	
4 Veteran, George Gregory, Capt.	64	491	11 Ardent, Richard R. Burgess, Capt.	74	
5 Monarch, V. Ad. Onslow, E. O'Bryen, Capt.	74	590	12 Bedford, Sir Thomas Byard, Capt.	74	
6 Powerful, William O'Bryen Drury, Capt.	74	590	13 Lancaster, John Wells, Capt.	64	
7 Monmouth, James Walker, Capt.	64	491	14 Belliqueux, John Inglis, Capt.	64	
8 Agincourt, John Williamson, Capt.	64	491	15 Adamant, William Hotham, Capt.	50	
			16 Isis, William Mitchell, Capt.	50	
Carried over, 552	4357		Total, 1066		

REPEATERS.

Beaulieu Frigate. — Cutters Rose, King George, Active, Diligent. — Speculator Lugger.

REPEATERS. — Circe Frigate. — Martin Sloop.

List and Disposition of the Dutch Fleet, October 11, 1797.

VAN			REAR		
Vice-Admiral Reyntjes, Commander.				Guns.	
	Guns.Men.			Brought over, 684	
1 Cerberus, Capt. Jacobsen,	68	450	13 Leyden, Captain Musquetier,	68	
2 Delft, Capt. Verdoorn,	56	375	14 Mars, Capt. Kolff,	44	
3 Jupiter, V.-Ad.Reyntjes and R.-Ad. Meures,	74	550	15 Waakzaamheid, Capt.-Lieutenant Nierop,	24	
4 Alkmaar, Capt. Kraft,	56	350	16 Minerva, Capt. Eilbracht,	24	
5 Haerlem, Capt. Wiggers,	68	450	17 Galatea Brig, Lieutenant Rivery,	18	
6 Munnikendam, Capt. Lancaster,	44	270	18 Atalanta Brig, Lieutenant Plats,	18	
7 Helden, Capt. Duminil de L'Estrille,	32	230	REAR.		
8 Daphne Brig, Lieutenant Fredericks,	18	90	Rear-Admiral Bloys, Commander.		
CENTRE.			19 Admiral Devries, Capt. Zegers,	68	
Admiral De Winter, Commander-in-Chief.			20 Hercules, Capt. Van Ryfoort,	64	
9 Wassenaer, Capt. Holland,	64	450	21 Brutus, Rear-Admiral Bloys,	74	
10 Batavier, Capt. Souters,	56	350	22 Beschermer, Capt. Hinxtt,	56	
11 Vryheid, (the Liberty,) Ad. De Winter Van Rossem,	74	550	23 Gelykheid, (the Equality,) Capt. Ruysen,	68	
12 States General, Rear-Admiral Story,	74	550	24 Ambuscade, Capt.-Lieutenant Huys,	32	
			25 Ajax Brig, Lieutenant Arkenbout,	18	
			26 Haasje, (Avijo,) Lieutenant Hartenfeld,	6	
Carried over, 684	4675		Total, 1266		

List of killed and wounded on board Admiral Duncan's Squadron.

Venerable, 15 Seamen, 2 Marines, killed ; 6 Officers, 52 Seamen, 4 Marines, wounded,   Total,
Monarch, 2 Officers, 34 Seamen, killed ; 9 Officers, 79 Seamen, 12 Marines, wounded,
Bedford, 2 Midshipmen, 16 Seamen, 2 Marines, killed ; 1 Lieutenant, 37 Seamen, 5 Marines, wounded,
Powerful, 8 Seamen, 2 Marines, killed ; 4 Officers, 74 Seamen and Marines, wounded,
Isis, 1 Seaman, 1 Marine, killed ; 3 Officers, 18 Seamen, wounded,
Ardent, 2 Officers, 33 Seamen, 6 Marines, killed ; 8 Officers, 85 Seamen, 11 Marines, 3 Boys, wounded,
Agincourt, none killed or wounded.
Belliqueux, 2 Officers, 20 Seamen, 5 Marines, killed ; 3 Officers, 63 Seamen, 11 Marines, wounded,
Lancaster, 3 Seamen killed ; 2 Officers, 13 Seamen, 3 Marines, wounded,
Triumph, 13 Seamen, 3 Marines, 1 Boy, killed ; 5 Officers, 50 Seamen and Marines, wounded,

Total of the killed and wounded,

The North Sea Squadron

IN 1795 HOLLAND was added to the number of Britain's enemies. The country had been overrun by the French, whose cavalry even captured a frozen-in Dutch fleet by galloping over the ice. The commander given the task of blockading the Dutch fleet was the impressive figure of Admiral Adam Duncan (1), who had quelled the mutiny aboard the *Venerable.*

Duncan's fleet was very much a cinderella force, scraped together at a time when most ships of the line in good condition were already allocated to the Channel, Mediterranean or West Indies stations. Most of the North Sea ships were not only in a poorer state, but also tended to be the older and smaller vessels: much of this

squadron was made up of 64-gun ships and 50s, the latter definitely too weak for the line of battle, and the former now widely regarded as less than ideal. Apart from the stretched nature of the Navy's resources, the main arguments for the allocation of such ships to Duncan were that his cruising ground was never far from a British base, so maintenance was easily accessible (in theory) for old and decrepit ships; but primarily, because the Dutch navy was itself comprised of ships that were small for their rate. Traditionally, the shoal conditions of the Netherlands coast are given as the reason for Dutch warships being small, but during the eighteenth century both the administration and ship design of the Dutch admiralties had failed to keep up with developments abroad.

The major part of the Dutch fleet was based in the Texel (2), and it was off this port that Duncan's blockading force, originally including some Russian ships, cruised. The shallow waters and shifting sandbanks of the southern North Sea made such a task very difficult, and from time to time the blockading squadron would be blown off station or have to return to its base at Great Yarmouth for re-supply. On one of these occasions, in February 1796, a small force of two Dutch 64s, two small two-deckers and some other ships escaped. They later came across an inferior British force whose only major ship was the 56-gun *Glatton*, but failed to take advantage of their superiority.

The *Glatton* was a curious ship, converted whilst building from an East Indiaman, and armed, at her captain's (Henry Trollope) insistence, entirely with short-ranged carronades, firing a very heavy shot for their weight, but with a short effective range (68pdrs on the lower deck, 32pdrs on the upper). The former had muzzles so wide they were virtually restricted to firing directly on the broadside, whilst there were no long guns at all and none of the carronades could be brought into position to be used as chasers, firing directly forward or aft.

Later the same year, off the Dutch coast, *Glatton* came across a squadron of eight French ships and boldly took them all on (3). The identification of these ships is not certain but they seem to have included the *Brutus*, a 74 cut down to a frigate, the *Rassurante*, an 18pdr frigate, the *Républicaine*, a 12pdr frigate and the *Incorruptible*, an experi-

3

mental 'frigate sloop' armed with 24pdrs, with between two and four smaller vessels. The *Glatton* seems to have done considerable damage with her heavy carronades and it was presumably their power that frightened the French off. They should have been able to stand off out of range and shoot the audacious British ship to pieces. Instead the *Glatton* was left with only two men wounded and her masts and rigging in a bad state (4). She had not had enough men to fire both broadsides at once and her crew had been divided into two with a group of loaders who loaded the guns on one side and then the other, the carronades being aimed and fired by a second group of picked men who also rushed from side to side.

The summer of 1797 saw most of Duncan's ships in a state of mutiny. At one time he only had his flagship, the *Venerable*, 74 and the 50-gun *Adamant* together with a cutter, to maintain the blockade, and he was forced to keep up the pretence of signalling to imaginary ships over the

horizon to keep the Dutch in port. Fortunately they remained there until well into the autumn.

---

1. 'Admiral Adam Duncan (1731-1804), 1st Viscount Duncan', oil painting by Sir William Beechey (1753-1839), no date.
NMM ref BHC2668

2. 'A Chart of the Coast of Holland exhibiting the situation of the Dutch Fleet at the time of the Engagement with Admiral Duncan, also the opposite coast of England including Yarmouth', coloured etching by W T Davies, published by John Fairburn, London, 24 October 1797.
NMM ref PAG8953

3. 'To the Right Honorable Earl Spencer . . . This Plate representing His Majesty's Ship Glatton . . . attacking a French Squadron consisting of six Frigates, a brig and a Cutter, on the night of the 15 July 1796', aquatint engraved by Robert Dodd, dated 19 December 1796.
NMM ref PAH7901

4. 'This Portrait of His Majesty's Ship Glatton . . . shewing her situation after Defeating the French Squadron, on the Night of the 15th July 1796', coloured aquatint engraved by Robert Dodd, dated December 1796.
NMM ref PAH7903

4

1

The battle of Camperdown, 11 October 1797

FRENCH PLANS for 1797 had included an invasion of Ireland covered by the Brest fleet, joined by the Dutch fleet from the Texel. By October of that year that plan was in abeyance, but the Dutch fleet, under Admiral De Winter, left the Texel notwithstanding. It is not clear whether he was going to join the Brest fleet, or merely to try conclusions with Duncan's fleet, most of which had recently been in a mutinous state; the most likely explanation is that the Dutch higher command were determined to make a gesture, against De Winter's

2

												Place
Venerable	Montagu	Russell	Glatton	Ardent	Repulse	Nassau	Belliqueux	Monmouth	Standard	Inflexible		Main
Albatross	Iris	Garland	Apollo	Stork	Warrior	Adrea	Vestal Kite	Martin Sea Gull	Billion Brilliant	Circe		Main
Ganges	Champion	Caesar	Triumph	Swan	Hound	Hawke	Nautilus	Redoubt	Naiad	Lancaster Inspector		Mizen
Pylades	Formidable	Endymion	Hydra	Bracket	Powerful			Veteran				Mizen
Brealius Lion	Bedford Hart	Agincourt	Isis Tisiphone	Espiegle Comet	Adamant Termigant	Agamemnon	Leopard	Weazle Persaphire	Director	Ranger		Fore
Trial	Cobourg	Rose	Active	Venus Black Joke		Nancy		Liberty	Rambler	Fox		Main

3

4

5

better judgement. His own fleet was not in the happiest of states either. It is not generally realised that there had been an aborted revolution in the Netherlands just before the French Revolution took place; but the result of this had been that there was a strong republican party in the country which were prepared to throw in their lot with the invading French. A substantial proportion of Dutch naval officers, including De Winter, were of this persuasion, but the great majority of the sailors were of the traditionalist party which supported the rule of the exiled Orange family. In the event the fighting power of both fleets does not seem to have been affected by these ideological splits, and both fought with the wholehearted (but far from vindictive) pugnaciousness that seems to have characterised battles between the British and Dutch.

The opportunity for the Dutch break out had arisen because Duncan and most of the fleet had retired to Yarmouth Roads to victual and refit, leaving a small observation squadron. It was there on 9 October that a hired cutter with news of the escape reached them (1). Duncan got under way immediately, and early on 12 October sighted the enemy fleet off their own coast near the village whose Dutch name, englished to Camperdown, is given to the battle. Neither fleets were in a neat formation, so both began forming a line of battle. The Dutch, however, were edging away into shallow water, and Duncan decided he had no time for careful

manoeuvring and signalled for his fleet to 'pass through the Enemy's Line and Engage from Leeward', after first hoisting the flags for 'General Chase' (2 shows the distinguishing pendants of the various ships of Duncan's fleet). With one exception (*Agincourt*, whose captain was court-martialled) his ships proceeded to engage the enemy as closely as possible, the general spirit being summed up by the short-tempered Scots Captain of

6

(appropriately) the *Belliqueux* who said: 'Damn . . . Up wi' the hel-lem and gang into the middle o'it'. They swept down in two groups, one led by Duncan's *Venerable*, the other by his second-in-command, Richard Onslow in the *Monarch* (3). As De Winter said later to Duncan: 'Your not waiting to form line ruined me . . . '. As it was the Dutch had managed to form a line, unusually (and sensibly) positioning frigates and brigs (in numbers of which they had an advantage) behind gaps in the line to help rake the British vessels as they came into action.

It was Onslow in the *Monarch* who first cut through the Dutch line. He then became involved in a battle with the Dutch *Jupiter*. Eventually nine of his ships came into action with five Dutch and overwhelmed them. Duncan's *Venerable* had aimed to break the Dutch line between the flagship *Vryheid* and her next astern, the *States General*, but the latter closed that gap, and so the *Venerable* went under her stern, firing a damaging raking broadside as she did so (4), and then ranged up alongside her originally intended opponent (5). Initially three other Dutch ships supported their admiral in this battle of the flagships, and *Venerable* had to withdraw from close action. By this time, however, the large British 74 *Triumph*, which had already battered the *Wassenaar* into surrender had come up and the 64 *Ardent* was also fighting De Winter (she lost more casualties than any other British ship as a result). Later Bligh's *Director* came up to fire the final broadsides against the much-battered *Vryheid* (6). William Bligh did well in this battle, though he is usually only remembered for his leading role in the *Bounty* mutiny.

With her masts gone (7) the embattled and surrounded Dutch admiral (8, 9) finally had to surrender. He had by then been abandoned by the remaining uncaptured Dutch ships which, seeing the British clearly winning, withdrew to the Texel.

7

1. 'HM Armed Cutter the Active J Hamilton Commander, Communicating by Signal to Admiral Duncan in Yarmouth Roads the intelligence of the Dutch Fleet being at Sea which led to the Glorious Victory of Camperdown', aquatint engraved by Edward Duncan after an original by John William Huggins, published 1830.
NMM ref PAG8957

2. 'Flag Table of the English Ships at Camperdown', watercolour by Nicholas Pocock (1740-1821), no date.
NMM ref PAD8873

3. 'An exact Representation of the Engagement & Defeat of the Dutch Fleet, by Admiral Lord Duncan', engraving and etching by Pass after an original by Godefroy, published London 13 January 1798.
NMM ref PAG7061

4. 'Battle of Camperdown, 11th October 1797', by Thomas Luny (1759-1837), 1803.
NMM neg no 9757

5. 'The battle of Camperdown, 11 October 1797', oil painting by Thomas Whitcombe (c1752-1824), signed and dated 1798.
NMM ref BHC0505

6. 'Director firing her last broadside, to which the Vreyheid struck', watercolour with etched base by Samuel Owen, 1798.
NMM neg no A3429

7. 'The battle of Camperdown, 11 October 1797', oil painting by Phillippe-Jacques de Loutherbourg (1740-1812), signed and dated 1801.
NMM ref BHC0504

8. 'Zeeslag. Tusschen de Bataafsche en Engelsche Vlooten op de Hoogte van Egmond den Elfdn. October 1797', etching by Reiner Vinkeles after an original by Gerrit Groenewegen, published by J Allart, no date.
NMM ref PAF4687

9. 'Battle of Camperdown, 11 Oct 1797', grey wash by Nicholas Pocock (1740-1821), no date.
NMM ref PAF5875

Camperdown: end of the battle

THE BATTLE had resulted in a series of individual fights between single ships and small groups. There were many dramatic moments. The Dutch *Hercules* caught fire and, though the conflagration was put out, had to throw her gunpowder over the side. Left defenceless she surrendered. The *Venerable* had her colours shot away, which were replaced by a young seaman, John Crawford (1). However, perhaps the most human moment of the entire battle was when, on the quarterdeck of the *Venerable* (2) Admiral De Winter offered his sword to Duncan, who refused it and shook his hand instead (3). De Winter then remarked on the extraordinary fact that both huge men, prominent upon the exposed quarterdecks of their heavily-engaged flagships during a very bloody action, had both escaped without a scratch.

The British fleet had consisted of seven 74s (the Dutch had three, plus a 72), seven 64s (the Dutch had the same number of roughly equivalent vessels, five 68s and two 64s), and two 50s (the Dutch three 56s and two 44s, one of them a cut-down vessel). By now most navies considered the 64 as rather small for the battle-line, and the small two-deckers of less than 60 guns as totally obsolete for that purpose. Both sides were roughly equal in numbers, but the Dutch ships were generally smaller and weaker. The British had more and heavier guns and slightly more men. The fact that the Dutch had considerably more small vessels (two large frigates, two 34s, four brigs and one despatch vessel as against one heavy

1

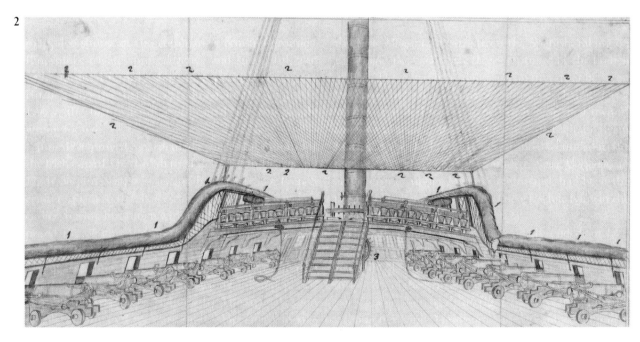

2

3

1. 'John Crawford of Sunderland, Durham, The Sailor who Nailed the Flag to the Main Top Gallant mast head, on board the Venerable, Lord Duncan's ship, after being Once shot away by the Dutch Admiral de Winter', coloured etching by Daniel Orme after his own original, published by the artist and Edward Orme, London, 21 November 1797. NMM ref PAD3447

2. A view of the quarterdeck and poop of HMS *Venerable*, brown pen & ink by John Little, dated 6 March 1799. The *sauve-tête* netting was rigged in action to protect the crew from debris falling from aloft. NMM ref PAF7977

3. 'The battle of Camperdown, 11 October 1797: Duncan receiving the surrender of Admiral de Winter', oil painting by Samuel Drummond (1765-1844), no date. NMM ref BHC0506

4. 'To the . . . Lords Commissioners . . . this representation of the Dutch Prizes . . . with the Flagships of the Admirals Visc. Duncan and Sir Richard Onslow, Bart, as stationed in the River Medway previous to the intended Royal Review', coloured aquatint and etching by J Wells after his own original, published by Robert Pollard, 29 December 1798. NMM ref PAH7912

frigate, one 28 and four hired cutters) did not compensate for this, despite their intelligent use of them during the battle. The result of the battle was that the British captured seven ships of the line, two 56s (of which one was then wrecked) and two frigates. Both frigates then went ashore, one of them being wrecked and the other recaptured and salved by the Dutch.

It was very noticeable that the Dutch had concentrated their fire on the hulls of the British ships, whose rigging was virtually undamaged, but whose hulls and crews had suffered considerably. British casualties were 244 killed or mortally wounded and 796 wounded, the Dutch figures being 540 and 620 respectively. The heavier Dutch casualties and the fact that all the prizes were dismasted when captured, or their rigging was so damaged that they became so soon afterwards, would argue that British gunnery was even more effective than the Dutch. It should be remembered, however, that the British had on balance heavier guns and more stoutly-built ships than their opponents. Certainly the hulls of all the prizes were considerably shattered and none of them was of much use for first-line service afterwards (4). However, Dutch ships, intended for use in shallow home waters, were built with flatter bottoms, shallower

draught, and usually both of lighter construction and smaller size than nearly all their contemporaries. This made them of lesser interest and use to the Royal Navy than French or Spanish prizes.

4

1

A global war

FOR MUCH of the nineteenth century in Britain, the period 1793-1815 was usually known as 'The Great War'–until eclipsed by an even more terrible conflict after 1914–for it was a truly global struggle, with naval warfare occurring in the remotest corners of Europe untouched by land fighting, and almost every place on the planet where European powers had colonies. After 1803 if anything it became even wider, but even in the early years its scope was remarkable. These pages feature a selection of actions away from the main theatres of war to demonstrate this geographical spread.

While convoying a small number of merchantmen to

2

3

Smyrna, the 50-gun ship *Romney* spotted the French frigate *Sybille*, 40 guns, Commodore Rondeau, lying with three armed merchant ships in the bay off the Greek town of Mykonos. On 17 June 1794 Captain Paget anchored near the French frigate and demanded her surrender, but although her main battery was only 18pdrs compared to the British ship's 24pdrs, the French vessel decided to fight. The opponents then battered each other at close range for over an hour until *Sybille* surrendered with 46 killed and 112 wounded; British loses were 10 and 28 respectively (1, 2, 3). Because she mounted extra carronades and could fight an extra main deck gun in a spare port, the theoretical firepower of the French frigate was not much less than that of the British 50 (380lbs to 414lbs), but the real advantage of a two-decker in concentrated fire can be seen in the very different casualties. The *Sybille* was a relatively new Toulon-built ship of 1091 tons which enjoyed a long active career in the Royal Navy under the same name (4).

4

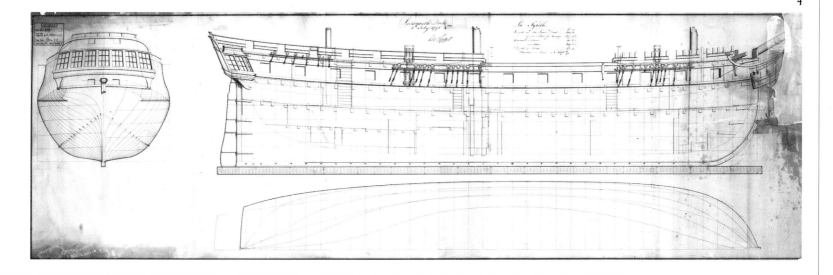

5

6

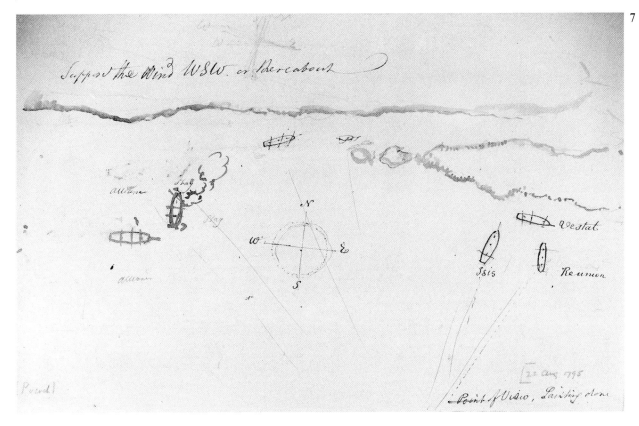

Nearly a year later, in May 1795, the British frigates *Thetis*, 38 and *Hussar*, 28 intercepted five armed storeships off Chesapeake Bay on the coast of the United States. The French squadron formed line of battle and one hoisted a commodore's broad pendant, giving the appearance of regular warships armed *en flûte* (with part of the armament, usually from the lower deck, unshipped). Nevertheless, the British attacked and captured the *Prévoyante* of 803 tons and the smaller *Raison* (5). Both prizes were commissioned as cruisers, but enjoyed only short careers; they were really only storeships and did not have the sailing qualities for a more active role.

French involvement in the Netherlands which lead to the establishment of the Batavian Republic and the flight of the Stadholder to Britain produced a range of new opportunities from January 1795. The political fiction was that Britain supported the legitimate government so no state of war could be declared, but orders were issued nevertheless to detain Dutch ships and occupy colonies belonging to the Netherlands, these being held in trust until the victory of the old regime. Dutch possessions stretched as far as modern Indonesia and Dutch trade was still among the most important in Europe. Part of this round-up of Dutch merchant ships included the taking of five rich East Indiamen off the South Atlantic way-station of St Helena on 14 June 1795 (6).

Traditionally, Dutch economic strength was heavily dependent on Baltic and northern trade, and on 22 August 1795 a Dutch commerce protection squadron of two 36-gun frigates and a cutter was discovered off Norway and pursued towards the port of Egeroe by a superior British force—the *Vestal*, 28, *Stag*, 32, and *Isis*, 50, under the command of Captain James Alms of the *Reunion*, 36. It was a complicated little action, and when Nicholas Pocock was commissioned to produce a painting of the event he first sketched a plan (7) showing how the cutter and the frigate *Argo* escaped into harbour, while *Reunion*, *Vestal* and *Isis* were forced to go about quickly to avoid running ashore; *Stag*, however, cut off and captured the Dutch frigate *Alliante*, 36, and Pocock's sketchbooks include two alternative compositions for a painting (8,9).

Similar encounters were occurring in the East Indies and the Indian Ocean, and probably the only sea free from any conflict by this time was the uncolonised vastness of the Pacific.

---

1. 'The Romney captures La Sybille 17 June 1794', anonymous pen & ink and watercolour, no date.
NMM ref PAG9683

2. 'Action of the Romney Captain the Honble. Wm Paget & La Sybille & 3 armed vessels–Commodore Rondeau June 17th 1794', black and watercolour pen & ink by J Livesay, no date.
NMM ref PAG9743

3. 'Action between Romney and Sibylle off Miconi, Grecian Archipelago, 17 Jun 1794', grey wash by Robert Cleveley, dated 1796.
NMM ref PAF5826

4. Sheer draught of *Sibylle* as captured. Admiralty Collection.
NMM neg 6139-33

5. 'To Capt the Honble A F Cochrane of . . . Ship Thetis, Captain Beresford of the Hussar . . . representation of their action with five . . . French Ships of War near Cape Henry June 17th [*sic*] 1795', coloured aquatint engraved by J Wells after an original by Nicholas Pocock (1740-1821), published by Nicholas Pocock 1 January 1801.
NMM neg no A4901

6. 'The Honble East India Company's Ship, General Goddard . . . with His Majesty's Ship Sceptre and Swallow Packet Capturing Seven Dutch East Indiamen off St Helena on the 4th of June 1795', coloured aquatint engraved and published by Robert Pollard, 21 January 1797, after an original by Thomas Luny (1759-1837).
NMM ref PAH7885

7. 'Plan of engagement between Isis, Reunion, Stag and Vestal and the Dutch frigate Alliante, 22 Aug 1795', pen & ink by Nicholas Pocock (1740-1821), dated 1795.
NMM ref PAD0397

8. 'Capture of the Alliance by the Stag Captain the Hon J S Yorke, 22 Aug 1795', graphite and wash by Nicholas Pocock (1740-1821), dated 1795.
NMM ref PAD0398

9. 'Action between the Stag Captain Yorke and two Dutch Frigates in which the Alliance was captured, 22 Aug 1795', graphite by Nicholas Pocock (1740-1821), dated 1795.
NMM ref PAD0399

POSTSCRIPT

THE FIRST five years of the war between revolutionary France and Britain had not presented the Royal Navy with difficulties comparable to those experienced during the war of the American Revolution. It was the triumphs of the French army ashore, especially its conquests in Italy, which caused the navy its greatest strategic problems. The near disaster of the French expedition to Ireland in 1796 was a salutary lesson in the need for a complacent service to rethink its fundamentals.

Ireland continued to present the French with an opportunity to knock Britain out of the war, but subsequent attempts to co-operate with the Irish independence movement were to be on a smaller scale, and were no more successful. The Irish rebel leader, Fitzgerald, was arrested before he could co-ordinate the plans for a military rising, which when it occurred was defeated before the French could bring support. In August of 1798 four of the line carried a small army of crack troops to Killala Bay in northern Ireland, but they were unable to keep the field on their own when a much larger British army was brought against them. In September another attempt was made, by Rear-Admiral Bompart with *Hoche* of 74-guns, and eight frigates. Thanks to the prompt action of Captain Keats in reporting the sailing to Bridport who was then at Torbay, Bompart was intercepted by Rear-Admiral Sir John Warren with three 74s and five frigates before he could get to Lough Swilly. In a rising gale and heavy sea a running fight developed and *Hoche* was forced to surrender. In her, Wolfe Tone was taken prisoner, and committed suicide to avoid being executed.

In 1800, when Admiral the Earl St Vincent took command, the Channel Fleet began continuous close blockade of Brest, in flexible formations which watched L'Orient, Rochefort, and the Spanish ports of Corunna, Ferrol and Cadiz. The powerful position which it thereby acquired over naval movement was more within reach because the British fleet had expanded rapidly, partly through capture from the enemy. In 1795 the Royal Navy had 512,000 tons of shipping compared to 284,000 tons in the French navy. In 1800 it was to have 569,000 tons compared to 204,000 tons in the French Marine. However, Spain's entry into the war in 1796 with a navy of 227,000 tons affected that calculation, although the operational consequences were not in proportion because of the tremendous difficulty Spain experienced in manning its fleet.[1] Probably more significant than the tonnage calculations was the experience St Vincent had had keeping the Mediterranean squadron at sea off Toulon and Cadiz. His careful attention to the health of his men reduced one of the principal dangers of blockade.

The opening years of the war had been all but disastrous for the French Marine. In the first five years it had lost twenty-six ships of the line to the enemy and another nine to accidents. Fifteen of them had been taken into service with the Royal Navy. Their Dutch allies had lost eleven taken by the enemy, of which ten had been commissioned in the Royal Navy, and the Spaniards had lost eight, of which five had been taken into the Royal Navy. Gradually, from 1796, the French Marine began to recover its discipline, and the dockyards began to recover their ability to send fleets to sea properly provisioned and fitted. The fleet which carried Napoleon to Egypt in 1798 was to be much more capable, even though it was to be defeated by Nelson at the battle of the Nile. When Napoleon came to power in France, he was able to attract back into the service some of the officers of the old regime who had resigned during the revolutionary years.

It was to be Napoleon who would provide Britain with its greatest challenge. To defeat a popular uprising 18 Fructidor 1796, General Hoche had used troops intended for the Irish expedition, supported by displaced military officers. Thereafter, the government had become increasingly vulnerable to the army it no longer fully controlled. The generals who had conquered in Italy and Germany ignored their instructions to return the occupied territories, preferring instead to set up vassal 'Republics' under their personal command. This prevented the Directory concluding a durable peace. On his return from his abortive Egyptian campaign, Napoleon succeeded in displacing the Directory itself, taking the reigns of power as 'First Consul', and then as 'Emperor'.

---

1. Jan Glete, *Navies and Nations: Warships, Navies and State Building in Europe and America, 1500–1860*, Stockholm: Almqvist & Wiskell, 1993, II, table 23; 35, p376.

SOURCES

Intoduction and general
William Laird Clowes, *The Royal Navy*, 7 vols (London 1897-1903)
Julian S Corbett (ed), *The Private papers of George, second Earl Spencer, 1794-1801*, Vols 1 & 2 (London 1914 & 1914)
William S Cormack, *Revolution and Political Conflict in the French Navy 1789-1794* (Cambridge 1995)
Patrick Crowhurst, *The French War on Trade: Privateering 1793-1815* (Aldershot 1989)
Norman Hampson, *La Marine de l'an II: Mobilisation de la Flotte de l'Océan, 1793-1794* (Paris 1959)
William James, *Naval History of Great Britain*, 6 vols (London 1837)
E H Jenkins, *The History of the French Navy* (London 1973)
G J Marcus, *A Naval History of England. The Age of Nelson* (London 1971)
Brian Tunstall (edited by Nicholas Tracy), *Naval Warfare in the Age of Sail: The Evolution of Fighting Tactics, 1650-1815* (London 1990)

The Nootka Sound crisis 1789-1790
William James, *Naval History of Great Britain*, Vol 1
William Kingsford, *The History of Canada*, Vol 7 (London 1894)
William Laird Clowes, *The Royal Navy*, Vol 4 (London 1898)
J Holland Rose, *William Pitt and National Revival* (London 1911)

First shots of the naval war
William Laird Clowes, *The Royal Navy*, Vol 4
William James, *Naval History of Great Britain*, Vol 1

The Low Countries, 1793-1794
J W Fortescue, *British Campaigns in Flanders 1690-1794* (London 1918)
William James, *Naval History of Great Britain* (London 1837), Vol 1
John Watkins, *A Biographical Memoir of His Late Royal Highness Frederick, Duke of York and Albany* (London 1827)

Ships of the Royal Navy: the First Rate
Brian Lavery, *The Ship of the Line*, 2 vols (London 1983-1984)
David Lyon, *The Sailing Navy List* (London 1993)

The Glorious First of June: preliminary skirmishes/the battle/aftermath
Oliver Warner, *The Glorious First of June* (London 1961)
David Cordingly, *Nicholas Pocock, 1740-1821* (London 1986)
Rear-Admiral T Sturges Jackson (ed), *Logs of the Great Sea Fights, 1794-1805*, Vol 1 (London 1899)
Michael Lewis (ed), *A Narrative of my Professional Adventures, 1790-1839 by Sir William Henry Dillon*, Vol 1 (London 1953)

A ship of the line in action
Brian Lavery, *Nelson's Navy: The Ships, Men and Organisation 1793-1815* (London 1989)
Michael Lewis (ed), *A Narrative of my Professional Adventures, 1790-1839 by Sir William Henry Dillon*, Vol 1

The Glorious First of June: the prizes
Jean Boudriot, *The 74-gun Ship*, Vol 3 (Rotherfield 1987)
David Lyon, *The Sailing Navy List*

'Dangers of the sea': fire
Captain Edward Pelham Brenton, *The Naval History of Great Britain*, 2 vols (London 1837)

Michael Lewis, *A Social History of the Navy, 1793-1815* (London 1960)

The Channel Fleet, 1794-1795
James Dugan, *The Great Mutiny* (London 1966)
Michael Lewis, *A Social History of the Navy 1793-1815* (London 1960), Ch XI
Colin Pengelly, *The First Bellerophon* (London 1966)

Bridport's action, 23 June 1795
Brian Tunstall (edited by Nicholas Tracy), *Naval Warfare in the Age of Sail*

The Channel frigate squadrons
James Henderson, *The Frigates* (London 1970)
William James, *Naval History of Great Britain*, Vol 1

Ships of the Royal Navy: the 18pdr frigate
Jean Boudriot, *The History of the French Frigate 1650-1850* (Rotherfield 1993)
Robert Gardiner, *The Heavy Frigate*, Vol 1 (London 1994)

West Indies 1793-1794/1795-1797
William Laird Clowes, *The Royal Navy*, Vol 4
Michael Duffy, *Soldiers, Sugar, and Seapower: The British Expeditions to the West Indies and the War against Revolutionary France* (Oxford 1987)
William James, *Naval History of Great Britain*, Vols 1 & 2

Commerce warfare in the West Indies
William James, *Naval History of Great Britain*, Vols 1 & 2

Capture of the Cape, 1795
William Laird Clowes, *The Royal Navy*, Vol 4
William James, *Naval History of Great Britain*, Vol 1

East Indies, 1793-1796
William Laird Clowes, *The Royal Navy*, Vol 4
William James, *Naval History of Great Britain*, Vol 1
C Northcote Parkinson, *War in the Eastern Seas, 1793-1815* (London 1953)

London, commercial capital of the world
R Davis, *The Rise of the English Shipping Industry in the Seventeenth and Eighteenth Centuries* (Newton Abbot 1962)
C Northcote Parkinson (ed), *The Trade Winds. A Study of British Overseas Trade during the French Wars, 1793-1815* (London 1948)
G Rude, *Hanoverian London, 1714-1808* (London 1971)

The cruise of a frigate
John Harland and Mark Myers, *Seamanship in the Age of Sail* (London 1984)

The Naval Officer: duties and privileges
W Falconer and W Burney, *A New Universal Dictionary of the Marine* (London 1815, reprinted London 1974)
W E May, *The Dress of Naval Officers* (London 1966)
N A M, Rodger, *Naval Records for Genealogists* (London 1988)

Occupation of Toulon
Political tangles
Evacuation of Toulon
John Barrow, *The Life and Correspondence of Admiral Sir Sidney Smith*, 2 vols (London 1848)
Brian Lavery, *The Ship of the Line*, Vol 1, App XI
J Holland Rose, *Lord Hood and the Defence of Toulon* (Cambridge 1922)

Lord Russell of Liverpool, *Knight of the Sword: The Life and Letters of Admiral Sir Sidney Smith* (London 1964)

The original Martello tower
Quentin Hughes, *Military Architecture* (Liphook 1991)

Fireships
W Falconer and W Burney, *A New Universal Dictionary of the Marine*
Robert Gardiner (ed), *The Line of Battle* (London 1992), Ch 5 [fireships]
Sir Richard Vesey Hamilton (ed), *Letters of Sir Thomas Byam Martin*, Vol 1 (London 1902)

Corsican Campaign, 1794
William Laird Clowes, *The Royal Navy*, Vol 4
James Hewitt (ed), *Eye-Witnesses to Nelson's Battles* (Reading 1972)
William James, *Naval History of Great Britain*, Vol 1
Tom Pocock, *Horatio Nelson* (London 1987)

Ships of the Royal Navy: flush-decked ship sloops
Robert Gardiner (ed), *The Line of Battle*, Ch 3

The Mediterranean Fleet under Hotham
James Hewitt (ed), *Eye-Witnesses to Nelson's Battles*

Britain withdraws from the Mediterranean
John C Dann (ed), *The Nagle Journal, 1775-1841* (New York 1988)

Battle of Cape St Vincent
Nelson's Patent Bridge
Colonel J Drinkwater Bethune, *A Narrative of the Battle of St Vincent* (second edition, London 1840)
Rear-Admiral T Sturges Jackson (ed), *Logs of the Great Sea Fights, 1794-1805*, Vol 1
Christopher Lloyd, *St Vincent and Camperdown* (London 1963)
Nicholas Tracy, *Nelson's Battles:The Art of Victory in the Age of Sail* (London 1996)

The Naval Officer: recruitment and advancement
Brian Lavery, *Nelson's Navy*
Michael Lewis, *A Social History of the Navy, 1793-1815*

Blockade of Cadiz
John C Dann (ed), *The Nagle Journal, 1775-1841*
James Hewitt (ed), *Eye-Witnesses to Nelson's Battles*

Santa Cruz de Tenerife, 1797
William Laird Clowes, *The Royal Navy*, Vol 4
James Dugan, *The Great Mutiny*
James Hewitt (ed), *Eye-Witnesses to Nelson's Battles*
William James, *Naval History of Great Britain*, Vol 2
Tom Pocock, *Horatio Nelson*

Close blockade
William James, *Naval History of Great Britain*, Vols 1 & 2

French naval bases: Brest
J Meyer & M Acerra, *Marines et Revolution* (Rennes 1988)
Simon Scharma, *Citizens* (London 1989)

The Irish Guard
William James, *Naval History of Great Britain*, Vols 1 & 2

The Naval Officer: life at sea
N A M Rodger, *The Wooden World. An Anatomy of the Georgian Navy* (London 1986)

Inshore warfare in the Channel
John Barrow, *The Life and Correspondence of Admiral Sir Sidney Smith*
William James, *Naval History of Great Britain*, Vols 1 & 2
Lord Russell of Liverpool, *Knight of the Sword: The Life and Letters of Admiral Sir Sidney Smith*

French naval bases: Cherbourg
J Meyer & M Acerra, *Marines et Revolution*
Simon Scharma, *Citizens*

Droits de l'Homme, 1797
C N Parkinson, *Edward Pellew, Viscount Exmouth* (London 1934)

The Black Legion invades Wales
Édouard Desbrière, *Projets et Tentatives de Débarquements aux Iles Britanniques*, Vol 1 (Paris 1900)
James Dugan, *The Great Mutiny*

Portsmouth—key to the Channel
J Coad, *Historic Architecture of the Royal Navy. An Introduction* (London 1983)
————, *The Royal Dockyards, 1690-1850: Architecture and Engineering Works of the Sailing Navy* (Aldershot 1989)
R J B Knight (ed), *Portsmouth Dockyard Papers 1774-1783: The American War* (Portsmouth 1987)
R A Morriss, *The Royal Dockyards during the Revolutionary and Napoleonic Wars* (Leicester 1983)

The Great Mutinies
James Dugan, *The Great Mutiny*
Conrad Gill, *The Naval Mutinies of 1797* (Manchester 1913)
Brian Lavery, *Nelson's Navy*

'Dangers of the sea': grounding
John Harland and Mark Myers, *Seamanship in the Age of Sail*

The North Sea squadron
Battle of Camperdown
Camperdown: end of the battle
Rear-Admiral T Sturges Jackson (ed), *Logs of the Great Sea Fights, 1794-1805*, Vol 1
Christopher Lloyd, *St Vincent and Camperdown*

A global war
William James, *Naval History of Great Britain*, Vols 1 & 2

Notes on artists, printmakers and their techniques
E H H Archibald, *Dictionary of Sea Painters* (Woodbridge, England 1980)
E Bénézit, *Dictionnaire critique et documentaire de Peintres, Sculpteurs, Dessinateurs et Graveurs* (Paris 1976)
Maurice Harold Grant, *A Dictionary of British Etchers* (London 1952)
Ian Mackensie, *British Prints: Dictionary and Price Guide* (Woodbridge, England, 1980)
Lister Raymond, *Prints and Printmaking* (London 1984)
Ronald Vere Tooley, *Tooley's Dictionary of Mapmakers* (New York and Amsterdam 1979)
Ellis Waterhouse, *The Dictionary of 18th Century Painters in Oils and Crayons* (Woodbridge, England 1980)
Arnold Wilson, *A Dictionary of British Marine Painters* (Leigh-on-Sea, England 1967)

NOTES ON ARTISTS, PRINTMAKERS AND THEIR TECHNIQUES

These brief notes cover most of the artists and printmakers who appear in the volume, as well as the principal printing techniques. They are intended only to put the artists in context with the period and readers wanting further information on their art and lives should turn to the sources; in many cases there is little more to tell.

Alexander, William *(1762-1816)* English watercolourist and architectural illustrator known mainly for his series on China which he visited in 1792. In 1807 he was appointed Professor of design at the Military College at Great Marlow.

Alken, Samuel *(1750-1815)* English engraver of acquaints *(qv)* of topographical scenes and sporting scenes.

Ambrosi, Francesco *(fl mid-late eighteenth century)* Italian engraver who produced mainly topographical views, but who also worked after Nicholas and Pierre Ozanne *(qv)* and Claude Vernet *(qv)*.

Anderson, William *(1757-1837)* Scottish marine painter who trained as a shipwright. He is known principally for his small river and estuarine scenes around Hull, but he also executed large-scale set pieces such as 'The battle of the Nile' and 'Lord Howe's Fleet off Spithead'. The British Museum hold sketch books of the battles of the Nile and Copenhagen.

Andrews, George Henry *(1816-1898)* English watercolourist of marine subjects who was trained as an engineer. He also did drawings of a number of journals such as the *Illustrated London News* and the *Graphic*.

Aquatint A variety of etching *(qv)* invented in France in the 1760s. It is a tone rather than a line process and is used principally to imitate the appearance of watercolour washes. The process involves the etching of a plate with acid through a porous ground of powdered resin. The acid bites small rings around each resin grain and gradations of tone are achieved by repetition of the biting process and the protection of areas of the plate with varnish.

Bailey, John *(fl late eighteenth and early nineteenth centuries)* English engraver of aquatints *(qv)* of topographical views and naval subjects after his contemporaries.

Baines, John Thomas *(fl late eighteenth and early nineteenth centuries)* English marine painter. As well as his naval subjects, such as 'Action between *Blanche* and *Pique*', he also painted views derived from a trip to Australia in 1855-56.

Baugean, Jean-Jérôme *(1764-1819)* French painter and prolific engraver best known for his collection of shipping prints, *Collection de toutes des Éspeces de Bâtiments*, which went through numerous editions in the early nineteenth century. Also well known is his depiction of 'The Embarkation of Napoleon onboard *Bellérophon*'.

Beechey, Sir William *(1753-1839)* English portrait painter who studied under Zoffany. He was made portrait painter to Queen Charlotte in 1793 and for the rest of his career produced a steady output of fashionable subjects. A contemporary portraitist, James Opie, said of his pictures that they 'were of that mediocre quality as to taste and fashion, that they seemed only fit for sea captains and merchants'.

Bendorp, Carel-Frederik *(fl mid-late eighteenth century)* Flemish painter and engraver who worked at Rotterdam and produced topographical views and historical and naval subjects.

Bowles, Carington *(fl late eighteenth century)* London engraver and publisher of decorative and allegorical subjects and topographical views.

Bowles, John *(fl mid-late eighteenth century)* English draughtsman and line engraver of topographical views.

Boydell, John *(1752-1817)* English engraver, publisher and print seller who was patron of most of the painters of his day whose works he engraved and supplied to every European market. This export market made him a considerable fortune and in 1790 he became Lord Mayor of London.

Boydell, Josiah *(1752-1817)* English mezzotint *(qv)* engraver mainly of portraits, and the nephew of John Boydell *(qv)* whose partner he became.

Briggs, Henry Perronet *(1792-1844)* English portrait and history painter who became a member of the Royal Academy in 1832.

Bromley, William *(1769-1842)* English engraver. He worked for the British Museum but is remembered principally for his portraits of Wellington and Napoleon.

Brown, Mather *(1761-1831)* American portrait and history painter, who settled in England in 1781 where he became a pupil of Benjamin West *(qv)*. As well as portraits of members of George III's Court, he also painted military and naval subjects such as his depiction of 'Howe on the Deck of the *Queen Charlotte*'.

Buttersworth, Thomas *(1768-1842)* English marine painter who served in the Royal Navy from 1795 until he was invalided out in 1800. His vivid watercolours of the battle of St Vincent and the blockade of Cadiz, painted while he was at sea, suggest first-hand experience. After leaving the Navy he devoted himself fulltime to his painting and created a very considerable body of work.

Cadell, Thomas *(1742-1802)* London publisher and bookseller, amongst whose publications was *Cook's Voyages, 1773-77*.

Carey, J *(fl late eighteenth century)* English engraver, principally of decorative subjects.

Cauvin, Thomas *(1762-1846)* French geographer and archaeologist.

Chesham, Francis *(1749-1806)* English draughtsman and engraver, principally of topographical views and naval subjects.

Cleveley, John the Elder *(c1712-1777)* English marine painter and father of John the Younger *(qv)*, Robert *(qv)* and James, who became a ship's carpenter. He worked in Deptford Dockyard and may have learnt his painting skills from the dockyard painters responsible for external ship decoration. He is best known for his scenes of dockyards and shipbuilding.

Cleveley, John the Younger *(1747-1786)* English marine painter, son of the shipwright and painter John Cleveley the Elder *(qv)*, and twin brother of Robert Cleveley *(qv)*. He was brought up in the Deptford Dockyard and learned his craft from his father and the watercolourist John Sandby. He travelled with Joseph Banks as draughtsman on his exhibition to Iceland in 1772, and again to the Arctic in 1774, and it is for his depictions of the Arctic that he is best known.

Cleveley, Robert *(1749-1809)* English marine painter, son of John Cleveley the Elder *(qv)* and twin brother of John Cleveley *(qv)*. He was Captain's Clerk in the *Asia* and served on the North American and West Indies stations in the 1770s. He is known mainly for his history paintings of the American Revolutionary War.

Colls, Ebenezer *(fl mid nineteenth century)* English marine painter of coastal and naval subjects.

Cook, Henry R *(fl the first half of the nineteenth century)* English engraver, mainly of portraits.

Cruickshank, George *(1792-1878)* English draughtsman and etcher and temperance preacher, celebrated for his caricatures and political and social satires. He produced an immense volume of work during his long life, following the tradition of Hogarth, Gillray and Rowlandson.

Daniell, James *(fl late eighteenth and early nineteenth centuries)* English mezzotint *(qv)* engraver and publisher, mainly of naval scenes, many after Singleton.

Daniell, Samuel *(1775-1811)* English draughtsman and engraver and younger brother of William Daniell, the eminent topographical, marine and architectural artist, for whom he worked.

Dodd, Robert *(1748-1815)* English marine and landscape painter and successful engraver and publisher, best known for his portrayals of the naval battles of the Revolutionary American and French Wars. His is also known for his formal portraits of ships in which three views are included in a single image.

Doumet, Zacherie-Félix *(1761-1818)* French marine painter, born in Toulon, who left that port during the siege to move to Corsica and then Lisbon, before returning in 1806.

Drummond, Samuel *(1765-1844)* English landscape painter and portraitist who served in the Royal Navy for seven years. Self-taught, and with first-hand experience of naval warfare, he painted a small number of naval subjects including the well-known 'Death of Lord Nelson'.

Drypoint Intaglio *(qv)* engraving *(qv)* technique in which the image is scratched into a copper plate with a steel needle which is held like a pen. Ridges —burr— are created around the lines which give drypoint its characteristic fuzzy effect. The burr is delicate and quickly wears away during the printing process so that print runs are short.

Duncan, Edward *(1803-1882)* English landscape painter and engraver of marine and sporting subjects as well as topographical scenes after his contemporaries.

Duplessi-Bertaux, Jean *(1747-1819)* French engraver and painter whose principal body of work depicted the events of the French Revolution.

Dutton, Thomas Goldsworth *(c1819-91)* Prolific English draughtsman and lithographer of ships and shipping scenes, after his own watercolours and those of his contemporaries. His huge and varied body of work gives a vivid impression of nineteenth-century shipping.

Durand-Brager, Jean-Baptiste-Henri *(1814-1879)* French marine painter and traveller. As well as official history paintings for the French Government of naval scenes, he also accepted commissions from the Czar and the Austrian Emperor.

Earle, Augustus *(fl early nineteenth century)* American-born history and marine painter who travelled widely to the United States, New Zealand and the Mediterranean in search of subjects. He was the draughtsman onboard the *Beagle*.

Edy, John William *(fl early nineteenth century)* Danish painter and engraver of topographical views and naval scenes after both his contemporaries and his own designs.

Elliott, Thomas *(fl late eighteenth and early nineteenth centuries)* English marine painter who worked in and around Portsmouth in the last decade of the century.

Elmes, William *(fl late eighteenth and early nineteenth centuries)* English draughtsman and engraver who made caricatures much in the manner of Cruickshank *(qv)*, including two of Napoleon, published between 1811 and 1816.

Emeric, F J *(fl late eighteenth century)* French naïve ship portrait painter.

Engraving The process of cutting an image into a block or metal plate which is used for printing by using a number of techniques such as aquatint *(qv)*, drypoint *(qv)*, etching *(qv)*, or mezzotint *(qv)*. An engraving is a print made from the engraved plate.

Etching An intaglio *(qv)* engraving process by which the design is made by drawing into a wax ground applied over the metal plate. The plate is then submerged in acid which bites into it where it has been exposed through the wax. An etching is a print made from an etched plate.

Evans, Benjamin Beale *(fl early nineteenth century)* English engraver, principally of portraits, who did work for John Boydell *(qv)*.

Faden, William *(1750-1836)* English cartographer and publisher, and the partner of Thomas Jeffereys *(qv)* whose business he ran in the Charing Cross Road after the latter's death in 1771. He is best known for his *North American Atlas*, published in 1777, *Battles of the American Revolution* and *Petit Neptune Français*, both of 1793.

Fairburn, John *(fl late eighteenth and early nineteenth centuries)* London publisher and geographer and map seller whose works include *North America* (1798) and *Spain and Portugal* (1808).

Flight, J *(fl late eighteenth and early nineteenth centuries)* English miniaturist painter who worked in London and exhibited regularly at the Royal Academy between 1802 and 1806.

Gear, Joseph *(1768-1853)* English marine painter, born in Portsmouth, who became marine painter to the Duke of Sussex and is best known for his views of the 'Grand Review at Spithead' (1815). He moved to America at an unknown date where he continued to paint, principally depictions of British ships.

Golding, Richard *(1785-1865)* English engraver, principally of portraits and genre subjects after his contemporaries.

Groenewegen, Gerrit *(1754-1826)* Dutch marine painter and etcher who trained as a ship's carpenter. After losing a leg he turned to drawing ships' draughts and then to watercolour paintings and etching *(qv)*. Author of a famous collection of etchings of shipping and craft entitled *Verzameling van Vier en tachtig stuks Hollandsche schepen* (Rotterdam 1789).

Huggins, John William *(1781-1845)* English marine painter who spent his early years at sea with the East India Company until around 1814 when he established himself as a painter. He produced an enormous number of ship portraits, many of them engraved by his son-in-law, Edward Duncan *(qv)*, as well as a number of large-scale naval battles, in particular the battle of Trafalgar. In 1836 he was made marine painter to King William IV.

Jeakes, Joseph *(fl early nineteenth century)* English engraver of aquatints *(qv)*, notably of topographical scenes, naval engagements after his contemporaries, particularly Thomas Whitcombe *(qv)* and his own designs.

Jefferys, Thomas *(c1710-1771)* English cartographer and publisher, and one of the most important map publishers of the eighteenth century. His huge output included *The Maritime Ports of France* (1761), and between 1751 and 1768 he produced important maps of America and the West Indies. After bankruptcy Robert Sayer *(qv)* acquired many of his interests and published much of his work posthumously, notably his *North American Pilot* and *West Indies Atlas* in 1775.

Jones, George *(1786-1869)* English history painter, particularly of battle scenes of the Napoleonic Wars, for example 'Nelson Boarding the *San Josef* at the Battle of St Vincent'.

Joy, William *(1803-1866)* English marine painter who worked mainly in collaboration with his brother John Cantiloe, and the two are often referred to as the 'brothers John'. As well as paintings of naval incidents they were commissioned by the Government in the 1830s to record and make drawings of fishing craft.

Jukes, Francis *(1747-1812)* English painter and etcher of aquatints. As well as his popular 'Views of England' and his sporting prints he was a prolific exponent of marine subjects.

Livesay, J *(fl late eighteenth and early nineteenth centuries)* English marine watercolour painter.

Livesay, Richard *(1750-1823)* English landscape and genre painter and pupil of Benjamin West *(qv)*. He was appointed the drawing master of the Naval Academy, Portsmouth, in 1796, and his first marine painting, 'Cornwallis's Retreat', was exhibited at the Royal Academy that year.

Loutherbourg, Philippe Jacques de *(1740-1812)* Born in Strasbourg, he moved to London in 1771 at the instigation of David Garrick, the actor, who employed him as scenic director at the Drury Lane Theatre. Though principally a landscape painter, his dramatic naval works and seascapes, notably the vast 'Battle of the Glorious First of June 1794', had considerable influence on marine artists in the early years of the nineteenth century, particularly J W M Turner.

Lithograph A print made by drawing a design on porous limestone with a greasy material. The stone is then wetted and ink applied to it which adheres only to the drawn surfaces. Paper is then pressed to the stone for the final print. Lithography was discovered only at the very end of the eighteenth century but quickly developed into a highly flexible medium.

Luny, Thomas *(1759-1837)* One of the leading English marine painters of his generation. A pupil of Francis Holman *(qv)*, he served in the Royal Navy until around 1810 when he retired to Teignmouth. His remarkable output amounted to some 3000 paintings and many of these were engraved.

Medland, Thomas *(1755-1822)* English draughtsman and aquatint *(qv)* engraver of landscapes, topographical views and naval subjects, who taught drawing at the East India College.

Mezzotint A type of engraving *(qv)* in which the engraving plate is first roughened with a tool known as a rocker. The rough surface holds the ink and appears as a black background and the design is then burnished onto it by scraping away the rough burr to create lighter tones and by polishing the surface for highlights. Thus the artist works from dark to light, creating a tonal effect which was particularly suited to reproducing paintings and had its heyday in eighteenth-century England.

Milton, Thomas *(1743-1827)* English aquatint *(qv)* engraver of landscapes and portraits after his own designs and those of his contemporaries, and son of a marine painter.

Orme, Daniel (*fl late eighteenth and early nineteenth centuries*) English aquatint (*qv*) engraver of decorative, military and naval subjects after his contemporaries.

Owen, Samuel (*1768/69-1857*) English marine painter, principally of watercolours of coastal and fishing scenes, some of which were produced in W B Cooke's *Thames* of 1829. His few large battle pieces, painted in oils, include a depiction of Jervis's action off Cape St Vincent, 1797.

Owen, William (*1769-1825*) English landscape and society portrait painter, who died from accidental opium poisoning.

Ozanne, Nicholas Marie (*1728-1811*) French draughtsman and painter of marine subjects and brother of Pierre Ozanne. He was made draughtsman to the French Navy in 1762 and is remembered chiefly for his accurate recording of maritime and naval events.

Pass, J (*fl late eighteenth and early nineteenth centuries*) English line engraver of topographical views, portraits and rural subjects after his contemporaries.

Pocock, Nicholas (*1740-1821*) Foremost English marine painter of his day. He was apprenticed in the shipbuilding yard of Richard Champion in Bristol before being appointed to command the barque *Lloyd*, setting sail to Charleston in 1768. This was the first of a number of voyages for which there are illustrated log books, some of which are at the National Maritime Museum. He was present at the West Indies campaign in 1778 or '79, and completed an oil painting in 1780, receiving helpful criticism from Sir Joshua Reynolds. Thereafter he devoted himself to his art and painted numerous depictions of the struggles with Revolutionary France

Pocock, Lt William Innes (*1783-1863*) English marine painter and a son of Nicholas Pocock (*qv*). Like his father he went to sea in the merchant service before spending ten years in the Royal Navy from 1805 to 1814, during which time he recorded incidents in sketch books, many of which are held by the National Maritime Museum. His oil paintings are very much in his father's style and suggest that he spent time as his pupil.

Pollard, Robert (*1755-1838*) English line and aquatint (*qv*) engraver of naval and historical subjects, as well as of portraits and architectural scenes. He set up business in London in 1781 and is known to have collaborated with Francis Jukes (*qv*).

Pringle, James (*fl late eighteenth and early nineteenth centuries*) English marine painter, mainly based in Deptford, who exhibited a number of naval works at the Royal Academy. The National Maritime Museum has a series of small drawings of warships which demonstrate skilled technical draughtsmanship.

Reynolds, Sir Joshua (*1723-1792*) Foremost English portrait painter whose early reputation was made with his portrait of Keppel with whom he sailed to Italy in 1749. He returned to London in 1753 and established himself as the leading portrait painter of his day. He was made President of the Royal Academy upon its foundation in 1768 and in his 'Discourses' —lectures—he endeavoured to create an intellectual foundation for English art.

Robertson, Archibald (*1765-1835*) Scottish portrait painter who studied at the Royal Academy under Joshua Reynolds (*qv*). He moved to America in 1791 where he painted Washington and his family and acquired a considerable reputation. He was the author of *Sketches of America*.

Sayer, Robert and Bennett, John (*fl mid-late eighteenth century*) London publishers, based in Fleet Street, of sporting subjects, topographical views and maps.

Schouman, Martinus (*1770-1838*) Dutch marine painter who is credited with reviving the tradition of marine painting in Holland in the nineteenth century. As well as dramatic seascapes, he painted a number of naval subjects.

Serres, Dominic the Elder (*1722-1793*) French marine painter, born in Gascony, who, after running away to sea, was captured by a British frigate in 1758 and taken to England. He became a pupil of Charles Brooking and was a founder member of the Royal Academy. Though a Frenchman he became one of the most successful marine painters of the Seven Years War and of the American Revolutionary War.

Serres, John Thomas (*1759-1825*) English marine painter and elder son of Dominic Serres, the Elder (*qv*). Though he painted a number of dramatic naval battle scenes in the manner of de Loutherbourg (*qv*), whom he greatly admired, his main activity was drawing the coasts of England, France and Spain in his capacity as Marine Draughtsman to the Admiralty. A selection were subsequently published in *Serres Little Sea Torch* (1801). He died in debtors' prison as a result of the pretensions and wild extravagances of his wife,

the self-styled 'Princess Olive of Cumberland'.

Sewell, J (*fl late eighteenth century*) English publisher and founder member of the short-lived Society for the Improvement of Naval Architecture.

St John, Georgina (*fl mid nineteenth century*) English land- and seascape painter.

Streatfield, Reverend Thomas (*1777-1848*) English topographical painter whose lasting monument is his fifty-volume history of the county of Kent held in the British Museum.

Stothard, Thomas (*1755-1834*) English history painter and one of the most important and prolific book illustrators of his day, completing some 5000 subjects.

Sutherland, Thomas (*fl late eighteenth and early nineteenth centuries*) English aquatint (*qv*) engraver of sporting, naval and military subjects and portraits after his contemporaries.

Tardieu, Ambroise (*fl late eighteenth century*) French engraver who did plans of harbours and fortifications, and published a number of atlases.

Tobin, J (*fl late eighteenth century*) English line engraver of figures and landscapes after his contemporaries.

Tomlinson, John (*fl early nineteenth century*) English engraver of landscapes who left England to work in Paris where he drowned himself in the Seine when drunk.

Turner, Charles (*1773-1857*) English aquatint (*qv*) and mezzotint (*qv*) engraver of portraits, military and sporting subjects and topographical views. His engraving of J M W Turner's 'A Shipwreck' in 1805 was the first one made after a Turner painting.

Vernet, Antoine Charles Horace called **Carle** (*1758-1836*) French painter and son of Claude Joseph Vernet (*qv*). Though he painted battle scenes and history subjects, he is best known for his equestrian paintings.

Vernet, Claude Joseph (*1714-1789*) French landscape painter who is probably best known for his series of paintings of the ports of France which he painted in the 1750s and 60s and which were engraved at the same time.

Vinkeles, Reinier (*1741-1816*) Dutch engraver of portraits and landscapes.

Wells, J G (*fl late eighteenth and early nineteenth centuries*) English aquatint (*qv*) engraver of landscapes and topographical views and naval and military subjects after his own designs and those of his contemporaries.

West, Benjamin (*1738-1820*) American painter who is now regarded as the founding father of the American school. He settled in London in 1763, and though he retained his contacts with his native land, he remained there for the rest of his life. His history paintings, as personified by 'The Death of General Wolfe', became an inspiration for young American painters depicting the history of their young nation.

Westall, William (*1781-1850*) English painter of landscapes and an illustrator and engraver of topographical views who was appointed by the Admiralty as draughtsman to accompany Captain Flinders in *Investigator* on an exploratory voyage around Australia between 1810 and 1813. On the return journey their ship was wrecked on a coral reef and marooned for eight weeks while his heroic captain sought help in an open boat.

Whitcombe, Thomas (*born c1752*) English marine painter who, like Nicholas Pocock (*qv*) and Luny (*qv*), was celebrated for his huge output of paintings depicting the French Revolutionary Wars. He contributed some fifty plates to the *Naval Achievements of Great Britain* and also painted numerous works for engravings. There is no record of his death.

Wilkins, William (*fl early nineteenth century*) English landscape painter who ventured into naval subject matter with his 'Battle of Cape St Vincent, 14th February 1797'.

Williamson, Thomas (*fl early-mid nineteenth century*) English engraver of portraits and decorative works after his contemporaries.

Yates, Lt Thomas (*c1760-1796*) English marine painter who entered the Royal Navy in 1782, leaving a few years later to become a painter. With the outbreak of the French Revolutionary Wars he began to engrave and publish from his drawings of celebrated naval actions. He was shot in a family dispute and few works remain from his short life.

INDEX

All ships are British unless otherwise indicated in brackets following the name

THE COMPLETE BO

UFOs

*An Investigation into
Alien Contacts and Encounters*

THE COMPLETE BOOK OF
UFOs

An Investigation into Alien Contacts and Encounters

PETER HOUGH & JENNY RANDLES

PIATKUS

First published in 1994 by
Judy Piatkus (Publishers) Ltd
5 Windmill Street, London W1P 1HF

Reprinted 1995
First paperback Edition 1995

*A catalogue record for this book is
available from the British Library*
ISBN 0–7499–1399–1
ISBN 0–7499–1506–4(pbk)

Edited by Esther Jagger
Designed by Paul Saunders

Cover photograph: After the *Freedom of Information Act*, the Spanish Air Force
opened up their UFO files and revealed some amazing cases. The photograph,
taken over Maspalomas, Gran Canaria, in June 1976 depicts an object also seen by
the crew of a naval vessel.

Set in ITC Cheltenham and Plantin Light by
Create Publishing Services, Bath
Printed & bound in Great Britain at
The Bath Press, Bath, Avon

CONTENTS

INTRODUCTION

The subject of unidentified flying objects (UFOs) is more popular today than it has ever been; its mounting interest to the general public has paralleled its increasing maturity and complexity. Sceptics were predicting in the 1950s that 'flying saucers' were just a fad that would quickly pass. Now, in the closing years of the twentieth century, that 'fad' has become an indelible mark, some would say stain, on world culture. UFOs are no longer a fringe interest, locked outside the mainstream of society and associated with 'cranks'. The phenomenon is now on the inside, woven into the fabric of day-to-day life. It has been a silent, subtle invasion.

UFO scenarios are used in television soap operas and major feature films. They appear in advertising and are the subject of late night discussion programmes. Men and women with scientific and military backgrounds talk openly and positively about the topic. The British Ministry of Defence has now publicly reversed its attitude: it regularly passes on cases to civilian organisations, and is ready to assist in providing relevant information to researchers. The subject is no longer derided but accepted as something 'alien', a phenomenon outside our understanding.

The release of official files in recent years reveals the seriousness with which UFOs were regarded at a time when government spokesmen rubbished them in public. Those files describe visual sightings and the tracking on radar of unknown aerial objects. They report the scrambling of military jets in futile attempts at chasing silver-coloured discs. These were not hallucinations or misidentifications. They resembled nothing on Earth. Sunlight often reflected off their hard shiny surfaces, and the best military pilots in the world found themselves out-manoeuvred.

UFOs may have always been around, but interpreted differently according to the culture of the time. This woodcut from a Swiss library describes an observation of strange globes that were seen in the sky by citizens of Basel on 7 August 1566.

We are not just talking from a historical perspective. Somewhere in the world, similar events are unfolding as you read these words.

In recent years UFO abduction experiences have come to dominate the subject. This has caused much controversy inside and outside of the UFO community. Abductions offer less objective evidence and some researchers believe it is a psychological phenomenon riding on the back of a genuine nuts and bolts anomaly. People are taken from their cars, or their beds, from crowded back streets, to a white room where they are experimented on by strange entities. Hidden 'memories' are accessed through the use of hypnosis. Is the abduction scenario a cover story for childhood abuse, as some sceptics believe, or does it demonstrate the complete control by an alien intelligence of the environment and every human being?

At last the prayers of serious ufologists are being answered. Specialists from all branches of science are becoming involved; they include psychologists as well as physicists. However, there is still no government funding for public research projects. Specialists give their expertise in their own time, at their own expense.

Our modern history begins in 1880. This was the time when UFOs were first perceived as futuristic flying machines, although in one form or another they have been with us all along. The book charts the development of the phenomenon and society's struggles to come to terms with something completely 'out of this world'.

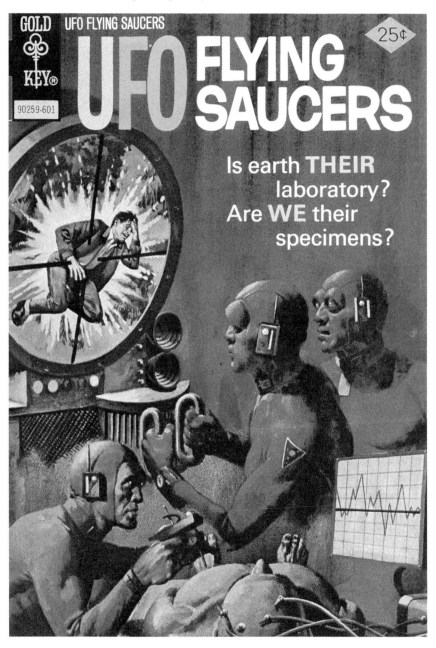

The cover of *UFO* magazine, dated January 1976.

Part One

1880:
ARRIVAL OF THE
AIRSHIPS

THE FIRST OF THE CIGAR-SHAPED OBJECTS

The modern UFO age began around 1880, at the height of the industrial revolution.

The modern UFO age began not in 1947, as many commentators suggest, but around 1880, at the height of the industrial revolution. Whether there is a link between the Western world's sudden advance in scientific and technological achievement and the simultaneous sightings of futuristic flying hardware is an intriguing speculation to which we shall return at the end of this book.

Of course, UFOs in essence have been around for much longer. Biblical history is littered with cryptic references to flying objects piloted by supernatural beings. But the period from 1880 up until the start of World War I saw one of the most clearly defined manifestations of the phenomenon. Our modern UFO history starts here. These early stories parallel modern-day UFO encounters, except that, instead of gleaming metallic 'spaceships' piloted by 'aliens', the sightings involved cumbersome dirigibles with human-looking crews.

Airship technology

Through the diligence of researchers on both sides of the Atlantic, numerous old newspaper accounts have come to light which describe sightings of mysterious airships. This was at a time when such machines were still on the drawing board, except for a few prototypes being tested in Europe.

Although the world's first powered, manned dirigible was flown on 24 September 1852, progress went haltingly after that. This steam-powered balloon (see opposite), designed by the Frenchman Henri Giffard, travelled approximately seventeen miles at 5 mph. Later attempts usually met with disaster, such as happened to the dirigible built by Dr Karl Wolfert in Germany; his machine, fitted with a small engine, crashed shortly after take-off. Dr Wolfert and his mechanic, Herr Knabe, died in 1897 during another attempt, when the gas envelope caught fire and exploded. In fact the first fully controlled air journey did not come about until 1903, when an airship flew thirty-seven miles over France.

It was after this date that airships slowly started to come into their own. On 15 February 1908, the US Army received its first tender for a dirigible from Captain Thomas Scott Baldwin. However, it was six years later before the *California Arrow* was built and tested. By this time the Germans had launched their first successful military mission using a Zeppelin, against the Dutch.

Aeroplane development was similarly beset with problems and disasters during this period. The first aeroplane to achieve man-carrying powered, sustained flight was the *Flyer* in December 1903. This was the culmination of four years' work by Wilbur and Orville

The first successful airship – constructed in 1852 by Henri Giffard.

Wright. Their aeroplane achieved flight for fifty-nine seconds and travelled just 852 feet.

As in modern UFO reports, the phantom airships of these times mimicked current flight technology but went several steps further. They attained remarkable speeds, demonstrating a manoeuvrability far outstripping anything built before World War II.

The sightings begin

Jerome Clark and Lucius Farish tell us that, according to the *Santa Fé Daily New Mexican*, a cigar-shaped craft driven by a huge propeller was seen by three men on the evening of 26 March 1880. These citizens of New Mexico described ten persons who laughed and shouted down at them from the strange object in an unrecognised language. Their general behaviour was of drunkenness. When one of them threw several items overboard, a beautiful flower and a slip of silk-like paper with oriental-type letters on it, together with a cup of 'very peculiar workmanship', were recovered.

The items were displayed at a nearby railroad depot. Within hours a stranger arrived and examined them. He pronounced them to be of Asiatic origin, and made the depot agent an offer of money he could not refuse. The man claimed to be a 'collector of curiosities', but it is common in modern accounts for strange men to visit UFO witnesses and procure any tangible evidence. These sinister figures are today referred to as Men in Black, because of their dark dress and strange demeanour.

All at sea

In that same year a close encounter occurred between a ship and an unidentified flying object, according to a Mr Lee Fore Brace writing in the December 1883 issue of the journal *Knowledge*.

On board the British India Company's steamer *Patna* while on a voyage up the Persian Gulf in May 1880, on a dark, calm night, about 11.30pm, there suddenly appeared on each side of the ship an enormous luminous wheel, whirling round, the spokes of which seemed to brush the ship along. The spokes would be 200 or 300 yards long. Each wheel contained about sixteen spokes, and made the revolution in about twelve seconds. One could almost fancy one heard the swish as the spokes whizzed past the ship, and, although the wheels must have been some 500 or 600 yards in diameter, the spokes could be distinctly seen all the way round. The phosphorescent gleam seemed to glide along flat on the surface of the sea, no light being visible in the air above the water. The appearance of the spokes could be almost exactly represented by standing in a boat and flashing a bull's-eye lantern horizontally along the surface of the water round and round. I may mention the phenomenon was also seen by Capt. Avern, commander of the *Patna*, and Mr Manning, the third officer.

The phenomenon spreads

Between November 1896 and May 1897, sightings were recorded in over nineteen states in America. Reports described large elongated objects with bright searchlights, and occasionally wings and propellers were noted. These apparently solid-looking machines flew against the wind; when sound was heard, it was a hissing or humming noise.

From October, newspapers began printing reports of unidentified craft in the backwoods of Nebraska. Late in that month a fruit rancher and his family near Bowman, California, observed an object with three brilliant lights, travelling at about 100 mph. Then on 17 November the phenomenon suddenly escalated into the airspace over Sacramento, with startling results. The *Sacramento Bee* recorded the flavour of those times:

Last evening between the hours of six and seven o'clock a most startling exhibition was seen in the sky. People standing on the sidewalks at certain points in the city saw coming through the sky over the house tops, what appeared to be merely an electric arc lamp propelled by some mysterious force. It came out of the east and sailed unevenly towards the southwest, dropping now nearer to the Earth, and now suddenly rising into the air again, as if the force that was whirling it through space was sensible of the dangers of collision with objects upon the Earth.

Some of the hundreds of witnesses who obtained a closer view said the object was enormous and cigar-shaped with large wings attached to an aluminium-type body. Shouts and laughter were also heard from the direction of the thing. A witness named R. L. Lowry and another man allegedly heard a voice call down: 'We hope to be in San Francisco by tomorrow noon!'

Airship reports also came from Canada. A glowing red ball was observed for fifteen minutes over Rossland, British Columbia, on 12 August, 1896. Many witnesses described how it approached the town, paused over a mountain peak, made several orbits then sped away.

The great plague of reports which followed took the press by surprise. These had all the trappings of a modern UFO 'flap' – a sudden rapid increase of sightings over a relatively short period. When occupants were seen, they appeared to be normal human beings. Usually they claimed to be secret inventors making test flights before unveiling their wondrous machines to the world. Needless to say, these 'inventors' were never heard of again.

A close encounter of the third kind

An incident comparable to a Close Encounter of the Third Kind, culled from the *Arkansas Gazette*, relates the experience of Captain James Hooten, a railroad conductor.

Not all of the airship pilots looked human. Two men told the Stockton Evening Mail *of their encounter near Lodi, California. They described three tall strange beings with large narrow feet and delicate hands. Each creature was hairless with small ears and mouth. Their eyes were large and lustrous. When they failed in their attempt to abduct two of the men, the beings fled into a cigar-shaped craft and left.*

I had gone down to Texarkana to bring back a 'special', and knowing I would have some eight to ten hours to spend in Texarkana, I went to Homan to do a little hunting. It was about 3 o'clock in the afternoon when I reached that place. Before I knew it, it was after 6 o'clock when I started to make my way back towards the railroad station. As I was tramping through the bush my attention was attracted by a familiar sound, a sound for all the world like the working of an air pump on a locomotive.

I went at once in the direction of the sound, and there in an open space I saw the object making the noise. To say I was astonished would but feebly express my feelings. I decided at once this was the famous airship seen by so many people.

There was a medium-size looking man aboard and I noticed he was wearing smoked glasses. He was tinkering around what seemed to be the back of the ship, and as I approached I was too dumbfounded to speak. He looked at me in surprise, and said: 'Good day, sir, good day.' I asked: 'Is this the airship?' And he replied: 'Yes, sir,' whereupon three or four other men came out of what was apparently the keel of the ship.

A close examination showed that the keel was divided into two parts, terminating in front like the sharp edge of a knife-like edge, while the side of the ship bulged gradually towards the middle, and then receded. There were three large wheels upon each side made of some bending metal and arranged so that they became concave as they moved forwards.

'I beg your pardon, sir,' I said, 'the noise sounds a great deal like a Westinghouse air brake.'

'Perhaps it does, my friend: we are using condensed air and aeroplanes, but you will know more later on.'

'All ready, sir,' someone called out, when the party all disappeared below. I observed that just in front of each wheel a two-inch tube began to spurt air on the wheels and they commenced revolving. The ship gradually arose with a hissing sound. The aeroplanes suddenly sprang forward, turning their sharp end skyward, then the rudders at the end of the ship began to veer to one side and the wheels revolved so fast that one could scarcely see the blades. In less time than it takes to tell, the ship had gone out of sight.

One can immediately see some remarkable similarities between this account and the more recent UFO scenario. Hooten came across the scene as if by accident, in an isolated area, and found the futuristic craft in some sort of mechanical trouble. This was a feature particularly of cases in the 1960s and 1970s: it was not uncommon for UFOs to suffer similar 'malfunctions', and provides a good excuse for someone to 'happen' to come across one.

A sketch of the 'airship' seen by Captain James Hooton at Homan, Arkansas.

As repairs are carried out by the crew, Hooten enquires about its motive power. The answer he is given fits the era and is tailored to Hooten's own interests, but is too general to be fully understood. Modern extraterrestrials prattle on about electromagnetic motors.

The British experience

Although the bulk of unearthed reports stem from North America, the phenomenon was not confined to that continent. Newspaper accounts have also been discovered in Britain, and searches made of newspaper files in other countries are showing that the airship phenomenon was global. In particular, many reports describe encounters in Scandinavia and New Zealand.

According to the Swedish newspaper *Dagens-Nyheter*, 'an unknown controllable airship' twice circled the Estonian city of Tallinn on Tuesday, 24 August 1909, before flying off towards Finland. Newspapers thought the object was 'probably Swedish', even though none like it existed. Exactly one month later a winged machine passed over the Castle Forest near Gothenburg in Sweden, just 100 metres above ground level.

The *South Wales Daily News* of 20 May 1909 referred to several Cardiff docks workmen who had sighted an airship in the early hours of the previous Wednesday morning. A little earlier, on the Tuesday evening, another witness got somewhat closer to the object.

Sweden and Norway, which was to be at the centre of a mystery aircraft wave in the 1930s, also played court to several airship reports around 1897. One of these featured a 'balloon' with an 'electric' or phosphorescent sheen.

Mr C. Lethbridge of Newtown, Cardiff, emphatically assured one of our representatives that on Tuesday evening while walking over Caerphilly Mountain, 'I saw a sight which frightened me, and which at first I thought was a big bird.' Lethbridge is an elderly man of quiet demeanour. He has a little Punch & Judy show, in which he travels about the country in the summer. He left Senghenydd with his show, on a handtruck, for Cardiff, and he reached the summit of Caerphilly Mountain when he saw the sight which frightened him.

'I saw,' said Lethbridge, 'a funny-looking object on the roadside, and two men who seemed to be at some kind of work close by. The object was long and like a big cigar. The men – two officers, were –'

'Officers? What made you think they were officers?'

'Well, they were tall men, military-looking men, and were dressed in thick fur coats and caps. Of course I didn't know they were officers, but they were two men – that's certain, and military-looking men, too.'

'How close did you get to them?'

'I was about twenty or thirty yards away when I first saw the men. The noise of my truck – it rattles a lot – must have disturbed them, for they commenced to speak very fast, some kind of lingo which I could not understand. They appeared to pick up something off the ground and jump into the object close by. Then it rose up like – like a switchback movement, and when it had got up a pretty good height it went straight in the direction of Cardiff.'

'What did you think it was?'

'I don't know. They frightened me. I thought first it was some big bird, but it must have been an airship.'

'What made you think that?'

'Well, after it had gone up a way two lights began to shine from it. They looked like electric lights. It made an awful noise – a – a whirring noise, and – '

The pressman had heard of that whirring noise. What did Mr Lethbridge mean by it?

'Well, ' he answered slowly, 'a noise like an engine working. Saw and heard it! I have no doubt about it, I was frightened I can tell you, and after watching it go away towards Cardiff I continued to walk home.'

Such is the story related by Mr Lethbridge of his strange experience between 10.30 and 11 o'clock on that Tuesday night. Interestingly, it received confirmation through the statements of residents in Salisbury Road, Cathays, Cardiff who said that: 'Between 10.40 and 10.50 they saw an object in the air which looked like an airship.'

The newspaper account goes on to narrate the testimonies of other witnesses to the airship. Lethbridge's vague description of the object as 'long and like a big cigar' has often been used in contemporary sightings. A search was made on Caerphilly Mountain at the location, where a red label printed in French was discovered along with a piece of mutilated notepaper and several other slips of paper – but these only served to confuse the issue.

The Caerphilly encounter was not an isolated incident but part of a huge flap lasting several months. On 21 May 1909, the *East Anglian Daily Times* came up with the headline: BRITAIN INVADED! AIRSHIPS IN EAST ANGLIA, WALES, AND MIDLANDS. PHANTOM FLEET. NORWICH AND SOUTHEND PAID A VISIT. What follows is a précis of the article uncovered by researcher Carl Grove.

The airship fleet which is invading England had a busy night on Wednesday. We speak of a fleet because, according to correspondents, there must be not only one, but half a dozen mysterious cigar-shaped machines with quivering lights and whirring mechanisms flitting about the country by night. Wednesday night's observers report manifestations at such widely divergent points as: Southend-on-Sea, Birmingham, Norwich, Tasburgh, Wroxham and Pontypool.

The mysterious airship has been seen in London. The fact has leaked out under extraordinary circumstances. The Aeronautical Society of Great Britain received a postcard on Thursday stating that a number of railwaymen at West Green had noticed the mysterious airship. They state they saw the airship on Friday last. The names of two of the men are George Walden and Joseph Cooper. Seen by a *London Evening News* representative, [Walden] said:

'Yes, it is quite true, we saw an airship. It was about 3.30am last Friday morning. We were at work coupling some trucks in the sidings. Suddenly my mate, Cooper, said, "What's that?" Pointing to a strange-looking object in the sky. "It looks like a policeman's truncheon, doesn't it?" I replied. "Yes, or a big cigar." It was travelling at a fast pace from the north-east. There were no lights attached to it. We were quite clear that it could not have been a cloud, as it was too regular in shape. It was also a very clear and cloudless night.'

A Southend correspondent telegraphs that on Wednesday evening at dusk, an airship was observed at a considerable height between Southend and Shoeburyness. It manoeuvred about for some time until darkness set in, and then disappeared.

Mrs Turner, of Norwich, was returning from the theatre on Wednesday night, and gives the following description of what happened about 11.30:

'As I came into my street, a flash of light came on me all of a sudden, and made the street look like day. There were two young people in the street – a youth standing near his bicycle, next to a young lady. I heard one of them say: "What's that?" I could hear a noise like the whirring of wheels. I looked up, and there I saw a big star of light in front and a big searchlight behind. It was flying very low, so low that it would have touched the pinnacle of Angel Road School had it passed directly over it.'

Mr Chatten, a grocer's assistant, was cycling home to the parish of Thurston about midnight on Wednesday night, when, he says:

'I was dazzled by a bright light shining from right above me. The trees and hedges were lit brilliantly. I have seen a naval searchlight at Harwich, and I should suppose that what I saw was something of that sort, but there was a bluish tinge about it, and it did not appear as strong as the naval lights. It seemed to be switched off after only a few

The major airship waves of the late nineteenth and early twentieth centuries lay undiscovered by ufologists for twenty years. Now they are the most widely researched historical cases in the field.

seconds. Getting off my bicycle I saw a long cigar-shaped object. It was soaring upwards, the tapering end going foremost, and was moving rapidly in the direction of Norwich. On the underside was what I should call a bar, supporting a sort of framework, a yellow light shining at each end.'

A Pontypool correspondent telegraphs that a mysterious airship was sighted at Pontypool on Wednesday evening by a number of people, including Mr Gath Fisher, architect, and his wife, who assert that it was cigar-shaped, and that it had a powerful light at each end. Men on night duty at Pontypool town forge declare that the airship floated over the forge and then darted off in another direction, frantically at right angles to that from which it arrived. It disappeared in the direction of Herefordshire. The airship carried a large sheet of canvas and a powerful light. Post Office officials and workmen corroborate the story.

For several nights people living in Small Heath, a suburb of Birmingham, have seen what is stated to be an airship passing over the district. It is described as cigar-shaped, but carried no light.

Barry Greenwood, editor of Just Cause *magazine, found a whole new group of airship sightings in Massachusetts as recently as 1992. The opportunity for newspaper archive research the world over still exists for dedicated people who do not mind eyestrain!*

Venus to enemy aircraft – the speculation continues

The airship sightings seemed to peter out after 1909, to surface for one final wave in 1913. Then, as now, Venus was cited as the explanation for some of the anomalous events. In the *Nottingham Daily Express* of 26 February 1913, the following appears:

In regard to the airship said to have been seen near Selby, Yorkshire. A glance at a map shows us Hambledon W to S, and Leeds W of Selby. These are precisely the azimuths of the plant Venus at the times given. Venus is now particularly bright, and suddenly appearing and disappearing behind wind-blown clouds, she gives the illusion desired. To hear the 'engines', shut your eyes, and a motorcar will rarely fail you. All the same it's rough on dear old Venus.

There must be no doubt that astronomical bodies accounted for some sightings, especially during a flap when people's awareness is heightened and they are more inclined to misidentify natural phenomena. Plainly, however, meteors burning up in the atmosphere, and bright stars and planets, could not account for the detailed description of nuts-and-bolts hardware witnessed at close quarters, sometimes by several people.

When the mundane failed as an explanation, society rationalised further and speculated that the sightings were of airships being test-flown by secret inventors. As we have seen, the phenomenon encouraged this belief by staging close encounters between witnesses and human-looking pilots. In the USA this idea proliferated, and individuals came forward claiming to be involved in the construction of the mysterious airships.

A character called Dr E. H. Benjamin confided to friends and relatives that he had constructed an airship near Oroville. The press began to hound him, and even his solicitors believed the story. A prominent San Francisco lawyer named Collins claimed to have seen the airship – some 150 feet long – ascend to about 90 feet under perfect control. The tale grew, although the only thing established with certainty was that Benjamin was a dentist from Maine.

There was also an enigmatic man named Wilson. According to witnesses in parts of Texas and Louisiana, a pilot aboard an airship had introduced himself as a Mr Wilson. During one of the encounters, Wilson mentioned an acquaintance called Captain Akers. When Akers was questioned, he admitted he had known a man of that name in 1876 and 1877, who was working as an aerial navigator. But Mr Wilson was heard of no more.

Modern UFO devotees will not be surprised to hear that airships were perceived as secret military aircraft. In Britain particularly, they were thought to be German reconnaissance ships. Arnold Lupton, MP for Sleaford in Lincolnshire and an explosives expert, sought to put people's minds at rest regarding a possible air attack. He pointed out that it would need 10,000 lb of dynamite to destroy the Bank of England. As this would necessitate a huge fleet of airships, it obviously was not practical, he stated in the *South Wales Daily News* of 20 May 1909.

Hoaxes

Some of the stories printed by American newspapers were hoaxes used by editors in the circulation war. Modern researchers have exposed several such tall stories.

On 18 April 1897 the Dallas *Morning News* printed a story of an airship which had allegedly crashed the day before at about 6am.

According to the story, the silver cigar-shaped object came down low over Aurora before crashing into the side of a hill. When observers rushed to the crash sight they discovered the disfigured body of the pilot; according to one man – an authority on astronomy – it was the body of a Martian! The alien was allegedly buried in Aurora cemetery.

In 1966 Dr Alfred E. Kraus of the Kilgore Research Institute at West Texas State University carefully investigated the story for the Condon Committee (see Chapter 18). He interviewed surviving citizens from that time, but they claimed to know nothing about the incident. Kraus discovered that, a few years before, an ageing telegraph operator had confessed to starting the hoax. A search of the crash sight with a metal detector uncovered nothing unusual, and there was no sign of the 'Martian's' remains.

Attempts to exhume the alleged alien body in the Aurora cemetry were met with fierce opposition by the local community. After a brief legal battle in 1973, the ufologists agreed not to pursue the matter.

Five days after the Aurora story was published in 1897 a prominent Kansas rancher, Alexander Hamilton, and two other men told reporters they had seen an airship hovering over a corral where he kept a herd of cows. They were startled to see a calf being pulled up into the cigar-shaped object, which then flew away. The following day a man called Lank Thomas found the remains of the animal, apparently dumped from the air. Other witnesses testified to Hamilton's honesty, and the tale became a classic case of animal mutilation by extraterrestrials.

However, the truth of the affair had been printed as far back as 1943, in an obscure Kansas newspaper. Apparently Alexander Hamilton and the publisher of the Fredonia *Daily Herald* had concocted the story between them – a tale that was to be retold in newspapers as far away as Europe. The article came to light in 1976 when it was brought to the attention of Bob Rickard, editor of *Fortean Times*, by Robert Schadewald. American ufologist Jerome Clark traced a survivor who knew the Hamilton family, and she confirmed the hoax but it was still being reported as true in some UFO books even during the 1990s!

The Clipper of the Clouds and other fictional inventions

Does art imitate life, or does life imitate art – or is one an interchangeable reflection of the other? In 1886 Jules Verne published a novel called *The Clipper of the Clouds*. Verne was already an internationally known writer with many previously successful works including *Journey to the Centre of the Earth*, *Twenty Thousand Leagues under the Sea* and

Around the World in Eighty Days. Clipper tells the story of a shadowy figure called Robur who builds a giant airship in which he has many adventures. Many people of the Victorian era must have been aware of Verne's futuristic romance. Indeed, he was not the first writer to propagate the idea – nor the last.

During the latter half of the nineteenth century a French painter and illustrator named Albert Robida produced a pictorial and written vision of the future. He described an imaginary world of the 1950s which included chemical and bacterial warfare, television, climate control – and airships.

In 1892 American writer Lu Senarens created a character called Frank Reade Jr, whose adventures were chronicled in the weekly magazine *The Boys of New York*. What was special about the adventures was Reade's mode of transport: he travelled about the world in a variety of airships. Many of them were electrically powered with rotors which operated similarly to modern helicopters. Remarkably, Lu Senarens was only fourteen when he made his first sale, and went on to produce an astonishing forty million words. When Reade had visited all the remote areas of the world, he built a new airship – one which transported him across the Milky Way!

One of those airships which never got off the drawing board was the *Avitor*, patented by an American called Dr Mariot. Drawings of the *Avitor* showed a cigar-shaped craft with fins and a smoke stack, indicating that it was steam-driven. It was against this background of human ingenuity and imaginative fiction that people believed they were encountering actual airships. After World War II the dream – or nightmare – was of visiting spacecraft; the UFO phenomenon obligingly structured itself accordingly.

A case, researched by ufologist Barry Greenwood, which illustrates in microcosm many of the components of the airship phase of UFO reports occurred in Massachusetts during the latter part of 1909.

It started with statements in the press that a man called Wallace E. Tillinghast had announced that on 8 September he had flown an airship from Worcester to Boston, then to New York where he circled the Statue of Liberty and back again, attaining a speed of 120 mph over a total distance of 300 miles. This coincided with sightings of an airship made at that time. Tillinghast was described as 'a prominent citizen and vice president of a Worcester Manufacturing concern' who offered 'the most remarkable claim ever made of the possibilities of human aviation'.

According to Tillinghast his machine was a monoplane weighing

In 1994 airships are once again filling the skies – only this time they really do exist. Hundreds have been exported from Florida around the world to be used for promotional purposes. They glow in the dark and have triggered dozens of new UFO waves that plague police, airports and UFO groups alike.

over 1,500 lbs, with a wing span of 72 feet. It was equipped with a 120 horse power gasoline engine, and in addition to himself carried a crew of two mechanics. Tillinghast claimed that while over Fire Island he developed 'motor' trouble. He flew up to 4,000 feet where repairs were carried out, the airship gliding unpowered for forty-three minutes!

Interestingly, William Leach, an employee of the Fire Island Life Saving Station, claimed that he had heard 'the rattle and hum of a high speed motor' passing overhead at 7.30pm on 12 December. If there had been no more sightings the story might have died there, but just a few days before Christmas the phenomenon returned in force.

The *Newburyport Morning Herald* reported that an 'airship' travelling at a rapid rate passed over Boston harbour just after 1am on 20 December. Immigration lawyer Arthur Hoe was alerted by a 'pandemonium' of ships' whistles in the harbour. According to the *Taunton Gazette* Hoe 'saw the dark frame of an aeroplane bearing lights come up against the wind and pass him going at a good pace. He heard the whir of some machine . . . and could plainly see the silhouette of some sort of large frame with the rays of the lights gleaming through its open work.'

It was suggested that Hoe had mistaken the masthead light of a steam liner, the *Whitney*, as she was sailing into harbour, but the lawyer was adamant that the phenomenon was high in the air, and sighted in a different direction from where the ship had berthed. But arguments over this particular sighting were quickly forgotten as a flap took hold of the Boston area during the next few days.

Below the headline AIRSHIP SEEN IN TWO CITIES the *Boston Globe* of 23 December said:

WORCESTER Dec 22 – Flying through the night at an average speed of 20 to 40 miles per hour, a mysterious airship tonight appeared over Worcester shortly before 6 o'clock, hovered over the city a few minutes, disappeared and then returned to cut four circles, meanwhile sweeping the heavens with a searchlight of tremendous power.

The glaring rays of its great searchlight were sharply defined by reflection against the light snowfall which was covering the city. The dark mass of the ship could be dimly seen behind the light which flashed in all directions.

The object attracted the customers of a restaurant and thousands more residents of Worcester who came out on to the streets to observe. After fifteen minutes the object departed, but returned just after 8pm, where

BOSTON EXCITED OVER PHANTOM AEROPLANE

Great Light Sweeping Skies Seen by Thousands

Following the report from Worc Wednesday night of the discovery that city of a strange moving apparently the searchlight of a d air craft, stories came from mam of the observance of similar li evening from villages east of and even from Bo⸱⸱on Comn

Scientists Think Venus Caused the Excitement

Some Claim Outlines of Craft Were Plain

While hundreds of people about Boston saw what they declare was an airhouse⸱ them

TILLINGHAST WON'T SAY WHERE HE WAS

an out of Worcester last night, up in the air. It may be that over the city, but that is my business.

hen I said recently that I had n from Boston to New York and n I said nothing but what was r I have an airship which will rr three or four persons and will ke the speed I claimed for it at is, about 120 miles an hour. "When I get ready I shall speak ally, and not till then."—Wallace E. Tillinghast.

TILLINGHAST ADMITS FLIGHT

Meanwhile, Wallace E. Tillinghast, the man who

Headlines from the *Boston Post*, 24 December, 1909.

once more it circled the city four times before disappearing in the south-east. It was also seen over Marlboro and Cambridge.

In Revere just after 7pm 'several responsible persons' also sighted the phenomenon. Samuel Gibby, Chairman of the Board of Sewer Commissioners, saw two fast-moving lights coming from the direction of Boston. He then saw that the lights reflected off the wings of an airship. He alerted a neighbour, and the two men then watched it hover overhead before turning round and disappearing. Fire Chief Arthur Kimball saw the object moving at the speed of an express train, and clearly saw its outline; this was witnessed by another fireman too. When the searchlight turned down on to the street, it made it as bright as day. Alexander Rampell, an aeroplane designer himself, told the *Boston Record*:

> As the aeroplane approached the beach it apparently slowed up and began to drop. At first I thought it was going to land on an aeroplane station I have established on the roof of my garage. The aeroplane

came down to within five hundred feet of the ground, its framework becoming plainly visible and the reports of its engines coming clear and distinct. The planes were, I should say, seventy foot across and the tail and propeller forty foot long. It became apparent that the aeronaut had come down merely to get his bearings, for rising rapidly as he passed over our heads, he passed out to sea towards Nahant.

In the small community of Lynn, Representative Matthew McCann and garage owner John Davis were emphatic on the physical reality of the airship. McCann told reporters: 'I saw it distinctly. I could hear the throb of the engine and could vaguely distinguish the outline. I could not tell how many persons were onboard. It had two lights on in front. It circled about in the air then disappeared in the direction of Salem, when it turned and went in the general direction of the Milton section of Dorchester.'

The sightings went on for several days, bringing some added colour to the Christmas festivities. Indeed, one newspaper suggested that the sightings were of Santa Claus! But what was it that drew thousands of American citizens out on to the frosty streets and convinced most of them they had witnessed a remarkable flying machine?

Anatomy of a phenomenon

A study of the Boston wave in the light of contemporary UFO flaps reinforces a truism believed by most responsible ufologists: that UFO encounters are never about just one thing. Once the belief – or realisation – creeps into a society that human beings are confronted by a phenomenon beyond their own technological capabilities, all sorts of psychological and sociological factors come into play. These factors include misidentifications of natural phenomena, hoaxing, the possible sighting of secret terrestrial flying craft and a genuine objective 'alien' anomaly. In 1909, the events at Boston included all of these.

Venus
Without a doubt many of the more mundane sightings were of the planet Venus and possibly the stars Castor and Pollux in the constellation Gemini. These astronomical bodies were visible over Massachusetts and the cold, frosty conditions would make them look spectacular. Certainly some of the descriptions sound like Venus. Professor William

H. Pickering of Harvard University told the press that the planet was visible from late afternoon until about eight in the evening.

Any object observed in the night sky for over two hours – as some of the witnesses claimed – has to be an astronomical body. But as Venus slipped out of sight over the horizon at about 8pm, it cannot account for sightings after that time. Although the psychological phenomenon of autokinesis can account for the apparent small movement of a stationary light, it is not an explanation for the obvious journey of an object across the sky. Nor can stars and planets project beams of light on to streets and buildings.

Hoaxers

The hoaxers were a combination of practical jokers and liars. For instance, there was evidence that someone – or several people – were sending up miniature hot air balloons. The lanterns which hung beneath these hot air-filled bags provided the spectacle of a light moving in the sky. The *Worcester Telegram* reported how one balloon had landed on a garage and started a fire; the remains of others were found around Worcester. Modern hoaxers also use this method. In a bizarre twist to the fire balloon theory, a man called C. D. Rawson claimed that the lights were lanterns attached to the legs of two large white owls! Rawson explained how he had ordered three dead owls for mounting, from North Carolina, but instead live birds arrived. He claimed that on deciding to release the owls he tied the small lanterns to their legs with string, so the birds could later free themselves.

Rawson told reporters he would publicly release the third owl in Only Square, Worcester, but first the weather and then other excuses were used to explain why the creature was not produced. Charles K. Reed, a taxidermist, stated that there were no white owls south of the Arctic, and in any case they would be incapable of carrying any weight.

'Secret' inventors

Were some of the sightings – particularly the close encounter cases – actual airships constructed by 'secret' inventors?

A man called G. F. Russell arrived in New York from Marblehead to announce he was the pilot of the mystery airship. Russell, who was only twenty-one, claimed that the machine operated on 'a new gyroscope-equilibrium invention'. However, when his employers were contacted – W. Starling Burgess, a yacht-building company – they denied the story. Although they had been working on several airships, none of them was ready for removal from the workshop – to say nothing of flying.

What was the truth behind the claims of Wallace E. Tillinghast, who told newspaper men he had made over one hundred trial flights in several machines?

With the upsurge of sightings in late December, Tillinghast found himself pursued by the press – which is perhaps what he had hoped for all along. Spies kept an eye on his movements, reporting that during the wave Tillinghast was sometimes at home and at other times missing. At one stage the press harassment became too much and he was reported to have slammed the door in the face of journalists. While not directly claiming to be responsible for the sightings, he did nothing to discourage belief either. When questioned about the phenomena observed over Worcester during the previous Wednesday evening, he told the *Taunton Gazette*: 'I was out of Worcester last night. Where I was is my own business. It may be that I flew over the city, but that is my own business too. I am not talking to the press or the public. When I get good and ready I will show the public that I have what I have claimed.'

Some newspapers saw the sightings as vindication of the engineer's earlier claims. A note was even secretly made of Tillinghast's car mileage counter to determine where the airship was based! While some newspapers carried stories supporting Tillinghast's story, others were openly sceptical – as were official bodies.

The Aero Club of New England issued a statement through its President, Charles J. Glidden, which was reported in the *Christian Science Monitor* and elsewhere. The statement related the results of the club's own investigation into the affair: Tillinghast's alleged speed of two miles a minute, and supposed gliding capability for over three-quarters of an hour, were impossible given the current technology. Other aeronauts in the Boston area had never heard of Tillinghast, and no one at that time was claiming to have seen his airship on the ground, taking off or landing.

Under pressure Tillinghast announced that his airship would be exhibited at the Boston Aero Show, to be held in late February 1910. This was the result of a visit by the show's promoter, Percy Edgar. In the meantime there was speculation that the machine was garaged on a farm in Boylston owned by Paul B. Morgan, who had also provided financial backing for the project. Reporters tried to get near a long wooden building, but were arrested for trespassing. The Boston Aero Show came and went without an appearance by the two-mile-a-minute monoplane.

Winston Churchill asked a parliamentary question about the airships in 1913. At the time it was speculated they might be German Zeppelins.

So was it all a practical joke by Tillinghast which got out of hand? Some months later, on 13 July 1910, the *Providence Journal* published a small piece that added some credence to the physical reality of an airship. It reported that Arthur M. Davidson, Secretary of the Worcester Board of Trade, had told them that he had visited Wallace Tillinghast at a secret location and been shown the airship. But when asked if he had seen it in flight, Davidson admitted that he had not.

The truth probably was that Wallace E. Tillinghast had built an airship. Equally probable was that the machine had never left the ground. The inventor hijacked the UFO reports out of vanity, and possibly in the hope that the publicity might attract additional backers for his project.

Fifty thousand people crowded the streets over Christmas 1909 looking for evidence of the phantom airship. Many of them, like witnesses today, mistook Venus. Did the rest really catch sight of an 'alien' phenomenon?

Ironically, the secret airship pilots are still with us, still taking credit for UFO reports! One of them approached Jenny Randles at a conference held in June 1993. He told her he was one of a network of inventors who carried out clandestine night-time flights over the British Isles. Apparently they wore silver jump suits to fool witnesses into reporting accidental sightings as UFOs. That way the Civil Aviation Authority would pay no heed to the reports, and they could evade prosecution.

Part Two

1919–39:
UP TO WORLD WAR II

GHOST FLIERS
AND OTHER PHENOMENA

In 1913, over the Struma Valley in Bulgaria, a huge 'fireball' was seen heading towards the frontier with Greece.

Reports of UFOs just before and during World War I are thin on the ground, although they do exist. Some of those that resembled airships have already been discussed; here is a selection of different-looking phenomena.

Fireballs over the Balkans

In 1913, over the Struma Valley in Bulgaria, a strange phenomenon was recorded just as the sun was sinking over the mountains. Prisoners in the valley saw a huge 'fireball' heading towards the frontier with Greece. What was remarkable was the slow descent of the object. According to a political prisoner named George Topîrceanu, it was as if it was descending on a parachute.

In the summer of that year, twenty-year-old François Zatloukal was travelling from Brnoyto Zidenice in Moravia (now part of the Czech Republic) when he was startled by something in the sky. It was between nine and ten in the evening when he saw six objects at high altitude resembling fiery red stars. They seemed to be under intelligent control, because they flew in an elliptical orbit in a clockwise direction. After six to eight minutes he continued on his journey.

A more bizarre series of encounters took place over the village of Bujoreanca in Romania, according to a schoolteacher. In the autumn of either 1914 or 1915 the man was having a meal in the garden with his family when everyone's attention turned to the sky. There they saw a spherical object with an 'exhaust pipe' protruding from it, not more than twenty-five metres above the ground, travelling east. As it passed over, the object caused some acacias and oak trees to bend in the turbulence. It left a trail of glowing sparks and made a whistling sound.

Over the next week the object reappeared several times and was witnessed by all the villagers. Strangely, it materialised over one house, then dematerialised over another. On one occasion it remained stationary over one of the houses, and a woman who lived there was afterwards found dead, apparently covered in burns.

A similar experience from these years was related by meteorologist Elizabeth Klarer of Natal, South Africa to investigator Cynthia Hind. In October 1917 Elizabeth and her sister were living on a farm in a valley nestling below the Drakensberg Mountains. It was near the Mooi River at sunset, at around 5.30pm, that they had their sighting. The girls were standing on a hill when an orange-red ball appeared in the sky; it seemed to be rushing in their direction, and Elizabeth thought it must be a meteorite. They then noticed a metallic sphere which circled around the ball three times, deflecting it from its course. In later years Elizabeth became a contactee and wrote a book about her experiences called *Beyond the Light Barrier*. It describes her regular contact with a non-human intelligence.

Back in the Balkans at a place called Colun in Romania, another interesting case occurred some time in 1926. A farmer called Ion Bunescu, was seeing to his horses at about 1am when over the pasture appeared an 'illuminated spear' which lit up the area. According to Bunescu it hovered for about twelve minutes, part of that time directly above him, before moving off towards Arpasul de Jos, some eight kilometres away. There it circled a small wood before suddenly becoming 'extinguished'. The farmer said it had made a whistling noise, was shaped like a boat, and was darker in the middle. He estimated it to be about three metres long and two wide. This is interesting in the light of modern animal mutilation cases where strange lights have been seen over fields just before the discovery of dead and injured animals (see Part Six).

That year also saw an early humanoid encounter. It occurred to a six-year-old boy in Lancashire, England, and was investigated by the authors in 1990.

The 'Three Wise Men'

Henry Thomson, a professional artist who has travelled around the world, has a photographic memory which allows him to commit to canvas with absolute accuracy scenes he witnessed decades ago. It also enables Henry to remember in vivid detail an incident from his childhood.

One evening in November 1926 Henry had been playing hide and seek with his pals. In their version of the game, half the group hid while the rest counted to fifty and then split up to begin searching. Grudgingly, Henry had had to leave the other boys because it was his bedtime.

As he lay under the covers he could hear the others outside, still playing, and he wanted to join them. He quickly dressed, then stealthily crept out through the back door to join his friends. This time he was one of the seekers, and volunteered to search the backs of Eustace Street and nearby Woodgate Street.

The back yards of the terraced houses all looked the same: dark and spooky, except where a chink of light spilled out through imperfectly closed curtains. As he walked down Eustace Street, something caught

'Standing, peering into the house, were three figures – and they did not look human.' This sketch by Henry Thomson depicts his mysterious encounter in November 1926.

his eye in the yard of number 21. He stopped and peeped around the opened gate. What confronted him was to remain indelibly etched on his memory for ever.

The light from the scullery window spilled out into the yard. Standing there, peering into the house, were three figures – and they did not look human. They were turned away from the boy, who stared in amazement. Two of them were around five foot eight, but the third, who stood in the middle, was several inches taller. They wore helmets and silver-grey suits ridged in thick padded horizontal bands, plus black boots. Tubes from a box mounted on each figure's back fed into the neck of the helmet.

Perhaps some small noise made by the boy alerted the figures, but they suddenly spun round. Three owl-like faces stared down at him. Their heads – or helmets – were doorknob-shaped, with two black slit eyes, no mouth, but a vertical slit where the nose should be. A loud gargling or mumbling sound issued from the tall one, and the three advanced towards Henry.

Henry ran home as fast as his legs could carry him. His parents thought his terror was due to being caught after slipping out of the house, and his story of 'three men in divers' suits' was met with disbelief. But Henry persisted, and over the coming months his family came to realise that something very peculiar indeed had happened to their little boy. Eventually his mother referred to the encounter as 'a visitation from the Three Wise Men' – a conclusion that Henry feels is a million miles from the truth!

High above the Himalayas

In his travel diary, published in 1929, Nicholas Roerich relates a very unusual experience. The book, entitled *Altai-Himalya*, records his expedition through India, Tibet, Sinkiang and Mongolia.

On August fifth – something remarkable! We were in our camp in the Kukunor district, not far from the Humboldt Chain. In the morning about half-past nine some of our caravaneers noticed a remarkably big black eagle flying above us. Seven of us began to watch this unusual bird. At the same moment another of our caravaneers remarked: 'There is something far above the bird.' And he shouted his astonishment. We all saw, in the direction north to south, something big and shiny reflecting sun, like a huge oval moving at great speed. Crossing our camp this thing changed in its direction from south to southwest, and we saw how it disappeared in the intense blue sky. We even had time to take our field glasses and saw quite distinctly the oval form with the shiny surface, one side of which was brilliant from the sun.

City sightings in the snow

In the winter of 1933 the *New York Times* published details of a sighting over the city which had occurred during a heavy snowstorm on Tuesday, 26 December. Witnesses described how they heard the sound of an aircraft circling above Park Avenue and 122nd Street at 9.30am; the phenomenon continued for five hours. Many witnesses contacted the National Broadcasting Company, and Newark Airport radio operators from the Department of Commerce offered help in the belief that a lunatic airman was trying to land. Field beacons were lit, and searchlights tried to probe through the falling blanket of snow. According to the newspaper, none of the flying fields had aircraft operating that day – indeed, the weather conditions made it impossible. At 2.25pm, when the sound stopped, nothing fell from the sky on to Manhattan.

Little more than two months later, on 2 February 1934, the London *Times* reported that the previous night an 'airoplane' had circled over the city continuously for two hours. The heavy note of the engines indicated it was a large machine, and its altitude was low enough for its lights to be seen. The Air Ministry stated it knew nothing of the flight, and civil aerodromes around London were equally baffled.

However four days later, when the matter was brought up in the House of Commons, Sir Philip Sassoon, Under Secretary of State of Air, offered an explanation. He claimed the aircraft belonged to the RAF and was on a training exercise in cooperation with ground troops. But on 11 June, two aircraft circled above the city, low enough for their outlines to be easily discernible. The Air Ministry admitted that the RAF frequently practised night flying, but it was forbidden to operate over London at less than 5,000 feet. They told *The Times* that the identity of the rogue aircraft was not known.

American researcher Charles Flood discovered a similar story dated 14 February 1936 in the *Oregonian*. It told how 'an unidentified airplane battled a raging blizzard and twenty below weather over Cody, Wyoming'.

The ship was heard roaring over the city at about 6pm. After it circled several times, the sound of its motors faded and it was not heard again for almost an hour. At approximately 7pm it was heard over the town again, the pilot accelerating his motor as he circled for several minutes.

Residents of the city fought their way through heavy snows to the airport, and circled the field with flares. Before the flares could be lit, however, the sound of the unknown plane's motor had again faded.

In a follow-up report, the newspaper stated that no explanation had been offered to identify the mystery aircraft.

The ghost fliers of Scandinavia

The last of Amundsen?

During the mid-1930s sightings of large grey aircraft were made by thousands of people across northern Scandinavia. They bore no markings and were the subject of intense searches by the military authorities of Finland, Norway and Sweden. These aircraft were able to outperform flying machines of that period and to operate in terrible weather conditions. The prelude to all this centred around an unidentified aircraft photographed on an island near the Arctic Circle.

In 1928 Roald Amundsen, the Norwegian explorer who in 1911 had been the first man to reach the South Pole, organised a fatal flight to the North Pole. His first attempt, in 1925, had nearly ended in disaster when one of the two aircraft his team were using crashed. This time, somewhere far north of the Arctic Circle his twin-engined Lathom aircraft must have come down, because it was never seen again.

Three years later a team of scientists flew over the Arctic Circle in the *Graf Zeppelin* on a photographic mission. Professor Paul Moltchanow discovered in one of his pictures an artificial object which no one had noticed at the time. Shaped like an aircraft, the object was resting on snow in the south-eastern part of the island of Novaya Zemlya. The professor told the *New York Times*: 'The plane was lying on a strip of snow. It is a monoplane with sharply rectangular wings and can be clearly seen. It is a two-seater and undamaged. It seems possible that it could be Roald Amundsen's plane, because he had a two-motor Lathom. We have no idea so far what it might be.'

However, Captain Walter Bruns, the founder of the Aero-Arctic Society, which had sponsored the expedition, disagreed with this hypothesis. He told the press that it was 'extremely unlikely' to be Amundsen's aircraft, as it had not carried enough fuel to have travelled

General Pontus Reutersward commanded the north Swedish military area. He wrote a secret seventeen page report to the Secretary of War concerning the ghost fliers. It said: 'The collected and analysed data ... has given me the impression that unauthorised air traffic has occurred.'

that far. Captain Bruns added that there was no record of any other aircraft missing in that area.

Further doubt was cast on the Amundsen explanation when German aviation experts announced that the object resembled a Dornier Wal seaplane. Was this the abandoned aircraft from Amundsen's first expedition? But it was thought impossible for the crashed aeroplane to have blown so far south – it had probably been crushed by pack ice where it lay. Then it was suggested that the mystery aeroplane was one of two Wals belonging to the Russian government. The Dornier factory in Friedrichshafen, Germany, who had sold the two planes to the Russians, stated that the aircraft were currently operating along the Siberian coast. The origin of the aircraft was to remain a mystery.

Invasion of the super planes

The parish priest of Lantrask in Sweden observed mysterious aircraft on several occasions during 1932 and 1933. In the summer of 1933 the craft flew over the area no fewer than twelve times. It always followed the same route, south-west to north-east. On four occasions it flew so low that he was able to observe it carried no markings or insignia. The machine was greyish with one set of wings. Once it skimmed just a few metres above the parsonage and he made out two figures in the cabin. As in the previous airship wave, the occupants were always described as normal-looking human beings.

An analysis was carried out by the General Staff in Stockholm of 487 Scandinavian cases between 1933 and 1934. They concluded that 46 were 'credible', 64 'probably credible', 273 'others' and 104 'unbelievable'.

Although there had been reports before 1933, the phenomenon intensified during Christmas week of that year. An article in the Swedish newspaper *Dagens-Nyheter* stated: 'A mysterious aeroplane appeared from the direction of the Bottensea at about 6pm, Christmas Eve, passed over Kalix, and continued westward. Beams of light came from the machine searching the area.'

The report was fairly brief, but it seems that the authorities must have received many similar unpublished sightings given that on the 28th the following announcement appeared in the press:

The ghost flier will be hunted by the Flying Corps Number 4 in Ostersund. Saturday, the Flying Corps received orders by telegraph to make contact with the police in the area. The flier was reported on Saturday, visible over Tarnaby, and this report was very interesting because the weather was clear.

The head of the Air Force received a telephone call asking for help in searching for the mysterious flier in Norrland. Information and detailed descriptions will be collected about the smuggler-flier.

At 6pm Saturday evening the ghost flier passed over Tarnaby. People saw it cross the Norwegian border, turn over Joesjo ... the place where he disappeared Friday evening. The last sighting was eastward towards Stensele.

On the day this report was released an aeroplane carrying three lights was observed at high altitude over Langmo Vefsn in Norway. Apparently it was similar to previous sightings from Hattefjallsdalen.

Two days later motorists near Gällivare in Sweden watched an aircraft which flew over the road at a height of around 150 feet. The authorities stated there were 'no ambulance planes or military craft in that area at the time'.

The New Year began with more reports and official comment:

The head of the Air Force, Major Von Porat, refused to speculate on the phantom flier except to confirm that he did exist. 'Specific details on this affair can't be published,' he said.

As late as Sunday morning a large grey aeroplane, bigger than any army plane, was seen in Sorsele. The machine flew in big circles over the railway station and vanished in the direction of Arvidsjaur.

Mr Olof Hedlund was taking a walk at 3.45am when he suddenly heard an engine roar from above. There was a full moon and visibility was very good. Mr Hedlund said the machine was about 400 metres up and in sight for about fifteen minutes. It was single-winged and enclosed, like a passenger plane, and was equipped with pontoons or some sort of skis.

No marks or insignia were visible. The engine stopped during the turns over the village. The noise seemed to emanate from the propeller. The machine was similar to a single-engined Junkers.

An old song set to a new tune

Over a hundred similar reports were uncovered in the 1970s by Swedish and American researchers. It is hard to imagine the impact of these reports on the Scandinavians, at a time when aviation lacked sophistication and was still a perilous pursuit. Like the phantom airships before them, the ghost planes seemed to be recognisable flying machines which possessed capabilities way beyond the technology of that time.

A feature of the mystery aircraft was to cast down blinding searchlights – a component of many modern UFO sightings. Arc lights came into being during the nineteenth century, but they required heavy generators and batteries which for a plane would have presented a weight problem beyond the technology of the 1930s. Aeroplanes were fitted with lights similar to car headlights, making night flying a rare and dangerous affair. The ghost fliers took to the air in appalling weather conditions, yet at that time instrumental and navigational equipment was so crude that most pilots preferred to remain grounded than to risk even a mild rainstorm. Over a third of reports referred to objects detected during snowstorms, blizzards and dense fog.

A lighthouse keeper named Rutkvist at Holmogadd in Sweden reported an aircraft which he had observed on two occasions. On Monday, 8 January 1934, he saw it hover over the island of Grasundet. After a time it spiralled towards the sea, stopped short, then ascended again – repeating the manoeuvre for an hour. On another date he observed an object flying in a blizzard against winds up to sixteen metres a second. He told journalists: 'I have never seen anything like it! It was a very strange action for an aeroplane.'

State of the art

Let us consider the evidence for where these craft might have come from. Most aircraft at that time had not advanced much since World War I: the majority were clumsy biplanes with open cockpits and a low range. But the ghost planes were larger than these. Radios were rarely employed, being heavy and difficult for a single pilot to use. Yet broadcasts by the phantom fliers were picked up all over Scandinavia.

The ghost fliers are a true mystery. It was not just a case of the misidentification of ordinary aircraft, or of secret military aircraft from a foreign country—although perhaps some of them were. In the 1930s Russia had no aircraft industry to speak of. Adolf Hitler broke the terms of the Versailles Treaty in 1933 when he began secretly building up the Luftwaffe; surely he would not have risked his meagre reservoir of ex-World War I pilots in pointless missions over Scandinavia. It was speculated that Japan might be the culprit, but that country was at war with China in the 1930s, and one would assume too busy to bother elsewhere. On top of that there was a worldwide recession.

Because of the very limited range of aircraft, any country carrying out a reconnaissance of Scandinavia would have had to set up fuel supply lines in hidden bases manned by aviation personnel. Aircraft carriers might be considered an alternative – but they were still only in the early stages of development. Even in America, the sighting of an aeroplane was still a rarity. Despite all this, the people of Norway, Sweden and Finland were observing large grey aircraft, sometimes in formations of threes, right up to 1937.

The military response

As far as the military were concerned, low-flying aircraft were over their territory for one reason only – to discover the location of forts, military and railway installations for a future war. The Swedish and Norwegian authorities were convinced they were dealing with a foreign power. They also knew the sightings were not explicable in terms of hoaxes and illusionary phenomena. In a report to General Virgin on 3 January 1934, Major Von Porat wrote: 'Many people of good repu-tation have seen the mysterious aeroplane with searchlight rays playing over the ground. Among the witnesses are two military men from the 4th Flying Corps.'

The ghost fliers seemed immune to accident – not so with their pursuers. When the 4th Flying Corps tried to shadow them across the mountains they lost two biplanes, which may have had something to do with the decision to call off the operation on 18 January. Army search parties nevertheless continued to search the snowy mountains on skis and snowshoes, and military investigators interviewed the many civ-ilian witnesses. The same measures were being taken in Finland, while Swedish and Norwegian ships were busy exploring the surrounding seas and remote islands for the airbases necessary to equip the anony-mous grey aircraft.

It is amazing how this hive of military activity has been mirrored in recent years by the hundreds of reliable sightings of phantom sub-marines which, with equal ease, have invaded Swedish territorial waters and escaped damage or capture. Before the collapse of the Soviet Union, these USOs – unidentified submersible objects – were thought to come from the Warsaw Pact countries. But Russia has always denied this. Despite the use of hundreds of depth charges, no USO has ever been forced to surface.

By February 1934 the authorities realised that the phenomenon was making fools out of them. They reasoned that if they were dealing with aeroplanes some of them would crash and a few of them would be captured, or at least their supply bases would be discovered. None of this had happened; so, they concluded, the ghost fliers were not air-craft. Many in the military preferred to think they did not even exist – a familiar story.

The authorities turned their backs, and the phantom fliers, as if sensing this, eventually lost interest and departed.

In 1937 the Finnish General Staff published a study of the 1933–1934 wave. Of 111 reports, 10 sightings and 5 sounds remained unexplained. The report said: 'The mysterious phenomena were usually observed for only a short time and never from two places at the same time.'

Part Three

1939–47:
WAR OF THE WORLDS

——3——

FOO FIGHTERS FROM MARS?

Whilst scattered sightings occurred throughout the war and across the globe, it was late 1943 before air crews began to realise that something odd was going on.

During World War II thousands of aircraft were flying above Europe and the Pacific on bombing raids, reconnaissance missions and other operations. Never before had so many people been above the clouds, scanning clear skies with eagle-eyed intensity on the constant look-out for enemy action. It is hardly surprising that the UFOs, which had probably always been 'up there', suddenly got spotted in great abundance. But as some worried people soon came to ask: were they fighting enemies from only *this* world?

Confusing the enemy?

Whilst scattered sightings occurred throughout the war and across the globe, it was late 1943 before air crews began to realise that something odd was going on. At first, those who reported these incidents were laughed at or told they must be suffering from battle fatigue. But such easy rationalisations soon had to be rejected.

Hilary Evans reports a sighting on 14 October 1943 when a bomber raid on an industrial plant at Schweinfurt in Germany was mounted by the American 384th. On their final bombing run many crew members observed 'a cluster of discs' dead ahead. These were 'silver coloured, about one inch thick and three inches in diameter'. They were 'gliding down slowly' in a tight group. One B-17 pilot, unable to avoid contact, feared imminent disaster as his plane sliced through the small lights. But to his intense relief the bomber continued on its way, unhindered and undamaged.

It is quite conceivable that some reports of this kind referred to 'chaff' – clumps of aluminium foil released by aircraft in an attempt to confuse enemy radar screens by producing false reflections. Yet this possibility does not seem to have prevented official investigations by worried intelligence units, particularly with the American forces based in Europe.

According to rumour, there was also a British investigation into the foo fighter reports called the Massey Project. However Air Chief Marshal Sir Victor Goddard – who was an outspoken believer in alien craft during the 1950s – flatly denied this and said that Treasury approval for such a minor exercise at a time when Britain was fighting for its survival would have been ludicrous.

More certain is that the sightings continued to bemuse pilots and were occurring not only in European skies. On 10 August 1944 there was a sighting from a bomber unit near Sumatra in Indonesia, who observed an object pacing their aircraft's wing. It was a red-orange sphere that kept up with all the evasive manoeuvres executed by the pilot. After several minutes it shot away at a 90 degree angle and accelerated into the night. Captain Reida of 792 Squadron filed an in-depth report with US Army/Air Force intelligence, 'thinking it was some new type of radio-controlled missile or weapon'.

More explanations have been suggested for foo fighters than any other UFO type – including meteors, ball lightning and small comets.

Not St Elmo's Fire

By autumn 1944 reports were so commonplace over France, Germany and surrounding areas that crews had nicknamed the lights 'foo fighters', apparently after a comic strip popular at the time. 'Foo' was, presumably, a corruption of the French word *feu*, which means fire.

Jenny Randles interviewed comedian Michael Bentine, who in late 1944 was an intelligence officer stationed in eastern England dealing with Free Polish troops. He had to debrief bomber crews after a raid on the German secret weapons site at Peenemünde on the Baltic coast where deadly aerial technology was developed.

Bentine reported how they described seeing these lights. He did not take them seriously until several crews had come back and told identical stories. They spoke of being 'pursued by a light which was pulsating and had flown round the aircraft'. He suggested that they were observing St Elmo's Fire, a static electrical discharge that sometimes creates balls of light around pointed metal objects like ship's masts. But the crews were insistent that they had seen St Elmo's Fire elsewhere and that these phenomena were nothing like it.

Bentine continued: 'As far as they were concerned it was some form of weapon. So I said: "What did it *do* to you?" And they said "Nothing." So I said it was not a very effective weapon!'

Foo fighters photographed over the Pacific theatre during World War II. These mysterious balls of light were some of the earliest officially investigated UFOs.

A couple of days later an American intelligence officer visited Bentine's unit to hear what his crews were observing. By now there had been more than half a dozen cases in just a few weeks. The American said that his men were seeing the same thing and added: 'They appear in daylight as well. We don't know what they are.' Michael Bentine told us that, in his view, 'It was probably the manifestation of what is now called a UFO.'

Tales of the 415th

The most widely quoted sighting occurred on 23 November 1944 and involved the 415th, an American night fighter unit flying out of France. They seem to have been the location of most of the best-known 1944–5 reports and were the source of the 'foo fighter' nickname.

On this date, Lieutenant Edward Schlueter was going from Dijon on an intercept mission to Strasbourg and Mannheim, flying mostly above the Vosges Mountains. With him were Lieutenant Don Myers and an intelligence officer, Lieutenant Ringwald. It was Ringwald who first spotted about ten balls of orange-red fire moving at great velocity in formation. The sky was very clear and Ringwald was an excellent and experienced observer: he had just spotted a freight train miles V-rockets then terrifying southern England, and the frantic Nazi race to develop intercontinental missiles to strike the American mainland away from their flight path, despite the fact that its boiler was shielded by blackout and only a plume of steam had given its location away.

The crew debated the lights. Were they misperceptions of stars? Could they be meteors? Perhaps their own aircraft was reflecting off clouds? They dismissed each idea in turn.

Then, as they closed in for the kill, the red fireballs simply melted into nothingness. Minutes later they reappeared, then vanished again. It was as if they were playing tag. The crew gave up and got on with their raid.

Many similar sightings followed. Radar stations and on-board radar in the aircraft showed that nothing was actually there. Yet the lights climbed up, chased the bombers, matched them for speed and manoeuvrability and then disappeared instantly. It is not surprising that the possibility of a 'secret weapon' became popular, despite the innocent nature of the events.

Three weeks later, on 2 January 1945, stories appeared in the press in many countries, using the term 'foo fighter' and still implying a weapon, but adding that nobody could identify what it was. Given the V-rockets then terrifying southern England, and the frantic Nazi race to develop intercontinental missiles to strike the American mainland

A montage of press cuttings about the 1945 foo fighters.

'Foo fighters' are what UFO experts now call 'lights in the sky' or LITS. They are the most common UFO type in the world, accounting for over sixty percent of all sightings.

(near to perfection when the war ended), the idea of an unknown German threat was far from absurd.

There were ground-based witnesses, too. We have a report from a former prisoner of war at the Heydebreck camp in Upper Silesia, Poland. At 3pm on 22 January 1945 a number of men were being paraded by the Germans before being marched away to evade the liberating Russian Army. A bomber appeared overhead, flying at about 18,000 feet, and the men gazed in horror at what seemed to be fire pouring from its rear end. Then they thought it might be a flare caught up in the slipstream of the aircraft. Finally, they realised it was neither of these things: the object was a silvery ball hugging the bomber, which was desperately trying to evade it. The foo fighter was still right on the tail of the aircraft as both passed into the distance.

A few weeks later the war ended, and nothing more was said. No secret weapons of this kind were found in German hands. Captured air crew, scientists and intelligence officers affirmed that Nazi fighters had also been seeing foo fighters (they called them 'feuer' balls). The Germans and Japanese had both assumed these things to be American secret weapons!

An undiscovered secret weapon?

When the first 'flying saucers' arrived a couple of years later, the secret files on foo fighters were re-examined by the US Army and Air Force to see if they might be the same phenomenon. Foo fighters were concluded to be rare electrical activity, such as ball lightning.

However, novelist W. A. Harbinson took a very different view in his fictional epic *Genesis*, based, he reports, on research initiated by foo fighter stories. He contends that there really was a German secret weapon – a small, jet-powered, remote-controlled disc, effectively a prototype of larger (manned) versions that would have flown had the war not ended when it did.

According to post-war German accounts that Harbinson traced, the device was designed by Rudolph Schriever in spring 1941, first tested in June 1942 and flown in earnest in August 1943. Schriever reportedly built a full-scale circular craft some 137 feet in diameter that was scheduled to fly in April 1945. The test was abandoned with the advance of the Allies on Berlin, the death of Hitler and the end of the war in Europe. But Harbinson found evidence that the working full-scale prototype was built in the Harz Mountains during 1944 and secretly flown on 14 February 1945.

Schriever originally believed that his papers and the prototype had all been destroyed to stop them falling into Allied hands; but subsequently, right up to his death in the late 1950s, he wondered if that were true. He had concluded that the by then persistent sightings of disc-like UFOs were the result of continuing secret development of his own invention, perhaps by Nazi scientists who had fled Germany and set up a base in some remote region.

Eventually, in January 1992, the truth about foo fighters and the USAF was revealed when Barry Greenwood, an excellent and objective UFO investigator specialising in digging into government files, gained limited access to still classified records on American war activity. Initially this comprised the unit summary and war diary of the 415th night fighter squadron – certainly the most involved of the US flight crews.

These papers credited Don Myers of the 23 November 1944 sighting with the first use of the term 'foo fighter' (although, oddly, this event was cited as having occurred in late October, and not the date the crew themselves had given in a December 1945 service magazine interview). Assorted lights (often red, sometimes green and also white) were encountered on frequent missions. Lieutenant Schlueter saw them more than once.

In September 1992 Greenwood started reading a three-feet-thick file of all the mission records for the 415th between autumn 1944 and spring 1945. He found that sightings continued right up to the end of the war. Intriguingly, among these documents – which were many years older than Harbinson's bizarre novel – were the records of American foo fighter sightings during February 1945. There were two of them – both within a few hours of the purported flight of that amazing Nazi flying disc from the reputed complex in the Harz Mountains!

By 1945 pulp science-fiction comic books were very popular with adolescents and often featured alien contact and even, occasionally, saucer-shaped objects in the sky.

4

GHOST ROCKETS IN THE SKY

Throughout the summer of 1946 the sightings escalated.

It was left to science fiction readers and tabloid speculators to think that there might be something supernatural behind the quickly forgotten foo fighter stories. The war ended and there were far more pressing matters for most people to contend with.

However, the UFO mystery was not about to go away. Whilst nobody had yet recognised how scattered pockets of activity, from the phantom airships to the foo fighters, reflected an unidentified aerial phenomenon that had been appearing in the sky for decades, another wave of strange events was about to hit the world.

These latest UFOs were not perceived as a scientific riddle to be resolved. They were not pursued with open and enthusiastic vigour. These new lights in the sky were decreed a military secret and treated yet again as a possible source of threat from a power very much of this earth – not one that was thought to come from somewhere decidedly off it.

Crowded skies over Scandinavia

The reports began as early as 26 February 1946, when a Helsinki radio story described 'inordinate meteor activity' in the far north of Finland. But it was late May before they spread further south and into Sweden, where greater population density ensured almost daily reports. Throughout the summer of 1946 the sightings escalated. By the autumn 996 reports had been officially logged by the Swedish defence authorities alone. A conservative estimate for sightings in Scandinavia that summer would probably reach several thousand.

Most witnesses referred to a light at night, briefly emitting flame from the rear. The speed varied from very rapid to quite sedate. There were daytime reports also, often describing missile—or dark lozenge-shaped craft. Often there was a short tail of fire. The objects moved horizontally but then often fell vertically downwards. However, mixed in with these reports were occasional sightings of spindle shapes or eggs and ovals – accounts more reminiscent of modern-day UFOs.

A good account in early August came from a meteorologist who had the good fortune to be using a telescope for observational purposes when he saw one of the lights above Stockholm. He watched it carefully as it passed overhead for about ten seconds, describing it as being 'at least 90 feet long. The body was torpedo-shaped and shining like metal. It had a tapered tail that spewed glowing blue and green smoke and a series of fireballs.'

The media reported the events quite extensively from late May – until ordered by the defence authorities in late July to stop for what they called 'strategic' reasons. Their fear was clear – these 'ghost rockets', as the media had named them, were believed to be secret weapons being test flown in (or – in some more hysterical quarters – deliberately aimed at) Sweden. There was only one realistic possibility for the sender of these missiles – the Soviet Union.

Indeed, in summer 1944 the first V-2 rocket successfully tested by Germany had landed in Sweden, crashing and exploding in a farmer's field. Debris had been collected, analysed and then sent to Britain for Allied assessment. This prototype ballistic missile was the first taste of the successor to the Nazi V-1 (or 'doodlebug') which was already devastating London. The V-2 (and the longer-range V-3, under development as the war ended) could carry bomb payloads hundreds of miles from their remote launch sites, such as Peenemünde.

By 1946 scientists were making their first tentative searches for extra-terrestrial life by scanning the heavens with radio telescopes.

High-level intelligence briefings

Worried defence chiefs in Scandinavia now believed that the USSR (which had captured control of Peenemünde in 1945) might have developed the technology and started trying out enhanced V-2s by 'bombing' supposedly friendly countries – although, thankfully, minus the warheads. There are persistent stories that during August 1946 top-level intelligence experts visited Sweden to discuss the problem, under the guise of trade missions or proffered aid for radar equipment. British war hero Douglas Bader and the general who had led the US bomber squadrons that had reported most of the foo fighters, James Doolittle, were two who visited Stockholm and had meetings at this time.

Legends about what they discussed have since abounded. But in 1984 Barry Greenwood attempted to find out directly. He wrote to Doolittle, who replied unambiguously on 29 August that he 'did know' about the ghost rockets, but seemed to scotch the claims that he had access to any higher-level data by saying that he had 'no firm knowledge of actual ... "ghost rockets" in Sweden' and that what he did know came 'largely by the press'. Of course, he may simply have been being discreet, given the fact that the matter has never received an official airing in the US public archives.

A British Air Ministry intelligence report, dated 8 September 1946, referred to 'bright, shining, luminous or fiery balls, or else cylindrical or cigar-shaped objects, sometimes with a bright light in the tail, occasionally in the nose ...'. It is interesting to note the phrase 'cigar-shaped' being used here in an official report a year before there were such things as flying saucers or UFOs. Some sceptics still cling to the view that colourful language like this is a product of imaginative witnesses in the modern age, basing their accounts on science fiction. But in fact it was originally used in a government report, and probably for the same reason that witnesses still use it fifty years later: it well describes what they see. Exactly the same applies to the term 'saucer-shaped', which has nothing to do with images of extraterrestrial spaceships, as has been assumed. It was first used, in fact, in a witness account during the 1896–7 airship wave!

Meteors – or lumps of coke?

The most impressive sighting from among all these ghost rocket events occurred on 9 July 1946, when over 250 reports were made in Sweden and the only known photograph was taken. A man named Erik Reutersward managed to obtain a single dim picture. The thing was described as being silvery but changing to blue-green in coloration as it plunged near-vertically towards the ground. The photograph opposite depicts a teardrop object with a short tail.

Most analysts have concluded that this sighting and the photograph relate to a bolide – an unusually bright daytime meteor – and it does have many of the characteristics of one. Indeed, there is little doubt that quite a number of the ghost rockets were probably a case of mistaken identity: other reports suggest meteors at night, yet others may be flocks of birds reflecting moonlight, and so forth. In fact, in the end even the defence authorities suggested that some 80 per cent of the reports came from people alerted to watch the skies in unprecedented

During 1946 Scandinavia was the subject of a wave of 'ghost rocket' sightings which received considerable attention from the military authorities but was never resolved. The only known photograph was taken on 9 July by Erik Reutersward and despite its limited quality was evaluated by investigators as probably depicting a daylight meteor.

numbers by the media hype, but who were seeing as a result what we would now call IFOs (identified flying objects).

But there were some real anomalies. For example, there were accounts where the object supposedly crashed into the ground. Many people saw an object plunge into Lake Kolmjarv in northern Sweden on 19 July. The authorities scoured the lake for days, but found nothing. Yet in a few other cases debris was picked up from the ground at the site of a supposed ghost rocket impact; it resembled lumps of blackened slag of some sort. For instance, at Bjorkon in Sweden on 10 July a rocket smashed into the beach, leaving a three-feet-wide crater with powder that burned the hands when it was touched.

Professor R. V. Jones, an expert in V-1 and V-2 rockets, and an Air Ministry scientist in Britain analysed some of the slag and other residues from such landings. Jones later reported that he was utterly unimpressed and that in his view these were irrelevant materials such as lumps of coke. People had found objects on the ground after seeing lights in the sky, but the materials had probably been there long before the ghost rockets flew and were completely unconnected.

It has recently been discovered that some ghost rocket sightings occurred in Soviet territory but were kept secret for many years.

On 10 October, with the sightings now far less frequent, the Swedish defence authorities issued their main public 'conclusion'. This dismissed all stories of crashes and residue, said that most sightings were unreliable misperceptions of mundane things, but that in a few cases 'clear, unambiguous observations have been made which cannot be explained as natural phenomena, Swedish aircraft or imagination . . .'. They added that precautions were being taken. In effect, all military authorities were under orders to report sightings of 'ghost rockets' (which some did make), and a low-level alert of the armed forces was in operation for a time afterwards.

An extensive investigation of ghost rockets, involving the scouring of official records in Stockholm, was made possible after declassification of these files in 1983. Swedish ufologists Anders Liljegren and Clas Svahn, who undertook this task, noted that the team of scientists and intelligence officers which the Swedish authorities brought together ended their work in December 1946. In their final report the team affirmed the high IFO ratio and said that 'despite the extensive effort which has been carried out with all available means, there is no actual proof that a test of rocket projectiles has taken place over Sweden . . . Even if the main part of the report can be referred to as celestial phenomena, the committee cannot dismiss certain facts as being merely public imagination.' In other words, some were *real* UFOs.

Conclusions from the evidence

So, what were the ghost rockets? In hindsight two things are obvious. The official conclusion that 80 per cent (plus) were really mundane things such as meteors is clearly valid; yet the unsolved cases were almost certainly not Soviet rocket tests. As later events were to demonstrate, most of the Nazi secrets and experts gravitated to the Americans, giving them a clear lead in the field of rocketry during the 1950s. Had the USSR been capable of launching ghost rockets in May 1946 it seems rather unlikely that they would have fallen as far behind in this aspect of the arms race as they quickly did.

Nor did the ghost rockets vanish after autumn 1946. Sightings of the same phenomena appeared all over the world in years to come, and reports are still being made as the millennium approaches (see pages 274–6 for some worrying modern-day examples).

We simply call these lights something other than ghost rockets . . . Today we call them UFOs.

Part Four

1947 onwards: INVASION OF THE FLYING SAUCERS

5

LIKE SAUCERS SKIPPING ACROSS WATER

O ver Washington State on the west coast of America, 24 June 1947 was a clear, sunlit day. The purity of the atmosphere enhanced the natural beauty of the Cascade Mountains which were visible from the cockpit of Kenneth Arnold's light aircraft. Arnold, with over four thousand hours' flying experience, was a thirty-two-year-old businessman who sold and installed the Great Western Fire Control System – an apparatus he had designed and patented himself. He was also a flying deputy for the Ada County Aerial Posse, an acting deputy Federal United States marshal, and a member of the Idaho Search and Rescue Mercy Flyers.

Searching for wreckage

That day started just like any other, as Arnold was later to explain.

> I had just finished installing some firefighting apparatus at Chehalis, Washington. The job finished, I began a chat with Herb Critzen, chief pilot for Central Air Service. We talked about the possible location of a lost Marine transport which had gone down in the mountains. I decided to look for it. It meant a $5,000 reward, and I hoped that via my proposed route to Yakima, Washington, I might be lucky enough to find it. I decided to spend enough time in the air in the vicinity of Mount Rainier to make a good attempt at locating the wreckage.

His own aircraft, a single-engined Callier, was specially designed for mountain work – capable of landing in rough fields and pastures. At 2pm Arnold took off to start his search for the Marine Curtess C-46

On 24 June 1947 pilot Kenneth Arnold observed a formation of UFOs flying over the Rainier Mountain range in Washington, USA.

Commando transport plane which had disappeared somewhere in the mountains and had so far eluded discovery. He figured his journey to Yakima would be delayed by about an hour while he searched the 14,400-foot-high plateau of Mount Rainier. Kenneth Arnold never did find that aircraft. But he found something else instead – or it found him.

It was during this search, and while making a turn of 180 degrees over Mineral, Washington, at approximately 9,200 feet altitude, that a tremendously bright flash lit up the surfaces of his aircraft. He was startled, and thought he was very close to collision with another aircraft whose approach he had not noted.

He spent the next thirty seconds or so searching urgently for that 'other aircraft' in an attempt to avoid an accident. He did indeed see another aircraft, which he identified as a DC-4 – probably on its regular flight from San Francisco to Seattle. But this was to the port side and rear of him, and surely much too far away to have caused the light phenomenon. So he conjectured that a P-51 – a USAF jet fighter – might have buzzed across his nose to give him a fright, and that the sun had reflected off its wings.

As he continued his search for this speculative other aircraft a second flash occurred, and this time he was able to pinpoint the direction it had come from. He followed the line of sight, and his brow furrowed in puzzlement. From the north, near Mount Baker, flying close to the mountain peaks at incredible speed, was a formation of very bright objects.

Arnold felt they were about a hundred miles away and therefore too distant to make out any features. However, they were approaching him at an angle and steadily nearing the snow line of Mount Rainier. 'All the time I was thinking that I was observing a whole formation of jets. In group count, such as I have used in counting cattle and game from the air, they numbered nine. They were flying diagonally in an echelon formation with a larger gap in their echelon between the first four and the last five.'

Tail-less aircraft

But Arnold noticed something disturbing. None of the aircraft had tails! Once more his rational mind sought out an explanation. He knew the Air Force were very good at camouflage. Had they perfected it to a degree that appendages such as tailplanes on an aircraft could be rendered as good as invisible?

They were now about twenty miles away. If they carried on their present course they would pass between Mount Rainier and Mount Adams. Using the mountains as markers, Arnold timed the passage between them using his wristwatch, hoping to work out their speed later.

I was fascinated by this formation of aircraft. They didn't fly like any aircraft I had seen before. In the first place, their echelon formation was backward from that practiced by our Air Force. The elevation of the first craft was greater than that of the last. They flew in a definite formation, but erratically. As I described them at the time, their flight was like speed boats on rough water or similar to the tail of a chinese kite that I once saw blowing in the wind. Or maybe it would be best to describe their flight characteristics as very similar to a formation of geese, in a rather diagonal chain-like line, as if they were linked together.

Another characteristic of these craft that made a tremendous impression on me was how they fluttered and sailed, tipping their wings alternatively and emitting those very bright blue-white flashes from their surfaces. At the time I did not get the impression these flashes were emitted by them, but rather that it was the sun's reflection from the extremely polished surface of their wings.

The direction of the flight never varied, although the individual objects did swerve in and out of the mountain peaks – flying in front of some, disappearing momentarily behind others. Between the two mountains lies a very high plateau; Arnold observed that, as the first unit of craft cleared the far southernmost edge of the plateau, the second part of the echelon was just entering the opposite, northern edge. That meant the formation was five miles long!

As the nine objects flew out of sight, he unsuccessfully tried to explain them away in his own mind as some sort of technological wonder belonging to the Air Force. They made him feel 'eerie', and he tried to focus his mind on the search for the downed C-46 which had crashed some months earlier with thirty-two Marines aboard. Somehow the $5,000 didn't seem important to him any more. 'I wanted to get to Yakima and tell some of the boys what I had seen,' he explained.

Captain Tom Brown, public relations representative for the Army Air Force said they did not know what the saucers were, but they did not believe that 'anyone in this country, or outside this country, had developed a guided missile that will go 1200 miles an hour as some reports have indicated'.

A flight of guided missiles?

At around four o'clock Arnold landed at Yakima, went straight to see Al Baxter, general manager of Central Aircraft, and asked to see him alone. When he had related his story and drawn some pictures, Baxter was bemused. He knew Arnold was neither crazy nor the type to pull a stunt: he was in fact a level-headed character and an experienced pilot. Besides, he had nothing to gain from making up such a story, and everything to lose. Yet Baxter could not disguise his feelings of incredulity. It was written all across his face, and Arnold saw it. *Was* there a rational explanation for the experience?

Baxter called in several of his helicopter instructors and flight pilots for their opinions. After listening carefully to the story, they discussed it amongst themselves. Arnold related what happened next. 'The high point of my enthusiasm got its top knocked off when one of the helicopter pilots said: "Ah, it's just a flight of those guided missiles from Moses Lake." '

Arnold returned to his aircraft and took off for Pendleton, Oregon. Was that the explanation? He was not even aware of a base at Moses Lake. Besides, he had not mentioned the incredible speed of the objects, nor the fact that one of the craft looked different from the rest. This had been darker, crescent-shaped, with a small dome on top. If they had indeed been missiles they were of a completely new and previously unknown design. The other eight objects had resembled pie pans – so shiny that they reflected the sun as well as a mirror.

As a matter of routine, the officials at Yakima had to notify those at Pendleton of Arnold's imminent arrival. With this information went news of the businessman's strange sighting. So when he landed a group of people were waiting for him, anxious to hear the story. Using the figures Arnold had recorded at the time of the incident, it was calculated that the objects had been travelling at around 1,300 miles per hour! The pilot was now certain of one thing. If they were terrestrial they were remotely controlled. The human body could not survive the terrific gravity forces generated at such speeds.

Armed with his maps and calculations, Arnold decided he should report the incident. 'I kind of felt I ought to tell the FBI because I knew that during the war we were flying aircraft over the Pole to Russia, and I thought these things could possibly be from Russia.'

The birth of the flying saucer

Ironically, when he arrived at the local FBI office he found it shut. So instead he went to see Nolan Skiff, editor of the 'End of the Week' column in the *East Oregonian*. Initially Skiff was sceptical, but the pilot's credentials and sincerity convinced him. Another journalist, Bill Becquette, was also present and, realising that the story would have national interest, sent off an Associated Press despatch. It was while Arnold was trying to explain the strange movement of the aircraft that he unwittingly gave the media a phrase they grew to love, but one which later ufologists loved to hate. 'They flew like a saucer would if you skipped it across water.' With those few words, the term 'flying saucer' was born.

The despatch which was to ensure Kenneth Arnold's place in history said:

PENDLETON, ORE, June 25 (AP) – Nine bright saucer-like objects flying at 'incredible speed' at 10,000 feet altitude were reported here today by Kenneth Arnold, Boise, Idaho, pilot who said he could not hazard a guess as to what they were.

Arnold, a United States Forest Service employee engaged in searching for a missing plane, said he sighted the mysterious objects yesterday at three pm. They were flying between Mount Rainier and Mount Adams, in Washington State, he said, and appeared to weave in and out of formation. Arnold said that he clocked and estimated their speed at 1200 miles an hour.

Enquiries at Yakima last night brought only blank stares, he said, but he added he talked today with an unidentified man from Utah, south of here, who said he had seen similar objects over the mountains near Ukiah yesterday.

'It seems impossible,' Arnold said, 'but there it is.'

A Gallup Poll of 19 August 1947 revealed that nine out of ten Americans were now familiar with 'flying saucers'.

It said a lot for Kenneth Arnold's credibility that the story was reported seriously and in a matter-of-fact way. But even Bill Becquette could not have realised the international ramifications of the incident, which captured the imagination of the media across the world. Arnold, like so many unprepared victims of anomalous phenomena, had unwittingly opened up his life to the media circus.

I could have gone to sleep that night if the reporters, newsmen, and press agencies of every conceivable description had left me alone. I didn't share the general excitement. I can't begin to estimate the number of people, letters, telegrams and phone calls I tried to answer. After three days of this hubbub I came to the conclusion that I was the only sane one in the bunch. In order to stop what I thought was a lot of foolishness and since I couldn't get any work done, I went out to the airport, cranked up my airplane, and flew home to Boise.

Arnold was naive if he thought the interest would leave him behind at Pendleton, and until he spoke to Dave Johnson, aviation editor of the *Idaho Statesman*, he was still convinced that the objects were of advanced terrestrial origin.

When I caught the look in his eye and the tone of his words, 'flying saucers' suddenly took a different and serious significance. The doubt he displayed of the authenticity of my story told me, and I am sure he was in a position to know, that it was not a new military

As a result of Kenneth Arnold's story about crescent-like objects skipping through the air like a saucer across water, the term 'flying saucer' was invented by a journalist. Most people assumed that this meant that UFOs were saucer shaped and this motif soon dominated. A few years later even the cover of Arnold's own book, pictured here, portrayed the UFOs as more saucer-like than he had described them.

guided missile, and that if what I had seen was true it did not belong to the good old USA. It was then I really began to wonder.

Dave Johnson told him that the Wright Field Base wanted a report so they could check it out. They were not the only ones. Journalists and TV crews besieged the home of Doris and Kenneth Arnold.

Other sightings

Around that time there were other sightings too. United Airlines pilot Captain E. J. Smith and co-pilot Ralph Stevens observed something unexplained during one flight. On 26 June, the *Chicago Tribune* reported a sighting made by a Pendleton couple. On the same day as Arnold's sighting, a prospector from Portland called Johnson claimed to have witnessed five or six discs around the region of the Cascade Mountains. There were 850 sightings reported between June and July.

All of this left Arnold confused. It seemed that everyone was jumping on the bandwagon. It was true that, prior to his headline sighting, the phenomenon of 'flying saucers' was not generally acknowledged. Why were all these reports coming in *now*?

Did Arnold's sighting act as a catalyst? No doubt some people caught up in the excitement were going out looking for saucers and then misidentifying aircraft landing lights, bright stars and weather balloons. Others, however, were perhaps observing something truly mysterious. All Kenneth Arnold had done was give people the confidence to speak out instead of skulking away afraid of ridicule.

Not that Arnold escaped ridicule himself. Once people started interpreting his experience as proof of an extraterrestrial invasion, the debunkers were not slow in coming forward. As he told ufologist Greg Long in 1981: 'These nameless, faceless people ridiculed me. I was considered an Orson Welles, a fraud. I loved my country. I was very naive about the whole thing. I was the unfortunate goat who first reported them.'

Investigation and theories

Some months later, he sent a detailed report to the Air Force, which carried out an investigation. At that time, astronomer Dr J. Allen Hynek was their UFO consultant. Many years later, after realising the government were hoodwinking the American people, Hynek founded CUFOS – the Centre for UFO Studies.

Dr Hynek found several discrepancies in the story. Arnold's estimate of a hundred-foot 'wing span' did not bear out for the alleged distances involved. At twenty miles away – never mind a hundred – something only 100 feet wide would be invisible to the human eye. This meant the distances must have been much less, which also reduced the calculated speed of the formation to subsonic figures. Therefore the objects could have been terrestrial aircraft. There was only one problem with that: everyone denied there were any aircraft in the area at that time. However, if it was the estimate of *size* which was wrong and the distance was about right, but the objects were much larger than Arnold had thought, then the speed of around 1,300 miles per hour was about correct.

The case was never solved, although there have been plenty of theories, including that of mirages. More recently it has been suggested that what Arnold observed were 'earth lights' – luminous balls of electromagnetic energy allegedly released into the atmosphere along fault lines in the Earth's crust during periods of underground stress.

As far as Kenneth Arnold was concerned, the formation of nine objects he saw moving across the crystal-clear Washington skies 'like a saucer would if you skipped it across water', was only the beginning of several more similar experiences. Although this is not generally known, Arnold experienced many more sightings. His eighth, in 1952, was of two objects – one of which was transparent. 'They looked like something alive,' he said. 'I've had the feeling with these things that they are aware of me, but they made no effort to come close.'

Then in 1966 he took some 16mm cine film of a glowing 'cylinder' over Idaho Falls, Ohio. Although the object looked similar to an atmospheric balloon, it was travelling at speed into a northerly wind.

Whatever he saw during the long day of 24 June 1947, Arnold retained his passion for the subject right up until his death in 1984. This would suggest that his experience was something much more tangible than just imagination. An FBI agent who saw Kenneth Arnold at the time thought so, too:

It is the personal opinion of the interviewer that [Arnold] actually saw what he states he saw in the attached report. It is also the opinion of the interviewer that [Arnold] would have much more to lose than gain and would have to be very strongly convinced that he actually saw something before he would report such an incident and open himself up for ridicule that would accompany such a report.

—— 6 ——

It Came from Outer Space

The Roswell incident of July 1947 is believed by experts to be the single most significant incident in UFO history.

The FBI are unimpressed

On 22 March 1950 Guy Hottel, a field officer with the FBI in Washington, sent a bizarre memo to his boss J. Edgar Hoover. Headed 'Flying Discs or Flying Saucers', it ran:

An investigator for the Air Force stated that three so-called flying saucers had been recovered in New Mexico. They were described as being circular in shape with raised centres, approximately 50 feet in diameter. Each one was occupied by three bodies of human shape but only 3 feet tall dressed in metallic cloth of a very fine texture . . . the saucers were found in New Mexico due to the fact that the Government has a very high-powered radar set-up in that area and it is believed the radar interferes with the controlling mechanism of the saucers.

Such an extraordinary story seems not to have been taken too seriously by the FBI hierarchy. They note that 'no further evaluation' was undertaken. Many researchers think the leak came via an unreliable source and related to a dubious story of an alleged UFO crash at Aztec, New Mexico. That event is widely considered a hoax. But the official memo is quite real.

March 1950 is very early for allegations about a UFO crash in this state, with the entities being small, humanoid and wearing silvery suits. The science fiction of the day did not feature this type of alien – which soon became the norm for American UFO reports of alien contact and abduction. When this memo was secretly circulating, the first UFO book – *Flying Saucers are Real*, a sensational charge of cover-up by ex-Marine officer Donald Keyhoe – had only been in print a few weeks.

Strange hieroglyphic markings

Another possible source for the memo is the Roswell, New Mexico incident of July 1947. This affair received minimum attention outside the American West and was rapidly forgotten even by ufologists. It would be thirty years before they researched it in earnest. From the declassified files we can now see what 'officially' happened and couple this with the evidence from the few public revelations in 1947.

On the night of 2 July 1947, barely a week after the Kenneth Arnold sighting, William Brazel heard an explosion in the sky above his large property near Corona, New Mexico. Corona is a fascinating location – a scrub desert area surrounded by rocky ridges, with the Los Alamos nuclear facility a hundred miles north, Socorro just west, and the atom bomb and missile test facilities of White Sands and Alamogordo/Holloman Air Force Base only a short distance south. It is also twenty-five miles from Vaughn – home to the startling green fireballs that were set to erupt upon the landscape some sixteen months later (see page 86). Anything odd going on within this sensitive area would shake the defences of the United States.

The explosion that Brazel heard came in the middle of a fierce thunderstorm but sounded unlike thunder, so next day he rode around the property to check on his sheep. He and a neighbour were amazed to discover an area about three-quarters of a mile across scattered with very odd-looking wreckage. A gouge in the earth looked as if some craft had skidded upon impact. The debris included a very light metal that could easily be lifted, yet was very tough. Bits of material were akin to balsa wood, and would not burn, plus some brown, parchment-like substances. Some of the debris bore hieroglyphic or geometric symbols, seemingly stained with a purplish or pink coloration.

House arrest and secrecy

Mystified, the men took pieces of this material back and showed it to family and friends. Someone thought he might get a reward for handing in the remains of a military device to the authorities, and Brazel was persuaded to take it into the town of Roswell on his next visit, on 6 July. When he told the sheriff, two deputies were immediately sent off to the 80-mile-distant site as vaguely described by Brazel. The rancher was then directed to the town's air base, which in 1947 was the only location in the world with an active bombing unit flying atomic weapons.

The Roswell deputies found no debris in the area, but did see a burnt circle as if a craft of some sort had touched down. An intelligence officer from Roswell, Major Jesse Marcel, together with a junior officer, Sheridan Cavitt, drove to Corona with Brazel. At the same time the bits that Brazel had brought in were flown to a regional command centre at Carswell Air Base in Forth Worth, Texas for expert analysis.

Back at Corona, Brazel, Marcel and Cavitt soon gave up the idea of collecting the rest of the debris – there was just too much of it. But they loaded some of it into the back of a pick-up and late on 7 July drove back to the base. Next morning base security met Brazel at the site to cordon off the area, and even turned away the local police. They collected up all the remaining debris and, to Brazel's surprise, took him back to Roswell where they kept him under voluntary house arrest for about a week. Friends who saw him during this time say he looked 'strange' and walked past without acknowledging their presence.

A rapid (or hasty) evaluation of the bulk of the debris was made at Roswell Air Base during the early hours of 8 July. Colonel William Blanchard arranged for Marcel to load up a B-29 and fly the stuff to Wright Patterson Air Force Base in Dayton, Ohio (soon to become the hub of all Air Force investigation into UFOs), calling off at Carswell to collect the test samples.

Blanchard appears to have been unable to identify the wreckage. As no government rules about UFOs were yet in force, the commander chose to tell the world what had been discovered. He was quickly censured for doing so by Pentagon sources keen to put the lid back on, but not before base officer Lieutenant Walter Haut had issued a wire message reading:

Apart from the UFO crash in the Roswell desert, about twenty other claims exist for similar accidents. Most of them are in the desert somewhere!

The many rumours regarding the flying discs became a reality yesterday when the intelligence office of the 509th bomb group of the eighth air force, Roswell Army Air Field, was fortunate enough to gain possession of a disc through the cooperation of one of the local ranchers and the Sheriff's office at Chaves county. The flying object landed on a ranch near Roswell sometime last week. Not having phone facilities, the rancher stored the disc until such time as he was able to contact the Sheriff's office, who in turn notified Major Jesse A. Marcel of the 509th bomb group intelligence office ... It was inspected at the Roswell Army Air Field and subsequently loaned by Major Marcel to higher headquarters.

Hughie Green's unfinished story

The story was picked up by local radio and press. It was these reports – and the subsequent retraction – that gave ufology all it knew before 1978. The one exception was the account of Hughie Green, later a leading TV entertainer in Britain, whose story first appeared in the UFO press in 1955.

Green said he was driving across the USA from west to east and heard the original radio broadcasts, which then suddenly stopped. Upon arrival at Philadelphia he tried to discover more but failed. He has intimated to both authors of this book that there may be more to his story, but has unfortunately not elaborated upon that point.

'National security item. Do not transmit...'

The next breakthrough occurred in 1978 when the USAF, FBI and CIA files on UFOs, including the original official release from the base and its subsequent retraction via the Pentagon, had just been released under new freedom of information (FOI) laws. Major Marcel, by then retired, and Lydia Sleppy, a teletype operator at a radio station in Albuquerque, had both been traced by UFO researchers and had a lot more to say about the matter.

Sleppy related how she had been receiving incoming data on the retrieval of the flying disc via Roswell when a further message came through reading: 'Attention Albuquerque: Cease transmission. Repeat cease transmission. National security item. Do not transmit...' At this point data stopped coming in from the base and she had to curtail all plans to release it through the news networks to the rest of the world.

This second official message came some hours after the first, with media sources already swamping Roswell. Marcel was now at Carswell with all the debris and General Roger Ramey had taken command upon his arrival, ordering Marcel off the B-29, instructing him to say nothing, replacing him as courier for the onward leg but (Marcel insists) still flying the wreckage on to Wright Patterson. Marcel was then flown back to Roswell immediately, and the story was issued that the flight to Dayton had been cancelled.

Ramey now sent out a second press release, stating that the whole thing had been a mistake. The debris was from a weather balloon with a radio device attached. A hurried press conference that afternoon showed the supposed weather balloon debris to the rapidly disenchanted media (see page 72).

In 1978 Marcel told ufologists that this balloon story was invented to

See opposite
A copy of an FBI teletype about the Roswell crash that first told the world about the UFO incident in July 1947, before it was hushed up and there was a backtrack to claim it was a balloon.

TELETYPE

FBI DALLAS   7-8-47   6-17 PM

DIRECTOR AND SAC, CINCINNATI   URGENT

FLYING DISC, INFORMATION CONCERNING. ████████, HEADQUARTERS

EIGHTH AIR FORCE, TELEPHONICALLY ADVISED THIS OFFICE THAT AN OBJECT

PURPORTING TO BE A FLYING DISC WAS RE COVERED NEAR ROSWELL, NEW

MEXICO, THIS DATE. THE DISC IS HEXAGONAL IN SHAPE AND WAS SUSPENDED

FROM A BALLON BY CABLE, WHICH BALLON WAS APPROXIMATELY TWENTY

FEET IN DIAMETER. ████████ FURTHER ADVISED THAT THE OBJECT

FOUND RESEMBLES A HIGH ALTITUDE WEATHER BALLOON WITH A RADAR

REFLECTOR, BUT THAT TELEPHONIC CONVERSATION BETWEEN THEIR OFFICE

AND WRIGHT FIELD HAD NOT ~~SCRANTICMS~~ BORNE OUT THIS BELIEF. DISC AND

BALLOON BEING TRANSPORTED TO WRIGHT FIELD BY SPECIAL PLANE FOR EXAMINATIO

INFORMATION PROVIDED THIS OFFICE BECAUSE OF NATIONAL INTEREST IN CASE .

~~XXXX~~ AND FACT THAT NATIONAL BROADCASTING COMPANY, ASSOCIATED PRESS, AND

OTHERS ATTEMPTING TO BREAK STORY OF LOCATION OF DISC TODAY. ████████

████████ ADVISED WOULD REQUEST WRIGHT FIELD TO ADVISE CINCINNATI

OFFICE RESULTS OF EXAMINATION. NO FURTHER INVESTIGATION BEING

CONDUCTED.

            WYLY
            RECORDED
END

CXXXX ACK IN ORDER

UA 92 FBI CI MJW

BPI H8

8-38 PM O

8-22 PM OK FBI WASH DC VH

OK FBI CI MJW

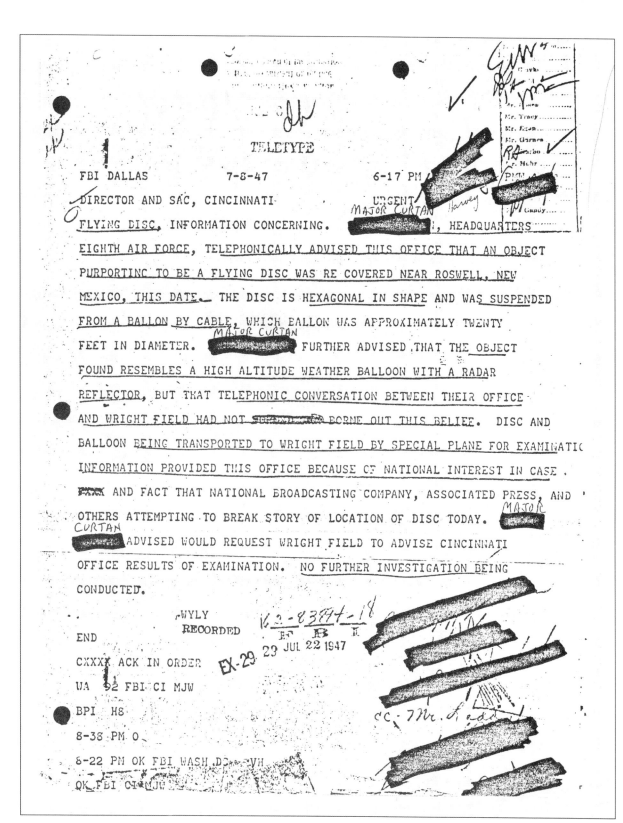

Debris from a weather balloon displayed to the media at Roswell.

deflect attention from the truth. Nobody knew what the debris was, but it was definitely not from a balloon. The US government wanted the opportunity to investigate the wreckage in secret, so it had to silence the media. On 9 July a dazed-looking Brazel was wheeled in front of the local press in Roswell to claim he had found the material on 14 June – not 3 July – and had discovered weather balloons on his land before. He later told friends, as confirmed by them in interview, that the military had asked him to say this.

Marcel was always adamant that the material he collected and handled for over twenty-four hours was incredible. All who saw it and who have been tracked down (at least a dozen people since 1978) confirm that it was very strange and unearthly. They talk of trying to dent some metal bits with a sledgehammer but failing, despite its extreme lightness and flexibility. Crates containing huge amounts that were carried on to the aircraft reputedly weighed almost nothing. And, as Marcel always argued, a weather balloon would not scatter over the huge area of desert which he saw in this case. He felt sure that some solid craft had exploded in mid-air and rained pieces down upon the landscape.

The secrets of Hangar 18

A second story surfaced in about 1950, and may be related to the March 1950 memo to the FBI. This came via Grady Barnett, a civil engineer with the Soil Conservation Service, who told friends that at the time in question he had been at Magdelena on the plains of San Agustin near Socorro, New Mexico, over 100 miles west of the Brazel ranch. He reputedly saw a crashed disc with small human-like bodies. They had no hair and large domed heads, and were lying dead outside the craft. A group of archaeology students led by a professor were in the area and saw this evidence too, but all the witnesses were ordered to remain silent by a team of military men who arrived to secure the site and take the bodies away.

This story has been influential within ufology. Rumours are persistent that it was the main craft which hit trouble over Corona and then impacted in San Agustin. The bodies were taken to Wright Patterson, where a secret 'Hangar 18' complex is supposed to have housed technology and bodily remains even before Project Sign was launched there some weeks later. It then moved, and is still at, Area 51 in the Tonopah Air Base complex, nestling within a remote area of Nevada 200 miles north of Las Vegas.

Indeed, many ufologists in the USA claim, as a result of this, that the alien nature of the UFOs was proven by the Roswell crash nearly fifty years ago. All the twenty-two years of Air Force study were a sham – a team of uninformed, low-level people putting on a public pretence of investigation. In 'truth' the greatest secret *never* told has been kept from the world ever since.

Unfortunately, the evidence to support the alien body claim within the Roswell story is hard to find. Many ufologists, even if they believe that an unknown craft did crash in the desert at Corona (as most do after extensive perusal of the evidence) are unpersuaded by the San Agustin allegations.

The Roswell Incident, a book published in 1980 by William Moore and Charles Berlitz, reported what little we knew about the matter at that time. It did enough to establish that a case had to be answered. Unfortunately Grady Barnett had died in 1969, and so was never interviewed by the Roswell investigators; the alien story remained a

The film Hanger 18 *(1980) was loosely based on what might have happened if a craft was captured at Roswell and kept under military guard ever since.*

secondhand, unsupported yarn. But the crash of some kind of object was established beyond reasonable doubt.

A debate arose about new witnesses who appeared after an NBC *Unsolved Mysteries* feature on the case in September 1989. In February 1992 a series of meetings were held in Chicago between both those favouring and those sceptical of the alien side to the story, and the debate was published in a monograph. Also in 1992 CUFOS published a whole series of reports, many by their investigators on the case, ex-Air Force officer Kevin Randle and researcher Don Schmitt, who discussed their continuing work, including field searches for debris scraps in the Corona scrub. Sadly forty years on nothing was found.

There are some claims that Brazel actually helped the Air Force discover a second location near Corona via aerial reconnaissance flights during the week that he was in custody. Not only the main 'disc' was found but also alien bodies – but, again, these are just unsupported rumours.

Schmitt and Randle cite some intriguing circumstantial evidence to verify this. A Roswell mortician fielded several enquiries from the base that week about preservation of bodily tissue, leading him to believe an air crash had occurred. He was then asked about the smallest coffins available! A base nurse later told the mortician that she assisted in transporting these child-sized bodies. The pilot of the aircraft that flew Marcel and the debris to Fort Worth also says he later took the bodies to Wright Patterson. This man ('Pappy' Henderson) kept the story even from his wife until 1982, after the Moore and Berlitz book had appeared. Feeling it was evidently no longer a secret, he chose to talk about it – though with circumspection.

Consistently these claims are that the entities were about four feet tall, had large domed heads, no hair, tiny mouths and big slanted eyes. The opinion of all those who claim to have seen them is that the affair proved the existence of alien craft arriving on Earth. The technology from the crashed object was so far beyond us that much is still undeciphered.

Japanese balloon bombs

Of course, there are critics of the case. Most sceptics argue that the weather balloon 'cover story' is true and the mistake came from excited air base officers presuming something stranger amidst flying saucer hysteria in the press. Others' ideas include a V-rocket astray from a nearby range.

By far the best-argued critical theory comes from within ufology itself – research by the influential writer John Keel. He says that the object that crashed in the Corona scrub was a Japanese balloon bomb!

In fact there is strong supporting evidence for his claim. During the latter stages of World War II the Japanese did launch large balloons packed with explosives across the Pacific. They drifted for days at great heights and, although most never completed the journey, some descended on the USA. The US government kept the fact secret because they did not want the Japanese to know their flights were a success. In an incident in the summer of 1945 six people were killed by an exploding balloon when it fell near their picnic area in Oregon.

Some years after the war balloon bombs were still being found – mostly in the western states, where they had lodged in rocky crevices. From late 1945 censorship was removed and people were warned what to look out for, but the story of the balloon bombs was fairly obscure even by mid-1947.

Keel's idea that the Roswell debris was from a Japanese balloon certainly has its advantages. The balsa wood, thin metal foil, parchment and rod-like metal bits covered with pink and purple stained picture writing (not unlike Japanese, one senses) all sound far more like a balloon than a spaceship that has crossed the universal void. Indeed, the very fact that the US government's blatant cover story about a weather balloon worked at all was only because the debris found by Brazel was rather balloon-like.

But Randle and Schmitt argue against Keel's thesis in their 1992 book, *UFO Crash at Roswell*, noting the most damning evidence such as the seeming indestructibility of the metal, the reputed gouge on the ground which no balloon could make, and the finding of the larger 'craft' and bodies. One would also expect the military authorities at Roswell to have recognised a balloon bomb. Nor does there seem to be any obvious reason why a cover story would be needed when the full truth could easily have been told in 1947 – or today, half a century after the war has ended.

It was Keel who proposed a rather fanciful idea of the balloon circling the globe for two years before descending on Corona – something that Randle and Schmitt find implausible. But Keel has since suggested a renegade Japanese military figure launching a solo attack on the USA because he could not accept his nation's defeat. If that idea were true (or even if suspected of being true at the time) it might indeed have incited a cover-up back in 1947. But why not release the records about this matter now, if that is all that took place?

Another idea that occurs to us is that the balloon bomb may have stuck in a ridge near Corona from 1945 but was released by the storm winds on 2 July 1947 and then hit by lightning as it drifted away. This would have caused the huge explosion in mid-air that Brazel heard, and the balloon may have rained its debris down on his ranch. But again – if this was what occurred – why not simply tell us so? The fact that there was, and remains, a cover-up and the insistence on the ludicrous weather balloon story implies that the truth was rather more startling.

The jury is out

In January 1994 Steven Spielberg was reported to be working on pre-production of Project X – his film about the Roswell crash, to be prepared in time for the 50th anniversary in July 1997.

With the multiplicity of books already published, the Roswell case is far more important to the ufologists of the 1990s than it was at the time of its occurrence. Most American experts believe it to be the single most significant incident in UFO history – the one that will eventually prove an alien presence on earth. Calls for congressional hearings periodically surface and, following the making of a movie and a TV documentary about the case, both scheduled for 1994 release, the fascination of this extraordinary event can only continue to grow.

Whether the truth will ever be known is quite another matter.

—— 7 ——

A SIGN OF THE TIMES

The waves of flying saucer reports in 1947 led to a top-secret investigation by the US Air Force.

Kenneth Arnold's sighting and the waves of flying saucer reports that followed had a serious effect on the US military authorities, regardless of the truth behind the Roswell affair that dominated its first few weeks. They had entered World War II after being caught with their pants down at Pearl Harbor. The danger of doing so again was not to be underestimated. So flying saucers were treated to a top-secret investigation in the hands of the US Air Force.

Few people outside the Pentagon knew how during the previous three years foo fighters and then ghost rockets had come to maximum strategic attention, both being perceived as potential secret weapons. Now exotic craft were being observed above the US mainland and had all the signs of being another rung up the ladder of technology, with capabilities well beyond anything the Americans possessed. If they were in the hands of an enemy power they were a major threat.

It would have been irresponsible not to take such a threat seriously. As a result, the investigation that was mounted and the secrecy that surrounded it were inevitable. Unfortunately, there were two unforeseen consequences.

Preconceived ideas

Once the mechanics of secrecy were in place they became almost impossible to dismantle, giving rise to whispers of cover-up and conspiracy – in effect that the US government knew the 'truth' (the alien origin of the discs) but were afraid to admit it. It seems unlikely that this was the case, unless there was a spaceship at Roswell. Bureaucratic secrecy feeds upon itself and breeds conspiracy theory. It was to be a long time before governments woke up to this and became more open about their UFO data.

The other problem is more subtle. By placing UFO study in the hands of military authorities from the start the answer to the mystery had been predetermined. These flying saucers were craft – that is, machines – powered by some living intelligence. As a result of such a premature conclusion it was equally presumed that the craft probably had pilots. In other words, UFOs were perceived by everyone – from governments to tabloid newspapers – as being products of a controlled and very strange technology.

This was an understandable, but serious, misjudgment. Whilst some UFOs may prove to be craft of unknown origin, by far the great majority of them are not. That lesson could have been learnt from the foo fighters and ghost rockets, where eventually it was found that the source of most reports was natural, not even supernatural, and certainly not extraterrestrial.

Yet the mind-set of 'UFOs as flying craft' gripped hold of popular imagination, and its stranglehold is scarcely broken today. Most people still regard UFOs and alien craft as synonymous terms. The question everyone asks is the same one that those first military investigators had posed in 1947: not the more correct and definitely more helpful 'What are these strange phenomena that people are seeing?' but 'Where do these frightening *machines* come from – and who the heck is flying them?'

Uneasy cooperation

Within a week of Kenneth Arnold's sighting there was furious military activity. We can piece together what went on from hundreds of documents released decades later under the US Freedom of Information (FOI) Act and from interviews with some of those who were involved at the time.

By early July Brigadier General George Schulgen, an Army/Air Force intelligence officer, was already requesting various military bases and intelligence agencies to cooperate in collating reports on the waves of UFO sightings. The press was full of them, but he wanted first-hand data.

On 10 July 1947, E. G. Fitch from the FBI circulated a memo under the heading 'Flying Disks'. He told how Schulgen had urged that every effort must be undertaken in order to run down and ascertain whether the flying disks are a fact and, if so, to learn all about them. According to General Schulgen the Air Corps intelligence are utilizing all of their scientists in order to ascertain whether or not such a phenomenon could in fact occur. He stated that this research is being conducted with the thought that [they] might be ... a foreign body mechanically devised and controlled.

Key people within the FBI appended their comments as to whether such cooperation with the military was appropriate. Assistant Director David Ladd was reluctant, referring to recent cases in which small discs had been found and investigated by military bodies but which as a rule were 'found to have been pranks'. The top man, however – none other than J. Edgar Hoover – added his own thoughts in a handwritten note, saying that he would recommend cooperation but that 'before agreeing to it we must insist upon full access to disks recovered. For instance in the La. case the army grabbed it and would not let us have it for cursory examination.'

This remark created all sorts of rumours when the file was declassified in 1977. Was Hoover referring to real UFO debris which had been captured by the US Army/Air Force in summer 1947, such as at Roswell? Sadly, the truth is more mundane:'La.' is the abbreviation for Louisiana, and from other declassified files we know that on 7 July, three or four days before Hoover penned these words, a case had occurred at Shreveport in that state. A small aluminium disc, not much more than a foot wide, was found amidst smoke on the ground. The military arrived and discovered that it was covered in wires and bore a crude motto on the side reading 'Made in the USA'. It was obviously a hoax – someone's idea of a joke following two weeks of intense flying saucer coverage by the press.

On 30 July the FBI issued instructions to all its agents to cooperate fully with the military – an arrangement which was to last barely a month. On 3 September an unfortunately phrased memo was circulated to Air Force bases, suggesting that the Air Force should do all the serious work and FBI agents be left to sift through the 'many instances which turned out to be ash can covers, toilet seats, and whatnot . . .' Not surprisingly, the FBI were not impressed and their cooperation ceased forthwith! Sadly, the level of tact and skill with which the US Air Force were to handle the UFO problem during the next twenty or so years was to show very little improvement. Nevertheless, the FBI involvement did bring in some impressive cases.

'Something is really flying around'

On 8 August a London agent reported an incident that had occurred on 16 January 1947 – five months before the Kenneth Arnold sighting. At 22.30 hours an RAF Mosquito was on night flying practice 100 miles out over the North Sea near the Dutch coast when a radar tracking was made of an unknown target. The aircraft was ordered to intercept at 22,000 feet and 'a long chase ensued'. This concluded at 23.00 hours over Norfolk. Two airborne radar contacts were established with the unidentified object, which took 'efficient controlled evasive action'. The British Air Ministry conclusion had been that the encounter was unexplained. UFOs were clearly nothing new.

It was strong evidence like this that formed the basis of a very early appraisal of sixteen American cases made by Lieutenant Colonel Donald Springer of Hamilton Field Air Base in California. All were dated between 19 May and 20 July 1947 and were very impressive. His analysis, dated 30 July, showed that ten of the sightings had occurred in daylight and almost all had been made by well-qualified observers. This was a sample of the 'best' of possibly dozens of cases received by military sources by that time.

These sort of reports show how the popular misconception that UFOs were 'flying saucer'-shaped was now taking root, thanks to the media. Of these sixteen cases, only one came close to being what we might now call disc-shaped. The rest were a mixed bag including 'a bright light', 'flat on base with top slightly rough in contour', 'like barrel head' and 'a wagon wheel'.

The conclusions of this first-ever attempt to conduct a serious investigation into UFO reports were amply supported by the data. The following remark was included in an appendix: 'This "flying saucer" situation is not all imaginary or seeing too much in some natural phenomenon. Something is really flying around.'

Springer further noted that he was puzzled by the 'lack of topside enquiries' – a decided disinterest from the highest level in government. Many similar statements have been made since then by military personnel or witnesses to major events. Springer became the first in a long line to speculate about a conspiracy, arguing five weeks into the UFO mystery that flying saucers might well be something 'about which the President, etc. know'.

Project Sign

Although sightings were falling off by late summer (as Schulgen himself rightly concluded, largely because the media were reacting less fervently towards them), analyses of data such as that made by Springer became very influential. They had persuaded Lieutenant General Nathan Twining, head of the AMC (Air Material Command), to request action. So on 23 September he wrote to Schulgen to conclude firmly that 'The phenomenon reported is something real and not visionary or fictitious.' He urged that a codenamed secret project should be mounted to study the data on a permanent basis, so as to allow the 'information gathered [to] be made available to other branches of the military and to scientific agencies with government connections'.

Twining's suggestion was endorsed by Schulgen; on 30 December the chief of staff at the Air Force, Major General Craigie, approved the project and ordered the creation of Project Sign. It was to be based at Wright Patterson Air Force Base at Dayton, Ohio (where the Roswell wreckage had been flown), and coordinated by AMC. Although its name was classified, the existence of the project was not secret because it needed reports. To the public it became known affectionately as Project Saucer.

Project Sign was officially launched on 22 January 1948 and got off to a traumatic start. A few days earlier, Captain Thomas Mantell had died as he climbed high into the air in his F-51 aircraft in pursuit of a silvery mass. This object was also reported by ground observers near Godman Field, Kentucky. His last words described seeing a large silvery metallic object trying to close in on him, and then there was silence. His plane was found smashed to fragments on the ground some hours later.

Sign employed various experts to assist – they ranged from intelligence officers to scientific consultants who were asked to comment on relevant cases. One of the first employed on an ad hoc basis was a young astronomer then at Ohio University, and later to become Professor at Northwestern University in Chicago. This was Dr J. Allen Hynek – roped in, as he admitted, for two principal reasons: he did not believe in flying saucers and would try very hard to find an answer to all sightings, and, by chance, he was the closest astronomer to Wright Patterson Air Force Base at the right moment. None the less, this invitation changed his life.

Speculation as to what 'Project Sign' stood for is rife. Was it a 'sign of the times' or a 'sign in the sky'? In fact it was simply next in the list of code words in the USAF manual.

The Skyhook tragedy

Hynek did his best with many sightings, but never compromised his scruples. If he could not find a credible solution, he said so. He could not find one for the Mantell crash and told the hierarchy at Sign of this failure. They had the media baying at their doors for a statement and desperately needed a solution, so they came up with the idea that the silvery object was the planet Venus.

Had a brave (if perhaps foolhardy) Mantell died trying to do the impossible and fly towards the stars in his plane? If so, eventually lack of oxygen in the cockpit would have led him to have suffered a blackout; the plane would then have gone into a steep dive and ultimately disintegrated.

There was only one thing wrong with this speculation. It is almost impossible to see Venus against a clear blue sky in the middle of the day – and even if you could do so it would definitely not look dramatic enough to qualify for the description of a large metallic object. The public refused to be fobbed off with a ludicrous solution cooked up to enable Sign to play for time, and this latest public relations disaster merely fuelled the belief that the government knew all about UFOs but would not tell the truth.

In reality, we now know that Mantell was almost certainly chasing a 'Skyhook' – a huge silvery device that was floating far too high in the atmosphere for his F-51 ever to have reached it. The Navy were testing these monster aerial devices secretly and had not told the Army/Air Force about their exercise.

Warring factions

Project Sign was soon convinced that some sightings were real, but its members split down the middle as to what that meant. The idea that they were Soviet missiles was quickly rejected – because it seemed ridiculous to imagine that the USSR would test secret devices deep within the US mainland.

This really only left one option – that the technology was not from any terrestrial source but from an extraterrestrial one. The UFOs, in other words, were alien spacecraft. Any Project Sign staff who could not stomach such a startling idea concluded the opposite: that the sightings were real enough, but must all be mistaken identity for various ordinary things like stars and planes.

For months the two factions were at loggerheads. Then an incident

An early case that impressed the official investigation involved an aircraft which engaged in a aerial 'dog fight' with a glowing disk over North Dakota. Sceptics argued that it was a balloon, but it convinced many of the investigators.

happened which was to tip the scales heavily in favour of those backing the aliens.

'A Flash Gordon rocket ship'

At 2.45am on 24 July 1948 Clarence Chiles and John Whitted were piloting an Eastern Airlines DC-3 at 5,000 feet on a beautiful moonlit night not far from Montgomery, Alabama, when they spotted a strange aircraft rushing towards them at great speed. In fact it was a ghost rocket, encountered for the first time at such close range. It was torpedo-shaped with two rows of windows on the side, glowing bright blue and with flames shooting out of the back. Whitted excitedly described it as a 'Flash Gordon rocket ship'.

The thing shot past them in just a few seconds without creating any air turbulence – something sceptics would use to show that it must have been much further away than the pilots believed. Yet it was so bright that it almost blinded them. Most of the passengers were asleep.

The most likely explanation for this event was a sighting of a very bright bolide, or fireball meteor. However, Chiles and Whitted categorically rejected the idea, saying they had often seen meteors in mid-air. In any case they were adamant that the object they saw was 'a man-made thing'. It was a flying craft built and flown – by somebody!

These witnesses were highly experienced air crew whose testimony therefore carried considerable weight. Indeed, Sign was quickly aware that there was still more to the story, because about an hour earlier a near-identical object had been secretly reported by a ground engineer at an air base in nearby Georgia. The object had a phosphorescent glow and was moving horizontally – exactly as the air crew had described their 'rocket ship'. A meteor or bolide descends at an angle into the atmosphere, so that answer looked shaky.

Sensibly, Hynek hedged his bets. He pointed out that if you took the report at face value there was no astronomical interpretation. However, he added that the ground engineer might have made a timing error and seen the object at the same moment as the Eastern Airlines crew. If so, this might support the view of an 'extraordinary meteor' giving off incandescent gases.

Few at Sign agreed with this theory. Edward Ruppelt (pictured on page 84), a later leader of the US Air Force project who had access to these secret files, said in 1956 that this case 'shook them worse than the Mantell incident'. It gave the believers in the ETH (extraterrestrial hypothesis) all the incentive they needed.

Captain Edward J. Ruppelt.

Codename Grudge

Within two weeks these people had produced a summary 'Estimation of the Situation'. Dated 8 August 1948, it used the Chiles-Whitted sighting as a cornerstone in its case, arguing that the best answer to the escalating evidence was that the flying discs were alien in origin. The file went to chief of staff General Hoyt Vandenberg, who rejected it, cogently arguing that it was based upon eye-witness testimony alone and had no physical evidence in support. Staff from Sign tried to change his mind, but he refused to budge.

The other faction at Project Sign now seized the upper hand and began to press their case that all sightings were explicable. The 8 August report was destroyed, although a few pirate copies appear to have been retained and Ruppelt read one of them about four years later. This 'holy grail' of ufology has never been found when requested under the FOI Act.

Staff who had backed the ETH hypothesis were reassigned. Six months later, in February 1949, Sign produced a rapid 'final' report. This stressed how many cases could be readily explained, suggested an increase in staff so as to place UFO officers on every air base, and implied that, given this sort of effort, most cases could probably be resolved and the entire mystery soon eliminated. But it did admit that it had failed to find a workable solution for about one in five of the 237 sightings it had investigated.

The Air Force chose to downgrade the project rather than increase its status. Effectively it became part of another, larger study and was given a new codename – Grudge. This word, some said, may have been intended as an expression of how the Air Force now felt about its UFO headache.

Grudge was a low-key affair with a clear brief. Captain Edward Ruppelt, who took over its reins in October 1951, minced no words in describing its role: he said that the team's task between 1949 and his takeover was to get rid of as many UFO sightings as possible. Grudge tried very hard to persuade responsible journalists to write negative stories in exchange for access to 'secret files', but the people they approached had examined the mystery and could not be convinced there was nothing going on.

By August 1949 Grudge published its final results – assessing 250 sightings and failing to identify 23 per cent (actually a worse performance than Sign, despite the new tactics!). Grudge warned that sightings might be used by Communist infiltrators to mask an insurrection – a curious argument which was to resurface later.

On 27 December 1949 the Pentagon announced that Grudge was to be axed (although in truth it was simply reduced to just one low-rank officer, effectively a filing clerk). It was to stay in limbo for two more years until Edward Ruppelt rode in like the cavalry to the rescue.

TWINKLE, TWINKLE, LITTLE UFO

A secret FBI memo of 31 January 1949 to J. Edgar Hoover mentioned night-time sightings which took the form of 'brilliant green lights'.

During the political games of the late 1940s and early 1950s, one of the best-kept secrets of the day had a profound effect on Washington's judgment of the UFO mystery. If there had merely been tales of lights in the sky, appearing randomly, doing nothing in particular and showing no threat, then no long-term investigation would have been maintained. But there was an extraordinary pattern developing that terrified the authorities: one secret memo used the term 'grave concern'.

Green fireballs – a new kind of spy

A specific type of UFO which came to be called the 'green fireball' was literally haunting key installations. These included top-secret missile sites, nuclear research facilities and atomic weapons testing grounds. It was as if an enemy surveillance of America's best-guarded facilities might be under way. The problem was that nobody knew who the enemy was – or indeed if that enemy was human!

On 31 January 1949 a secret FBI memo to J. Edgar Hoover summarised data accrued to that point from a conference headed 'Protection of Vital Installations'. This had involved the OSI (an Air Force intelligence unit) and the ONI (the Office of Naval Intelligence). The military had reported how lately there had been 'day-time sightings which are tentatively considered to possibly resemble the exhaust of some type of jet-propelled object. Night-time sightings have taken the form of lights usually described as brilliant green, similar to a green traffic signal or green neon light.'

One witness – a pilot from Sante Fé, New Mexico – offered a graphic account to an Air Force investigator some time later: 'Take a soft ball and paint it with some kind of fluorescent paint that will glow a bright green in the dark. Then have someone take the ball about 100 feet out in front of you and about 10 feet above you. Have him throw the ball at your face as hard as he can. That's what a green fireball looks like.' The January 1949 memo added that the objects were moving at between three and twelve miles per second – in other words, astonishingly fast!

As the document wrily noted, '... these phenomena have not been known to have been sighted, however, at any intermediate point between Russia and Los Alamos, but only at the end of the flight toward the apparent "target" ...'. Los Alamos in New Mexico was a highly sensitive nuclear facility. It is no wonder the US government were worried by all of this.

Although superficially these swift-moving green lights are similar to meteors , the report added that 'some nine scientific reasons are stated to exist which indicated that the phenomena observed are not [meteors]'. It then concluded that scientific opinion amongst the intelligence staff was that the green fireballs were either 'hitherto unobserved natural phenomena or that they are man-made. [But] no scientific experiments are known to exist in this country which could give rise to such phenomena.'

Thus, as Project Grudge was telling the public that UFOs were all easy to explain away, some of the top intelligence experts and scientific advisers to the US President were studying a stream of repetitive sightings of unknown objects overflying secret atomic bases. Their conclusions were that these objects were not only unexplained but also highly disturbing.

The experts are baffled

Piecing together the story of the green fireballs, we see that they began in late November 1948, although it seems that the first major events took place on 5 December. Within days so many experienced personnel, including Air Force pilots in mid-air and scientists on the ground, had seen these things that nobody at Los Alamos ever doubted that a mystery was afoot.

The man called in by the military intelligence was Dr Lincoln La Paz, a world authority on meteorites and a professor at the University of Albuquerque. La Paz had top-secret clearance and, some evidence suggests, had been one of the advisers consulted by the US government in July 1947 regarding the infamous Roswell UFO 'crash' (see Chapter 6).

La Paz and his team tracked down witnesses, interviewed them, plotted bearings on maps and followed a technique they had used successfully many times before to find meteorite debris on the Earth's surface. Again and again they visited the spot where green fireball debris should be. Again and again they found nothing. Yet reports were showing an alarming and very consistent flight pattern. The green fireballs overflew the atomic and nuclear facilities at Los Alamos, Sandia and so on – and then simply vanished!

Within one week, on 12 December 1948, Dr La Paz saw a green fireball for himself. It moved horizontally across the sky and had many other characteristics that did not match those of a meteor. He estimated its light output as 5218 angstroms, and inferred that the colour resulted from a high copper content. Much later that view was affirmed when considerable copper dust was recovered from beneath green fireball flight paths. Copper is hardly ever found in meteorite falls.

From all this evidence Dr Lincoln La Paz had absolutely no doubt that the green fireballs were unknown objects. In a secret report he wrote down his preliminary findings: the fireballs were moving too slowly, were too low in the sky, gave out no sonic boom despite their supersonic speed and proximity to witnesses, and did not leave a trail of sparks from the rear as meteors do. These things were utterly baffling.

On 8 February 1949 Dr Joseph Kaplan, a leading geophysicist and specialist in phenomena within the atmosphere, visited Albuquerque. He too had security clearance and was allowed to examine the now extensive data, after which he told the Air Force scientific advisory board that he found the matter 'unsettling'.

A home-grown mystery?

It was now felt necessary to convene a Conference on Aerial Phenomena, as it was termed, to debate this matter. The top scientists who attended included Edward Teller, one of the masterminds behind the building of the atomic bomb. At last UFOs were getting the right kind of respect, though they have never fully recaptured it since. Project Grudge were invited, but amazingly did not bother to send a representative – a fact that upset the scientists, who decided to keep Grudge only summararily informed in the future.

The problem was that Grudge's newly reconstituted operation was still reeling from the rejection of their 'estimate of situation', and the team were under orders to explain as many cases as possible as mundane things. This meant focusing on easily resolvable sightings – of which ufology, then as now, had plenty. It may have had no choice but to distance itself from something being endorsed by world-famous scientists.

As Edward Ruppelt said, when head of Air Force investigations into UFOs, this February 1949 gathering at Los Alamos was 'one conference where there was no need to discuss whether or not this type of UFO, the green fireball, existed. Almost everyone at the meeting had seen one.'

La Paz tried to persuade the assembled scientists that the objects were no known natural phenomenon, but Teller and others felt that they had to be some new process such as plasmas or electrical effects in the atmosphere. Teller added that the characteristics of the report suggested an optical rather than a physical phenomenon, akin to an ionised glow.

Teller, in particular, had access to data that would have told him had these objects been secret test launches – perhaps guided missile experiments with a 'need to know' classification. He assured the meeting they were not US technology. In the end La Paz carefully phrased his own conclusions – saying, in effect, that the fireballs were not meteors, nor did he, personally, believe they were natural phenomena. He felt that they were projectiles of an unknown technology, he hoped American. If 'friendly' they need not then be investigated – a view he 'doubted will be taken seriously' – but, if the powers above his head *knew* that these things were not American projectiles, as he clearly thought they did, then 'intensive, systematic investigation should not be delayed'.

'Project Twinkle' was the first scientific experiment to seek UFOs but it was not to be the last. The quest for proof is never ending.

Project Twinkle

One hint that the Americans were perhaps behind the green fireball sightings after all comes in several references from FBI memos; intelligence staff reported that they were twice warned of the probability of new sighting waves being imminent, including just prior to the first outbreak in late November 1948. A wave of reports had followed each tip-off. The warnings came from sources 'high up' in the chain of government, causing one to question how they knew what was about to happen unless they themselves were in control of the green fireballs?

However, this attractive solution is countered by the fact that Dr Kaplan was charged with the responsibility of a further detailed study in the wake of the Los Alamos meeting. A codename, Project Twinkle, was assigned and he spent much of 1949 setting up ideas for a further discussion meeting held in October – visiting, for example, the Cambridge scientific research laboratories of the AMC in Massachusetts to devise practical experiments.

The green fireballs pictured on the front cover of *Fate* in July 1957 were seen by thousands over the stadium at Santa Fé, New Mexico.

Following the October 1949 meeting Twinkle contracted Land-Air Incorporated to develop an automatic system to enable the fireballs to be filmed by two cameras at once, which would provide much useful data about the objects. Spectrographs and equipment to measure electromagnetic emissions were also obtained. Twinkle operated the cameras near Holloman Air Force Base in New Mexico during 1950 and 1951 for a total of eighteen months. If they were US weapons this expensive government-funded project makes no sense.

Sadly, a whole host of things went wrong with Twinkle. The Korean War intervened, taking away the military personnel who had been trained to use the more sophisticated equipment. There was much human error, lack of inter-departmental communication and sheer inefficiency, which meant that even when green fireballs did appear they were not adequately documented by the experiment.

Worst of all, the fireballs played games and Project Twinkle was led by the nose around the New Mexico landscape, rather than staying put and waiting for the UFOs to fly past their equipment. They set up their twenty-four-hour monitor where most green fireballs had been seen. But the numbers had dwindled by early 1950 when the project finally got up and running. After fruitless weeks they heard of sightings now occurring some distance away and so they upped sticks and followed the trail, only to arrive at their new stake-out soon after the wave was over! Then the fireballs returned to Vaughn, and so the game continued.

By late 1951 Twinkle closed down without reaching any firm conclusions. In 1953, when Edward Ruppelt had taken over the helm at a newly invigorated Air Force UFO project, he saw Dr Joseph Kaplan at a meeting. The professor's first question was 'Whatever happened to Project Twinkle?' Ruppelt did not know, as the work had largely been routed past his predecessors at Grudge, but this encouraged him to find out what he could.

Kaplan, whilst saying that he disagreed with the findings of Lincoln La Paz, suggested that Ruppelt (a man passionately interested in the truth behind the UFO sightings) should visit the meteor expert in Albuquerque. Later in the year Ruppelt visited Los Alamos and spent several hours discussing the matter with scientists and technical staff at the atomic research centre there. They came up with various ideas about the fireballs, but each worker accepted the reality and strange nature of the objects, which were still occasionally seen. All of them had witnessed at least one, and some had seen several. The consensus at Los Alamos was that these were possible projectiles fired from an alien craft in Earth orbit as some kind of long-range surveillance probe!

In his memoirs, published in 1956, Ruppelt reported that 'Two years ago I would have been amazed to hear a group of reputable scientists make such a startling statement. Now, however, I took it as a matter of course. I'd heard the same type of statement many times before from equally qualified groups.'

Ruppelt finally did meet Lincoln La Paz. He was very forthright, but considered carefully before he answered the key question as to what he thought the green fireballs had to be. According to Ruppelt: 'He didn't think that they were a natural phenomenon. He thought that some day one would hit the Earth [i.e. crash] and the mystery would be solved. He hoped that they were a natural phenomenon.'

The fireball enigma continues

In September 1954 Dr La Paz had said that sightings of green fireballs had disappeared. But the archives of UFO research groups contain records of many such phenomena from around the world, and from far more recent times than the days of Project Twinkle. Often they are associated with major military or industrial complexes, exactly as they were half a century ago.

In May 1978 an RAF pilot was driving near the massive oil refinery plant at Carrington in Greater Manchester when he saw three green fireballs whizz past. He was later 'regressed' by hypnosis to see if he might have been abducted by them! This enthusiastic, if improbable, experiment ended in failure. The man recounted in detail the passage of the fireballs, but there was no hidden story of an alien kidnap – just another sighting to add to the ever-growing list of a mystery intractable as ever even after fifty years.

In 1993 a new attempt was mounted by a group called CSETI who tried to establish contact with aliens at key UFO and crop circle sites by beaming light up at the sky. It had scientific support.

Again green fireballs focused in October 1983 around the controversial nuclear plant at Sizewell in Suffolk, an area ringed by secret establishments with strong British and American connections. These facilities include electronics research centres, over-the-horizon radar and the twin NATO air bases of Bentwaters and Woodbridge.

It may well be very significant that two US air bases make persistent claims that they have hosted contact between aliens and the US government in modern times. These are Holloman Air Force Base in New Mexico (1964) and Bentwaters in Suffolk (1980) – see pages 212-18 – both are focal points of the most intensive green fireball activity known. Indeed, during the infamous close encounter at Bentwaters in December 1980 the sighting of many 'comets in the sky' – a new wave of strangely behaving fireball activity – proved a vital part of the story.

The green fireball mystery is far from a thing of the past.

—— 9 ——

THE ALIEN INVASION OF WASHINGTON

1952 saw the biggest ever wave of UFO activity in the USA, triggering massive global interest in the subject.

After two years in the wilderness Project Grudge received a massive shot in the arm when in October 1951 Captain Edward J. Ruppelt became the latest Air Force officer to pick up the task. Like his predecessors, he was not a believer in UFOs but a thorough investigator who would seek out rational explanations. He was brought in, as he was told, 'for just a few months' in order to 'sort things out'.

It took little time for Ruppelt to realise that something unexplained was going on, and before long he was recommending improvements and better resources. The Air Force hierarchy liked him. Some thought he could get rid of the problem of UFOs entirely. Others – in the minority, but a strong view none the less – remained sure that behind these pesky UFOs lay an alien vision and that Ruppelt could be just the man to prove it.

Project Blue Book takes off

So, for a variety of reasons, the top brass assisted in fulfilling some of Ruppelt's requests and the project became more active and more responsible than before. He secured its independent status again as the Aerial Phenomena Group, with a new codename – it became Project Blue Book in March 1952. As Ruppelt said; 'The word "grudge" was no longer applicable . . . the code name "Blue Book" was derived from the title given to college tests. Both the tests and the project had an abundance of equally confusing questions.'

The great 1952 wave

Hardly had Ruppelt's feet got under his desk at Wright Patterson Air Force Base than the USA was hit by the biggest wave of UFO activity ever. Although reports escalated from April onward, it was the last two weeks in July 1952 that were to see the height of the 'great flap'. This event was to have very profound effects: it would permanently alter the US government approach to UFOs, a term that Ruppelt first started to use as replacement for the presumptive 'flying saucer', and typical of his sensible approach. However, perhaps more important, the 1952 wave would create massive global interest in the subject – triggering official (and secret) investigations in countries like Britain which had been content to sit and watch what happened in the USA. The wave was also to make a deep impression on the minds of young children then growing up alongside regular accounts of these strange things in the sky – particularly given their widely perceived origin as alien craft.

The ufologists, the space enthusiasts who catapulted humanity towards the moon and the lovers of science fiction were all enraptured by the events of July 1952. A flood of UFO-related movies swiftly followed, notably *Earth Versus the Flying Saucers* of 1955. Without the 1952 wave space travel might have been slower in arriving, and very possibly the UFO mystery would have gradually ebbed away. As it was, this dramatic course of events virtually assured immortality for the dream of alien contact. The UFO mystery just happens to be a convenient mode of expression for a huge public desire that as a species we should have companions out there in the vastness of space.

A vital prelude to the wave was an article called 'Have We Visitors from Outer Space?' which appeared in *Life* magazine in March 1952. Coming from such an influential and unsensational publication, it was stunning. Ruppelt tells of the media clamour and how he had to issue what he called a 'weasel worded' public statement that *Life*'s opinions were their own, when in truth he knew that 'the Air Force had unofficially inspired [the article]'.

Indeed, Blue Book had supplied the best case material. The article cited key figures as saying: 'Maybe they're interplanetary.' This Ruppelt insists, reflected the personal opinion of several very high-ranking officers in the Pentagon at that time – 'so high that their personal opinion was almost policy'. The gradual escalation of all the evidence, despite every attempt to wish it away, was a factor in this shock verdict, as was the realisation that attention was settling on the seat of government – Washington DC.

Visitors to Washington

In May 1952 a high-ranking member of the CIA held a garden party not far from headquarters in Langley, Virginia. Suddenly a UFO flew right overhead, put on an aerial ballet and disappeared in front of many gaping influential guests. The impact was, of course, enormous.

After rushing quickly to nearby Washington to investigate the matter, Ruppelt notes that there was not very much he could do except stamp the file 'Unknown'. Then a CIA scientist told him that analysis was suggesting that a major event was imminent. It would occur in the capital. Blue Book had been monitoring the build-up also and had come to the same conclusion.

On 14 July, at 8.12pm, a Pan-Am DC-4 flying through the Washington area had a close encounter. Its veteran pilots, William Nash and William Fortenberry, had a close view of six coin-shaped objects that glowed red on top. At first these were below the aircraft; then they moved in a strange path across the sky, switching direction and finally climbing upwards to shoot away past the passenger aircraft as it flew south en route to Miami. The pilots last saw the lights 'flip' off one by one, possibly as they came out of range of the sunlight that was creating these reflections.

Hardly had the concerns about this worrying case died away when radar screens all around the capital started to pick up UFOs. This

In the summer of 1952 Washington DC was struck by a major wave of sightings that shook up both the US and British governments. Later this photograph appeared reputing to show the lights above Washington encircling the Capitol building. Investigation revealed them to be 'lens flares', ie street lamps outside the Capitol bouncing off the camera lens system.

began at 11.40pm on Saturday, 19 July, and lasted until after dawn. The sets were checked for faults within minutes of the blips appearing, as the control of air traffic over this location was a vital matter. The radar was working perfectly.

There were three systems in the area – the long-range set-up, which tracked aircraft passing through; the short-range radar at Washington Airport tower, which dealt with local landings and take-offs; and a military installation just across the Potomac River into Virginia. All three recorded the objects that night, often simultaneously. They comprised various targets moving slowly like aircraft, which then suddenly accelerated and zipped off-screen – one tracked at the then fantastic speed of 7,000 mph (about six times what Concorde can achieve today).

The 1952 Washington waves had more impact on the world than any other sightings in history. They also produced record numbers of witnesses – over 2000.

Many experienced radar officers viewed these targets and they were all baffled. When the UFOs started to fly through restricted airspace over the White House and Capitol, panic resulted. The nearest military base was undergoing runway repairs and was out of action. Three calls were made to urge the Air Force to send some interceptors into the area. Finally, one jet was scrambled – but it was nearly 3am before it reached Washington. By then aircraft arriving, departing and passing through the city's air space were seeing strange lights cavorting about the sky in total disregard of the tight security.

As the senior radar controller, Harry Barnes, said in his report: 'We knew immediately that a very strange situation existed.' Howard Cocklin, the radar controller in the tower at Washington Airport, looked out above the city as the blips rushed around the sky. He could see a big orange light right where one of the targets was indicated. A similar object 'like an orange ball of fire trailing a tail' was reported by phone by an airman to Andrews Air Force Base; an officer at the base went outside and saw it too, 'unlike anything I had ever seen before'. As he tried to bring others to watch it stopped dead, then shot off at an incredible speed and vanished.

A Capital Airlines DC-4 was vectored towards the lights from radar trackings. This was at about 1am. They saw several, but each time they closed in on the objects they shot away both visually and on radar. Later Barnes described the UFOs' behaviour as 'like a bunch of small kids out playing'.

Government inactivity – or was it?
The radar and Air Force personnel were extremely puzzled by the slow response of the government authorities, who took a very long time to do

very little. Indeed, when the interceptor from Delaware finally arrived, three hours into the affair, the UFOs had vanished – just minutes before, in fact. The jet flew around Washington for a while, using up fuel and seeing nothing, then returned to base. Almost as soon as it left the area the UFOs returned to the radar screens!

The events subsided as the sun rose, leaving a lot of baffled people. Yet nobody told Blue Book. In fact, Ruppelt flew by chance into Washington Airport just over twenty-four hours after the incident. When he bought a paper from the news-stand he found himself reading about these close encounters for the first time. He called his contact at the Pentagon from an airport phone booth to ask what was going on, but everyone there seemed as much in the dark as he was!

Although later that morning Ruppelt did interview personnel who were involved, this incredibly lax performance by the powers that be is as mystifying as the sightings themselves. But it has happened in other crucial cases since. This leaves the strong suspicion that in such instances there is a higher-level, top-secret, investigation unit, so far above operations like Blue Book that the small fry have no 'need to know' about its activities.

In cases such as this one – above the nation's capital city – someone must have been doing something. One wonders if for once they simply forgot to tell the dummy in the shop window what went on at the back of the store.

Official obstructiveness

Ruppelt tells how at the Pentagon that Monday every journalist and his cat was calling to get more information. Opinion was divided on whether to put out any solution they could think up or just to say they were investigating. The end result was 'No comment', which not surprisingly provoked accusations of a cover-up. Eventually it was accepted that Blue Book had to investigate, so Ruppelt agreed to extend his one-day visit to Washington and 'work all night' if necessary. He called back to Dayton, where nationwide sightings were pouring in – many better than the ones of the past thirty-six hours above Washington. But Ruppelt decided that national interest was best served by focusing on the case that the world's press were clamouring after.

So he planned his visits – to the three radar sites, to airline offices to speak to air crew, to the interceptor bases and to the weather bureau to check out possible solutions. Then he hit a brick wall. Nobody would give him an Air Force car to get to these sources as quickly as possible. He tried to hire one, but his expenses chits were refused. Instead he was told to take the bus – impossible, as speed was vital that morning. Finally he was reminded that he had written orders only to visit the city for the day, and would be classified as AWOL unless he went back to Dayton right away!

In Earth versus the Flying Saucers *the sightings over Washington were given liberal interpretation as a UFO crashes into the monument!*

The by now deeply frustrated Ruppelt – supposedly the one person charged by the US government with handling the most significant UFO sightings yet on record – was aware that he was being manipulated. He called his boss at the Pentagon, told him what he thought and added: 'I decided that if saucers were buzzing Pennsylvania Avenue in formation I couldn't care less ... I caught the next airliner to Dayton.'

An unlikely theory

A week later, on the evening of Saturday, 26 July, the radar screens went crazy again and Washington was hit by a second flood of lights. Yet again Ruppelt, busy dealing with reports of nationwide UFO activity back at Dayton, got the news secondhand from a journalist who called him to ask what the Air Force were doing about the 'invasion'. One can sense his anger when he reports that instead of the expected 'No comment' he told the reporter: 'I have no idea what the Air Force is doing. In all probability it's doing nothing.'

Being the good investigator that he was, of course, Ruppelt put the case ahead of his personal feelings. He alerted Washington and within minutes three officers connected with Blue Book were on their way to the airport – a press officer, Al Chop; Ruppelt's right-hand man, Major Dewey Fournet; and a navy intelligence electronics expert called Holcomb. They all got to the airport in time to see the majority of the radar trackings (again recorded by all the area radars that night) and the arrival of two F-94 interceptor jets who were in constant radio contact with these men.

The media had arrived at the airport as the lights in the sky were being reported publicly. Ruppelt describes how they were ordered out of the operations room 'on the pretext that classified radio frequencies would be used' that night. Actually this expulsion occurred because 'not a few people in the radar room were positive that this night would be the big night in UFO history – the night when a pilot would close in and get a good look at a UFO – and they did not want the press to be in on it.'

An incredible game of cat and mouse resulted. At first there was a duplication of the previous week's farrago. As soon as the jets reached the area the UFOs vanished, both visually and on radar. They turned up instead at Langley, Virginia, where a passing Air Force jet and several people on the ground saw them. When the interceptors left Washington, the UFOs returned there – so more F-94s were scrambled! This time they got a radar lock on one of them, but as they closed in the UFO sped off too fast to catch. Finally one jet managed to get a good visual close-up of the object, so the pilot put the jet on afterburner and flew straight at the thing. As he approached it, the UFO shot away at an incredible speed. The pilot, Lieutenant William Patterson, later reported: 'I chased a single bright light which I estimated about 10 miles away. I lost visual contact with it at about 2 miles.'

Fournet briefed Ruppelt the next day as he headed for Washington to handle the expected media flak. It was clear that all of the experienced personnel working in the radar room that night were satisfied that the targets they were tracking were real. They were not radar equipment defects or the result of a temperature inversion that was causing a mirage – one theory that had been mooted as a possible solution. Fournet added that these men thought the objects were 'metallic'.

Two days later the biggest-ever peacetime press conference was held by the USAF, but with none of the officers who had been eye witnesses. Instead, a radar expert was flown in that day. He had met no witnesses but tentatively put forward the inversion theory. It was gratefully embraced by the Air Force.

The Blue Book conclusion, thanks to Ruppelt, was that these reports were unexplained. The radar experts at Washington who had seen the targets insisted that inversion echoes regularly appear all summer long and look quite different from those appearing on their scopes for those two nights.

Indeed, and possibly far more relevant, the US Weather Bureau failed to back up the vaguely proffered temperature inversion/radar mirage theory – noting that the radar experts who described the targets were reporting things unlike the behaviour commonly known in the weather trade as an 'angel'. It seems that – whatever the Air Force wanted the public to believe – these 'angels' were not caused by the forces of nature.

Fifteen years later, the men in the radar rooms at Washington DC told the same story to experts from the University of Colorado funded by the US government to try to debunk UFOs into oblivion. The radar officers were again adamant that the July 1952 sightings in Washington DC were quite inexplicable. They insisted that, whatever occurred on those mysterious nights, they are amongst the most important UFO sightings in history.

10

ENTER THE CIA

1953 saw the involvement of the CIA in the UFO investigation.

The aftermath of the Washington DC wave was incisive. Some people were bought off by the weather inversion theory, but not within the corridors of power. The CIA, for example, were sufficiently perturbed to get involved in the matter.

Their concern stemmed less from what UFOs might be and more from what they might do to the harassed intelligence network. After the Washington debacle an Air Force general had pointed out that normal communications channels were clogged by the flood of incoming UFO data. This was the era of the McCarthy witch-hunts against Communist sympathisers, and the height of the Cold War: the CIA perceived a real danger to its operations. A UFO wave would provide excellent cover for any enemy invasion, which made UFOs a big threat – whatever they were.

An analysis based on newly recovered records of the time was recently made by ufologist Barry Greenwood (pictured opposite). This suggests that to some extent the hysteria over the Washington flap may have been manipulated. It was difficult to persuade citizens to participate in ground observer watches for Communist activity, yet in the wake of the UFO sightings recruitment shot up and everyone started watching the skies. Perhaps, Greenwood suggests, the wave was allowed to develop so as to fulfil that function. Were the slow response times in sending interceptors and seeming disinterest in bringing Blue Book into the picture part of a CIA scheme?

In early 1952 Ruppelt made a number of suggestions to improve Blue Book. One of the most important was to employ a prestigious scientific research facility – the Battelle Memorial Institute – to make an intensive statistical appraisal. This impressive long-term project ran until 1954.

Ufologist Barry Greenwood,
speaking at a conference.

High-level deception

When the US Air Force subsequently informed Ruppelt that a panel of
top scientists would be convened to review the best UFO data, he
thought this was another success for his attempt (backed by Allen
Hynek) to upgrade the science within Blue Book. What he did not
know was that the CIA were behind this latest initiative, and that the
experts would be working for them towards a hidden agenda.

Battelle were by this time well into their far more detailed project and
when they heard about the planned CIA meeting they urged that it be
put on hold until their data was ready. Like Ruppelt they falsely
assumed that the panel would meet to discuss UFOs, not secrecy
behind them. The Battelle scientists' plea was ignored and the CIA
team met for five days in Washington in January 1953. Even Hynek,
Air Force science adviser since 1948 and the only scientist at that date
to have real experience of UFO investigation, was merely invited to
some sessions and excluded from others because he had no CIA
clearance.

The Robertson panel, as this team were called, was headed by Dr H.
P. Robertson, a relativity physicist who had been involved in the
Manhattan Project to build the atomic bomb. The four others were

Luis Alvarez (a future Nobel prize winner), Lloyd Berkner, Sam Goudsmit and Thornton Page – all experts in physical sciences, emphasising the government view that UFOs were a material phenomenon and not hallucinations. Hynek, Ruppelt, Fournet and others directly involved in the data gathering at Blue Book presented evidence to the conference – which lasted for only twelve hours. The entire last day was spent writing and rewriting the statement to be issued in conclusion.

Thirty cases were investigated, with only a few minutes devoted to each one. Probable solutions were offered for some. Others were left as insoluble.

In the wake of the Roberston panel meetings in Washington, Project Blue Book began to explain away as many sightings as possible. It is now accepted by most serious ufologists that they were often right to do so and that ninety percent of all UFOs are really IFOs (identified flying objects). This UFO, photographed in Spain, is actually an unusual cloud formation.

Ruppelt, sadly unaware of how he was being duped by his superiors, was optimistic about this group. He said: 'Although the group of scientists would not be empowered to make the final decision, their recommendations were to go to the President if they decided that UFOs were real. And any recommendations made by the group of names we planned to assemble would carry a lot of weight.' The betting in an unofficial sweepstake at the Blue Book office just before the panel met was 5 to 3 in favour of them finding UFOs real (which in most eyes meant finding them extraterrestrial). In the end, of course, the panel were never interested in such questions.

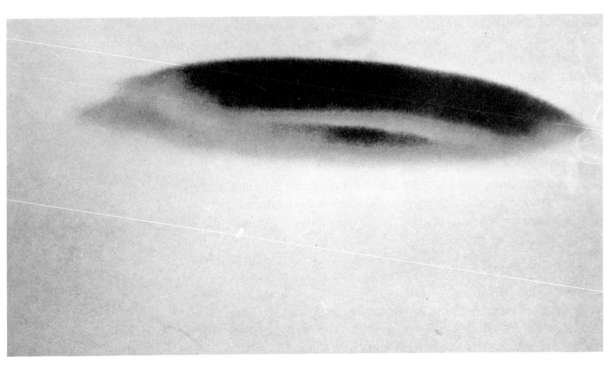

Manipulating the public

Their carefully discussed conclusions (again kept top secret, of course, even – it seems – from Ruppelt) were extraordinary. They agreed that communication channels could become 'overloaded', and that the US government should start a campaign to debunk the subject so as to 'result in the reduction in public interest in "flying saucers"'.

Suggested methods included allowing Walt Disney to make propaganda films, as well as TV programmes and press articles. The object of their two-year plan was to 'reduce or eliminate' public concern about UFOs as far as possible. However, the panel did warn that the newly founded civilian UFO groups 'should be watched because of their potentially great influence on mass thinking if widespread sightings should occur'. Adding to this was the curious idea that enemy agents could infiltrate UFO groups and use them for devious ends!

Such CIA tactics were rapidly put into play. Less than a year later, on 17 December 1953, a secret memo notes how 'the definite drop in the number of sightings' was 'attributed to the actions following the [panel's] recommendations'. Amazingly, Blue Book statistics suddenly showed that from unknowns totalling 20 per cent or more in previous years, only 1 or 2 per cent of cases per year were now being considered unidentified. The public were told that this showed how the UFOs had gone away. The real truth emerges from a careful study of the files, released in 1976. Identifications were being invented with abandon so as to wish away countless cases on a whim. Evidence to support each conclusion was regarded as an unnecessary luxury.

Nor is this a thing of the past. A CIA memo from 1976 tells how the agency is still having to 'keep in touch with reporting channels' in ufology (in other words, to spy on UFO groups). And in a November 1983 conference at the University of Lincoln, Nebraska, where Allen Hynek and Jenny Randles were amongst the lecturers, delegates were confined to the campus for the duration of the event following warning phone calls. A claim was made by an influential critic that the thrust of the conference could inadvertently aid Communist sympathisers by daring to discuss whether there was a cover-up of UFO data!

The Battelle results

Ruppelt knew none of these things. He was simply told that Blue Book was being upgraded in the wake of the Robertson panel, but his 1955 book makes it clear that he was never told of the secret directives. However, he quickly sensed the new regime. He left the Air Force in late 1953, writing positively on the subject and two years later publishing his devastating memoirs in which, ever the loyal officer, he pondered: 'Maybe I was just the front man for a big cover-up.'

It should be stressed that Ruppelt never became a member of the UFO community. He remained outspoken against the claims of writers such as Donald Keyhoe – then openly making charges of major conspiracies – and was greatly disillusioned by the contactee movement in the mid-1950s. This took hold just after the Robertson panel had met, and its value to the debunking cause was recognised in secret CIA memos. Some historical analysts think that the sudden arrival of countless Americans claiming contact with 'space brothers', and the quirky behaviour of some of them, may not be coincidence. Were some of the more extreme cases planted by the CIA as a way to speed up the Robertson panel requirements? They definitely tarnished UFO credibility.

If so, the move certainly paid off with Ruppelt. Four years after publishing his excellent book he produced a 'revised' edition in which he completely changed its emphasis. Now he said that UFOs were a space age myth and were all explicable. So dramatic was the turnabout that some think he must have been leaned on by the government, which may have threatened his new career in the aviation industry. Sadly, he died soon afterwards from a heart attack, aged thirty-seven, and was never able to answer the charges. But his widow insisted that it was the extent of the lunatic fringe within the contactee movement in California which demolished his faith in UFO reality.

This summary of the Robertson panel has excellent support. A fuller version was previously read by a panel member, Dr Thornton Page, who affirmed that it accurately portrayed what he recalled.

In contrast to these manipulations the Battelle study – by sceptics, it should be said – was a masterpiece of scientific research. It was subjected to intense secrecy. Hynek was told that even to mention it in public would result in him losing his prized contract with the Air Force.

The study was secret partly because its results were so positive – although, noting the lack of physical evidence, the Institute argued that they failed to prove an alien reality. Special Report 14 – as it was called when later released – took all 4,000 cases on Blue Book files to the end of 1952, selected the 2,199 that had the best data, and subject these to intense scrutiny. Every one was tabulated according to minute factors such as age, sex, observational experience of the witness, size of the object and so on: a very tough task when computer technology was not what it is today.

A Battelle scientist then assigned each case to one of four categories – excellent, good, doubtful and poor, according to quality of the evidence. Next it was put into an evaluation category. Every case was then given to an evaluation panel of Battelle scientists who met regularly to study batches of cases and reach their own conclusions. They did not know the outcome of the first evaluation. A team of experts – in fields like astronomy, radar and meteorology – were called in by the panel when significant cases appeared.

If the evaluation of the panel matched that of the lone Battelle analyst, then that conclusion was adopted. If not, discussions focused on that single case alone until a consensus was reached. On every case where the conclusion 'unknown' was adopted by either party, a full meeting of personnel was called to thrash it out until everyone was satisfied.

The results of the study provided some startling data. Most people expected the unknown cases to offer the least information (they were considered unknown only because there was insufficient data to identify them). When such missing data was provided, the case would be far more likely to be explained away. Sceptics still cling to this view.

In fact just under 10 per cent (about 200 cases) were rated as excellent data by Battelle. Of these, one third qualified for an unknown classification after rigorous investigation. Yet of the cases rated poor less than half were ultimately considered 'unknown'. All told, Battelle found that in just four years no fewer than 261 cases where the calibre of data available was viewed as either excellent or good qualified as an unknown phenomenon. This was overwhelming scientific evidence that something unexplained lay behind the UFO data. Yet the Robertson panel were only given a brief glimpse of a handful of these baffling cases.

Before freedom of information made the data available, the Air Force used the Battelle analysis to bizarre effect to try to counter Ruppelt's book. They reported that a study had proved UFOs to be invalid, because its data included only 'a few surviving unknowns'. In fact Battelle considered 22 per cent of its 2,199 cases to be unknown – which hardly justifies the tag 'a few' survivors! A government memo soon afterwards noted that the disclosure of this finding from Battelle was 'serving well the purpose for which it was intended'.

More dramatic still was a parameter for parameter analysis that Battelle had carried out. They looked at factors such as duration, shape and speed of the reports in both the identified and the unidentified categories. When an unknown case has no explanation, logic suggests

Despite claiming no interest in UFOs, Freedom of Information Act requests for data show that the CIA have regularly collected reports of UFOs.

The 1993 American TV series X-Files *is a drama based, reputedly, on 'true' files from the secret services. The agents regularly confronted UFOs and aliens in claimed reflections of genuine intelligence unit investigations – labelled the 'X-Files' – where X stands for the Unknown.*

that it may well simply be an example of an identifiable event which has not yet had the fortune to be resolved. But if so, then it would match up on this kind of parameter study.

For instance, all oranges are round and are coloured orange. If you have an object that you think might be an orange but you cannot prove that it is one, it will still match up to all other oranges in a parameter study of its shape and colour. Of course, things are a lot more complex in terms of multi-faceted UFO data, but the principle is the same.

Battelle studied its many cases to find the chances that the unknowns were identifiable objects (such as aircraft) but which had not had the fortune to be resolved. The outcome was that the chances were rather low – in fact the odds were an incredible one in a billion!

Such results imply that the unsolved cases were going to remain unsolved whatever investigation was carried out. They were genuinely unknown phenomena. But this could not prove, or even support, the view that the reports were describing an alien technology. That required a very different level of as yet unseen physical evidence. Even so, the Battelle results were a vital step forward.

Part Five

1950s:
ALIEN CONTACT

11

THE CONTACTEES

The contactees of the 1950s actually met aliens and took trips in their flying machines.

Controversy still rages over the contactees of the 1950s – men and women who were the precursors of the New Age channellers. Where modern channellers describe mental communications, much in the way that clairaudient mediums converse with 'spirits', the contactees actually met aliens and took trips in their flying saucers.

The contactee phenomenon is a rich treat for anthropologists, sticky with conscious and unconscious deceit, naive romanticism, and both sincere and sincerely deluded individuals. Were the contactees in touch with anything other than their own internal fantasies? Were the core experiences – stripped of all the third rate science fiction trappings – evidence of genuine 'alien' contact?

In the 1950s space exploration had hardly begun, and little was known even about our nearest neighbours. The contactees encountered extraterrestrials from planets in our own solar system – humanoid beings who apparently lived on Venus, Mars, Saturn and Neptune. It was conceivable at that time, because mankind was yet to learn how inhospitable these planets really are. Does this make the contactees tall story-tellers, or, as some ufologists believe, were the contactees being lied to?

The man who met a Venusian

The most famous contactee of all was George Adamski, a Polish American whose adventures with the 'space people' were chronicled in several books beginning with *Flying Saucers Have Landed*. This self-made man, who had an interest in astronomy and oriental philosophies, was out with some friends on 20 November 1952. They were picnicking in the Mohave Desert in California when they noticed a cigar-shaped object which was chased away by military jets – but not before it had ejected a silver disc which landed some distance away.

Adamski drove out near to where the saucer lay and was approached by a 'man' dressed in a one-piece suit. They communicated using telepathy, and Adamski learned that the being was from Venus. He said his race were concerned about the radiation from atomic bombs reaching into space and harming other worlds. The alien also informed Adamski that Earth was being visited by races from other planets in the solar system and beyond.

The witnesses to this encounter, observed through binoculars, signed affidavits. Meetings with other humanoids ensued, who took him on flights into space and around the dark side of the moon. But his description of wooded valleys was not borne out by subsequent space missions from Earth.

Adamski's photographs of cigar-shaped 'mother ships' and close-ups of the smaller disc-shaped 'scout craft' (see page 110) caused a lot of controversy. Critics compared the latter variously to part of a vacuum cleaner, a chicken feeder and a bottle cooling machine made in Wigan, Lancashire. This turned out to have been designed *after* the photographs were released, and purposely engineered by a fan of Adamski's to look like the scout craft. However, none of these items exactly matched the image captured on film.

In his defence, even sceptics were impressed with Adamski's apparent sincerity. Science journalist Robert Chapman wrote in *UFO – Flying Saucers Over Britain*: 'Adamski was so damnably normal and this was the overall impression I carried away. He believed he had made contact with a man from Venus, and he did not see why anyone should disbelieve him. I told myself that if he was deluded he was the most lucid and intelligent man I had met'.

Others around the world who have never heard of Adamski had sighted identical objects to the scout craft. One of them was a schoolboy named Stephen Darbishire, who with his cousin took two pictures in Coniston one day in February 1954 (see page 111). Leonard Cramp, an aeronautical engineer used a system called orthographic projection to prove that the object depicted in Darbishire's and Adamski's photographs were proportionally identical. In a recent interview with Darbishire, now a professional artist, he confirmed to Peter Hough and Dr Harry Hudson all the details of his original story.

On his first trip into space Adamski observed 'manifestations taking place all around us, as though billions upon billions of fireflies were

According to Flying Saucers Have Landed, *Adamski had his first sighting in 1946 – a year before Kenneth Arnold's.*

George Adamski was the first man to become famous as a claimed contactee with alien entities. To back up his story he produced many controversial photographs reputed to show the UFOs flown by the Venusians and Saturnians that he met. Many investigators doubt the credibility of images such as this 'mother ship' disgorging several 'scout ships' taken near Mount Palomar in California.

flickering everywhere ...'. This is not something that would readily emerge from the imagination to be included in a space yarn. When astronaut John Glenn orbited Earth on 20 February 1962, he commented that '... a lot of the little things I thought were stars were actually a bright yellowish green about the size and intensity as looking at a firefly on a real dark night ... there were literally thousands of them'. Russian cosmonauts reported the same phenomenon, which turned out to be caused by billions of reflective dust particles. How could George Adamski have guessed that?

This son of a Polish immigrant generated a worldwide following. By the mid-sixties, however, his popularity was on the wane as his claims became more and more outlandish. Just months before he died, on 26 February 1965, he was staying with a couple at their house in Silver Spring, Maryland. That afternoon Adamski and Madeleine Rodeffer saw something hovering through some trees. A car drew up and three men told Adamski: 'Get your cameras – they're here', before driving

off. Adamski grabbed the Rodeffers' ciné camera and produced some 8mm colour footage of a scout craft which seemed to be suffering a distortion effect down one side. Was this meant to revive public interest in Adamski, or was it evidence that the contacts, on some level at least, were 'real'?

Stephen Darbishire's famous photograph, taken in Coniston in 1954. Some UFO researchers feel that the in focus upright object in the front right of the picture is the pin or stick holding up a UFO model or drawing. Stephen Darbishire, however, denies this.

Daniel Fry

George Adamski may have been the first contactee to maximise his commercial potential, but Daniel E. Fry pre-dated his initial contact by two or three years. Fry was employed at the White Sands Proving Grounds in New Mexico. Like some contactees, he exaggerated his credentials: he described himself as an 'internationally known scientist, researcher and electronics engineer, recognised by many as the best informed scientist on space and space travel'. But Philip Klass discovered that Fry was in fact a skilled instrument maker who had designed and built small devices used in missile control systems.

Fry had his first contact at White Sands on 4 July 1949 or 1950 – ten years later, he was not certain of the date. That night, he said, he missed the bus which was to take him into town to see the traditional fireworks, so he walked out into the desert instead to enjoy the cool night air. As he looked up he noticed that the stars were being blotted out by something descending. Shortly afterwards a metallic object, oblate spheroid in shape, settled on the desert floor about seventy feet away from him. As he approached to investigate, a voice speaking in American slang warned him to keep away from the hot hull. At this Fry fell over a root, and the voice attempted to calm him. It belonged to an extraterrestrial called A-lan who was communicating with him telepathically. In fact the craft was remotely controlled from a mother ship orbiting the Earth, and was there to collect air samples.

A-lan invited the Earthman inside, whereupon the craft took off and travelled to New York City and back in half an hour. This would have meant attaining a speed of 8,000 miles per hour, yet Fry felt nothing except a slight motion. He was released back into the desert with the promise that there would be further contacts. Fry was given the task of preaching the aliens' philosophy of 'understanding' to human society. The beings turned out to be the descendants of a previous Earth civilisation which had emigrated into space in the distant past.

One of Daniel Fry's 'spinning UFO' photographs.

Fry produced several books and clear daylight photographs of space-craft (see opposite) and founded a quasi-religious order called Understanding, in order to spread the word. His first book was published just after Adamski's, and given his scientific background should have up-staged his rival's. However, Fry agreed to take a lie detector test on live television – and failed it. The result of a polygraph test is open to interpretation by the operator, but it damned Fry in the eyes of the media. Yet it is hard to conclude that the scientist was a hoaxer: he had a good, well-paid job and must have known that his claims of meetings with the space brothers would ruin his career.

George King – 'primary terrestrial mental channel'

Born in Wellington, Shropshire on 23 January 1919, taxi driver George King had a strange experience in his London flat when he was thirty-five. But having practised yoga since 1944, he was mentally prepared when a voice commanded: 'You are to become the voice of the inter-planetary parliament.' His first contact was with an alien from Venus called 'Aetherius', and out of this grew the Aetherius Society. It still thrives in many countries including Britain, the USA, Canada, Australia, New Zealand, Nigeria and Ghana. Many years ago 'Sir' George King vacated the damp London climate for the foothills of California.

After that initial contact King became a direct voice medium for the extraterrestrials. One of his contacts was Jesus Christ, who apparently now resides on Venus. He claims to have met Christ on a hill where he emerged from a spacecraft; the Messiah gave him some new teachings called 'The Twelve Blessings' to pass on to mankind.

The Aetherians use various paraphernalia including a 'prayer battery'. Richard Lawrence, the society's European secretary, described the apparatus in an interview with Peter Hough: 'With this we can do something which the Vatican cannot. Two hundred members highly trained in Buddhist mantra and Christian prayer regularly meet, charging up the battery with great prayer energy. In a matter of minutes, this beneficial energy can be directed to any location in the world.'

Indeed, the Aetherians claim that many natural disasters around the world would be even worse if it was not for the release of prayer energy from these batteries. The internal construction of the apparatus is secret, and no outsider has been allowed to examine it.

In his book *You Are Responsible*, written in the fifties, King describes a visit in an out-of-body state to Mars, where he is wounded by a dwarf with a ray gun. Later, he is commandeered to help the Martians destroy an intelligent meteorite which is attacking their space fleet. King finally defeated the sentient lump of rock 'with a weapon of love'.

Many Aetherians, including those with a scientific background, believed and continue to believe this rather far-fetched sounding scenario. How did the Aetherius Society cope with the information from space probes in the sixties and seventies, when it was discovered that conditions on Venus and Mars could not support advanced, oxygen-breathing life forms? Their answer was that the Master Aetherius and his colleagues became spiritual entities, not beings of flesh and blood. But in that case, why do they need space vehicles? Lawrence claims that the beings can manipulate energy and matter by tuning it to different vibrations, making it appear sometimes 'solid' and at other times more insubstantial and 'ghostly'.

Richard Miller and the spaceship *Phoenix*

One of the lesser-known contactees of the 1950s was a man called Richard Miller. He had his initial close encounter in 1954, after contacting extraterrestrials on short-wave radio. They instructed him to go to an isolated location near Ann Arbor in Michigan, where after fifteen minutes a disc-shaped object appeared and landed nearby. This, he was to learn, was called *Phoenix*. A doorway opened in the base of the vehicle and a staircase descended. Miller described what happened next. 'There, standing at the head of the stairway, was a young man dressed in a brown one-piece suit. He beckoned me to enter the ship, which I did. I was standing in a large circular hallway which seemed to encircle the whole craft. Although nothing had yet been said, the young man radiated a kind of friendliness which put me at ease.'

Miller was taken to the control room of the ship where he met the alien commander, Soltec, who greeted him in perfect English. He explained that their planet, Centurus of the Alpha Centauri system, belonged to the 'Universal Confederation', a group of over 680 planets which earned the right to membership by their evolutionary progress.

The contactee was told that, before Earth could become a member, mankind would have to awaken to higher spiritual values: 'When love of your fellow man becomes established, then will the Sons of Light appear and the Kingdom of your God will reign on Earth.' The 'Sons of Light', Miller was told, were what the Bible referred to as 'angels'.

Sceptics often ask why intelligent aliens would contact ordinary men and women and not some higher, more influential authority. Through Soltec, Miller provided an answer to this criticism. The extraterrestrials *had* contacted government heads and top scientists, he was told, but they had spurned the aliens, not wanting to give up their power base in the coming New Age; a cover-up had been agreed by the establishment. So Soltec and his friends sought to contact general members of the public, in the hope that they would spread the word and that the resultant pressure would force governments to change their policies.

Soltec went on to describe how the Atlantians had fought a nuclear war with their neighbours, the Lemurians, which was a result of material greed. Referring to modern civilisation, Soltec said: 'There is a much safer way to utilise the power of the atom than by trying to split it or break it up. Do they not realise that by destroying matter, they are opposing the will of the Creator?'

Soltec also explained about the 'Big Bang' theory, which holds that whole galaxies are travelling through space following a central explosion which brought about the creation of the universe. Currently, he said, the Earth was moving through a cloud of radioactive particles. The alien spacecraft, in orbit around the Earth, were reflecting the radiation away before it could pierce our atmosphere.

Richard Miller's contacts continued for over twenty years, all meticulously recorded in a library of writings and tape recordings.

The strange tales of Frank Stranges

Dr Frank Stranges, like Daniel Fry, is academically well qualified, making it hard for sceptics to understand why he should involve himself in 'space age gobbledegook'. An evangelist, he combines the teachings of his faith with the teachings of extraterrestrials gleaned from his various contacts.

Since 1956 Stranges has claimed many encounters with UFOs and their occupants, which are described in three books. One of them, *My Friend from Beyond Earth*, is similar in many particulars to Kenneth Arnold's famous sighting (see Chapter 5). In a later book, *Stranger at* the Pentagon, Stranges describes his meeting with Val Thor, a man from Venus, in the Pentagon Building in Washington.

> I then saw one lone man … It was as though he looked straight through me. With a warm smile, and outstretched hand, he slowly started towards me. I felt strange all over. As I gripped his hand, I was somewhat surprised to feel the soft texture of his hand … like that of a baby. His eyes were brown and his hair wavy brown, also. He was to all appearance like an Earth man, but *he had no fingerprints*.

The Venusian knew Stranges' name, and was there with the knowledge of American officials who were doing some tests on his clothing. 'He produced a one-piece garment that glittered as he brought it towards the sunlight streaming through the window. I asked him how it held together. He demonstrated by holding the front together, passing his hand as though to smooth it out, and I could not even locate the opening. It was held together by an invisible force.'

Val Thor was some sort of interplanetary missionary on behalf of 'the Lord'. He and his kind felt that man had drifted too far away from God and needed some help to get back there. The alien even hinted to Stranges that he might be Jesus Christ.

Truman Bethurum was taken aboard a flying saucer by a platoon of little men. There he was introduced to their female captain, Aura Rhanes, who could pass for human. Bethurum wrote in 1954 that she 'tops in shapeliness and beauty.' He later saw her in a restaurant, sipping orange juice, but she ignored him.

The contactee circus

There were many other contactees, including George Van Tassel, Truman Bethurum, Gabriel Green and Reinhold O. Schmidt. Many modern ufologists, such as Jerome Clark, view the contactee era as an embarrassment, a circus of deluded and perhaps over-imaginative men who preyed on the hopes and fears of others. Certainly they took to the lecture circuit like a duck to water, peddling stories of alien contact to a receptive audience who were willing to pay to hear what they wanted to hear.

This all happened in the immediate post-war era, when the world understood that man now had the power to destroy the entire planet. The aliens who courted the contactees were angelic beings who wanted to help us save ourselves from the holocaust. Many of the contactees were sincere people who brought hope and solace to their audiences and readers. But did the contactees have anything to do with ufology, or was it just a scam riding on the back of genuine UFO reports?

There are some researchers who think the contactee phenomenon was part of the CIA anti-UFO plot (see Chapter 10). What better way

Flying Saucers Have Landed – the book which tells the story of George Adamski's encounters.

of defusing intelligent public interest than by encouraging people to peddle tales so outlandish that they were guaranteed to quieten respectable members of society. In the meantime the authorities could continue their clandestine investigations unimpeded by enquiring busybodies. Even more important, it allowed governments to keep the lid on the pot. This probably contained a stew of potentially damaging ramifications should any government have to admit the reality of UFOs. Such an admission of impotence could bring about sociological and financial chaos around the world.

So what was behind the contactee phenomenon – fraud, delusion, disinformation or genuine contact with 'aliens'? It is quite possible that all of these things played their part. Certainly there were people out to make a fast buck, and there were individuals who wanted to believe they had been chosen as disciples of an intergalactic order. Just as likely is the probability that many were the witting or unwitting puppets of government security agencies. But were there actually any aliens?

Many commentators poured scorn on the names of George Adamski's extraterrestrial brothers – Orthon, Ashtar, Firkon and Kalna. But Adamski claimed they did not have names: they were an invention of his ghost writer to make the story more digestible to the public. One wonders just how much of the original story was sacrificed for commercial reasons. Stripping away some of the layers reveals a darker side not generally acknowledged at the time.

Fundamentally, it seems reasonable to conclude that some of the contactees were dealing with an objective phenomenon – an intelligence. This could have been extraterrestrial, but more likely something masquerading as such.

—— 12 ——

ALIENS OVER EUROPE

In October 1954 Europe experienced its first major UFO wave.

According to Ralph Noyes, then a British diplomat and later head of the Ministry of Defence section that handled UFO data, the Washington flap of 1952 had a profound effect across the Atlantic. RAF intelligence officers flew to the Pentagon to find out what was going on. Ruppelt recalled the visit, referring to a six-page list of questions that they had brought with them!

Recent data obtained by ufologist Gary Taylor from the British Public Record Office gives clear evidence of government activity at the time. Winston Churchill wrote from the Prime Minister's office on 28 July 1952 demanding of his Secretary of State for Air: 'What does all this stuff about flying saucers amount to? What can it mean? What is the truth?' (A copy of the memo is reproduced on page 120.) In response, intelligence staff were sent to the USA and the Prime Minister was advised by the Air Ministry on 9 August that a 'full intelligence study' into UFOs had been carried out in 1951. From this they had concluded that 'all the incidents reported could be explained' (citing astronomical and meteorological phenomena, balloons, birds, optical illusions, psychological delusions and deliberate hoaxes). They added that the Americans had told them that they had found the same in 1949 (Project Grudge, which of course was by no means as straightforward as Churchill was misinformed).

Now, as Britain and America consulted over new developments, the UFOs conspired to establish their global nature. In September 1952 a major NATO exercise was under way in eastern England and the North Sea. Called Operation Mainbrace, it involved aircraft and ships of various Allied powers. But was a third party taking part in these war games?

Subject File B.7.6.8.52   Defence (Research).

PRIME MINISTER'S
PERSONAL MINUTE

5

SERIAL No. M. 412/52

SECRETARY OF STATE FOR AIR

LORD CHERWELL

What does all this stuff about flying saucers amount to?   What can it mean?   What is the truth?   Let me have a report at your convenience.

W.S.C.

28 July 1952

Playing tag with the RAF

On three consecutive days – 19, 20 and 21 September – major close encounters took place amidst the exercise. On the 19th, at 10.53am, a 'silver and circular' object was seen following an RAF Meteor jet as it overflew a base near Dishforth in Yorkshire. Five air crew were witness to the event. One of them, Flight Lieutenant John Kilburn, described how it was 'swinging in a pendulum fashion' as it descended. This is an early reference to the so-called 'falling leaf' motion (he even used the term 'similar to a falling sycamore leaf'). UFOs often display this unusual flight pattern, which can be mimicked if you drop a plate into a bowl of water.

The Dishforth UFO then gave up its pursuit of the landing jet, hovered in mid-air, rotating on its axis, and left 'at an incredible speed towards the west, turning on a south-easterly heading before disappearing'. Such changes in direction and speed defy identification as a balloon.

The base commander at RAF Topcliffe received a number of reports from residents in the York and Thirsk area who had evidently also seen the UFO. A man at Easingwold spoke of a bright silver object that kept appearing, then disappearing; it hovered and finally shot away at great speed.

The next day a photographer aboard a US Air Force carrier in the North Sea was taking official film of an aircraft when he saw officers staring at the sky. He looked up and saw another silvery disc, of which he took several photographs. That film has not been released.

Twenty-four hours later no fewer than six RAF jets over the North Sea observed a similar silvery object in daylight. They closed in on the target and it accelerated away. Then it played tag with one Meteor, turning as it turned, before growing tired of the game and streaking away far beyond the capabilities of the RAF. This form of behaviour was becoming repetitive.

Ruppelt says an RAF intelligence officer then based at the Pentagon told him that the Operation Mainbrace reports led to official recognition of UFOs by the British government – especially since it followed swiftly on top of the Washington flap.

Official suppression

RAF encounters became quite common. In many cases the crews were advised to say nothing as the matter was covered by the Official Secrets

See opposite
Winston Churchill's memo to the Secretary of State for Air, Lord Cherwell.

Act. Ralph Noyes has confirmed that he has seen gun camera film of UFOs that were captured by pursuing RAF jets. None has been released.

There are various references in the archives of the Public Records Office to letter FC/S.45485/Signals (13 January 1953). This appears to have been about the implementation of new policy arising after the envoys had returned from the Pentagon. Clearly it was decided to upgrade UFO study in Britain considerably.

A restricted memo of 16 December 1953 sent to senior air staff in southern England told how sightings of UFOs by 'Royal Air Force personnel are in future to be reported in writing by officers commanding units immediately and direct to Air Ministry (DDI Tech) with copies to group and command headquarters'. This report also noted that 'the public attach more credence to reports by RAF personnel' and, as such, 'it is essential that the information should be examined at the Air Ministry and that its release should be controlled officially'.

Military personnel who dared tell their story of a close encounter after many years have often referred to the order to remain silent. We now have proof of that order, as this 1953 memo added: 'All reports are, therefore, to be classified "restricted" and personnel are to be warned that they are not to communicate to anyone other than official persons any information about phenomena they have observed.' So, in Britain, an official cover-up of the best-quality UFO evidence had been ordered right from the top and was in force by 1953 as a direct result of the events in Washington and during Operation Mainbrace.

Typical incidents during this intense period include the encounter over Salisbury Plain one winter's day in early 1953. Flight Lieutenant (later Wing Commander and an MoD radar specialist) Cyril Townsend-Withers was at 55,000 feet aboard a Canberra stripped bare to avoid weather effects on the new radar equipment. Suddenly he spotted an object dead ahead – both visually and on radar – which he termed 'a reconnaissance device from somewhere else'. It was a flat silver disc with two small 'fins'. As the jet made a radial turn the object sat there waiting for them to fly straight at it. They closed in and prepared for evasive tactics, but the UFO flipped into a vertical mode and shot skywards at an unbelievable speed.

Townsend-Withers awaited the required expiry of thirty years under the Official Secrets Act before he could talk. The radar system was thoroughly checked and was working perfectly. The RAF told the officer that a top-secret project was investigating the many sightings like his own at RAF Farnborough and was working on the premise that they could be alien craft.

The British magazine Flying Saucer Review *was launched in 1955 in the aftermath of the wave and became the first successful international UFO journal to be published regularly.*

Definitely not a balloon

Then, on 4 April 1957, a spectacular series of radar spottings occurred at RAF West Freugh in south-west Scotland: three separate bases tracked the object as it crossed the region. News was briefly made public, as some of the operators had been civilians. The Civil Defence organisation was put on alert before the subject was quickly hushed up. The commanding officer at West Freugh, Wing Commander Walter Whitworth, merely stated; 'I have been ordered by the Air Ministry to say nothing about the object.' A later press story stated that the UFO could have been a balloon, and this idea was generally accepted by sceptics. Only with the release of the official reports after they had come out of the jurisdiction of the thirty-year rule could it be seen that this theory was never remotely tenable.

The object was at a fantastic height (70,000 feet was recorded by Balscalloch radar, but this information was concealed because it exceeded aircraft capabilities of the day). The UFO changed course when 'it made a very sharp turn . . . to the SE at the same time increasing speed', said a secret Air Ministry report dated 30 April 1957. The UFO moved at 70 mph, then accelerated to 240 mph. As the same report concluded: 'There were not known to be any aircraft in the vicinity nor were there any meteorological balloons. Even if balloons had been in the area these would not account for the sudden change of direction and the movement at high speed against the prevailing wind.' It seems that the Air Ministry were learning well from the 'debunk at all costs' tactics then in use by Project Blue Book in the USA.

Furore in Whitehall

However, by far the most important UK sighting of the decade was never made public – at least, not until the University of Colorado study of UFOs in 1967 found it by accident. The USAF officer who told them assumed that the scientists would already know all about it, because – according to public statements by the White House – the team had complete access to all the US government's UFO data. The USAF officer knew the matter had been investigated eleven years earlier. What he did not know was that this vital case had never become part of the Blue Book or MoD public records.

The events occurred over the night of 13–14 August 1956. Three separate ground radars – at the RAF/USAF bases of Lakenheath and Bentwaters in Suffolk and the RAF command centre in East Anglia at Neatishead – all tracked an object which was seen by ground staff as well as from above (air crew looking down upon it from a USAF transport plane).

Squadron Leader Freddy Wimbledon – in charge of battle alert station that night – has subsequently told how he scrambled two RAF Venom fighters into the area in response to the USAF sightings. The first jet, he alleged, used the correct codes, locked on to the target with its airborne radar and also saw the light – which instantly swept around to the back of the plane and began to follow it. We have also tracked down and talked to civilians in Cambridgeshire who apparently saw the Venom streak overhead with the UFO in hot pursuit near Ely and Lakenheath!

It is hardly surprising that this case created a furore in Whitehall. Ralph Noyes says that the whole place was buzzing with it, and when in 1969 he came to take on the task of heading an MoD department which received UFO data he was fully briefed and shown the gun camera film taken by the Venom. Whilst this apparently only depicts a fuzzy light visible for a few seconds, it is further proof of the value of this most extraordinary encounter – especially as the MoD continue to choose not to release the film.

The scientists at the University of Colorado – whilst rejecting any validity to UFO sightings in general – concluded of this particular case that it was 'the most puzzling and unusual' in their files, adding that 'the apparently rational, intelligent behaviour of the UFO suggests a mechanical device of unknown origin as the most probable explanation'.

Yet the MoD says of this affair that it has 'lost' all record on its files, that it was never among the fifteen thousand cases on the Project Blue Book archives declassified in 1976, and that its gun camera film remains secret forty years later. Indeed, but for a fluke we would not know that this incident had ever occurred. How many others like it are out there somewhere?

Oddly, despite the fact that this classic case must have generated rainforests of paperwork, the Public Record Office files contain only one brief reference which appears to relate to it. This comes in an Air Ministry briefing paper offering assistance to a minister facing questions in the House of Commons. Some of these came from the then MP, NATO defence committee officer and future President of BUFORA (British UFO Research Association), Major Sir Patrick Wall. The paper is dated 2 May 1957 and describes radar contacts with UFOs during the past year.

It refers to three radar contacts during 1956. One was picked up on the airborne radar of a Vulcan bomber, but the crew saw nothing

visually. A second involved a radar lock by an aircraft sent to intercept an object tracked by Weathersfield radar. The third was 'an unusual object on Lakenheath radar, which at first moved at a speed of between two and four thousand knots and then remained stationary at a high altitude'. These latter two (whilst undated) may both refer to the night of 13–14 August 1956, as some details do match.

Claims that aircraft were sent in pursuit of UFOs were common during the early 1950s. Some photographs (from then and later) do exist, but sometimes the UFO is suspected to be a defect on the film that was accidentally in shot when the aircraft was being photographed.

18,000 mph!

In 1991, by more good fortune, we discovered that there was a sequel to this 1956 incident which the minister was never briefed about. A retired RAF fighter pilot contacted Jenny Randles and reported an episode which befell him, his navigator and the two-man crew of a similar Javelin fighter during the afternoon of 30 August 1956 – just two weeks after the Lakenheath/Bentwaters affair had rocked Whitehall and Washington.

The pilot again assumed that he was now free to talk about the matter since thirty years had elapsed. Investigations by Paul Fuller and others have uncovered data from official records and other sources that go some way to verifying this story. We even have his duty log book for the day in question, in which he had noted alongside his mission details: 'UFO !' Yet public records contain no reference to this case, despite its obvious importance – suggesting that it may be one of many.

At the time the two Javelins were practising air intercepts: one aircraft was used as a target while the other tried to fly across its path in mid-air. They were just south of the Isle of Wight at 45,000 feet, well above cloud cover and in perfect visibility.

The navigator manning the radar preparing to lock on the target aircraft picked up an object some nineteen miles north-east. Looking visually, the crew saw a glint in the distance as they closed in on their pre-planned position. They requested permission to abandon the exercise and pursue this object, which was granted. The target aircraft caught up with them, to fly alongside. In the meantime the UFO had moved ahead of them to cross their path and had slowed down to a near halt.

By now the crew and both radars had a lock on the object and the jets went into a steep bank to intercept the target. Radar showed it to be almost stationary and they were closing in fast. They obtained a good visual sighting of a grey metal disc.

Then – at eight miles from intercept – the UFO suddenly shot vertically upwards and left the radar scopes at the unbelievable speed of almost 18,000 mph! The four crew members were told to report the matter to the Air Ministry. A secret ground radar station at Sopley near Bournemouth confirmed that it too had tracked the object.

Official excuses, public hysteria

Evidence is overwhelming that there were many dramatic sightings such as these occurring throughout the 1950s – both in the UK and in the USA, and almost certainly high above many other countries too. They must have confirmed to the authorities that UFOs were real phenomena with amazing abilities and utterly inexplicable. Further secrecy was guaranteed by them.

As these cases were influencing judgment in Whitehall, the Pentagon and elsewhere in secret, Blue Book was debunking everything in sight. Governments almost everywhere else were explaining away sightings as fast as they were made or hiding the best data. Contactees created amusing headlines, and hysterical protestations about massive cover-ups kept coming from popular writers and the countless private UFO groups now springing up all over the world.

The official view was always that UFOs were nonsense. The public outcry from the extremists was that aliens had landed and the world governments knew this fact for certain. The truth probably lay somewhere in the middle – that unexplained and baffling UFO events were happening frequently, but nobody really knew what was causing them.

The Nordics and the Greys

Amidst all this, in October 1954, the first major wave outside the continental USA struck in France and Italy, spreading also into other countries, including Britain. For the first time reports of alien entities were coming in. But these were not from contactees meeting friendly space brothers; they were made by highly credible witnesses.

France took the brunt of these reports. Many involved small figures, under four feet tall, wearing silvery diver's suits. At Quarouble on 10 September 1954 a man was alerted by his dog barking furiously; when he investigated, he found an object that had landed on railway tracks by his house. Heavy indentations in the sleepers were later recorded by the police. Two entities fired a beam of light at the witness, who was endeavouring to chase off what he assumed were vandals. The beam 'froze' him in place until it was turned off.

Several more French cases during September and October included paralysing beams – sometimes fired from small objects like flashlights held by the entities. From this time, too, came the first well-attested reports of the engine and lights of motor vehicles failing in the presence of a UFO.

At Torpo in Norway on 23 November 1954 three witnesses saw a round object with a transparent dome on top. Inside this was a human-like figure operating controls and wearing goggles. The object shot upwards, hitting a power line as it did so and sending a shower of sparks down to Earth.

The most impressive sighting in Britain during this particular wave occurred on 21 October 1954 at an isolated house near Ranton in Staffordshire. Mrs Jessie Roestenberg hid with her children under the table as a large object with a transparent dome circled around, giving off a pulse of ultra-violet light. In the dome, as if curious tourists, were two 'ski-suited' men with blond hair.

The flood of such cases settled into a clear pattern. There were two basic types of entity, and they behaved in a remarkably consistent way.

First there were the tall, or near human height, figures such as at Ranton, often with blond or white hair and blue eyes (sometimes

Over two-thirds of the autumn 1954 wave in Europe were focused in France, which subsequently became the leader of European research into the subject.

127

Photographs of aliens began to appear during the early 1950s – including this image of a landed object and spacesuit-clad figure reportedly taken in July 1952 on the Bernina Mountains of Italy by Giampiero Monguzzi. It is widely believed by ufologists to be a table-top model photographed in close focus.

described as looking oriental or like a cat). In appearance they resembled the popular idea of Norse gods, and were therefore nicknamed 'Nordics' by UFO buffs. These entities tended simply to observe, to be compassionate or even friendly, and to display near-magical powers like wizards (such as walking through walls, possessing ESP, materialising and dematerialising). They became particularly common in Europe.

The other entities were much smaller – usually around three and a half feet tall or slightly more. They often wore silver suits and had large heads and huge round eyes. They behaved with rather less concern for any witnesses than the other group, and not infrequently rendered

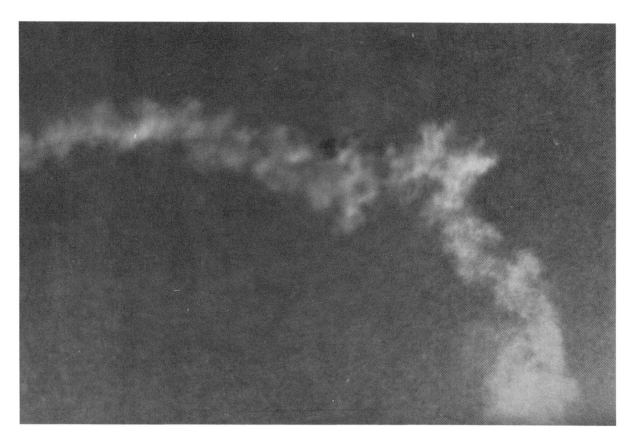

victims unconscious with a weapon of some sort. Later they became the kind of entity most frequently involved in alien abduction stories and were given the name 'Greys' because of their greyish skin colour.

The entities issue warnings

A gynaecologist in Venezuela was visited by the Nordics, who arrived in a magical flash of light and professed concern about human progress and our abuse of nuclear power. The doctor was told that these aliens would not interfere but would try to help in subtle ways (genetic engineering was even hinted at).

On the other hand these friendly Nordics knew about the Greys, whom they described clearly and claimed to have come from Orion. They were reputedly up to no good. Earth should guard against them, we were warned!

This photograph is one of the few considered truly impressive by UFO experts. It is one of a series of three taken by a postman at Namur, Belgium, on 5 June 1955. The disc-like object had reportedly ejected a vapour trail into which the object climbed. This image, showing UFO and vapour trail intermixed, is important because a vapour trail cannot form lower than several thousand feet making the size of this object too great for a model as might be used in a hoax.

THE SPACE GENERATION

Late October and early November 1957 saw an enormous amount of UFO activity.

One of the most significant periods in human history occurred in late October and early November 1957. We became an interplanetary species – perhaps in more ways than one!

In early October the Soviet Union freed mankind from the bonds of Earth by launching Sputnik 1. It was only a tiny capsule which simply went up and down, but it represented the start of a new age. Rather more significant was the mission on 2–3 November of Sputnik 2, which took the first living thing into orbit – a dog called Laika. This historic event made headlines around the world over the next few days.

Did man's space missions create UFO response?

Throughout this four-week period, and especially the key night of 2–3 November, UFO activity was enormous. If UFOs are in any way connected with intelligent beings observing humanity, then they must have noted the importance of this time. Either what took place during that period is an extraordinary coincidence, or it is strong evidence that UFOs are being intelligently controlled and made a direct response to these shattering events.

On the night that Laika (see opposite) became our first space traveller, fantastic things were afoot. The most astonishing set of close encounters struck the USA in what appears to be a blatant demonstration of superior technology.

The wave focused on New Mexico and Texas, the area where dramas had already unfolded the decade before. It was here that the Roswell events had occurred (the supposed UFO crash in 1947). The region contained sites, such as Vaughn and White Sands/Alamogordo, where the green fireballs had baffled top scientists. And in this same

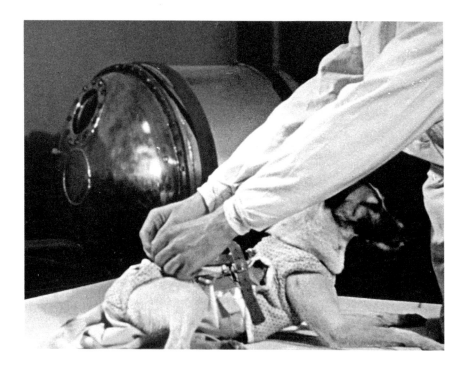

A technician prepares Laika, the bitch who became the first animal in space, for her launch aboard Sputnik 2 on November 3, 1957.

scrub desert location was Las Cruces, where the only twentieth-century scientist to discover a new planet (Professor Clyde Tombaugh, who discovered Pluto) had experienced his own UFO sighting.

The scene of this eminently topical UFO wave could also hardly have been more appropriate for other reasons. Here the first atomic weapons were detonated. Here missile and rocket technology was under intense development. There could have been no more likely place for any intelligence worried by our first foray into space to take a personal and very specific interest.

Electrical systems put out

Between 31 October and 6 November no fewer than thirty-six cases were reported of vehicles experiencing close encounters with glowing objects that impeded or destroyed their electrical systems. This was unprecedented. Undoubtedly the most astonishing came as a series of independent events that occurred between 10.40 pm on 2 November and 1.30 early the following morning – directly before the Laika mission. As many as twenty sightings occurred within a ten-mile radius of the border town of Levelland, and half of them involved physical effects created by the UFO.

Pedro Saucedo and Joe Salaz were driving a truck when four miles outside town they spotted a flying object heading straight for them.

Saucedo reported: 'When it got nearer the lights of my truck went out and the motor died. I jumped out and hit the deck as the thing passed directly over.'

There was a huge blast of wind and a wave of heat. Then the object shot into the sky, looking like a torpedo. In a semi-hysterical state the two men drove into the nearby town of Whiteface and called the sheriff's office at Levelland. The officer who took their call assumed they were drunk, but he was very soon to realise his mistake.

Under an hour later another call came in and by midnight there had been several. Soon half the town was seeing these oval balls of light roaming around the sky. Virtually every vehicle that came near one – as it sat on the road blocking the path or lay in wait by the sidewalk – was stopped dead in its tracks by some mystery force.

The sightings were unusually consistent. As soon as the object shot into the air, the ignition and lighting systems on the vehicle involved were said to have returned to normal.

By now Sheriff Weir Clem had set off with two deputies to find the intruder. At 12.15 Frank Williams, driving near Witharall, saw a yellow-red ball dead ahead and felt the power drain from his engine and lights. The object pulsated in rhythmic fashion, like lights in a disco accompanying the music. Williams's car headlights faded in and out. Then there was a terrific roar and the object shot skyward. The car now worked perfectly once more.

As each case was radioed through, Sheriff Clem sped off to the location to try to find the UFO. He failed, until at 1.30 he reached the spot where a few minutes before truck driver James Long had become the latest victim of the power-sucking UFO. Here Clem found a 'brilliant red sunset' across the highway. He drove towards it but could not catch up, and the police car suffered no interference. The object just ahead of him creating the glow was 'like a huge football', Clem reports, and shot away at great speed.

At the time Clem was in a convoy of three vehicles. Another police car with his deputies inside was behind him and saw the whole thing; they too suffered no ill effects. Ahead of Clem was fire marshal Ray James, whose truck suffered partial loss of power and lighting, but quickly returned to normal as the object streaked away. These were to be the final encounters of the night.

After the local media reported the matter, the sheriff's office received over a hundred calls from local residents who had seen the object during that three-hour spell. Newell Wright, on the road east of Levelland at 12.05, had noticed how his ammeter jumped to 'discharge', as if suddenly overloaded, then fell back to normal, taking with it all the car's power and lighting. Real, hard, scientific evidence about the power source was being gathered at last. Wright had inspected his engine but could find no fault. As he was doing so he noticed a green, oval mass dead ahead. As soon as the object vanished the car returned to normal as with all the others.

Ball lightning: another theory

Project Blue Book sent an investigator to the town three days later. He spoke with only two witnesses and quickly decided that because it had rained on the night *after* the events the UFO was sheet lightning exaggerated by hysteria. Later an idea grew that the UFOs were ball lightning – a rare form. At first this theory was supported by Allen Hynek, who later said he was ashamed of doing so – adding that, had he made any investigation, he would have discovered that specialists in this field knew that car stoppages do not result from ball lightning, and that this phenomenon is always isolated and extreme, never repeating on a regular basis.

Sadly, had anyone even checked the weather records – as Dr James McDonald, atmospheric physicist at the University of Arizona, did – they would have found that there was no storm nor any possibility of lightning anywhere near Levelland that night. Indeed, the conditions were mild and 'completely antithetical to conductive activity and lightning of any sort'.

Sheriff Clem says his investigation did what Blue Book failed to do and asked a local meteorologist about the lightning theory. The weather man said it was ludicrous. Of course, in 1957 Blue Book were aiming to debunk: they just needed an answer to this case that could superficially fool the public, not one that had any proper scientific credibility.

The Levelland events might have been a strange atmospheric phenomenon; but if so, it was one that science knows little about. Indeed, were the Levelland incidents seen in isolation (as Blue Book saw them) then the concept of such a phenomenon appears sensible. Yet there must still be disquiet about how the UFO 'showed off', almost acting like a naughty child playing with cars on a road. This sequence of events has a real hint of an intelligence behind it – as if it were a form of UFO poltergeist.

Indeed, hundreds more similar car-stop cases have occurred since 1957 all around the world, and that same feeling recurs with many of them. They seem to single out cars, toy with them, never provoke a serious accident, and then disappear rapidly. Lightning, on the other hand, avoids cars due to a physical law called the Faraday cage effect.

Car-stop cases in Britain

Exactly ten years after the Levelland events – in late October and early November 1967 – Britain suffered a major wave, with police cars chasing UFOs. Questions were asked in Parliament. Two classic car-stop cases occurred during the wave. The most impressive was at Sopley, right beside the secret MoD radar base involved in the August 1956 jet fighter chase (see page 123).

At 1.30am on 6 November a Leyland Comet diesel truck and a Jaguar car (driven by a local vet who had been out on a call) were both affected by a purple-red 'rugby ball' that hovered in front of the two of them and above a phone booth as they waited either side of a road junction. The Jaguar lost power to both its engine and lights, while the Comet truck only lost electrical power and its diesel engine continued to tick over. The object gave off a pungent odour (seemingly ozone from ionised gases in the atmosphere) and emitted a high-pitched humming noise.

The police were called to the scene immediately, and the witnesses claim the MoD sent investigators to follow up this case. Next day the road surface at the location was covered with fresh bitumen, the phone booth was repainted and scientists with geiger counters pored over the scorched grass on the embankment. Yet the MoD claim to have no record of any of this.

The truck driver was taken by police to collect his lorry from a compound in Christchurch. It had to be towed out to get it started. All the electrical circuits had burnt through and it required a new dynamo, starter motor, regulator, ammeter, batteries and bulbs.

Cases like this offer the strongest possible evidence for the physical reality behind some UFO events and tell us a great deal about the science that makes these UFOs real. It is scandalous that the University of Colorado team completely ignored the Levelland events in their two-year study project of 1967–9 (see page 174).

A UFO demo?

In early November 1957, even as Blue Book prevaricated, the Texas/New Mexico triangle was alive with more car-stop incidents. In daylight on 4 November there was a repeat run of the Levelland events, which seems to rule out any chance of their being a freak of nature. Ten different cars and pick-ups were stopped on a remote desert road between Orogrande and Alamogordo, New Mexico by a very similar-looking oval object.

Alamogordo is where the atom bomb was first exploded in 1945. White Sands, adjacent to it, is where rockets and missiles were being secretly developed. Indeed, one of the victims of this latest episode was James Stokes, an engineer working on the science of the upper atmosphere with the US government at the nearby missile development centre.

He was driving along when his radio faded and then his engine cut out after spotting a 'light colored egg-shaped object making a shallow dive across the sky'. As the thing passed at its closest Stokes could feel a kind of heat wave that made his skin tingle and hair stand on end, but, he added, 'There was no sound … When I got back in my car and checked the engine I found it intact but the battery was steaming.' The UFO flew into clouds, causing them to disperse like Moses parting the Red Sea! Presumably the electrostatic force associated with this object was causing the particles of cloud vapour to become charged and repel one another like tiny magnets. When he got home Stokes found that his skin was badly sunburnt.

The focus on such a strategically sensitive area has the hallmarks of a demonstration. Indeed, at 3am on 3 November 1957, just an hour and a half after the Levelland affair, a huge oval had been spotted descending on to the desert floor by two military policemen. They called in reinforcements, who also watched as the object pulsed in and out before departing. In this case the UFO seemed to be goading the military by its presence – right next to the disused bunkers at the Alamogordo range where the first atomic bomb had been detonated some twelve years before!

The most famous fictional space traveller, Captain James T. Kirk, alias William Shatner of Star Trek, *claims to have seen a UFO in the Californian desert.*

A further extraordinary coincidence

If coincidence has not already been stretched to breaking point by all these independent reports, the strangest is yet to come. There were no atomic explosions at the Alamogordo site in autumn 1957, but there had just been a new series of tests elsewhere in the world.

At the western Australian desert site of Maralinga, three atomic weapons were fired during September and October 1957 by the British military authorities. Derek Murray, now working as a photographer for the Home Office, was at the time a member of the RAF crew that ran these experiments.

We do not know the exact date (again the MoD claim to have no records of this incident), but it was during the last couple of days before the RAF team left the outback after their final test. They departed on 4 November, so the UFO event was very closely (possibly even exactly) coincident with the amazing episodes in the Texas/New Mexico triangle. The Maralinga event occurred at four o'clock on a hot afternoon, which equates to the middle of the night in New Mexico. They may even have occurred simultaneously!

Derek Murray was playing cards with some fellow officers when a man came rushing in to say that there was a UFO hovering over the site where the bombs had been exploded. Everyone laughed, until they saw that he meant it. Out they went, and found a flat metal disc with a dome on top, which had a clearly visible row of windows in it. It was 'perched there like a king sitting on his high throne looking down on his subjects ... it was a magnificent sight,' Murray confessed.

The thing hovered at a 45 degree angle in an aerodynamically impossible manner, as if daring somebody to do something about its audacious presence. The air traffic controller looked at it completely stunned, then dashed off to call Alice Springs. Nobody had any air traffic in this area of the Nullarbor Plains, hundreds of miles from civilisation.

Derek Murray says that the object was so real, so blatantly there and undeniable, that trained military personnel stood watching openmouthed. It then shot silently upwards and disappeared at the sort of astonishing speed that many pilots have reported during aerial encounters down the years.

The still stunned witness says of all this many years later; 'I swear to you as a practising Christian this was no dream, no illusion, no fairy story – but a solid craft of metallic construction.'

The abductions begin

Within days of the launch of Sputnik 1 in mid-October that year the first alien abduction had occurred in Brazil (see page 141). The UFO phenomenon had entered a new phase and set in motion a programme that may still be going on today. According to testimony, it involves the taking of genetic samples from humans for what is reputedly the creation of a hybrid space baby. Absurd as this is, some consistent threads do weave many of these early alien contact cases together, as you will discover later in this book.

The genesis of this bizarre story occurred right in the middle of the four-week spell between the two Sputnik launches. It adds more intrigue to the news of the reaction shown by UFOs in New Mexico and western Australia.

Although the Villas Boas story in Brazil was not investigated until January 1958 and not published in UFO records for five years, only days after Laika had breathed her last in Earth orbit there was another extraordinary alien contact case that seems to have had remarkable and related features.

The Nordic and the suburban housewife

It began in a suburban house in Fentham Road, Aston, Birmingham, on 16 November 1957. Twenty-seven-year-old Cynthia Appleton, mother of two daughters aged three and one, experienced what we would now call a 'time lapse'. She lost all memory for about an hour and was later told that there had been a failed attempt to contact her by some visiting aliens.

The failure lasted only two days. For at 3pm on the 18th, a strange 'atmosphere like a storm' filled the air with charged electricity and a rose-pink hue filled the air (all of this is very similar to what was reported at Levelland). Then there was a high-pitched whistling noise. A smell like ozone filled the room and a figure materialised inside Mrs Appleton's lounge on top of a discarded newspaper left scorched black by the electrical discharge.

The lighting conditions returned to normal and the young mother found herself staring at a tall humanoid creature with elongated eyes, pale skin and long blond hair (a classic Nordic-type entity). He wore a silver one-piece suit with a covered helmet. In Cynthia's own words, the figure looked like 'a Greek athlete'.

She was stunned at first, but then he began to communicate with her by telepathy, saying 'Do not be afraid', and a long conversation resulted. The gist of this was that he came from a planet they called Gharnasvarn (but which she thought was Venus) and wanted to interact peacefully, but could not do so because of our atomic weapons and earthly aggression.

The entity opened its arms wide and created what seems to have been a hologram in mid-air. In 1958, when this was first documented by Mrs Appleton to psychologist Dr John Dale, holograms had not been invented, but that seems to be what she was describing. Three-dimensional images of UFOs and atomic explosions appeared in this space.

This was simply the first of what turned out to be fourteen months of visits – a total of eight up to his final one on 17 January 1959. Only on the first two did the alien arrive in the pyrotechnical haze. On the others he came through the front door (having reputedly driven there!) wearing an old-fashioned suit and, on one occasion, even a homburg hat!

During these visits masses of information was conveyed to the woman. She was told that she had a brain which they could 'tune into' that allowed them to communicate better than with other people. She was given lectures about the structure of the atom, how to cure cancer by realigning the vibrational rates of sub-atomic matter, how time was an artificial concept, and even news of the development of a laser beam (documented with Dr Dale before such a discovery was made on Earth). Most of this was way above her head, and Mrs Appleton could never understand why such information was conveyed to her. She had no desire to become a media star or to set up a cult as the contactees had done; in fact she seemed rather embarrassed by the whole thing, but accepted what had occurred.

Dr Dale was very impressed and visited her several times. So did a clergyman, the Reverend G. Tiley, who said that he went out of spiritual curiosity and concluded that she was 'a very trustworthy woman. I believe her story from beginning to end.'

Her husband Ronald Appleton, a metal welder, was never present during any of these visits but stood by his wife's sincerity. On the other hand, a rather condescending doctor had suggested to her that she was suffering post-natal depression and fantasising the whole thing.

Even though Ronald saw nothing, Cynthia's older daughter, Susan, did. She was four at the time of the last visit and recalled being present when the entity arrived and said he had burnt his hand. Her mother put some jelly on to it that the man gave her, and then bathed it in water.

After the entity departed, a large piece of skin was left in the water and taken away for analysis. Birmingham University studied a sample, but failed to identify its nature. Dr Dale took some home to Manchester, where university scientists examined it under an electron microscope. They concluded that it was more like animal skin than human, but its exact form remained unidentifiable.

A twentieth-century Immaculate Conception?

The most extraordinary visit was the penultimate one, in September 1958. Mrs Appleton was doing the washing when the alien arrived at her door and calmly announced that she was going to have a cosmic child! He added: 'The baby's father will be your husband but the child will belong to the race on Gharnasvarn.' He did not specify how any of this was to come about, but told her that they knew all the details of the forthcoming baby. He (for it would be a boy) would be born in late May 1959, would weigh in at 7lb 3oz, and would have fair hair. They told her what name to give him. He would grow to become a powerful world figure.

There was one problem with this diagnosis. So far as Cynthia knew, she was not pregnant. However, she went to the doctor for a test and soon discovered that the alien was right – even though she had been less than a month into the pregnancy when he had called.

All of this was unequivocably documented before the baby was born. Ron Appleton, perhaps a little perturbed about any possible intergalactic paternity suit, stuck admirably by his wife – even when the baby was born. It was a boy, did have fair hair, was the right weight (within an ounce) and was born within a few days of the predicted date.

Ron Appleton said after the birth (naturally called what the aliens had suggested!) that Cynthia should ask the folk on Venus to cough up some money to help raise the child. In response (by a telepathic message) she was informed that they do not use money on Gharnasvarn. Ronald was quoted in *The People* newspaper as saying about the alien: 'If he shows up I'm going to tell him I'm [the boy's] father.'

Several times since its foundation, NASA (the American space agency), has been asked to mount a UFO study programme. It has always said no.

Towards a better human race

So what are we to make of any of this? Throughout the 1950s the first alien contact stories warned witnesses that the earth's misuse of atomic weapons was causing great concern, especially as we were taking our first tentative steps towards exporting deadly technology into outer space. Our visitors claimed to have superior powers, but could not (or would not) use them to stop us. We had to learn by our own actions what was right and what was wrong.

Within days of the first-ever projectile leaving Earth and entering outer space a systematic programme was reportedly set in motion, in places as diverse as a Brazilian ranch and a Birmingham street. This offers the first signs of an alien plan to improve humanity genetically – to hoist us up by our own bootstraps towards becoming a better race.

They were allegedly taking samples to try to create an alien—human hybrid and they told an English woman who would later gave birth to a perfectly normal child that she was somehow being used by them. We do not know how.

Sputnik 2 carried the first-ever living thing into Earth orbit and suddenly UFOs demonstrated their superior technology in a huge way, showing how our electrical systems can be rendered useless with ease. This demonstration focused on the centre of our missile and atomic weapons technology – the cutting edge of Western space and atomic science at that time. Indeed, to further emphasise the point dramatic appearances were set up – possibly at exactly the same time on the same day, and certainly just as Laika floated in orbit as a symbol of our earthly threat. These demonstrations were at the precise locations where the world's very first and the world's most recent atomic detonations had taken place.

Maybe this was all just a coincidence, but it certainly has the ring of something far more remarkable than that.

—14—

VILLAS BOAS AND THE ALIEN SEDUCTRESS

The night of 5 October 1957 saw a sinister shift in the alien contact phenomenon of the 1950s.

The tail end of the 1950s saw the alien contact phenomenon shift gear from an innocuous persona into a more sinister phase. It is significant, perhaps, that the flood of abduction reports in the 1980s are rooted in a case that seemed to bridge the gap between contactee stories and modern tales of alien genetic experimentation. In 1957 a Brazilian was relieved of sperm through forced copulation with a 'space woman'. Today, the aliens use more sophisticated means to remove sperm and ova from the men and women they have 'borrowed'. In the closing years of the twentieth century we would expect nothing less.

The story of the kidnapped Brazilian farmer was first brought to the attention of the English-speaking world in a 1965 issue of the magazine *Flying Saucer Review*. It was based on a report by Dr Walter Buhler of Rio de Janeiro, who had interviewed the percipient in 1961. Dr Buhler supplied to editor Gordon Creighton a full transcript of the man's declaration and a medical report compiled by Dr Olavo Fontes. These documents were dated 22 February – just a few months after the encounter.

Arrival of the intruders

Antonio Villas Boas (pictured on page 145) helped manage the family farm near the town of Francisco de Sales, in the state of Minas Gerais. Of mixed Portuguese and Amerindian origin, the twenty-three-year-old man possessed little formal education but was taking a correspondence course around the time of the incident. He was later evaluated as an intelligent individual.

A silvery fluorescence

There had been a family celebration on the night of 5 October 1957, after which Antonio and his brother João, with whom he shared a room, went to bed at 11pm. Antonio decided to open a window because the night was so warm, and on doing so observed that the yard outside was lit with a silvery fluorescence. At first the brothers decided to ignore it, but eventually Antonio's curiosity got the better of him and he went to the window again. As he watched, the light moved towards the farmhouse. He slammed the shutters to, which woke up his brother, and the two young men watched the light penetrating the wooden slats before moving over the roof, shining down between the tiles.

Nine days later between 9.30 and 10pm, the brothers were using a tractor to plough a field. Suddenly they saw an intensely bright red light at the northern end of the field, hovering about 300 feet above the ground. Antonio's brother stayed put while he went over to investigate. As he drew near, the light suddenly moved to the southern end of the field. Antonio followed it there, and the light skipped back to its original position. It did this twenty times in all. Antonio gave up and returned to João. The light remained where it was for some time, occasionally giving off rays and bright flashes, before disappearing.

Seized by aliens

The following night, Antonio was out on the tractor alone. At exactly 1am he observed a large red 'star' in the sky. Suddenly the light grew larger as it swooped down towards him. An object now hovered above him, emitting a light so bright that it swamped the tractor's headlights. This was from a red 'headlight' set at the front of the craft. The farmer thought of escape, but realised that the low speed of the tractor would make this futile. Escape on foot was similarly out of the question on the muddy, churned up soil. As he remained on the tractor in a state of terror, the craft dropped to the ground a few feet in front of him. Now the farmer was able to see it in detail, as he told Buhler.

> I could see the shape of the machine clearly, which was like a large elongated egg with three metal spurs in front (one in the middle and one on each side). They were three metal shafts, thick at the bases and pointed at the tips. I could not distinguish their colour, for they were enveloped by a powerful reddish phosphorescence (or fluorescent light, like that of a luminous sign) of the same shade as the front headlight.
>
> On the upper part of the machine there was something which was

revolving at great speed and also giving off a powerful fluorescent reddish light. At the moment when the machine reduced speed to land, this light changed to a greenish colour, which corresponded – such was my impression – to a diminution in the speed of rotation of that revolving part, which at this point seemed to be taking on the shape of a round dish or a flattened cupola.

I saw three metal supports (forming a tripod) emerge beneath the machine when it was at only a few metres from the ground. I totally lost the little self-control that I had left. Those metal legs were obviously meant to take the weight of the craft when it touched the ground on landing. I started up the tractor (its engine had still been running all this time) and shifted it round to one side, trying to open out a route of escape. But I had only travelled a few metres when the engine suddenly died and, simultaneously, the tractor lights went out. I tried to get the engine to start again, but the starter was isolated and gave no sign of life.

Antonio opened the tractor door and started to run when 'someone' grabbed his arm. In his desperation the farmer swung round and managed to throw his pursuer off balance, but three more caught up with him and hoisted him into the air. The creatures were shoulder height to him, and dressed in grey, tight-fitting coveralls with a helmet that obscured all their facial characteristics except the eyes, which were visible through lenses. They wore boots and gloves, and three tubes ran from the back of the head to the body. Antonio was carried struggling up a ramp and into the craft.

Inside, he found himself in a small square room lit as bright as day by square lamps set in the metal ceiling. The door closed so completely that there was not even a seam in the wall where it had been. One of his kidnappers indicated for him to follow into another room, which he did, not having any real choice.

We left the little room and entered a much larger one, semi-oval in shape. I believe this room was in the centre of the machine for, in the middle, there was a metal column running from ceiling to floor, wide at the top and bottom and quite a bit narrower in the middle. It was round and seemed solid. The only furniture that I could see was a strangely shaped table that stood on one side of the room, surrounded by several backless swivel chairs. They were all made of the same white metal.

Preparation for sexual intercourse

The young man was held in the room while the beings observed him and talked in a series of barks similar to a dog's. Then they forcibly undressed him and spread over his body a thick liquid which quickly dried. Two of the beings escorted Antonio into another room where blood was taken from him through a long tube. They then left him alone, and he lay down on a grey couch to rest. Suddenly he began to feel nauseous, and noticed a vapour coming out of some tubes in one of the walls. Antonio went into a corner where he was violently sick.

After a further period, the Brazilian was surprised by the entrance of a 'beautiful' naked female entity. She had blonde hair and a wide face, which came to a point at the chin. Her blue eyes were elongated and her lips quite thin. She had a slim waist, but broad hips and large thighs. Her breasts were high and well separated.

The 'woman' moved towards Antonio and rubbed herself against him. The farmer became aroused and sexual intercourse took place twice. Antonio enjoyed the experience, although it was almost spoilt when the 'woman' started grunting, 'giving the disagreeable impression that I was with an animal'. Shortly afterwards the door opened, and one of the 'men' appeared on the threshhold and indicated for the female to leave: 'But, before going out, she turned to me, pointed at her belly and then pointed towards me and with a smile, she finally pointed towards the sky.'

This indicated to investigators that she was telling him she was going to bear their child on her home planet. The female left and the other entity carried Antonio's clothes over to him, gesturing him to dress. He was taken back into the central room where several of the creatures were now seated. Antonio was left standing while they grunted amongst themselves. He decided to take an instrument, resembling a clock, to present as proof of his adventure. But no sooner had he picked it up when it was angrily snatched away from him.

Eventually the abductee was taken outside, along a catwalk, and given a conducted tour around the craft where certain features were pointed out to him. Afterwards he was allowed back into the field and the object took off. He had been on board the craft for four hours and fifteen minutes. The young man told his mother of the event – but no one else until he contacted journalist Señor João Martins, who had published an article about UFOs.

Evaluation by the investigators

Dr Fontes commented on the farmer's account:

Right from the outset it was obvious he presented no psychopathic traits. Calm, talking freely, revealing no nervous tics or signs of emotional instability, all his reactions to the questions put to him were perfectly normal. At no moment did he ever falter or lose control of his narrative. His tendencies corresponded precisely to what could be predicted in an individual who, in a strange situation, could find no explanation for certain facts. At such moments, even though he knew that the doubts expressed by him on certain questions might lead us to disbelieve him, he answered quite simply: 'I don't know about that', or, 'I can't explain that.'

Symptoms of radiation poisoning

In his medical report, Dr Fontes records that Villas Boas arrived home exhausted and slept for most of the day. For the next two nights he could not sleep and was plagued by a dreadful headache and nausea, causing him to lose his appetite. During the second sleepless night he felt a burning sensation in his eyes, followed by continual watering. From the third night Villas Boas experienced excessive lethargy for about a month, which caused him to keep nodding off. Small wounds appeared on his arms and legs which left scars, and two yellowish patches manifested on his face. It was speculated that these were symptomatic of radiation poisoning. If they were, they did not lead to any long-term health problems.

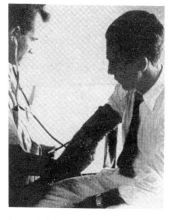

Antonio Villas Boas being examined after his abduction.

This case, and others which later emerged, were met with extreme scepticism at the time. Up until then people's experiences had been limited to objects sighted from a distance, or contacts with human-like extraterrestrials possessing the most gentlemanly manners. Antonio Villas Boas helped introduce terror and a new scenario where contactees became victims, not the chosen few.

As remarked earlier, the case bridged contactee claims and modern abduction accounts; but it was not a straight precursor for what was subsequently reported. Villas Boas remembered vividly being carried up a ramp and into the craft, while modern abductees suffer 'doorway amnesia' and have no recollection, even under hypnosis, of how they got inside.

The medical examination is central to most accounts. In many contemporary American cases, however, sperm and ova are taken from victims using medical procedures, where Villas Boas was relieved of sperm in a more natural way. Most American investigators believe the material is used to breed hybrid beings, to help reconstitute an alien race which is dying due to a reduced genetic pool. In the 1960s, investigators postulated that the female who copulated with the Brazilian farmer was such a hybrid. It is interesting that the broad face, pointed chin and thin lips exactly describe modern alien entities. However, the detailed description of the ramp and the copulation seem to have more in common with the technological and sociological expectations of the 1950s than with a hypothetical visiting extraterrestrial spaceship.

Villas Boas update

In 1978 Antonio Villas Boas broke twenty-one years' silence and was interviewed for a Brazilian television show. His private studying had evidently paid off because he was now Dr Villas Boas – a respectable lawyer living near Brasilia, married with four children. He had decided to break his silence because he was annoyed at the way his case had been treated over the years. He reaffirmed the experience with no contradictions, but added that, after having intercourse with the 'woman' for the second time, she had used a container to collect a sperm sample. Before his recent death, Villas Boas also confirmed that in the 1960s he was also invited to the USA by 'security forces' to view wreckage of a UFO. He constantly declined to discuss this further, even with his family.

Part Six

1960s:
Cosmic Watersheds

THE HILL ABDUCTION

The Hill abduction of September 1961 set a precedent for the use of hypnosis regression as a tool for exploring periods of 'missing time'.

The Betty and Barney Hill UFO abduction was the first case of its kind to be thoroughly investigated by ufologists and medical professionals. It set a precedent for the use of hypnotic regression as a valid tool for exploring periods of 'missing time' and laid down arguments still with us more than thirty years later.

'They're going to capture us!'

The Hills, a mixed race couple (pictured opposite), were returning to New Hampshire from holiday in Niagara Falls on the night of 19 September 1961. As Barney drove through the White Mountains on Route 3, traffic was sparse. Close to midnight the couple noticed a peculiar light in the sky which began to move. Barney stopped the car and Betty exercised their dog, Delsey, while he observed the object through binoculars. He told his wife it was probably just an aircraft heading towards Montreal.

As they continued, the object seemed to remain with the car, causing them to speculate afresh at what it might be. It was definitely moving, so that ruled out a star or bright planet, and if it was an aircraft or even a satellite it should have slipped over the horizon long before.

Then the light suddenly changed direction and drew closer. Betty picked up the binoculars and saw it was a disc-shaped object with a band of light around its circumference. They stopped the car once more and Barney climbed out for a better view. He was still trying to rationalise it, thinking at this point it might be a military helicopter having fun by scaring them, but he could not understand why it was completely silent. Then his wife heard him repeating over and over: 'I don't believe it! This is ridiculous!'

The object was now so close that he was able to see several figures staring down at him through lighted windows. One in particular made him very afraid. Suddenly he lost control and panicked. He cried out: 'They're going to capture us!' Barney raced back to the car and put his foot down hard on the accelerator. The next thing the couple were aware of were several 'bleeps' like the sound made by a microwave oven.

Betty and Barney Hill had an abduction experience while driving through the White Mountains on 19 September 1961.

Stress and nightmares

The following day Barney noticed some unexplained blotches on the body work of his car. There was also a soreness at the back of his neck and his shoes were badly scuffed. Some time later the Hills realised they could not account for two hours and thirty-five miles of their journey. They began to suffer from stress, but had no idea why. Betty experienced horrible nightmares in which she was taken into a room and examined by strange beings.

Hypnotic revelations

They sought medical expertise and saw two doctors in the space of more than a year. Finally they were passed on to Dr Benjamin Simon, a prominent Boston psychiatrist specialising in hypnotic therapy. In an effort to explore their anxieties, Dr Benjamin used hypnosis, regressing them separately so that neither would know what the other had said. However, so much time had passed since the event that it was never clear to what extent their stories were intertwined. They had discussed the sighting and Betty's dreams between themselves, and with others, long before they saw Dr Simon.

A terrifying story emerged that filled in the period of amnesia. Over several months an account was pieced together which told how their car was stopped by a group of strange-looking 'men' with pear-shaped heads and large wrap-around eyes. These beings forcibly carried the couple into the lighted object, where they were taken into separate rooms. Was this how Barney's shoes had become scuffed? After the 'men' had stopped his car, they 'assisted' him out of the vehicle and he suddenly felt very weak and cooperative: 'I can't even think of questioning what is happening to me. And I am thinking of a picture I saw many years ago, and this man is being carried to the electric chair. And I think of this, and I think I am in this man's position. But I'm not, but I think my feet are dragging, and I think of this picture.'

During their separation the couple underwent various tests by the entities, which included the taking of hair and skin samples. Under hypnosis, Barney described how a device was put on his genitals to extract semen. He developed a ring of warts around that area, and these became inflamed during the hypnosis sessions.

Betty claimed that a needle was inserted through her navel – this, according to her abductors, was a 'pregnancy test'. This detail caused Dr Simon to comment to investigator John Fuller: 'There's no such medical procedure. This is the sort of thing that makes me doubt the

A year before Betty and Barney Hill were abducted, a memo was sent out by the Secretary of the USAF to all base commanders. It contained these words: 'There is a relationship between the Air Force's interest in space surveillance and its continuous surveillance of the atmosphere near Earth for Unidentified Flying Objects – UFOs.'

story of the abduction.' But in later years a similar procedure was used to test the amniotic fluid cells in pregnant women for chromosomal aberrations – Down's Syndrome. Although the test had been developed in the 1950s, it was not in use until the mid–to late 1960s.

Certainly the extraction of reproduction material was the forerunner to countless similar abduction cases which surfaced strongly in the mid-1980s. They went one step further than either the Villas Boas or Hill cases. More recent abduction victims are shown their hybrid offspring by entities who had reabducted them and removed the foetuses for development 'elsewhere'.

The Hill story was very effectively presented by Fuller in his book *The Interrupted Journey*. Dr Simon concluded that the Hills were not lying, hallucinating nor suffering from any detectable psychosis. He told Fuller during their first meeting: 'You are going to have your hands full with this story. There are many things that are unexplainable in this case. I threw many kinds of tests at them during the months of therapy. I couldn't shake their stories, and they were definitely not malingering.' However, Dr Simon was later to conclude that the incident was an unconscious fantasy.

Barney Hill became so emotional under hypnosis when he was 'reliving' certain episodes that he had to be held down by several people. The authors have witnessed similar distressing abreactions with modern abductees. It seems hard to imagine an internal fantasy causing such emotional trauma in people who are not particularly interested in 'aliens' or unidentified flying objects.

A TV film was made of the Hill case. Entitled The UFO Incident, *it was shown in several countries during the mid 1970s.*

Betty Hill's 'star map'

One of the pieces of tangible evidence was a 'star map' that Betty Hill recalled seeing inside the craft.

> There were all these dots on it. And they were scattered all over it. Some were little, just pin-points, and others were as big as a nickel. And there were lines, they were on some of the dots, there were curved lines going from one dot to another. And there was one big circle, and it had a lot of lines coming from it. A lot of lines going to another circle quite close, but not as big. And these were heavy lines. And I asked him what they meant, and he said that the heavy lines were trade routes. And then the other lines, the solid lines, were places they went occasionally. And he said the broken lines were expeditions.

Later, under post-hypnotic suggestion she was able to reproduce the map. In 1974 Ohio schoolteacher and amateur astronomer Marjorie Fish published the results of her studies of the map, which Betty Hill had said was three-dimensional.

Ms Fish wondered if the map might correspond to a star system. She restricted her search to a thousand stars situated within fifty-five light

The front cover of *UFO Review*, issue 9, which featured Betty Hill.

years of our sun. Next she concentrated on those stars which astronomers thought might have planets capable of nurturing intelligent life. After five years Ms Fish thought she had a match. Indeed, one of the stars was the sun, and the alien's home planet appeared to be Zeta Reticuli.

However, she could not match up all the dots on Betty Hill's map. Meanwhile another astronomer came up with an even better match. But when noted astrophysicist Carl Sagan compared the Fish map using a more accurate computer program, he found there was little similarity.

Mixed marriage anxieties

Much has been said of Barney Hill's general anxieties due in part to his colour and marriage to a white woman. Indeed, Barney was referred to by his wife as a natural worrier. On the journey home, before the abduction, the Hills stopped at a restaurant. These were his feelings about that visit, as expressed during hypnosis:

> There is a dark-skinned woman in there, dark by Caucasian standards, and I wonder – is she a light-skinned Negro, or is she Indian, or is she white? – and she waits on us, and she is not very friendly, and others are there and they are looking at me and Betty, and they seem to be friendly or pleased, but this dark-skinned woman doesn't. I wonder then more so – is she Negro and wonder if I – if she is wondering if I know she is Negro and is passing for white.

The fact that the abduction 'memories' matched Betty's nightmares has been used to support the theory that there was nothing to the experience but dreams which she communicated to Barney while in a state of anxiety, resurfacing later through the medium of hypnosis. Others believe that the nightmares were a leaching through of repressed memories, later more fully released with the aid of hypnosis. But Betty did herself no favours in the years that followed Barney's death in 1969: she started seeing UFOs behind every tree and in every cloud.

Conclusions

Because of this, sceptics reasoned that the original encounter was also a misidentification of a bright star or planet, even though a nearby Air Force base had tracked an unknown object on radar that night. Perhaps

Betty's later bogus sightings are not surprising. A victim of any major trauma will find their life permanently affected by it. The victim of a knife attack will see knife men hiding around every corner, but no one ever questions the reality of the original crime.

The Hill abduction contains elements to be found in both later and contemporary cases. Apart from the medical examination and extraction of genetic material there is the common description of the entities, a floating, almost out-of-the-body sensation experienced by the couple, and of course the period of amnesia. Some ufologists have tried to separate the Hill case from other abductions, but there are too many common factors. If one falls, they all fall. Ironically, even though Betty Hill is adamant that her own experience was real, she believes that some of the contemporary cases are purely psychological.

—16—

MEN IN BLACK

In 1964 the concept of Men in Black entered the harsher reality of the UFO debate.

The concept of Men in Black (or MIBs as they are abbreviated) began as murky folklore, but in 1964 entered the harsher reality of UFO data. Although some suspect links with demonic forces far into the past, the real basis of the MIB legend began in April 1952 when a horror and science fiction buff, Albert K. Bender, latched on to the new UFO craze and created the 'International Flying Saucer Bureau' in Connecticut. It quickly spread to the rest of the world – indeed, the Bristol-based British Bureau still exists, as the world's oldest UFO group.

Broken promises

Bender's pioneer group was short-lived. After recruiting a gaggle of acolytes such as Gray Barker (who went on to become a witty writer on weird ufology), he announced the break-up of the team in September 1953. Bender confided 'the truth' to a few close friends. He said he had been visited by three men in dark suits driving a Cadillac and who had warned him to cease ufology. They explained that the US government had known about the alien origin of UFOs since 1951 and knew all of the reasons behind it. They would reveal these within five years, and civilian UFO study was dangerous.

In the coming months a few other figures associated with the old UFO group quit suddenly, and rumours spread about these mysterious 'men in black'. The legend took firm hold. In 1956 Barker gathered it together in an entertaining – if poorly documented – book entitled *They Knew Too Much about Flying Saucers*.

That might have been the end of the matter, except that in 1962 Bender finally broke his silence. The UFO truth had not been revealed.

The promises made had not been kept. Now he came out with a startling treatise entitled *Flying Saucers and the Three Men*. In this he told how the MIBs were really monstrous aliens in human disguise, on Earth to extract sea water; they had flown him to the Antarctic and scared him into submission. But in 1960 they left Earth, leaving the ufologist free to talk.

Even Gray Barker said he found it hard to believe Bender's second version of 'the truth'. To some it reinforced the mythology but Bender's book firmly ensured that an already dubious side alley of the subject was effectively rebuked by sceptics and ufologists alike.

The intruder in the photograph

But then, on 24 May 1964, Jim Templeton, a fireman from Carlisle in the North of England, took his young daughter out to the marshes overlooking the Solway Firth to take some photographs. Nothing untoward happened, although both he and his wife noticed an unusual aura in the atmosphere (seemingly reminiscent of that described by Cynthia Appleton before her 1957 encounter). There was a kind of electric charge in the air, though no storm came. Even nearby cows seemed upset by it.

Some days later Mr Templeton got his photographs processed by the chemist, who said that it was a pity that the man who walked past had spoilt the best shot of Elizabeth holding a bunch of flowers. Jim was puzzled. There had been nobody else on the marshes nearby at the time. But sure enough, on the picture in question (see opposite) there was a figure in a silvery white space suit projecting at an odd angle into the air behind the girl's back, as if an unwanted snooper had wrecked the shot.

The case was reported to the police and taken up by Kodak, the film manufacturers, who offered free film for life to anyone who could solve the mystery when their experts failed. It was not, as the police at first guessed, a simple double exposure with one negative accidentally printed on top of another during processing. It was, as Chief Superintendent Oldcorn quickly concluded, just 'one of those things . . . a freak picture'.

A few weeks later Jim Templeton received two mysterious visitors. He had never heard of MIBs: the subject was almost unknown in Britain then. But the two men who came to his house in a large Jaguar car wore dark suits and otherwise looked normal. The weird thing about them was their behaviour. They only referred to one another by numbers and asked the most unusual questions as they drove Jim out to the marshes. They wanted to know in minute detail about the weather on the day of the photograph, the activities of local bird life and odd asides like that. Then they tried to make him admit that he had just photographed an ordinary man walking past. Jim responded politely, but nevertheless rejected their idea, at which they became irrationally angry and hustled themselves into the car, driving off and leaving him. The fire officer had to hike five miles across country to get home.

A section of the photograph taken by Jim Templeton showing the mysterious figure standing behind his daughter Elizabeth.

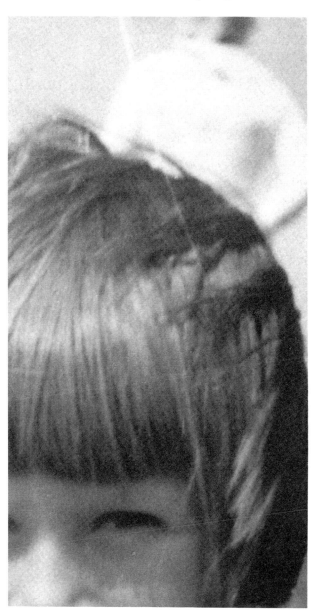

The MIB evidence

Men in Black are common in Britain and America but almost unknown in the UFO records anywhere else.

In fact, this little-known (and long unpublicised) version of the MIB story is far more the stereotype than the Bender saga. There are rarely three visitors – two is much more common. They often look very normal, except for their dark clothing. Their car, if they have one, whilst usually large and imposing, is rarely the black Cadillac so beloved of the apocryphal tales.

By far the most notable feature that singles these visitors out as more than just members of a UFO group or curiosity seekers is their irrational and eccentric behaviour. They seem uncomfortable with the English language, use strange grammar, ask bizarre questions, know a considerable amount about the background of the witness and frequently attempt to argue them into accepting a mundane solution. When they fail (usually because the theory they offer is highly improbable) they tend to respond in an unexpected manner – either leaving in a huff or getting up and walking away without another word. They seem part of the mystery, not apart from it. The fact that the real MIB scenario is less known than the early 1950s' version that gets most publicity (even in UFO books) tends to suggest that there is some substance to it.

It is certainly worth noting that, in the Appleton case, Cynthia said that after the first two visits (when her visitor was clearly identified as an alien in strange clothing) the remainder occurred in true MIB style: the being wore ordinary clothing, came in a car and sometimes brought a colleague. Had it not been for the first two visits, when the alien origin of the encounter was expressed directly to Mrs Appleton, this 1957 case would itself be better described as a typical MIB episode.

Demonic manifestations and other theories

Between 1965 and 1967 there was a new spate of MIB activity in the USA. John Keel wrote about much of this in his books *Operation Trojan Horse* and *The Mothman Prophecies*. Indeed, towns in Ohio and West Virginia where strange lights and alien entities were being seen in alarming numbers had almost as many visits from MIBs. Keel himself professed some experience of nocturnal meetings with these entities.

It was from such a maelstrom that he developed the then heretical view that no aliens were visiting us in spaceships, but that an almost demonic or interdimensional manifestation was occurring, using the extrasensory perception of witnesses. This view, whilst still very unpopular in the USA, gained ground elsewhere and now has many adherents in Europe.

Another view is that the MIBs are, like alien contacts, an act for the benefit of witnesses. What if, for example, UFOs were flown by time travellers from the future observing our society? Perhaps in cases where hard evidence of their presence is obtained, such as a photograph, they later return disguised as MIBs to try to retrieve it or to learn more about the mistakes they made.

Jim Templeton made a common assumption: that his visitors were Ministry of Defence investigators. In the USA rational witnesses presumed that MIBs who called on them were US Air Force intelligence staff. Indeed, in about half the MIB cases in both the USA and UK proof of identity claiming governmental allegiance has reputedly been shown. Names and identities have even been proffered. Unfortunately, on no occasion has any organisation who were named confirmed that these visitors are their agents. Indeed, when checks are made firm assurances to the contrary are usually issued.

On 1 March 1967 Lieutenant General Hewitt Wheless, assistant vice chief of staff to the US Air Force, even issued a secret memorandum (see page 160) to all senior personnel and divisions. It was headed 'Impersonations of Air Force Officers' and shows that the USAF were as concerned as ufologists about the matter. It cites how:

> In one reported case an individual in civilian clothes, who represented himself as a member of NORAD (the North America Radar Defence Network), demanded and received photographs belonging to a private citizen. In another, a person in an Air Force uniform approached local police and other citizens who had sighted a UFO, assembled them in a school room and told them that they did not see what they thought they saw and that they should not talk to anyone about the sighting. All military and civilian personnel and particularly information officers and UFO investigating officers who hear of such reports should immediately notify their local OSI offices.

American MIB cases tend to stress the 'alienness' of the visitor, whereas British reports of the MIB almost invariably describe them as being ordinary humans supposedly from the MoD or RAF.

What, if anything, the Air Force's intelligence unit (the OSI) found out about these matters has never been made public.

Threats, hoaxes and deceptions

Further extraordinary cases have continued to occur. Indeed, in Britain they seem more common than ever. In August 1972 a landed object

DEPARTMENT OF THE AIR FORCE
OFFICE OF THE CHIEF OF STAFF
UNITED STATES AIR FORCE
WASHINGTON, D.C. 20330

1 March 1967

REPLY TO
ATTN OF: AFCCS

SUBJECT Impersonations of Air Force Officers

TO ADC   AFSC   HQCOMD USAF   SAC
    AFCS   ATC   CAC   TAC
    AFLC   AU   MAC   USAFSS

Information, not verifiable, has reached Hq USAF that persons claiming to
represent the Air Force or other Defense establishments have contacted
citizens who have sighted unidentified flying objects. In one reported
case an individual in civilian clothes, who represented himself as a member
of NORAD, demanded and received photos belonging to a private citizen. In
another, a person in an Air Force uniform approached local police and other
citizens who had sighted a UFO, assembled them in a school room and told them
that they did not see what they thought they saw and that they should not
talk to anyone about the sighting. All military and civilian personnel and
particularly Information Officers and UFO Investigating Officers who hear of
such reports should immediately notify their local OSI offices.

HEWITT T. WHELESS, Lt General, USAF
Assistant Vice Chief of Staff

Official Air Force Document regarding appearance of individuals disguised as official agents trying to falsely obtain photos and other valuable information from civilians without authorization.

During the 1960s 'Men in Black' came to be reported in connection with UFO sightings. Witnesses would allege being visited by mysterious strangers who knew a great deal about their (often unpublished) story and would ask them bizarre questions. For a time the US Air Force became concerned as these visitors often claimed a military origin. This memo warning air bases about the 'impersonations' by men in black was circulated in March 1967.

was seen by two witnesses beside the top-secret National Security Agency telecommunications base at Menwith Hill in Yorkshire. The local police investigated right away, then called a press conference. But it never even started, because two men arrived in a large car, flashed identification that claimed they were from the MoD, told the journalists present to leave and then interrogated one of the witnesses on just one very minor aspect of the case (the method by which the UFO door opened). They had no interest in any other part of the story. The MoD deny that the visitors were anything to do with them.

Then in January 1976 a young woman in Lancashire had a terrifying encounter. After strange phone calls to her unpublicised address two men arrived and gave her a grilling in the presence of her parents (who claim they felt strangely powerless to act, as if they were 'under a spell'). The men were typically bizarre. One sat and said nothing, simply holding a strange black box close to his person. The other had only one arm, merely called himself 'The Commander', and asked peculiar questions of oblique relevance to the sighting. As in other cases they tried to get the witness to accept a mundane solution, and grew angry when she stubbornly refused to change her view of what she had seen.

In September 1976 a doctor who had been called in to consult and hypnotise a UFO witness in Maine, USA, found himself visited by two strange MIBs (actually one was a WIB – a woman in black). The man had lip gloss on his mouth and lipstick smears; he also wore ill-fitting clothes. The woman was physically lopsided. At the conclusion of the by now routine sequence of inane questions this far from UFO-obsessed witness, Dr Herbert Hopkins, was told by the MIBs that they had to go as they were running low on energy!

The extent to which witnesses report the MIBs possessing secret personal knowledge is illustrated by a former police officer who took a photograph of an entity over Ilkley Moor (see page 243). In January 1988 only about four people, two of whom were the present authors, knew about this case, let alone had the confidential witness's address or unlisted phone number. But then the MIBs arrived.

The film Hanger 18 *mystified many viewers by listing actors in its credits under the designation MIB-1, MIB-2, etc!*

The two men wore business suits, professed to be with the MoD (and showed photo identity cards to confirm this). They gave their names as 'Jefferson' and 'Davies' (*sic!*). The witness's wife was present and confirmed the meeting. The men then asked him to tell his story, which the witness did – but without mentioning the photograph. The men asked for the negative. Fortunately Peter Hough had this, as investigation was under way. The men left without any attempt to find out where the photograph was.

The following morning the witness received a phone call professing to be from a national newspaper which knew all about his case and was going to publish it. This terrified him so much that he almost abandoned the investigation on the spot, only being reassured when Jenny Randles spoke discreetly to both the London and Manchester offices of the paper in question (which never did feature the story). It was clear that they had not made any phone calls about a UFO story that morning.

Was this whole business a complex attempt by the MIBs to silence the witness, playing on his fear of publicity by making a bogus phone call? The MoD will not admit responsibility for Jefferson and Davies; and even so, how was the witness traced when his story was then secret? As with all of this accumulating evidence, if this MIB story is true then we still must ask major questions about the true origins of these mysterious visitors.

The selectivity with which MIBs are supposedly involved is curious.

An artist's impression of a 'man in black'.

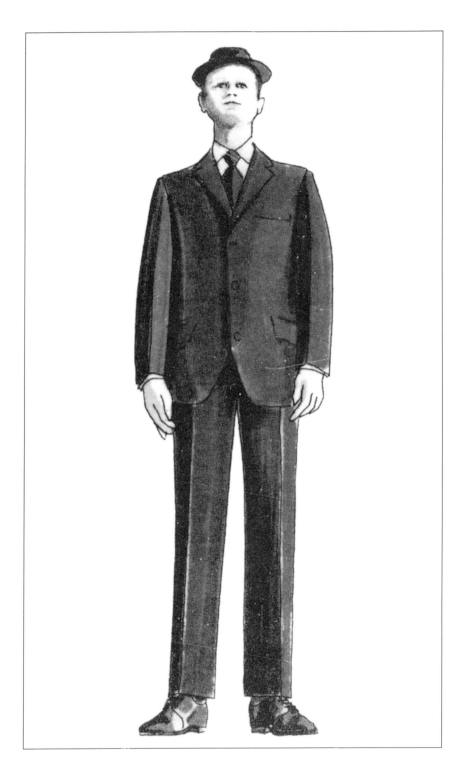

Only a handful of cases feature such visits, and they tend to be those with something unusual about them. A very credible abduction, for example, might not attract a visit. A close encounter with a small feature never reported before, such as a door that opens like a letter 'T', will . Photographic evidence seems a particular lure to such visitors, reinforcing the thought before that they mean to try to stifle new evidence.

Of course, a government investigation team might keep a look-out for cases with unusual features. If you know a lot about UFOs already, these may be just the ones to provide valuable clues. We may also understand the concern when events occur near sensitive sites, such as the 1967 event by the Sopley radar site and the 1972 landing at Menwith Hill.

There are a few occasions where MIB stories have simple explanations. In 1982 a UFO group in Swindon were given warnings to stop their investigations. Using a clever system with an automatic camera they baited a trap and photographed the MIB in live action. It was a rival ufologist!

In 1989 a series of lights were witnessed by police officers and an ambulance crew at Heywood in Lancashire. Police called in the local UFO team within minutes, and a few hours later Peter Hough and two other men from the group visited the site to interview the officers involved.

This case was, in fact, a result of rare atmospheric conditions, but a UFO magazine later published the amazing claim that another investigator had tried to interview the officers and suspected that they had been 'got at'. When he arrived at the scene three MIBs in smart suits left hurriedly. Unfortunately, the said MIBs were neither from the government nor from Mars but from the group MUFORA, suitably business-like and professionally dressed for their on-site investigation!

On the other hand, in July 1993 a man who took film of some lights of a UFO on his camcorder from an east coast town loaned it, on their request, to a UFO group. They provided no identification or a receipt (as all reputable groups will do), and the film disappeared without trace. That UFO group, as later enquiries established, does not exist.

There are countless stories of films disappearing in this manner, which is why bona fide ufologists have set up procedures to avoid them. In 1989 even Jenny Randles fell victim when a journalist arrived to make a radio programme for the BBC. At his insistence she gave him an important tape recording of an encounter at a military base. He refused to take a good-quality copy instead of the original. In fact, luckily, he was given another better-quality copy – not the original, as he believed. The programme never appeared, and extensive checks with the BBC could identify neither him nor his work.

Glasnost at the MoD

However, there are certainly times when legitimate activity by the defence authorities can be misconstrued. In October 1993 a man in a remote croft near Lockerbie in Scotland observed some lights and filmed them with his camcorder. He reported the matter to Prestwick Airport. Then a call came to his home from a man who claimed to be investigating UFOs at the MoD. He requested a copy of the tape, but suggested that if the witness was interested in a fuller investigation he should also contact a UFO group. Within the hour the witness was talking to Jenny Randles and an investigation had begun.

In the past the MoD would almost certainly have denied that they would display such overt interest or offer cooperation with a UFO group, such as giving out unlisted phone numbers. Another legend about an MIB impersonating an MoD officer could easily have been born from this simple story.

In fact there was no mystery here. A new policy at the MoD has ensured that actions like this are becoming commonplace. Indeed, in this new era of ufological glasnost the name of the MoD official involved was quickly and freely given by him – and he does exist!

—17—

ALIEN MUTILATORS

Animal mutilations hit the headlines in America in the late 1960s.

Even on a good day the UFO phenomenon barely manages to hide its dark, sinister side. When the sugar-coated candy of the contactee and channeller messages are digested, what remains is a bitter pill. At least the Men in Black display a farcical face to soften their threats and intimidation. But what of the mutilation of animals, claimed by many ufologists to be the work of aliens – where is the humour there?

In the late 1960s animal mutilations hit the headlines in America. In succeeding years the body count soared and the phenomenon spread into Canada and across to Europe – albeit in a variation of the American experience. By the close of the 1970s it was estimated that around ten thousand head of cattle had fallen victim to a methodical, skilled, cold, intelligent and unknown predator. Animals were found drained of blood, with their organs surgically removed. No one saw or heard this butchery, but UFOs were connected with it by many witnesses who observed strange lights hovering over paddocks just before the discovery of dead animals.

Yet the precursor to all of this was not a cow, but a horse – an Appaloosa saddle horse belonging to a Mrs Berle Lewis on a ranch in a remote area of Colorado's San Luis Valley.

The Lady killers

Lady – erroneously called Snippy by reporters and in several books – was given the run of the ranch in Alamosa to wander through miles of chico bush. On the evening of 7 September 1967, she arrived as usual at the ranch house for a dole of grain and a drink. She seemed in good health, but it was the last time Lady was seen alive.

The following evening she failed to turn up, and when dawn came

Memorandum

TO : Mr. Adams

FROM : R. J. Gallagher

Miscellaneous - Non-Subversive

SUBJECT: MUTILATION OF LIVESTOCK
STATE OF COLORADO
INFORMATION CONCERNING

DATE: September 12, 1975

1 - Mr. Adams
1 - Mr. Gallagher
1 - Mr. O'Connell
1 - Mr. Cooke
1 - Mr. Sheer
1 - Mr. Bowers

In response to a telephone call from Honorable Floyd K. Haskell, United States Senator from Colorado, to the Director 9/11/75, I contacted Senator Haskell telephonically today, 9/12/75.

Senator Haskell indicated his concern for a situation occurring in the western states where cattle have been discovered mutilated. The bizarre mutilations involve loss of left ear, left eye, sex organ, and the blood drained from the carcass with no traces of blood left on the ground and no footprints.

Senator Haskell repeated his request that the FBI enter the investigation. The provisions of the Interstate Transportation of Stolen Cattle Statute, Title 18, U. S. Code, Section 2311, were explained to him. It was poi... ...ere must be an interstate ... Senator ...

Part of an official memo concerning mutilation of livestock in Colorado in 1975. What could have caused such bizarre injuries?

Ben King, Mrs Lewis's brother, called his sister and they went in search of the horse. When they discovered the carcass they could not believe their eyes: the neck and head had been completely stripped of flesh, but there was not a drop of blood on the ground. More than a month later, a Denver pathologist carried out an autopsy on the animal. He was shocked to discover that the abdominal, brain and spinal cavities were empty. The killers had removed the internal organs with surgical precision.

Mrs Lewis's husband arrived not long after the animal was discovered and noticed a strange, medicinal smell and a substance resembling tar around the body. They noted a lack of hoofprints, footprints and tyre tracks. Nearby chico bushes had been flattened to just ten inches high, and there were several circular 'exhaust' marks and six identical holes in the ground. Ben King, an expert tracker, found the hoofprints of three horses which showed that the animals were in a headlong flight towards the ranch. The tracks split, with one set heading away. These stopped abruptly and mysteriously 100 feet away from where Lady's body now lay.

On 16 September, Mrs Lewis and some friends discovered in a bush a piece of flesh with horse hairs hanging to it. When it was prodded, the skin split and a green viscous matter spilled on to her hand, causing it to burn.

The macabre death was picked up by the media and eventually spread through the global wire services. Sheriff Ben Phillips, who declined to examine the remains, declared that Lady 'was probably killed by lightning'. A veterinary surgeon who did examine the carcass declared that the horse had collapsed due to a leg infection. He speculated that a passing Samaritan must have found Lady suffering and had put her out of her misery by cutting her throat. Natural predators had then moved in and stripped the neck of flesh and eaten away the internal organs.

Duane Martin of the Forestry Service arrived on 23 September with a geiger counter. The carcass showed normal background radiation, but some distance away, and around the 'exhaust' marks, the readings were higher. The mutilation of Lady was not as mundane as the sceptics reported, but was it as bizarre as many believed?

The UFO connection

Prior to Lady's death there had been a spate of unidentified lights over the area. It was these that caused Mrs Lewis to comment: 'I really believe that a flying saucer had something to do with Lady's death.' Her eighty-seven-year-old mother reinforced the belief when she was interviewed. Mrs Agnes King lived in a cabin just a quarter of a mile from where the horse was found. She told reporters that a large unidentified object passed over the cabin on the evening Lady did not show up for her feed. Mrs King was judged to be remarkably alert for her age.

However, most ufologists were cautious. As late as 1980 the Aerial Phenomena Research Organization (APRO) reiterated: 'APRO does not claim that Lady was killed by "flying saucer people", rather that she died in a very strange manner and that her death has yet to be satisfactorily explained.' Others, though, are more convinced of the UFO connection. The Doraty abduction case is a CE4 (close encounter of the fourth kind, see page 183) with an added dimension.

Judy Doraty, her daughter Cindy, and her sister-in-law were driving back home from Houston, Texas after an evening out in May 1973.

Charles Fort, a collector of curiosities, recorded the slaughter of sheep during May 1810 at a farm in Ennerdale, Yorkshire. No bodily parts were missing, just blood, which apparently had been sucked out through a wound in the jugular vein.

The night was clearly illuminated by a full moon. Suddenly they were aware of a strange light in the sky. At some point Judy stopped the car and climbed out for a better view, although the family were not unduly concerned about it.

Afterwards, however, Judy suffered headaches and feelings of extreme anxiety. In the award-winning documentary *Strange Harvest* produced by Linda Moulton Howe (pictured below), psychiatrist Professor Leo Sprinkle hypnotises Judy and takes her back to 'relive' the journey. Under hypnosis she describes a scenario that apparently has been edited from her conscious recollection. She starts with a description of the light and then comes a surprise: 'It's like a spotlight shining down on the back of my car. And it's like it has substance to it. I can see an animal being taken up in this. I can see it squirming and trying to get free. And it's like it's being sucked up.'

Then she feels she is in two places at once – still standing beside the car, yet now also in a strange room. 'It's taken into some sort of chamber. And I get nauseated at watching how they excise parts. It's done very quickly, but the calf doesn't die immediately.'

She then describes how the excised organs have needles, or 'probes', pushed into them. Two small entities with large eyes explain to her that the work is necessary 'for our betterment'. Then horror is heaped on horror when she sees her daughter placed on a slab and the beings examine her. She begs them to stop, convinced they are going to mutilate the child too, but they only take samples from her.

Linda Moulton Howe produced the award-winning documentary *Strange Harvest* on animal mutilations in the USA. She believes they are being carried out by extraterrestrials. The documentary drew the largest audience for a locally produced programme in the history of Denver. Demand was so great it was repeated just four months after its original broadcast.

It was not until 1990 that Cindy Doraty was regressed. The hypnosis was carried out by a psychiatrist called John Carpenter in Springfield, Missouri. Cindy confirmed, for what it's worth, her mother's testimony of seeing the calf rising up into the craft in a beam of yellow light.

There have been other cases where people have apparently observed UFO entities in connection with the procurement or mutilation of animals. In 1989 Linda Moulton Howe was contacted by a security guard in Denver, Colorado, who claimed to have observed from his truck a large circle of lights over a pasture. He kept silent because he did not want to lose his job. The following day he saw a farmer gather up two dead and mutilated cows from the same pasture. Linda also investigated the case of Myra Hansen and her young son, who in 1980 had observed two white-suited beings mutilating a cow which was bellowing with pain. When she tried to interfere, she and her son were abducted for a while.

In more recent years, Linda Moulton Howe created the popular TV series Sightings.

During January 1978, four poachers received a shock on the banks of the River Weaver in Frodsham, Cheshire. They were chasing pheasants when one of them noticed a silver balloon-like object floating on the water. As they watched, it took off and landed in a nearby meadow where some cows were grazing. Shocked, they watched several figures emerge from the object; they were dressed in silver suits and wearing headgear which included what looked like miners' lamps. They approached one of the cows, which seemed to become paralysed. A 'cage' was then constructed around it, and the entities seemed to be measuring the animal.

The men had seen enough and started to run, but their escape was impeded by a force which tugged painfully at their genitals. Afterwards, one of them had a mark on his leg similar to strong sunburn.

In Japan at a farm near Saga prefecture, the mutilated corpse of a cow was discovered on 29 December 1990. It lay in the cowshed, half its tongue missing, teats cored out from the udder. On 4 January 1992, the same farmer was alerted by the furious barking of his dogs. He ran to the cowshed and saw a small white object, similar in appearance to a jellyfish, suspended in the air. It flew outside and vanished. A cow was discovered on the floor with a badly broken leg.

The killing fields

The publicity surrounding Lady's macabre demise opened the flood gates to a wave of reports by other pet owners and farmers previously too embarrassed to say anything. In some cases the organ removal was so good that veterinarians at Oklahoma State University said they were unable to produce students capable of duplicating such expertise.

Mutilated animals were turning up in Brazil, Puerto Rico and Spain as well as the USA and Canada. They included horses, cats, dogs and sheep. Cows were the predominant victims in the southern states of America. As the 1970s rushed towards a conclusion, the human players in this affair became polarised in their views. On the one side were the ranchers and local sheriff's departments who were convinced there was no rational explanation, and on the other were the sceptics and government departments like the Colorado Bureau of Investigation. The latter claimed that the animals had died of natural causes, and then been mutilated by coyotes and magpies. But ranchers, who had been around animals for many years, knew this could not be the explanation; yet when the CBI took away tissue samples for analysis, the conclusion 'done by predators' invariably came back.

Elbert County Sheriff George Yarnell, suspicious of this, cut off a piece of hide with a sharp knife and sent it to the CBI for analysis. As he predicted, the subsequent report said the cut was the work of natural predators . . .

Another explanation was that Satanists were removing bodily parts for use in rituals. However, no one has been convicted of mutilating, and for the scenario to be viable, a whole army of occultists would have to be involved to account for all the killings. Even Carl Whiteside, Director of the CBI, did not think this could be the explanation when he commented in 1979: 'The thing which has always bothered me is the absence of any physical evidence. In my experience of cult type organizations, whether it be occult, organized narcotics trafficking, or anything which involves groups of people, sooner or later you will have someone who is a member of that group who will come forward and provide information. That hasn't happened.'

A number of cases included the sighting of unidentified helicopters. It was speculated that the mutilations were carried out by a secret government department testing for pollution and radioactive contamination. Other commentators think the helicopters are disguised UFOs. Whatever the explanation, the mutilations go on unabated.

The spread of mutilation

Since the beginning of the 1980s hundreds of horses have been found mutilated in southern England and Sweden. Is this an old song set to a new tune, because the injuries are much cruder than those inflicted across the Atlantic? Or is the 'obvious' explanation the real answer – that the injuries are carried out by individuals with a psychopathic hatred of horses?

Approximately half of the animals have died, or had to be destroyed because of their injuries. These consisted mainly of cuts around the sexual organs, causing some people to resurrect the spectre of Satanic cults. Apart from a couple of arrests, the attacks remain an enigma and continue at an increasing rate. A mainstay of this mystery is that, despite guard dogs and alarm systems, horses are still mutilated. Owners wonder how someone can avoid detection and then attack a horse which apparently does not struggle or make a noise.

In August 1993, a horse was found in Oxfordshire with its hide cut from its body in squares. Sixties' pop star David Jones discovered two mutilated horses on his farm in the Meon Valley in Hampshire during July 1992. One of them had suffered an object being forced up its vagina. In response to horse mutilation, the Automobile Association brought out a special insurance policy in 1993. Stan Forbes, Regional Manager for AA Insurance, said: 'There is a sickening trend for mutilation, yet most policies don't cover it.'

Other animals, too, have been discovered mutilated in recent years. Thirty seals, were found on a beach in the Orkneys in 1991. Someone – or something – had removed their heads. According to Mike Lynch, an inspector with the Scottish Society for the Prevention of Cruelty to Animals, the heads had been removed with surgical precision.

In January 1985, forty-four ewes were slaughtered at a farm near Ballymoney in Northern Ireland. They had not been mauled, but all of them had puncture marks on the neck. Collector of curious stories Charles Fort recorded several similar cases from the nineteenth and early twentieth centuries – sheep with puncture marks through which the blood had been extracted. Peter Hough investigated a case at a farm near Rhayader, mid-Wales, where thirty-five sheep were attacked in August and October 1988. Farmer's son Charles Pugh said: 'This has been happening just three hundred yards from us, but no one has seen or heard anything. It's the strangest thing we've encountered in forty years of sheep farming.'

Are UFO entities responsible for these bizarre killings? If so, is it to extract genetic material, as some ufologists have suggested, in order to manufacture biological entities – flesh and blood robots? If so, why leave the evidence behind? Is it because they do not care, and know that no one will accept the evidence left right under their noses?

—18—

THE END OF THE ROAD

1969 saw the cessation of Air Force investigation work. Hot cases – like the Lakenheath/Bentwaters affair – have still not been declassified.

Throughout the first twenty years of UFO study there was a twin-edged attack from disparate groups with very different, even incompatible, aims.

Private UFO organisations obtained much publicity, but in the main they were believers – not investigating what UFOs might be, because they already 'knew' that they were alien spacecraft. They collected UFO reports just as others might collect stamps, and attacked the authorities because of a perceived cover-up of the truth. Ufology had become a political football, not a scientific endeavour.

The military, on the other hand, had grown weary of UFOs. In 1947 they had been charged with the secret responsibility out of fear of a threat that had never materialised. Yet some UFO sightings puzzled their scientific experts and, try as they might to squirm free, they were ordered to maintain a vigil on the data – just in case. Scientific input was minimal – Allen Hynek in the USA (by now a convert to the view that some UFOs were real, but being discreet so as to retain access to the secret data) or the occasional intelligence staff expert called upon to write a position paper in other countries such as Australia and Britain.

Attempts to pass the buck

During the early 1960s the US Air Force tried to dump the problem on to somebody else (hardly a sign that they considered an alien invasion to be imminent). Their primary target was the newly created NASA, set up to coordinate US space activity. NASA were not to be snared. But this does show the mind-set that perceived UFOs as alien or nothing. NASA became the chosen ones because their expertise was space flight.

Fortunately, as the evidence grew in stature during the 1960s with some quietly impressive cases, aided by the decreasing levels of media hysteria, the need to transfer UFO study to scientific research was gradually realised.

In late 1965 the US Air Force convened an independent review body, headed by optical physicist Dr Brian O'Brien, to assess its work. For the first time it comprised a respectable array of physical and non-physical scientists, including psychologists. One member was cosmologist Dr Carl Sagan, whose later TV spectaculars made him a household name.

The O'Brien commission met for just one day in February 1966 and came out with a host of excellent proposals. They urged that, to defuse public outcries of 'cover-up', all official UFO files should be declassified and handed over to scientists. Further, they suggested that several teams be set up at universities around the USA, with at least one psychologist and one physical scientist at each to review the best of the incoming data. In this way UFOs would finally get the sort of objective appraisal required.

Whilst this was being digested by the government, a major outcry occurred when a series of sightings hit the state of Michigan. Allen Hynek, following typical Blue Book orders to debunk on sight, suggested that swamp gas (floating pockets of glowing methane) might have been responsible for some sightings. He was probably right, but the media exaggerated this into an attempt to explain everything away. The row spread to Congress.

The most influential figure in this debate was then US Congressman and future President Gerald Ford. His insistence ensured that some of the O'Brien panel ideas were taken up, but sadly in a limited form.

Just one man was put in charge. Universities were invited to tender to do the job professionally, but only one would be selected. It was stated that the chosen university would be given full access to all government records. However, that was clearly untrue. We have already seen how one of the most impressive cases – the Lakenheath/Bentwaters radar/visual from August 1956 – was not handed over (see page 123). There are also good grounds for arguing that other major cases never were.

Colorado project

The Condon Report *is the most widely quoted UFO book ever published.*

A number of scientific establishments were on the government shortlist during 1966, but the job went to the University of Colorado in Boulder. Given the task of coordinating the project was Dr Edward Condon, a quantum physicist who was a member of the team that built the atom bomb. He had high security clearance and was to some degree 'the government's man', but he had earlier challenged government sources over a toxic poisoning scare, which gave him the credibility that the project needed to gain public acceptance. Condon built his team with a hefty grant from taxpayers' money. Indeed the Condon project, which began work in October 1966 in a blaze of publicity, was extended well into the summer of 1968, with a total budget of half a million dollars, then a good deal of money. Its members then sat down to prepare its final report, which was to be released to worldwide anticipation in January 1969. But major traumas were to split the Condon team apart before then, which left the project irrevocably tarnished.

It later emerged that many more prestigious scientific bodies, such as the famous MIT (Massachusetts Institute of Technology) all turned down the chance to participate before Colorado got the contract. Unfortunately, just a few weeks into the project Condon was quoted as saying: 'It is my inclination right now to recommend that the government get out of this business. My attitude right now is that there is nothing to it.' He added with a smile; 'But I'm not supposed to reach a conclusion for another year.' His views on UFOs were thus never in much doubt.

Equally, the selection of cases to be studied by the scientists left a lot to be desired. Only fifty-nine were researched in depth for the final report. These excluded much impressive data such as the phenomena at Levelland in 1957, and included personal choices from Condon such as a ridiculous story about aliens from a universe populated by bears.

The problem, clear to some rapidly disillusioned scientists who were involved, but not obvious to others until the final report was issued, is that Condon focused on the wrong questions. The report asked if UFOs offered evidence of an alien visit to Earth. It concluded, not unreasonably from the evidence then, that the answer was no. But the real issue is whether any UFO sightings represent unexplained phenomena. The answer to that proved much more open. Of course, because most people continued to equate UFOs with alien spacecraft they assumed that the report's negative findings about their extraterrestrial origin translated into a debunking of the entire phenomenon.

The 'trick memorandum'

Matters took a catastrophic turn when a group of renegade scientists within the project discovered lurking in the files, a memo written two months before the contract was awarded. Written by the university administrator Robert Low, and entitled 'Some thoughts on the UFO project', it was instrumental in persuading Colorado to go for the contract. In this devastating document Low had justified taking on the work by saying that the study 'would be conducted almost exclusively by non-believers' who 'could and probably would add an impressive body of evidence that there is no reality to the observations. The trick would be, I think, to describe the project so that, to the public, it would appear a totally objective study...'

The so-called 'trick memorandum' was leaked to scientists within UFO groups to prove that there was honour left within the Condon ranks. So certain were the disillusioned project members that the final report would recommend deeper analysis that they agreed not to make this memo public. To everyone's credit, it was withheld, and known only to a select few. However, in January 1968 an atmospheric physicist at the University of Arizona, Dr James McDonald (one ufologist who was shown the memo), mentioned it in passing in a letter he sent to Low and Condon. They hit the roof.

The scientists who had leaked it to McDonald, Hynek and others were fired from the project forthwith under accusations of treachery. Others walked out in sympathy and disgust. This team, led by mathematician and psychologist Dr David Saunders, gave the memo to the prestigious magazine *Look*, who featured it strongly. They also set about writing their own rival report to challenge the official version about to be edited by Condon!

There is clear evidence that the Low memorandum did form the basis of the project. He went on to become its administrator. His memo recommended that the work should stress the psychology of UFO witnesses rather than 'the old question of the physical reality of the saucer' and that, if this were done, 'the scientific community would quickly get the message.' The university psychology department were given the casting vote in whether to take on the project, and a questionnaire issued to witnesses by the team was twenty-two pages long – just one page discussing the sighting, and twenty-one asking about the psychological and social background of the witness!

In 1967, the only full year of project operation, the main thrust of UFO activity was not in the USA but centred on Europe, especially in Britain, including a debate in the Houses of Parliament because of the many high-quality sightings. Low, soon after publicly dismissing UFOs as 'nonsense', went to Europe on project business but refused to look at any British cases, talk to leading researchers or chase up data on events being studied. Instead Low visited Loch Ness and justified this decision by saying that the monster did not exist and neither did UFOs, so he needed to examine how people in Scotland were trying to research a non-existent phenomenon.

Rival reports with ironical results

The Saunders alternative project report (*UFOs? Yes!*) was first out by three months. It took a devastating view of how evidence was squandered and opportunities lost. Jenny Randles has visited Boulder in the company of Allen Hynek and his wife Mimi, where she met one of the scientists who had assisted Saunders, Dr Richard Sigismund. He affirmed much inside information about how the Colorado University team went about their task. Like many others, he had become convinced that UFOs were a real mystery.

Condon wrote the conclusions to the thousand-page official report by himself. These were cleverly put at the front, and the entire bulky text then given to the press only hours before release. Most reporters only had time to read the summary rather than the densely argued evidence (which lacked even basic facts and figures).

Whilst this all put over a very negative view, the report itself is in fact, one of the most important documents about UFOs ever produced. Most people who have read it through have reached entirely the opposite conclusions to those that Condon himself seems to have done.

Almost a quarter of the cases are considered unexplained, often in very direct terms. Typical phrases from these conclusions are 'the probability that at least one genuine UFO was involved appears to be

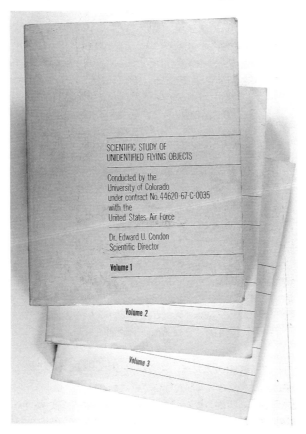

SCIENTIFIC STUDY OF
UNIDENTIFIED FLYING OBJECTS

Conducted by the
University of Colorado
under contract No. 44620-67-C-0035
with the
United States Air Force

Dr. Edward U. Condon
Scientific Director

Volume 1

Volume 2

Volume 3

The original Condon report.

fairly high', or 'this unusual sighting should therefore be assigned to the category of some almost certainly natural phenomenon, which is so rare that it apparently has never been reported before or since' (which seems a near-perfect description of a genuine UFO), or the quite explicit 'all factors investigated, geometric, psychological and physical, appear to be consistent with the assertion that an extraordinary flying object, silvery, metallic, disk-shaped, tens of metres in diameter, and evidently artificial, flew within sight of two witnesses'.

Quite how Condon could argue, after evaluations like this, that there was nothing to the UFO mystery is rather difficult to grasp. Yet Condon even urged that children should have marks deducted if they mentioned UFOs in their school work. Later he was quoted as saying that authors of UFO books should be publicly horse-whipped!

Until his dying day, Dr Edward Condon did not publicly accept that there was anything of scientific value in the UFO mystery.

Jenny Randles has taught the subject in schools to the benefit of young children. Finding out how UFOs interact with meteorology and astronomy is a positive step for many of them, who learn through a topic that interests them. This illustrates the narrow-mindedness of Condon's approach.

Fortunately many scientists saw through the façade to the heart of the report. The American Institute for Aeronautics and Astronautics formed a sub-committee of eleven scientists and challenged its findings. Then, in December 1969, the American Association for the Advancement of Science (the AAAS) gave it the ultimate thumbs down by staging a UFO seminar in Boston.

Condon was distraught. Indeed he tried desperately to stop it, even appealing to a personal friend (the then Vice-President Spiro Agnew). Agnew politely refused for the White House to interfere. Figures like Hynek and Sagan were lecturing. Thornton Page, who had been one of the CIA's Robertson Panel debunkers sixteen years earlier but had made a reassessment after seeing the full evidence, was also taking part. So were the chief analyst for photographic evidence in the Condon team, William Hartmann, and a host of scientists including atmospheric physicist James McDonald from Arizona. His brilliant in-depth and independent reinvestigation of the Lakenheath/Bentwaters case put the Condon project into sharp perspective.

A very fine, well-balanced book entitled *UFOs: A Scientific Debate*, edited by Sagan and Page, emerged from the proceedings in 1972. It was everything that the half-million-dollar Condon report should have been. A vital outcome was a declaration signed by thirteen top scientists, including all those who participated in the Boston meeting. It urged the US government to preserve the UFO archives and hand them over to a recognised scientific institute for open assessment by any qualified researcher.

Sadly, this wish was completely ignored. Indeed, as recently as 1993 Barry Greenwood located some files that had been retained by a Condon report archivist.

The US government fought back. Days after the Condon report was published, Allen Hynek was notified that his twenty-one-year tenure was over. Blue Book was closing down following the recommendations of the Colorado report. But the news was withheld from the public for the moment.

Years later, under the US Freedom of Information Act, documents about this closure process surfaced. An Air Force memo signed by Brigadier General C.H. Bolender discussing the procedure and dated 20 October 1969 gives some devastating news which was long suspected but never before confirmed in writing. The closure of Blue Book was the termination of a sham operation. Indeed, the closure itself was a sham!

Bolender reported that, even with the termination of Blue Book, 'reports of UFOs' would still 'continue to be handled through the standard Air Force procedure designed for this purpose'. And, affirming that this meant what it seems to mean, he noted that 'Reports of unidentified flying objects which could affect national security' (citing the appropriate coding procedure) 'are not part of the Blue Book system.'

In other words, all the hot cases between 1947 and 1969 – those, like the Lakenheath/Bentwaters affair, with serious implications – bypassed Blue Book altogether, were handled in other ways and (as of 1994) have still never been declassified. Furthermore, despite the alleged shutdown of any Air Force interest, all important UFO data was still to be collected by whatever department seemingly did the really significant work in secret. Blue Book had for a long time been just a public relations exercise.

Interestingly enough, after sitting on the closure for some months the US government chose to call a press conference and describe their alleged termination of all UFO interest immediately prior to the start of the AAA symposium in Boston. It seemed calculated to achieve indirectly what the Vice-President had refused to do for Condon – defuse the gathering.

If that was the plan, it failed miserably. The cessation of Air Force investigation work freed many scientists, like Hynek, finally to go public. The Condon report worked in the opposite direction to that which was anticipated. The AAAS symposium built a platform on which serious, scientific study could at last be searched.

Thornton Page reports that, a few years after the AAAS debacle, he called Condon for help when he (Page) was asked to write the entry on UFOs for the *Encyclopedia Britannica*. The ex-CIA scientific adviser and one-time UFO debunker was now writing an objective appraisal, and says in a 1984 letter that Condon's response to his telephoned request was very explicit: 'He shouted at me ... then there was a bang, and silence. I am told that he threw the phone on the floor with such violence that it broke.'

Part Seven

1970s:
UFOs Top Secret

THE WALTON STORY

The rehabilitation of Hynek

Following the closure of Project Blue Book and the new wave of scientific interest, Dr J. Allen Hynek was quick to launch his own organisation. CUFOS – now named the J. Allen Hynek Center for UFO Studies in honour of the late ufological pioneer, who died in 1986 – began as Hynek's definitive book *The UFO Experience* hit the bookstands in 1974.

The private groups now had a virtual monopoly on the public relations front, but the internal squabbles that rent the Condon report apart have since been duplicated within many UFO organisations, and these battles have seriously distracted from the work in hand. Mindful of this, Hynek built the group around scientists from an underground movement (the 'invisible college', as it was termed).

Close encounters with Spielberg

Hynek became the guru to whom the media would automatically turn. The astronomer never shirked that responsibility, but it was sometimes difficult to match it with his wider ambitions. He turned down offers to appear in TV commercials advertising beer, but let Steven Spielberg use his book to develop the multi-million-dollar 1977 movie *Close Encounters of the Third Kind*. This weird title comes from the classification scheme adopted by Hynek in *The UFO Experience*, and is still largely used today in expanded form. (Hynek defined three types of encounter. Later, working with Jenny Randles, these were slightly modified and the fourth category was added. *Close encounters of the first kind* are close up visual observations of UFOs where the object interacts with the witness or environment in some way. *Close encounters of the second kind* further involve the leaving of some physical evidence after the sighting, i.e. landing traces. *Close encounters of the third kind* not only provide sightings of a UFO but also of their crew, e.g. alien occupants. *Close encounters of the fourth kind* are alien abductions in which the entities interact with the witness and take them into the UFO or another dimension.) Hynek even appeared in cinema trailers explaining what close encounters were and had a cameo role in the movie itself, where the ufologist is seen watching in awe as the aliens land.

Hynek was a thoroughly honest and cautious man, which meant that even after forty years he was still struggling to accommodate the wilder shores of ufology, and he made these moves because he believed the time was right. Spielberg was personally interested and did make an excellent UFO movie, with many of its scenes based upon real cases. The director also indirectly aided the launch of the Center; although Hynek later suffered through arguments about whether he had given away the movie rights to his non-fiction book.

Despite the fine intentions, Spielberg's strange combination of science and showbiz had an uncertain effect on the blossoming UFO subject. In particular, the public presentation of a close encounter in such blatant fashion to an audience of millions around the world was bound to affect the data coming in.

Movies: the damaging effects

However, Spielberg's *Close Encounters* was not the first UFO movie. That distinction probably goes to the American low-budget TV feature *The UFO Incident*, a plodding but accurate portrayal of the Betty and Barney Hill abduction from September 1961. The movie premiered on US television in late October 1975 and reached much of the rest of the world just before Spielberg's incredible big-budget epic knocked them for six.

The entities in both these movies are quite similar, as they were based on the real reports gradually coming in from the USA. Witnesses spoke of small humanoids with large domed heads, huge dark eyes and white or pasty skins. The impact of screening to such vast audiences what 'real' aliens looked like began to ensure that even hoaxers described them like this, which removed an important control test. Reports began to even out after this time – worldwide, more and more took on the form of the American prototype, whereas before these movies there had been considerable variety. It is difficult to imagine this as mere coincidence.

By the time that *The UFO Incident* hit American TV screens there were perhaps a dozen well-attested abduction cases that had been studied by ufologists – including one (that of police officer Herb Schirmer at Ashland, Nebraska) which had been explored by the Condon team in December 1967. This was the day before the dam broke. Within five years there would be two hundred. By 1993 that number was in four figures and rising so fast it was termed an epidemic.

The Travis Walton affair

Probably the final case to occur before things became irrevocably altered through these movie images was the unparalleled incident of 5 November 1975. It came a couple of weeks after the Betty and Barney Hill story had aired on local Arizona TV, and included features otherwise rare in the UFO archives. However, the main protagonists of the Arizona abduction claim not to have seen *The UFO Incident* beforehand.

At the time the case was a minor sensation because of its unusual features. But in 1993 Tracy Torme, a former scriptwriter with *Star Trek: The Next Generation*, convinced Paramount Pictures to finance a movie about this old case, called *Fire in the Sky*.

Travis Walton had been a member of a seven-man logging crew working on a contract in the Sitgreaves National Forest near the small town of Snowflake. Leading the gang was Mike Rogers, whose sister would later marry Travis. Rogers was struggling to complete this major contract for which the crew had been paid some cash up front. They had missed one deadline, partly through work with other contractors and partly through unavoidable problems.

As darkness fell on 5 November they left the forest in their large truck, bouncing along the rough tracks. Suddenly they saw a glow in the sky and rounded a corner to confront a strange blue diamond shape hovering above a clearing. Most of the men were terrified, but young Travis Walton was not. He leaped out and stumbled towards it, staring upwards. Then, as he stood beneath the huge mass, fixed within its spotlight beam and trapped like a rabbit by hunters, a ray of light shot from the object's base. The woodsman was hit in the midriff and thrown several feet into the air. He crashed on to the ground as if he had been struck by lightning.

Walton lay motionless and his colleagues believed him dead. The UFO was still there and unsurprisingly they panicked, quickly fleeing the scene. Only some minutes later did Mike Rogers realise it had been

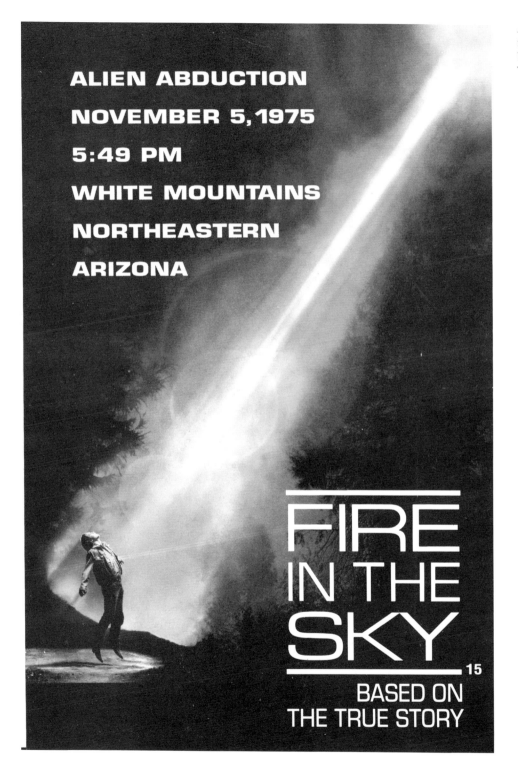

A promotional poster from the 1993 film based on the story of Travis Walton.

wrong to leave their friend and turned the truck around. But there was no sign of the UFO or of Travis Walton.

Lie detector tests

This part of the story and its aftermath is handled exceptionally well by the Paramount movie. Back in town the shocked men came under suspicion that they were covering up a murder, and next day a major search was mounted to find Walton's body. Protesting their innocence, the men eventually took lie detector tests. All bar one (who had a past record and was nervous) convinced the operator that they did not know where their colleague was.

Never before or since has an abduction begun in this overtly hostile manner or has the victim vanished for days on end with police squads out searching. Of course, that is what gives the case its Hollywood edge, but, paradoxically, it is also what creates difficulties from a UFO perspective. It is an atypical CE4 (close encounter of the fourth kind) which bucks the trend so much that it worries some investigators; although others defend it staunchly.

Rival ufologists

A few hours after Walton returned, a UFO was recorded visually and on radar at the Canadian Forces installation at Falconbridge, Ontario. NORAD informed the media that two F-106 jets were scrambled but no contact was made with the object.

Travis Walton was missing for five days and then telephoned from a nearby town where he 'awoke' with no memory of what had taken place. The police remained unhappy, still thinking that a crime might have been committed. They considered taking action but were unable to come up with any hard evidence to support the idea that Walton, Rogers and the other men were not simply telling the truth as they had seen it.

After the police released Walton, Rogers and their families, the UFO groups moved in. Two in particular fought a war of attrition. Walton chose to cooperate with one but not the other, who were rather more sceptical. So that team set about reporting evidence that might discredit the case. They found, for example, that Walton had taken (and failed) a lie detector test soon after his return. It was paid for by a national tabloid who were promoting his story. The paper decided not to make this public and asked the supporting UFO group not to do so either. Later they gave Walton a second test, which he passed, and publicised that outcome instead.

Walton, not unreasonably, pointed out that he was heavily stressed in the immediate aftermath of his experience and that this could easily have affected him during the first test. Lie detector experts and psychologists who talked to the witnesses disagreed on the credibility of the story, and it eventually just fizzled out as something that you could either believe or not.

UFO debunker Philip Klass fought very hard over the years to prove that this case was just a hoax. He suggested that the men knew they could never finish the logging contract before the extended deadline and so invented the story to get them out of the deal. An 'act of God' clause gave them the right to quit if there was something unforeseen that prevented them returning to the forest; otherwise they might forfeit money owed. The crew never did finish the job. Klass also noted that the foresters received a considerable cash sum from the media source which bought their story.

How you evaluate any such facts is another matter, of course. One cannot blame anybody for accepting sums proffered by the media if their story is true, nor for cashing in via book and movie deals afterwards. This may offer a possible hoax motive in the first place, but it is also a natural consequence of any case like this even if the story were true. In addition, Arizona ufologist Jim Speiser conducted an impressive follow-through in 1993 after the movie's release, and sceptics tried to prevent the use of the term 'a true story' in advertising campaigns.

Speiser not only spoke at length with Mike Rogers about the logging deal but also talked to the then contractor and his successor in the Sitgreaves Forest. Most of what he found seems to support the Rogers and Walton story. Indeed, Rogers and the then contractor, Maurice Marchbanks, both confirmed that the 'act of God' clause was never actually enforced in 1975, nor was this invocation requested by Walton and Rogers – which makes it unlikely that this was part of a plan concocted to get out of the logging contract. Of course, it might be argued that under the circumstances nobody from the logging company was going to press the issue. The crew were simply allowed to walk away from the deal, and so may never have needed to invoke any clause within the contract. Either way it was not a major factor.

After his return Travis Walton did get a few flash memories about what had happened to him during those missing five days. Hypnotic regression later plugged a few more gaps. Again these images were curious – including being taken to a giant hangar with lots of UFOs and being probed by odd looking aliens in unusual clothing. But these images were very confused.

Fact and fiction part company

This is less of a problem than it seems. The recall of abductees is often cloudy and filled with what are called 'screen memories' that appear to be cover stories or even fantasies masking deeper, more painful thoughts which they repress into their subconscious. However, in the movie *Fire in the Sky* these patchy and rather weak memories were considered inappropriate. So Tracy Torme found it necessary to write a letter to fellow ufologists, apologising for having to go along with a directive to alter this part of the script. The final sequence in the film is more like a fantasy, rather than Travis Walton's memory of what took place inside the UFO. When the woodsman visited Britain in June 1993 he said that these scenes made a point, but were not meant to be accurate. However, the horror-inspired images of needles being stuck into eyeballs and giant cocoons trapping his body do detract from this otherwise sensible account of the case.

The affair will probably always be shrouded in controversy, but if it did happen – as a quite unassuming Travis Walton and Mike Rogers unflappably insist that it did – then it forms a watershed. It links the scattered and rather limited abduction cases of the later 1960s and early 1970s with the nightmare invasion of alien kidnappers who seemed bent on widescale medical experimentation. This latter scenario was about to become the terrifying norm.

—20—

MILITARY ENCOUNTER OVER IRAN

On 19 September 1976 the Imperial Iranian Air Force command post received four telephone calls from people saying that they had seen strange objects in the sky.

One of the most dramatic cases to come to light through the Freedom of Information Act in America contained details of an air confrontation between military jets and possibly several UFOs. The theatre was the air space over Tehran in September 1976, not long before the Shah was deposed. A report of the incident was sent by the Defence Attaché at the US Embassy to the Defence Intelligence Agency (DIA). Here are some direct quotes from the report:

A. At about 12.30am on 19 Sep 76 the Imperial Iranian Air Force (IIAF) command post received four telephone calls from citizens living in the Shemiran area of Tehran saying that they had seen strange objects in the sky. Some reported a kind of bird-like object while others reported a helicopter with a light on. There were no helicopters airborne at that time. The command post called B.G. Yousefi, assistant deputy commander of operations. After he told the citizens it was only stars and had talked to Mehrabad Tower he decided to look for himself. He noticed an object in the sky similar to a star bigger and brighter. He decided to scramble an F-4 from Shahrokhi AFB to investigate.

B. At 0130 hrs on the 19th the F-4 took off and proceeded to a point about 40nm north over Tehran. Due to its brilliance the object was easily visible from 70 miles away. As the F-4 approached a range of 25nm he lost all instrumentation and communications (UHF and Intercom). He broke off the intercept and headed back to Shahrokhi. When the F-4 turned away from the object and apparently was no longer a threat to it the aircraft regained all instrumentation and communications. At 0140 hrs a second F-4 was launched. The backseater acquired a radar lock on at 27nm, 12 o'clock high position with the vc [rate of closure] at 150 nmph. As the range decreased to 25nm the object moved away at a speed that was visible on the radar scope and stayed at 25nm.

C.   The size of the radar return was comparable to that of a 707 tanker. The visual size of the object was difficult to discern because of its intense brilliance. The light it gave off was that of flashing strobe lights arranged in a rectangular pattern and alternating blue, green, red and orange in color. The sequence of the lights was so fast that all the colors could be seen at once. The object and the pursuing F-4 continued on a course to the south of Tehran when another brightly lighted object, estimated to be one half to one third the apparent size of the moon, came out of the original object. This second object headed straight toward the F-4 at a very fast rate of speed. The pilot attempted to fire an AIM-9 missile at the object but at that instant his weapons control panel went off and he lost all communications (UHF and Interphone). At this point the pilot initiated a turn and negative G Dive to get away. As he turned the object fell in trail at what appeared to be about 3–4nm. As he continued in his turn away from the primary object the second object went to the inside of his turn then returned to the primary object for a perfect rejoin.

D.   Shortly after the second object joined up with the primary object another object appeared to come out of the other side of the primary object going straight down, at a great rate of speed. The F-4 crew had regained communications and the weapons control panel and watched the object approach the ground anticipating a large explosion. This object appeared to come to rest gently on the earth and cast a very bright light over an area of about 2–3 kilometers. The crew descended from their altitude of 26 m to 15 m and continued to observe and mark the object's position. They had some difficulty in adjusting their night visibility for landing so after orbiting Mehrabad a few times they went out for a straight in landing. There was a lot of interference on the UHF and each time they passed through a mag. bearing of 150 degrees from Mehrabad they lost their communications (UHF and Interphone) and the ins fluctuated from 30 degrees – 50 degrees. The one civil airliner that was approaching Mehrabad during this same time experienced communications failure in the same vicinity (Kilo Zulu) but did not report seeing anything. While the F-4 was on a long final approach the crew noticed another cylinder shaped object (about the size of a T-Bird at 10 m) with bright steady lights on each end and a flasher in the middle. When queried the tower stated there was no other known traffic in the area. During the time the object passed over the F-4 the tower did not have a visual on it but picked it up after the pilot told them to look between the mountains and the refinery.

E.   During daylight the F-4 crew was taken out to the area in a helicopter where the object apparently had landed. Nothing was noticed at the spot where they thought the object landed (a dry lake bed) but as they circled off to the west of the area they picked up a very noticeable beeper signal. At the point where the return was the loudest was a small house with a garden. They landed and asked the people within if they had noticed anything strange last night. The people talked about a loud noise and a very bright light like lightning. The aircraft and area where the object is believed to have landed are being checked for possible radiation.

A classic case

The White House, Secretary of State, National Security Agency and CIA were sent copies of this remarkable report. Additional to the report was a DIA Defence Information Report Evaluation, which concluded that the case was 'outstanding'. The evaluator wrote that it was a 'classic', meeting 'all the criteria necessary for a valid study of the UFO phenomenon'. The criteria included multiple witness sighting from various locations and viewpoints, highly credible observers, confirmation of sightings by radar, electromagnetic interference with three aircraft, physiological effects, and outstanding manoeuvrability exhibited by the objects.

The report was originally released by the DIA to a Berlin ufologist and American High School teacher in Germany named Charles Huffer. When Ray Boeche, an American UFO investigator, also requested the document, it was (perhaps significantly) missing the evaluation report.

Almost two weeks after the aerial encounter, the *Iran Times* ran a story based, they claimed, on recorded communications between the first pilot and ground control. His name was Lieutenant Jafari and he was twenty-three years old. The article fleshed out the official report by describing, first, how Jafari attempted to catch the object, breaking the sound barrier in hot pursuit, but failing. When ground control suggested he abandon the mission, he agreed, then radioed: 'Something is coming at me from behind. It is fifteen miles away ... now ten miles away ... now five miles ... it is level now. I think it's going to crash into me. It has just passed by, missing me narrowly.' Lieutenant Jafari was so shaken by the near miss that he had to be guided back to Shahrokhi Air Base.

This is a significant case in our official history of the UFO phenomenon. Psychological and sociological theorists need not apply here. The objects exhibited intelligence and a technology superior to our own. Yet this demonstration of an apparent nuts and bolts phenomenon only serves to muddy the water of the ufological pond.

— 21 —

FREEDOM OF INFORMATION

From late 1976, as a result of the Freedom of Information Act, *previously secret UFO files began to pour out.*

D espite the appeals of scientists after the AAAS symposium, seven years elapsed before their cries were heard. The UFO data in the government archives remained locked away until the introduction of a Freedom of Information (FOI) Act gave the authorities little choice. From late 1976 the ex-secret UFO files began to pour out.

The FOI Act assured citizens access to all data unless national security would be compromised by its release. Since the government's public stance for many years had been that there was nothing sensitive (indeed nothing much at all) to the subject of UFOs, there would appear to have been little room for argument if they had tried to withhold many of these files.

The secrets of declassification

The Blue Book data was declassified on many reels of microfilm – allowing sight of fifteen thousand UFO cases collated between 1947 and 1969, and the varying degrees to which these had been pursued. Much valuable material came forth in that way, showing the inadequacy of early methods. Photographs now so obviously dubious had not been rejected – indeed, sometimes they were endorsed. But conversely, promising cases had been left dangling through lack of time and money.

The Ruppelt era shone like a beacon of sober investigation. For the rest of the time, disgruntled officers with no scientific training were doing a job that most seemed to regard as the military equivalent of being sent to Siberia.

It was not long before the files of other secret organisations were being sought. The FBI, CIA and other authorities were petitioned.

WITH 32 PAGES OF OFFICIAL PHOTOS

THE TOP SECRET **UFO** FINDINGS REVEALED!

PROJECT BLUE BOOK

A MAJOR DOCUMENT!

AFTER NEARLY THIRTY YEARS THE AIR FORCE FILES ARE OPEN— THE UFO WHITEWASH IS OVER!

EDITED BY

Brad Steiger

Ballantine
Nonfiction
26091
$1.95

Sometimes they would deny having data, then succumb when ufologists were persistent. But many obstacles were placed in their way. For a time the battle for FOI documents became the focal point of ufology, but it should have been obvious that nothing of any real importance would be released, even if it had ever existed. If it did, it was clearly going to be subject to the national security codicil applied to all FOI releases.

Doing battle with the NSA

The big fight was with the NSA – the super-secret National Security Agency. They employ satellites to intercept phone calls and have the most sensitive operation in the USA, with outposts all over the world. In Britain a base at Menwith Hill near Harrogate was and still is NSA-operated. As their job was to bug the world for sensitive data, this meant two things: first, that anything they had about UFOs was likely to be fascinating, but second, that the chances of very much being releasable without compromising the NSA's procedures were slim.

Initially the NSA denied having any files about UFOs. Then, after much pressure, they agreed that they had a few. A figure of several hundred eventually emerged, but the request for access was refused. As a sort of sop a document entitled 'UFO hypotheses and survival questions' was released – its relevance to the NSA UFO data seems curious, and it poses many questions about what the actual data might contain. The document effectively surveys key options for what UFOs might be and seems to favour the view that some objects are extraterrestrial.

Despite many appeals, the NSA files themselves were still kept secret. The FOI Act allows protests all the way up to the US Supreme Court, however, and many ufologists backed a fighting fund to pay for the costs of doing just that. But even the top security-cleared judge who presided over the case was not allowed to see the files. Instead, the NSA issued a twenty-one-page statement for his eyes only, explaining why their UFO data had to be kept secret.

One assumes that this document went beyond the publicly presented reasoning that the data is unimportant but the methods used by the NSA to collect it have to be secret. Sadly, we do not know what else it said, as the judge rapidly agreed that to release the files would 'seriously jeopardise the work of the agency'. That effectively was that.

The document that the judge saw was then appealed for by an inspired FOI fighter. After much hassle, on 27 April 1982 it was made

After the introduction of the Freedom of Information Bill there were so many requests for UFO data that the US government began to charge serious sums for the work involved in the hope that it might deter people!

public – or rather a sanitised version of it was released. This is one of the most astonishing UFO files ever revealed. Eleven of the twenty-one pages were totally blacked out by the censor's pen, and most of another six were similarly treated. Only four pages still contained any moderate-sized sections which were readable – principally the opening paragraphs of the document.

We learned that one of the denied files concerned an NSA agent's secret visit to a UFO conference (unreleased as it was said to be 'irrelevant'!). Typical of what *is* visible through the sea of black ink is reference to a file by the author of the 'Survival Questions' paper. He penned another of the 239 secret documents entitled 'UFOs . . .' (the title goes on for a line and a half, but the rest of what it was called is rated as unreleasable!). We are told that 'In this document the author discusses what he . . .' (three inches of missing text follow).

It seems clear that in both these instances the denial of the material is unconnected with the methods used by the NSA to gain access to it. The title of the paper and a summary of its overview appear to be considered too sensitive because of what they say – not because of the means by which what they say was accrued. The same may be true in many other cases, for all we know.

'Surprise material'

After a further struggle to get access to minor snippets, such as the dates and locations of intercepted UFO messages without any reference to how these messages were intercepted, just a few extra words in the affadavit were freed for public scrutiny. In these we discover that the NSA use an odd term for UFO data – 'surprise material', which suggests that they have made unexpected discoveries as a result of their access to it. What a pity the rest of the world is being denied a sight of the sort of surprise that these NSA agents have had.

Although the search for FOI files has abated, except in connection with specific cases, the belief in a 'smoking gun' to prove alien reality still persists. No smoking gun has appeared, despite the desperation, but there are hints that someone on the fringes of the UFO movement may have felt the need to invent one. Bogus documents have begun to flood American ufology.

The search for the missing link

American researchers seek the file that will prove there was a secret investigation team with access to all the better evidence – up to and including alien spacecraft wreckage and the captured bodies of their alien crew. The belief that such things do exist remains undented in American culture; although it is far less accepted outside that country, where UFOs and spaceships are not viewed as automatically synonymous terms.

The Bolender memo from 1969 proved that there were other procedures by which UFO data was processed. Who handled these cases, and where are their files? More important, who decides which cases threatened national security and should be routed past the USAF?

We knew that a case like the Lakenheath/Bentwaters 1956 radar-visual was one such example from the time when Blue Book operated and which seems to have gone through the national security channels. From the lack of data supposedly available on the equally extraordinary Rendlesham Forest saga in 1980 (see page 212) it seems that, even long after Blue Book's closure, this is the type of case which qualifies for exclusive handling.

The big question is this. How many other files are out there somewhere, and what degree of material evidence do they possess?

In 1992 Dr Jacques Vallée published the so-called 'Pentacle' memo, written in January 1953 by a source at the Battelle Institute during the time they were doing lengthy top-secret research on UFOs. This seems important because it refers to thousands of cases under investigation. Where are those files? However, it might just be a minor dispute over semantics, as Battelle had over four thousand USAF files to select from even in 1953.

This urgency is typical of the desperate search in the USA to find that missing link which so many ufologists believe must exist. That belief stems from the fact that the FOI files which have been released are on the whole very disappointing to them.

UFO researcher Jacques Vallée.

Of course, disappointment rather depends upon what you expect to find within these files in the first place. They seem to reflect a puzzled administration with little clue as to what is happening and not much idea of how to deal with it. Might that not be exactly what was happening?

Australia introduced a similar FOI Act soon after the USA, and ufologist Bill Chalker was one of the first to make use of it. Learning from the American experience, the Australian government in Canberra invited Chalker to access all their records and extract and copy whatever he wanted. If they let him report all of this to the UFO world it would save them the effort of fielding hundreds of individual requests.

Chalker did an excellent job, but the same pattern emerged – many

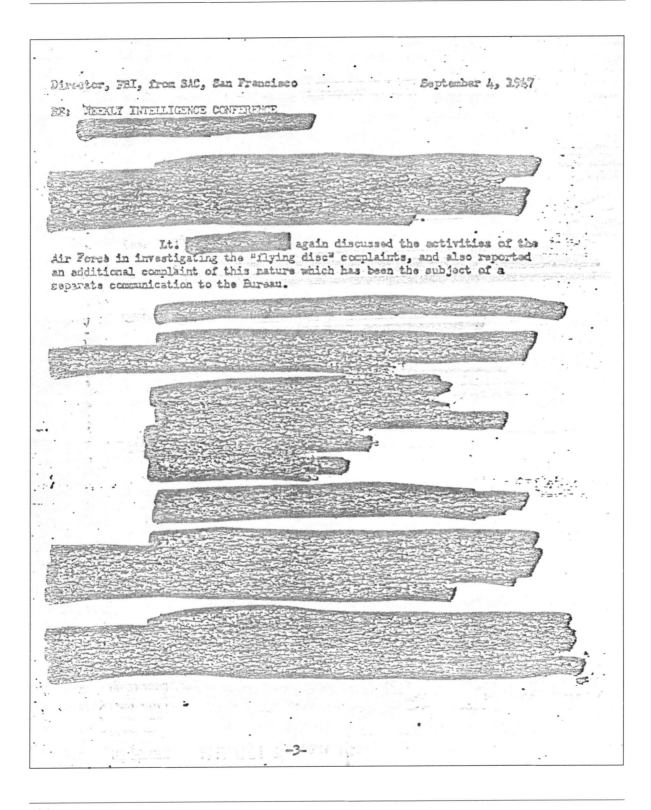

Director, FBI, from SAC, San Francisco   September 4, 1947

RE: WEEKLY INTELLIGENCE CONFERENCE

Lt: ▮▮▮▮▮▮▮▮▮ again discussed the activities of the
Air Force in investigating the "flying disc" complaints, and also reported
an additional complaint of this nature which has been the subject of a
separate communication to the Bureau.

-3-

odd cases, inadequate investigations, occasional memos from baffled experts speculating on wild theories of origin, vain attempts to make cases disappear by explaining them away, but ultimately a continuing series of reports that defied resolution. This all remained undented by changes in public mood or UFO credibility. The essence of the UFO phenomenon shines through, just as it does in the databases of private UFO groups all over the world.

Everything we know, from BUFORA and CUFOS to the CIA and Canberra, tells us that most UFO sightings are readily explained, but just a few are not. With these unsolved cases, nobody has a monopoly on truth and hard answers are much thinner on the ground than endless speculation. This covers many theories from alien spaceships to altered states of consciousness.

Of course, there are those who can say, and have said, that Chalker was only shown what the Australian government wanted him to see and that the real 'hot stuff' was held back. But he was satisfied with the assistance that he received and appears to believe that the authorities played fair. If there was a smoking gun or a secret cache of Australian files, these were outside the province of the bureaucrats and administrators who are charged with the responsibility of collating UFO data. These people, on the whole, seem as puzzled, confused and full of curiosity as are most responsible ufologists.

Confusion in Europe too

As we shall see, the French data reveals a very similar picture, as do sporadic releases from other countries – such as Spain, where military files about radar trackings, air force jet chases and unsolved sightings have been released from time to time over the past fifteen years. These all establish the same level of mystification. But it adds no great new insights. There seems precious little evidence about some massive global conspiracy to withhold vital solid evidence that would prove alien reality to the world.

Indeed, in December 1993, when the energy commission of the EC passed a proposal by an Italian delegate to request funding for a European UFO commission, there was an outcry. Yet the idea was a sensible one. Most people saw this in terms of a search for 'little green men'. What they did not see was that, if some UFOs are natural physical phenomena (and there is strong evidence that they are), then energy and power might be harnessed if we can investigate them properly. The funding requested makes sound economic sense.

See opposite
This memo is typical of the data revealed under *Freedom of Information Act* requests – showing the sea of censorship. This particular memo dates from before the US government were even officially investigating UFOs (ie four months before Project Sign began). But it's clear to see how little they are prepared to release even half a century later!

In 1976 the Spanish Government invited journalist Jose Benitez to Madrid. Benitez was introduced to an Air Force Lieutenant-General who was Chief of Staff of the Air Ministry. The journalist was handed documentation on twelve of their best cases. This included film taken by Spanish Air Force pilots.

In strict terms, government investigations are as hamstrung as private ones by lack of money and insoluble questions about UFO origin. Yes, there is a cover-up, but it hides a lack of certainty and much confusion as to what UFOs might be. There is no sign of any desperate rearguard action to prevent the world from learning incredible secrets about an alien invasion.

— 22 —

THE FRENCH CONNECTION

In 1977 France became the first world government to create a full-time, permanent team of scientific ufologists.

Although many of the major historical developments took place in the United States, one of the most important did not. In 1977 France became the first world government to create a full-time, permanent team of scientific ufologists, and in the mid-1990s it is still operating.

Its origin goes back to March 1974 when the then Minister of Defence, Robert Galley, went on French national radio with an interview that should have provoked global headlines, yet oddly did nothing of the sort. Galley assured the French people that his Ministry took UFOs very seriously and was studying them. He reported that there had been radar trackings and that French Air Force jets had chased these objects. Whilst many sightings could be accounted for, others could not. He added that, if people were able to see the extent and quality of the data that was coming in to the authorities, they would be properly disturbed.

It was an astonishing admission and probably represents the honest views of most nations. But France, not tied to the USA by the NATO defence treaty, had simply chosen to be the first to speak out.

Galley seems to have taken advice from scientific staff, notably Dr Claude Poher from the French Space Agency at Toulouse. He and another colleague, astronomer Dr Pierre Guerin, had evidently been impressed by the Condon data, the AAAS symposium, Hynek's appearance in the public arena and first-hand observation of cases being channelled through to them for evaluation by the French Defence Ministry.

Soon after Galley's speech Poher completed a major statistical analysis of UFOs and Guerin wrote a position paper. These scientists published their work in English in the then prestigious journal *Flying Saucer Review*.

A scientific riddle acknowledged at last

On 1 May 1977 the French government created GEPAN, which translates as Study Group into Unidentified Aerospatial Phenomena. It was placed under the directorship of Poher with the collaboration of others who included Guerin.

Coming as it did when Spielberg and Hynek's movie *Close Encounters of the Third Kind* was starting its journey around the world, and just as the US government had finally begun to release once secret UFO files through the new Freedom of Information Act, it was perceived as a very important step forward. Ufology had come visibly further in the few years post-Condon than it had done in the previous quarter-century. The main reason was that at last it was being treated as a scientific riddle and not as a military headache.

In the early days GEPAN was very interactive with the UFO world. Sadly, most English-speaking ufologists were ignorant of this data and mainstream science journals never mentioned it. However, for those who took the trouble to access GEPAN reports their significance was obvious.

The *gendarmerie* were specially trained to deploy units to follow up cases and call in GEPAN if it felt necessary. A number of scientific laboratories were on standby to handle samples or other physical evidence. Everything was extremely efficient and open.

Confirming the Battelle results

During 1978 354 reports were sent to GEPAN (by 1985 the total was over 1,600) and of these more than half represented close encounters rather than just lights in the sky. This was partly because less productive cases had been filtered out by the police.

A quarter of the cases were evaluated by GEPAN as genuine UFOs. As their first status report, published in 1979, pointed out, 'these reports ... pose a real question'. Even more important than this honest admission was the fact that GEPAN duplicated the Battelle research from twenty-five years before and made the same finding: the more data made available on any case, and the better the calibre of the reporting witnesses, then the *more* likely it was that the event would remain unexplained.

But there was more still. For example, they found that puzzling UFOs were more prevalent given better atmospheric clarity. This is significant because if UFOs were simply misperceptions then the opposite would be true. Equally, if UFOs are hallucinations or fantasies they would have no correlation with the quality of the atmosphere. That the incidence of unidentified UFOs increased in better viewing conditions was strong support for their physical reality.

Based on this evidence, two years into their project GEPAN sought more funding and expressed the view that their work was proving that witnesses were really seeing UFOs. However, there was a price to pay for the upgrading of the project: increased secrecy. One of the last published GEPAN reports about internal discussions with the French government noted that the results were proving disconcerting and that presidential scientific advisers were recommending 'great vigilance' in publication.

This advice seems to have been enforced from about 1980. Dr Poher 'retired to sail around the world' and a new young astronomer, Dr Alain Esterle, took command. He was far more circumspect, but still retained some links with the UFO world. Jenny Randles met him in London in May 1981 and he intimated that scientists on the project were starting to think that some evidence might actually support the alien nature behind some cases.

In early 1983 Jenny went to France and was able to get hold of some new GEPAN data. They were publishing limited-edition 'Technical Notes' in a regular series (each one was stamped with an individual identifying number under 100). These incredibly detailed documents, which included photographs, site measurements, laboratory data and so on, consisted of almost book-length treatments each focusing on a single investigation. The cases were classic encounters such as an incident of 26 January 1981 when an object with portholes hovered over a farmer's car, caused its engine to fail and then damaged its electrical circuits. GEPAN's conclusion was that this case was 'in the proper sense, an unidentified aerial phenomenon'.

In 1983 British and French ufologists tried to initiate an annual series of entente-cordiale *joint meetings. So few British ufologists could understand French that this laudable move soon failed.*

GEPAN goes underground

Ironically, on the very day that Jenny went to France, 21 February 1983, the *Sunday Times* (which had mentioned none of GEPAN's positive research) carried a small item quipping 'Flying saucers sought no more'. It claimed that as an economy measure the Mitterrand government was closing down GEPAN because the group was viewed as 'an expensive folly'. French ufologists, Jenny found, generally believed that GEPAN was merely going underground and had stopped all cooperation with the public. However, GEPAN was far from on the point of extinction. It was revamped in 1983, but retained its status in

Toulouse. The *Sunday Times* never seem to have corrected their earlier claim that it was completely dead and buried.

Later in 1983 Pierre Guerin issued another position statement. In it he argued that the powers-that-be used various tactics to try to 'put it into the minds of the scientists to deny the existence of UFOs' – or at least, he added, the majority of scientists 'who are not sufficiently interested in the matter to search through the records for themselves'.

From what we have seen of the history of UFOs throughout this book, such an assessment has merit. Science has been manipulated into discounting UFO evidence by a host of reasons, ranging from the ufologists' own sad obsession with extraterrestrial invasions to governmental desire to restrict research to a few militarily controlled appraisals. Of course, if you are interested in UFOs not for what they are, but rather for how you can use them to build some sort of weapon, then the very last thing you want is for scientists all over the world who have not signed allegiance to the MoD or NSA to think there is something worthwhile connected with the data.

The landing at Trans-en-Provence

A truly dramatic case that GEPAN came across was the landing at Trans-en-Provence; it was certainly subjected to one of their most intensive investigations. In June 1987 Jenny met, in Washington, engineer Jean Jacques Velasco, the new head of GEPAN. Velasco was very impressed by the calibre of the Provence case (which Alain Esterle, GEPAN director at the time, had also enthused about, saying: 'We have a combination of factors which induce us to accept that something akin to what the witness described actually did take place.')

It seems that on 9 January 1981 police at Draguinan, a town in south-eastern France long plagued with UFO sightings, received a new report. It came from a farmer called Renato Nicolai in the nearby village of Trans-en-Provence. The man's house sat astride a slope built into a series of terraced orchards in the valley of the River Nartuby. The police visited Nicolai and he showed them the site.

At 5pm the previous day he had been working outside on the terraces when he had heard a 'faint whistling'. He turned to see 'a device in the air at the height of a big pine tree ... not spinning, coming lower towards the ground'. It was like a slightly elongated egg with four circular openings on the base. As he walked towards it he saw that it had touched down on the slope. It was there for a very short time and 'right away it lifted off, still emitting a slight whistling sound'. It 'kicked off a

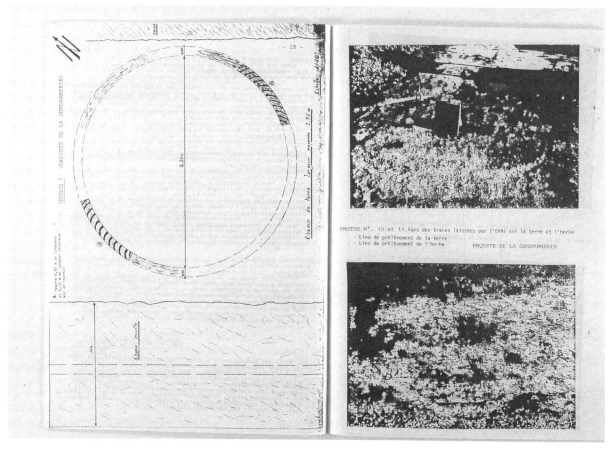

little dust when it left'. The object – slightly smaller than the size of a car – climbed about twenty feet up and then sped away to the north-east.

Nicolai said it was 'the colour of lead. The device had a ridge all the way around its circumference.' Two of the holes 'could be reactors or feet. There were also two other circles which looked like trapdoors.' There were two small legs at one point on the base. He had no doubt that it was a constructed machine.

A near-identical object had landed on the snowy slopes of a hillside at Meanwood, West Yorkshire, in February 1979 amidst a major two-day flap. That weekend a UFO also landed at a quarry in nearby Bacup and US Air Force jets chased an object out to sea between Southport and Blackpool. Blackpool pier shook (according to reports from a security guard), and a caravan park at Scarisbrick was damaged by the noise. This led to questions in the house by then MP (and future TV celebrity) Robert Kilroy Silk. The parallels between these two cases are quite strong.

Part of the GEPAN report detailing the Trans-en-Provence case.

Back at Trans-en-Provence the police did not merely have Nicolai's story but also physical evidence. For there was a curious ring in the earth where the object had landed. It was several inches wide and over six feet in diameter. They took samples.

GEPAN were contacted three days later and the *gendarmerie* were instructed to take further, more specific samples, including controls from outside the ring area. Scientists from GEPAN then made their own study.

A leading expert in plant damage, Michael Bounais, supervised the analysis work at the National Institute for Agronomy Research. Many major findings appeared. The chlorophyll content of the plants in the landing zone had altered markedly. The leaves on the grass had aged 'in some way that neither natural processes nor laboratory experiments could duplicate'. There were also major deformations of the ground which could not be explained. GEPAN said in conclusion; 'We cannot give any precise or specific interpretation for this remarkable set of results . . . But we can state that there is nevertheless confirmation from them that a very sigificant incident took place on this spot.'

It was soon after the completion of the research on this case that GEPAN went underground. In Washington, Velasco reported that the Trans-en-Provence landing was very important. He suggested that an electromagnetic field, rather than an irradiating energy source, was more likely to have caused the plant and soil changes.

In a paper written for the *Journal of Scientific Exploration* in 1990 Bounais himself also had his say about these effects. He was baffled, he said, because; no normal method such as ionising, thermal or hydro factors could explain the changes that he had found.

In November 1988, ufologist Dr Jacques Vallée visited the site and interviewed Nicolai in the company of plant specialist Bounais. Samples were taken back to California where a prestigious scientific institute conducted further tests on Vallée's behalf. The institute wished to remain anonymous because it preferred not to be publicly associated with UFOs (which is, sadly, still a common problem). It could offer no mundane explanation, even after bombarding the material with X-rays and testing it under an electron microscope.

GEPAN/SEPRA discredited?

On 15 July 1991 Robert Galley, now retired from government duties, gave a new interview to the respected journal *OVNI Presence*. He explained how in his 1974 interview he was not proclaiming a belief in little green men, simply that 'There certainly are, even now, within the atmosphere luminous phenomena which do not have an immediate explanation.'

Galley was also questioned about the wave of triangular objects sighted in Belgium between 1989 and 1991 (see page 268) and about the idea that these may have been American stealth aircraft. He seemed very open-minded on the possibility, citing an instance in which an American spy plane flew over French territory to photograph a uranium enrichment plant at Pierrelatte. Galley intercepted the mission and sent a French Air Force colonel to Ramstein Air Force Base, where the jet landed, and had the negatives promptly confiscated! They had not publicly accused the Americans of this, but, Galley implied, if it could happen once then it might have happened above Belgium with a new type of aircraft that resembled UFOs.

Another responsible French journal, *Phenomena*, published a devastating appraisal of GEPAN (or SEPRA as it has been retitled to take account of a newly expanded role that includes orbital space re-entry investigations). This journal, unlike much of French ufology, had been restrained in criticism. Whilst Velasco and others had attended overseas UFO conferences, GEPAN seemed reluctant to support events closer to home. Quite a few researchers were openly accusing them of being closet debunkers. Physicist Jean-Pierre Petit had said in 1988, for example, that GEPAN had been set up after a wave of sightings and the impact of Galley's public endorsements not to research the UFO matter but rather to 'extinguish the problem'.

Now Perry Petrakis, a moderate French ufologist, was saying that after giving GEPAN/SEPRA the benefit of the doubt they had to face the truth. He cited various impressive cases where the scientists seem to have been either reluctant to get involved or disinclined to speak out.

On 2 September 1990 a Boeing 727 heading from Strasbourg to Algeria picked up a UFO on radar. The crew tracked it for three minutes, travelling at around 5,000 mph! As it flew over Algeria, ground radar was temporarily jammed. Despite access to military sources, SEPRA were silent on the case.

Then on 3 October 1991 the Dordogne region was hit by a major wave of reports of a weird 'cloud' which created electromagnetic disturbances, affecting TV transmissions for instance. Strange lights were also seen. The following morning police were called by residents because a white, filament-like material had been sown over power lines and trees. This so-called 'angel's hair' was common in sightings during the 1950s and emitted by mysterious clouds; it had not been reported

SEPRA officially gets funding to study unusual atmospheric phenomena, which includes UFOs. This avoids the scientific row that would develop if government money from a science budget was allotted to UFO study.

In October 1954 Europe was subjected to a major UFO wave. In France there were several cases involving a rare type of physical evidence – so-called Angel's Hair. This white fibrous material fell from the sky after the passage of a UFO and has appeared only in a very few cases since. It is variously argued to be either spiders' webs or some kind of meteorological residue.

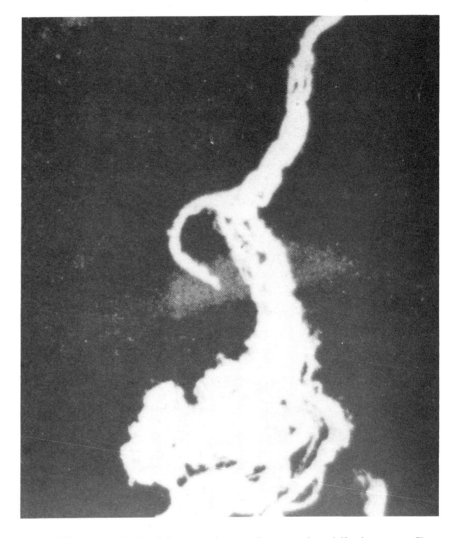

since. The case looked impressive and created public interest. But SEPRA fell silent. It took many months of investigation by the ufologists to establish that a military exercise had deployed the fibrous material as a form of electromagnetic decoy, and this was the source of the angel's hair and the reported odd effects. SEPRA could have prevented wasted effort had it used its internal contacts to dispel public concern from the start.

Then, on 8 July 1992, a military helicopter flying from Le Luc to Aurillac had a close encounter in daylight with a black diamond or lozenge shape. It was crossing at 6,000 feet above the town of Brignoles. This case is remarkably similar to a series of mid-air encounters over southern England involving commercial jets coming into close proximity with dark cylinder shapes. More than half a dozen are known since April 1991 (see Chapter 34).

The military allowed ufologists on base to interview personnel. The object was about fifteen feet long, moving at about 300 knots towards the south-east. The group sent a fax to SEPRA, but nothing emerged. They also claim that, when they tried to report the case on TV, SEPRA expressed concern, saying that they could not approve discussion of a military matter in public. These, of course, are the personal opinions of some French researchers. We can only note from our experience – particularly during its days at GEPAN – that SEPRA officials were helpful and provided us with useful data on their work. Now, sadly, but perhaps not altogether surprisingly, they seem more constrained.

Petrakis closed his report on the world's only official UFO team by asking of GEPAN/SEPRA; 'What are their results ... other than the Trans-en-Provence case which is twelve years old? Can one accept that a public service such as SEPRA, funded by public money, be such a secretive or inefficient group? We do not think so and no longer trust it.'

During February 1994 outraged reaction by British MEPs and a hostile media temporarily blocked EEC plans to fund an expansion of SEPRA into a 'common market' wide European UFO research centre.

Part Eight

1980s:
GLOBAL
PENETRATION

THE RENDLESHAM FOREST AFFAIR

During the last few days in December 1980 an English pine forest was host to an amazing case. It was either 'one of the most important in world history', as one researcher termed it, or 'a ghastly embarrassment to ufology' as a leading astronomer and sceptic has claimed.

Rendlesham Forest is a large woodland area on the quiet, sandy coastland of East Anglia eight miles north-east of Ipswich. The Forestry Commission 'farms' it for its hardwood and it is home to wildlife such as deer and rabbits. But equally it has a rather sinister aspect.

To the north is Sizewell, with several controversial nuclear power stations. A coastal spit called Orford Ness runs along its eastern rim. Apart from a lighthouse this has housed secret American research units linked to the super-sensitive NSA (National Security Agency). Officially this is home for new 'Over the Horizon Radar'. However, the locals are more suspicious about possible electronics experiments. South of the forest, at Martlesham Heath, is a communications HQ, and at RAF Bawdsey radar was first developed during the mid-1930s and secret research continues. There are tales of strange lights in the sky, mystery hummings and explosions, and weird effects on house lighting and other power sources such as cars.

However, right in the heart of the forest itself are two air bases – RAF Bentwaters and the smaller RAF Woodbridge. Until the end of the cold war these were leased to the Americans for NATO defensive duties. Staffed by hundreds of American personnel as a rearward maintenance site for any possible war in Europe, they had a token RAF 'caretaker' but were otherwise like small American towns transported across the Atlantic.

- **Colonel's top secret report tells the facts**
- **Mystery craft in exploding wall of colour**
- **Animals flee from strange glowing object**

UFO LANDS IN SUFFOLK

And that's OFFICIAL

A UFO has landed in Britain— and that staggering fact has been officially confirmed.

Despite a massive cover-up, News of the World investigators have proof that the mysterious craft came to earth in a red ball of light at 3 a.m. on December 27, 1980.

toward the depressions.

3. Later in the night a red sun-like light was seen through the trees. It moved about and pulsed. At one point it appeared to throw off glowing particles and then broke into five separate white objects and then disappeared. Immediately thereafter, three star-like objects were noticed in the sky, two objects to the north and one to the south, all of which were about 10° off the horizon. The objects moved rapidly in sharp angular movements and displayed red, green and blue lights. The objects to the north appeared to be elliptical through an 8-12 power lens. They then turned to full circles. The objects to the north remained in the sky for an hour or more. The object to the south was visible for two or three hours and beamed down a stream of light from time to time. Numerous indivi-

There are some fascinating similarities between the strategic importance and wealth of modern technology at this particular location and the area surrounding Roswell, Alamogordo and White Sands in New Mexico, where the infamous Roswell 'crash' occurred in 1947.

The Roswell incident was followed by the green fireball and car-stop events that struck the area between 1949 and 1957. Rendlesham Forest is a mere ten miles across but in recent years has also generated both car-stop cases and green fireball events. In 1980 it was the scene of Britain's only 'UFO crash' and the main rival of Roswell in terms of credibility and support.

So much has been pieced together about this affair from many years of research that several full-length books have appeared. But the main interest has been outside of Britain – where the public know little.

Headlines from the *News of the World*.

Mysterious warnings

Jenny Randles (who has written two books and been involved almost from the start) can personally attest that several planned documentaries – including one where a transmission date had been scheduled – were mysteriously cancelled at the last minute. It is also the only case over which she has had to risk prosecution under the Official Secrets Act by using Whitehall documents to which she and colleagues were denied access by the MoD but which were secured under FOI rules in the USA. She was even 'warned off' (Man in Black-style) by a government scientist who told her how dangerous he believed this type of investigation to be and how he, personally, would not follow it up any more. He claimed she was 'messing with something for which you can end up at the bottom of the Thames'.

At times the investigation of the matter was more like a James Bond movie script than a UFO case. Anonymous phone calls came in the night. Top-secret documents and tape recordings were leaked to investigators. Exchanges between senior political figures included US Senators and British MPs such as David Alton, Michael Heseltine, Merlyn Rees and Lord Trefgarne. Secret documents were claimed stolen during a robbery, meetings with 'spies' were set up in country parks and deserted railway stations, and claims about the 'truth' behind the incident abounded, ranging from captured satellite engines to a stray nuclear missile, and an alleged mind-scrambling experiment using a new 'psychotronic weapon' (a combination of electronics with a brain-affecting psychological warfare beam).

Sightings over southern England

We do know that late on the evening of 25 December 1980 many strange objects, which resembled comets breaking up or bright fireballs, appeared in the sky over south-eastern England. Civilian aircraft saw and reported them. The main activity was blamed on the re-entry of a Soviet satellite, but the British Astronomical Association list other events between 9pm and 3am which constitute a sequence of less than fully understood phenomena.

At Sudborne a man putting his dog into the outhouse for the night saw a huge glowing mass pass over, hover briefly, then vanish into the forest. On a small road through the woods between Orford and Woodbridge a courting couple saw the sky light up as an object plunged from the heavens into the trees. Other travellers saw it, too. Moments later

When the British public first heard about the events in Rendlesham Forest, via the News of the World *in October 1983, the story was so big that it even relegated top-rated soap opera* Coronation Street *to a support story on the front page.*

```
            HANSARD EXTRACT

          24 OCTOBER 1983


               Col. 62


       RAF Woodbridge (Alleged Incident)


   Sir Patrick Wall asked the Secretary
of State for Defence (1) if he has seen
the United States Air Force memo dated
13 January 1981 concerning unexplained
lights near RAF Woodbridge;
   (2) whether, in view of the fact that
the United States Air Force memo of 13
January 1981 on the incident at RAF
Woodbridge has been released under the
Freedom of Information Act, he will now
release reports and documents concerning
similar incidents in the United Kingdom;
   (3) how many unexplained sightings or
radar intercepts have taken place since
1980.

   Mr. Stanley: I have seen the memorandum
of 13 January 1981 to which my Hon. Friend
refers.  Since 1980 the Department has
received 1,400 reports of sightings of
flying objects which the observers have
been unable to identify.  There were no
corresponding unexplained radar contacts.
Subject to normal security constraints,
I am ready to give information about any
such reported sightings that are found
to be a matter of concern from a defence
standpoint, but there have been none to
date.
```

An excerpt from *Hansard* regarding the House of Commons' debate on UFOs and the Rendlesham case raised by MP and NATO defence committee member Major Sir Patrick Wall and responded to by armed forces minister, John Stanley.

Woodbridge base sprang into full alert, with jeeps and trucks running everywhere.

A farmer was also alerted by this incident when some of his cows were sent rushing into the road. A taxi returning from a Christmas party hit them, and he and another farmer had to herd up the injured animals and get them away. Next day he complained to the base that a huge white light that he had seen must have been an aircraft. He demanded compensation, but they claimed no aircraft were flying. Days later he heard the UFO rumours, went back to the base and said it was still their fault because the Air Force should have protected him from the UFO. Soon afterwards the farmer had moved hundreds of miles away and was allegedly paid compensation. When traced two years later he would only say about this claim of being 'paid off' (which the USAF deny) that he did get money and (in his own words) 'whatever it were, it weren't enough!'

The Air Force communicates with UFO entities

Fifty miles away the object had been tracked on radar at RAF Watton as it cut the coast and vanished towards the ground. The matter would have been forgotten had it not been that a few days later US Air Force intelligence officers took the radar film for scrutiny and explained that Watton might have tracked a UFO that landed in the forest. It was confronted by senior officers from Woodbridge – one of whom communicated with small beings floating underneath. The event had been taped live by a senior commander.

Local ufologists Brenda Butler and Dot Street were contacted within days by one of the USAF security police on the base. He explained how he had been in a party of men sent out to the site in response to a report made from the perimeter fence. In the woods they found a landed object about the size of a car; small creatures with domed heads were suspended inside a beam of light underneath. Senior officers had come out and communicated using sign language. The UFO had been damaged by impact as it fell through the trees, but the aliens repaired it and left. It was as if the UFO was expected.

All of these stories, and many others, were offered independently. There was no publicity (not even in the local press). The MoD denied everything until 13 April 1983 when the British caretaker – Squadron Leader Donald Moreland – admitted that the stories were correct (except for the involvement of aliens). Without warning, the MoD confirmed in writing to Jenny Randles that the case was genuine and said they had no explanation for what had happened.

See opposite
In December 1980 a mysterious object crashed into woodland outside a USAF base in Suffolk, England. After three years of denials by the British government the official report about this incident, which had been submitted days later to the British Ministry of Defence, surfaced under the US Freedom of Information laws. The British government then confirmed its accuracy and that no explanation had been forthcoming. Speculation rose as to how many other significant cases it was keeping from the public.

DEPARTMENT OF THE AIR FORCE
HEADQUARTERS 81ST COMBAT SUPPORT GROUP (USAFE)
APO NEW YORK 09755

(E109

REPLY TO
ATTN OF: CD

13 Jan 81

SUBJECT: Unexplained Lights

TO: RAF/CC

1. Early in the morning of 27 Dec 80 (approximately 0300L), two USAF security police patrolmen saw unusual lights outside the back gate at RAF Woodbridge. Thinking an aircraft might have crashed or been forced down, they called for permission to go outside the gate to investigate. The on-duty flight chief responded and allowed three patrolmen to proceed on foot. The individuals reported seeing a strange glowing object in the forest. The object was described as being metalic in appearance and triangular in shape, approximately two to three meters across the base and approximately two meters high. It illuminated the entire forest with a white light. The object itself had a pulsing red light on top and a bank(s) of blue lights underneath. The object was hovering or on legs. As the patrolmen approached the object, it maneuvered through the trees and disappeared. At this time the animals on a nearby farm went into a frenzy. The object was briefly sighted approximately an hour later near the back gate.

2. The next day, three depressions 1 1/2" deep and 7" in diameter were found where the object had been sighted on the ground. The following night (29 Dec 80) the area was checked for radiation. Beta/gamma readings of 0.1 milliroentgens were recorded with peak readings in the three depressions and near the center of the triangle formed by the depressions. A nearby tree had moderate (.05-.07) readings on the side of the tree toward the depressions.

3. Later in the night a red sun-like light was seen through the trees. It moved about and pulsed. At one point it appeared to throw off glowing particles and then broke into five separate white objects and then disappeared. Immediately thereafter, three star-like objects were noticed in the sky, two objects to the north and one to the south, all of which were about 10° off the horizon. The objects moved rapidly in sharp angular movements and displayed red, green and blue lights. The objects to the north appeared to be elliptical through an 8-12 power lens. They then turned to full circles. The objects to the north remained in the sky for an hour or more. The object to the south was visible for two or three hours and beamed down a stream of light from time to time. Numerous individuals, including the undersigned, witnessed the activities in paragraphs 2 and 3.

CHARLES I. HALT, Lt Col, USAF
Deputy Base Commander

Within days the USAF affirmed this to American ufologists and by June had released the official report submitted to the MoD by the deputy base commander, Colonel Charles Halt. This explained that the crashing object had left a gaping hole in the pine tree canopy (already described to us by a forestry worker who had found it a few days later) and three indentations in a triangle formation where the legs of the landed object had been. Radiation of two to three times the normal background count was recorded here. As these marks were being explored by base personnel, further UFOs returned and were seen by many officers including Halt. It was astonishing testament.

Despite further denials, the tape made during this site investigation was released a year later direct to British researchers. It told how photographs and samples were taken (none of which has ever been released) and how during the second encounter beams of light had been fired from the UFO towards the airmen as they chased it through the woods. At the end their voices broke up in terror and they headed back towards the base.

Much later, on interviewing some of those involved in the tape (who had been reluctant to talk until the story went public), it became clear that there was time missing from their full recall. At least one man may even have been abducted.

The sceptics allege that the UFO was a meteor, that the object in the forest the Orford Ness lighthouse beam, and that the physical traces were left by scratching rabbits. Most ufologists and all the witnesses find this idea absurd.

A 1993 documentary about the UFO cover up and the Rendlesham Forest case was made by SKY TV. This programme, No Defence Significance, *scored ratings so high that it beat many popular dramas such as* LA Law.

—— 24 ——

DEADLY RENDEZVOUS

Photographs released by MUFON showing the extent of the injuries sustained by Betty Cash and her grandson on the night of 29 December 1980 are horrifying.

Some cases seem to indicate that UFOs can seriously damage your health. A number of incidents have occurred, after which the witness is left with clear physical ailments. Such cases seem to provide strong evidence of UFO reality. Few were better in this respect, or received a bigger public profile, than the Cash/Landrum encounter.

Restaurant owner Betty Cash heard that a competitor was opening up in her area, so on the night of 29 December 1980 she decided to check them out. With Betty was her friend and senior staff member, Vickie Landrum, who brought along her seven-year-old grandson, Colby. They were driving towards Dayton, Texas, through a pine forest at around 9pm when they noticed a fiery object in the sky. It quickly descended to treetop height and hovered menacingly over the road ahead, forcing the car to a halt just 135 feet away.

Descriptions varied. Betty described it as a very bright light with no distinct shape, but her friend thought it was elongated with a rounded top and pointed lower half. Colby went one step further and said it was diamond-shaped. The witnesses climbed out of the car for a better look, even though they were very afraid. Bursts of flame, accompanied by sounds similar to a flame thrower, jetted down from beneath the object. There was also a roaring and bleeping noise that lasted throughout the encounter.

The whole thing was too much for the little boy, who pleaded with the women to get back in the car with him. He was very distressed, so Vickie got inside with him. Betty remained looking at the object for a little longer. When she took hold of the door handle, it was so hot it was difficult to grasp. The heat from the UFO was fierce and burned her wedding ring into her finger. Inside the car the little boy was hysterical and his grandmother thought it was the end of the world.

The object began to move off and the witnesses decided to follow it. As they did so they noticed around twenty-three twin-rotor helicopters, later identified as Chinooks, which were following the object. The helicopters never got closer than three-quarters of a mile. After stopping a few more times to observe the spectacle, the two women and the child went home. Betty arrived at 9.50pm after dropping the other two off.

Radiation symptoms and cancer

Within hours horrific symptoms similar to radiation poisoning manifested in all three of them. Young Colby suffered 'sunburn' on his face and eye inflammation. His grandmother also had inflammation of the eyes, plus some odd indentations across her fingernails and temporary hair loss. Betty, who had been exposed longest, suffered the most.

In the first four days she complained of blinding headaches, nausea, vomiting and diarrhoea. She also experienced neck pains, swollen eyes and blisters on her scalp, which burst releasing a clear liquid. At the end of this period she was admitted to Parkway General Hospital in Houston as a burn victim. Specialists who were called in to examine her were unable to diagnose her complaints. After leaving hospital she soon returned, as she was no better: now her hair was falling out in clumps. In just two months her medical bill amounted to $10,000. But that was not all. Betty developed breast cancer and was forced to have a mastectomy.

The photographs released by MUFON showing the extent of the injuries are shocking. There is absolutely no doubt that the women and the little boy were confronted by something which resembled nothing within the framework of their previous experience. It was unrecognisable as an aircraft, or as a permutation of any conventional terrestrial flying machine. When the victims of this potentially lethal object learned that the American government did not recognise the UFO phenomenon (at least publicly), they decided that the object which had caused them so much physical damage must belong to that government and decided to sue for $20 million.

The case dragged on for several years in the US District Court in Houston. During this time the story generated numerous newspaper articles and television documentaries. Incredibly, despite its high profile in America, the case was totally ignored by the British media.

In court were representatives of NASA, the Air Force, Army and Navy. The judge dismissed the case in August 1986 on the grounds

Incidents like the Cash/Landrum affair and Michalak's encounter illustrate the deadly potential of the phenomenon. There is a growing body of cases in which victims are damaged psychologically and physically, perhaps even killed. If abductions also turn out to be real, we are looking at a phenomenon which controls, takes, abuses and damages humans without conscience or regret. Angelic beings from outer space these are not…

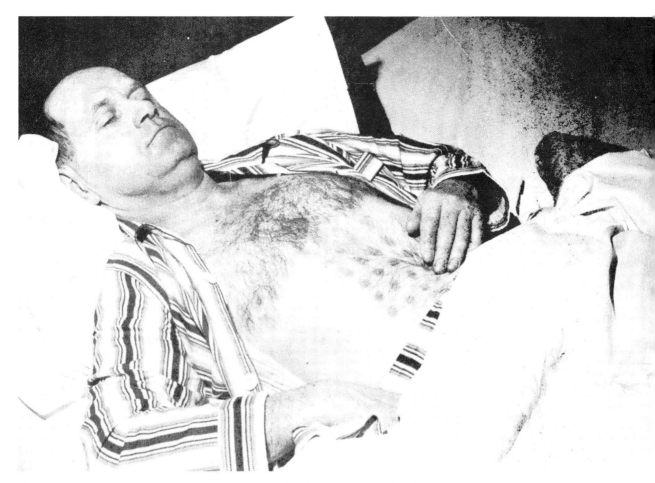

that no such device was owned, operated or listed by any branch of the American government. The case was investigated in their part-time capacities as UFO researchers by NASA scientists John Shuessler and Dr Alan Holt. Schuessler told British ufologist Timothy Good: 'Judge Ross Sterling considered the expert testimony to be sufficient reason to dismiss the case. That means he will not meet Betty Cash, Vickie and Colby Landrum, and he will not hear evidence they wanted their attorneys to present.' Schuessler also pointed out that the evidence regarding the helicopters was virtually ignored. Despite the statements of additional witnesses in the area, no agency would accept liability for the Chinooks!

What are we to conclude about this? Is it significant that the encounter occurred at about the same time events were unfolding across the Atlantic in Rendlesham Forest? Was it a cover-up of some very sensitive prototype vehicle? Rumours abounded that the object was an

This photograph remains one of the best examples of injury caused by a UFO. Canadian prospector Steve Michalak was in a remote location near Falcon Lake, Ontario, in May 1967 when he says that he inspected a landed UFO. This let out a blast of hot air which burnt a checker pattern into his skin. Michalak was treated in hospital and his story is one of the most graphic pieces of physical evidence for the reality of UFOs.

experimental nuclear-powered space shuttle which was experiencing difficulties, or that it was a retrieved alien craft which was being test-flown. It is now several years since the incident happened. If it was a new fledgeling Earth technology, why have we seen nothing more of it? Surely it would have been refined by now?

The military helicopters provide a new twist to an old dilemma. There is a painting of a man swimming in the sea. He has one arm outstretched to attract the attention of people on the beach. The title of the picture is *Drowning not Waving*. On that night of 29 December, were the helicopters 'Escorting not Chasing' or 'Chasing not Escorting'? Either way, three victims bear the physical and mental scars which prove they were escorting, or chasing, *something*.

—— 25 ——

ABDUCTION MANIA

Abduction mania was rife by 1982.

By the early 1980s there had been over a hundred cases of alleged alien abduction and a pattern was forming. To some extent that was because 90 per cent of these cases were from the USA and so were very consistent in outline.

Overseas there were far fewer cases. Many countries, such as Australia, had had none at all even by the mid-1980s. In places like Britain the trend was different from the USA. The entities tended to be tall, blond-haired, and blue-eyed – similar to those relatively friendly Nordics which featured in non-abduction cases from Europe throughout the 1950s.

However, this discrepancy went largely unnoticed, as did other patterns that were turning up. In the Far East, for instance Malaysia, entities were only a few inches in height, while South America had a plethora of cases where the aliens were said to be dwarf-like and covered in hair.

The American experience

Ufologists readily ignored this, because the American abduction cases received most publicity. All the movies made about the subject were based on American cases, and it was in the USA that most of the serious abduction research was being conducted. This created an illusion that the type of abduction story emerging from America was identical with what was occurring worldwide. It was not, although there were broad similarities in the scenario reported.

A typical American abduction case would involve a witness (usually alone, although occasionally as part of a couple or rarer still in a family group) who was driving on a lonely road late at night when a strange light was spotted in the sky. There were problems with their engine or lights, and they may then have heard odd noises or felt peculiar sensations in their mind. Then they would 'come to' at a different location and suddenly discover that a period of time (perhaps fifteen minutes, or even up to a couple of hours) had simply vanished from their recall.

During the course of days and weeks dreams or flashback images might hint to the witness about a hidden memory of alien contact. A ufologist would probably suggest they underwent regression hypnosis, using the methods already explored through the Hills' 1961 encounter and various successors.

This hypnosis almost always uncovered 'memories', or rather what were interpreted to be memories by the investigator (and therefore the witness). A story of an apparent abduction by strange creatures crystallised. This tended to involve a medical examination, increasing claims that genetic samples such as blood and tissue were being taken, and other common patterns such as being shown three-dimensional films about the fate of the Earth.

Of course, almost all of these features of the American abductions had already been well publicised after the emergence of the Hills case in 1966. The aliens were a slightly evolved variant of a four-feet-tall figure with a large domed head, pasty skin and huge dark eyes – a type known as the Greys.

A little-known film gem touches on UFO abductions and focuses on the military response to UFO activity. The Disappearance of Flight 419 *is arguably the most intelligent film drama about UFOs yet made.*

Sprinkle and Hopkins

The first abduction researcher was psychologist Dr Leo Sprinkle, who carried out the hypnosis on officer Herb Schirmer for Condon's team at the University of Colorado in 1968. Sprinkle was ensnared by the phenomenon and has conducted many experiments. He was reaching intriguing conclusions.

He hosts annual gatherings of abductees and feels they are somehow undergoing a spiritual progression. The ethos of the cases that he was uncovering was very positive, as if aliens were giving us a hand up the ladder of evolution. Many witnesses had psychic backgrounds, experienced other strange phenomena and took an active interest in the environment.

Budd Hopkins followed in Sprinkle's footsteps. He was neither a scientist nor a psychologist – in fact a celebrated New York artist. Unlike Sprinkle he went public in a very big way. His first book, summarising a dozen cases from 1975 onwards, was entitled *Missing*

Time. It appeared from a small publisher in 1982 and had minimal impact outside the UFO world; but within ufology, especially in the USA, its effect was tremendous.

The problems of hypnosis

Hopkins worked with a psychologist at first but has since done his own regressions; some people have been critical of this because he lacks a medical background. In 1982 the British UFO Research Association imposed a code of practice on all members, banning hypnosis without medical supervision, and in 1987 it introduced a voluntary moratorium on all use. It never received any credit from the sceptics for this act, even though they were vociferous about the abuse of hypnosis as a tool in abduction research.

The problem with hypnosis was recognised by Dr Benjamin Simon, who had first used it within ufology on Betty and Barney Hill. He showed that it was not 'a royal road to truth' but could reveal fantasy as easily as hidden memory. Experiments by countless psychologists (and some work since in UFO situations) have readily proven that about 50 per cent of checkable 'facts' retrieved from regression hypnosis are imagination: they never really happened. Witnesses can be subtly coerced into thinking something is a memory when it was implanted by suggestion under hypnosis in an unconscious way. Because of this, hypnosis is rarely used in criminal prosecutions.

Alien contact is a subject for which you can never check the facts since nobody knows what they are! So the value of hypnosis is diminished further. At least one sincere abductee (police officer Alan Godfrey, abducted in Todmorden in West Yorkshire in November 1980) has admitted that, whilst he did see a real UFO, his subsequent alien kidnap story retold under hypnosis is, he feels, far less reliable. It could be a fantasy based on books he had read. This kind of contamination is so serious that hypnosis cannot be trusted.

Hopkins is undoubtedly sincere and widely considered to be a researcher with the best of motives, keen to assist witnesses who approach him, but there are some who have expressed concern about his use of regression hypnosis, particularly given his lack of medical background. Hypnotic regression back to alien abduction is a deeply contentious issue. Some people feel that we must draw back from what can fairly be termed an 'abduction mania' that has swept through much of world ufology since the early 1980s.

Clearly something puzzling is going on in these cases. The question is whether widespread hypnosis illuminates the way towards a solution or shrouds the evidence in a blanket of fog.

Budd Hopkins's second book was published in 1987, by which time he was well known through the media and as a lecturer around the world. This book, *Intruders*, had huge sales and discussed one particular case from Indiana. A TV mini-series based upon it was made in 1992 and has been shown all over the world, ensuring that the American stereotype image is deeply engrained in the minds of billions. It has gradually killed off nearly all other variants on the theme.

The 'goodies' and the 'baddies'

It is interesting that Hopkins's witnesses more frequently report 'Greys' than do Sprinkle's. The pattern of medical examination and genetic adaptation is there, but his cases are generally more terrifying. He claims to find little sign of psychic overlap and his witnesses seem more like victims with negative after-effects. They have been likened by psychologists to women who have been raped, with similar post-traumatic stress symptoms. The scenario that emerges from Hopkins's cases is of a group of alien scientists involved in a secret invasion and out to create some kind of genetic hybrid baby via their (mostly female) crop of abused abductees.

The comparison between these two sub-groups of data can be likened in fiction to a 'war of the worlds' scenario (Hopkins) versus the far more pleasant theme of Spielberg's 'close encounters of the third kind' (in Sprinkle's cases). Since Hopkins's version has had far more media attention in the past decade, it has become almost irrepressibly dominant worldwide.

However, these differences cannot be ignored. The fact that since 1987, when Greys were popularised on a global scale by people like Hopkins and Strieber, the data outside the USA has adapted to this pattern is clear evidence of a human dimension behind the reports. The way in which the form and behaviour of the entities previously tied in with the culture from which they emerged was another clue, as was cultural tracking – meaning that cases never display technology in advance of our own, but just at the very edge of it.

American abductees see domineering scientists who want to change the world to conform with their own concept of it. South Americans encounter mythological figures who are hirsute and aggressive. British and other European witnesses have tended to meet genteel, civilised but rather wishy-washy aliens who seemed afraid to do too much because it might upset the universal balance.

It was left to non-American abduction researchers to point out such problems. In 1980, before Australia was swamped with a run of 'Grey' abductions, Keith Basterfield published a book entitled *UFOs: The Image Hypothesis*, suggesting a psychological theory that did not dent American ufology. He proposed that the experiences were a form of vivid and unusual hallucination. Later he worked with psychologist

Fate magazine 1992. This special issue on UFO abduction shows the modern abduction mania.

Dr Robert Bartholomew to pioneer the concept that witnesses to abductions were what are called 'fantasy-prone personalities' – a small section of humanity known to possess such vivid fantasy lives that they find it hard to distinguish some of their imaginative memories from real ones. This theory is in retreat, but it was important that such a concept should be tested by ufologists.

In 1988 Jenny Randles published a book entitled *Abduction* which had minimal impact in the USA. It pointed out the human dimension to the abduction, the psychic overlap, the way in which witnesses were being found to have a high level of visual creativity and the need to seek a solution that explained all such aspects of the mystery as well – not just the domineering but rather one-dimensional approach of American research.

Almost no alien abductions are known from India, Japan and other eastern countries. Nobody knows why.

Some feel that positive and negative outcomes can occur, and the rather hackneyed format of the 'little grey scientists performing medical experiments' is a direct result of this evaluation being imposed upon the data by ufologists, notably in the USA. In other cultures where that is less prevalent witnesses evaluate their experiences differently and tend to have other (often more user-friendly) types of spacenapping encounters.

A beacon of hope also emerged from folklore researcher Dr Eddie Bullard at Indiana State University. He attempted to establish that the abduction was a modern mythology by comparing it with the genesis of folk tales throughout history. He failed to prove this and believes there is an underlying reality to these cases. But he did stress the importance of the anomalous findings and conducted a major study of eight hundred abduction cases that were available by 1992. This finally persuaded some elements of the American UFO movement that the situation was a lot more complex than it might seem.

Also in 1992 psychologist Dr Kenneth Ring from the University of Connecticut discovered the human side to the abduction mystery. He had been a leading expert in the NDE (near death experience), where people on the verge of death but who survive to tell the tale were frequently reporting vividly real visions. These included bright lights, abduction into a strange world and contact with entities. The comparisons with alien abduction had already been spotted by some ufologists, but Ring used his influence in a major comparative study of the psychological profile of each group. His conclusions appeared in *The Omega Project* and proposed that both NDE and abduction were part of a spiritual puberty through which some 'advanced' members of the human race were passing. Whether his theory eventually proves any more valuable than the simplistic view of alien spacenappings, Ring has again emphasised the work of non-American ufologists for the American audience and may have ensured that more sophisticated work will continue in the future.

The alien abduction phenomenon is a deeply mystifying experience. It may not even relate to the UFO phenomenon in its basic form at all – except by the modern cultural inference that it must do. It shows many differences from simple lights in the sky. These may well be physically real, even if spacenappings are 'only' phenomena of an inner space reality.

26

CIRCULAR REASONING

Although alien abductions dominated ufology in the USA during the 1980s, another issue was to the fore in Europe, especially in Britain.

Flattened crops

In August 1980 a farmer at Westbury in Wiltshire discovered three swathes of gently flattened oat crop on his land. They formed circles about sixty feet across, with neat swirled centres and edges still standing erect. It looked as if something had descended from the skies and squashed the field: the resemblance to a UFO was obvious. The area was inspected by ufologists, including Ian Mrzyglod from the group Probe. Then the farmer harvested the fields and the mystery was over.

Mrzyglod and his team checked the matter sensibly. After consulting physicist Dr Terence Meaden, a specialist in wind damage from tornadoes, they concluded that the circles were probably the result of an unusual type of rotating air vortex called a 'fairweather stationary whirlwind'.

Sporadic circles appeared in 1981 and 1982 at other locations in Hampshire and Wiltshire. Reports in the *Journal of Meteorology* dismissed the idea of a spaceship which was being voiced by some ufologists.

Then, in July 1983, everything changed. Suddenly a dramatic five-pattern formation appeared – with a central circle and four satellites. It looked blatantly artificial, but Dr Meaden sought the cause in more complicated air vortices. Further examples appeared during the next few days as public interest grew.

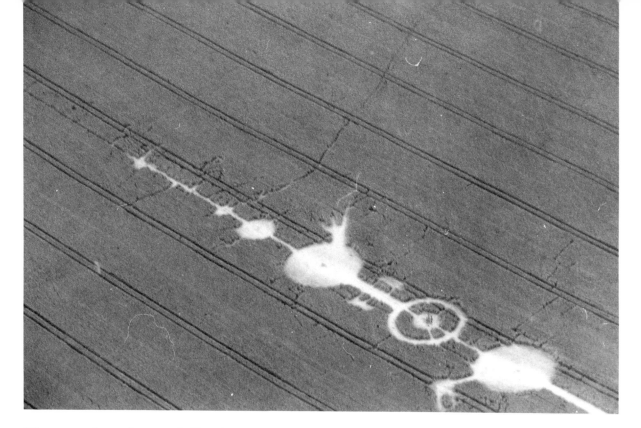

The weather theory falls down

Ufologist Pat Delgado took the story to the media, stressing the idea that an intelligence (presumably alien of some sort) might be producing the marks for unknown reasons. Immediately a new subject was born. The weather theory, which worked well for simple circles, looked feeble in the face of these 'quintuplets' and the media revelled in the silly season story that they were handed, linking the marks with the popular movie *ET* which was then on release.

Delgado later joined forces with another newcomer, Colin Andrews, and wrote pieces for *Flying Saucer Review* magazine which sought evidence to support such ideas. Each summer brought new formations and increasing numbers via aerial surveillance, usually focused on southern England. Rings appeared around circles, then double and triple rings. The image of someone having a joke at the expense of the eager media and growing band of circle watchers (many of them former ufologists) is obvious in hindsight.

Some ufologists gave strong support to Meaden's weather theory for the simpler patterns but began to uncover a trend of hoaxing. Mrzyglod exposed the first, in August 1983, when a national newspaper paid for the creation of a quintuplet to try to fool a rival paper. This was never reported, as the media had soon lost interest. A real mystery was left in people's minds.

By the end of the decade the crop circle mystery was an internationally recognised phenomena with tourists flocking from all over the world to see the latest formations in southern England. Complex formations such as this co-called 'pictogram' began in 1989 and enterprising farmers charged entrance fees for people to walk inside them. This is a famous pattern found at Alton Barnes, Wiltshire in July 1990.

Cerealogical celebrities

In 1989 Andrews and Delgado, with the help of pilot 'Busty' Taylor, produced a book full of spectacular aerial photographs. *Circular Evidence* played on the mystery, adding many side-issue stories (from dogs getting sick inside circles to aircraft crashing in nearby fields long after the circles were harvested). This, plus the undoubtedly challenging visual enigma which was there for all to go and see each summer, ensured that their clarion call for circle research became a bestseller.

The two men were now celebrities in their own new field, soon christened cerealogy: it spawned three magazines and countless societies. Meaden produced *The Circles Effect and Its Mysteries*, a scientific text which he published himself. Only a few took seriously his theory that the weather could explain virtually everything, including the increasingly complex circular formations.

Hoaxes

Ufologists Jenny Randles and Paul Fuller self-published their own thesis, the only book to explain the social background and take hoaxing seriously. It suggested that Meaden's vortex was creating some circles and hoaxes others, notably the more recent weird shapes. But it still undersold the importance of hoaxing, which nobody had recognised.

The circles changed in direct response. From 1990 they became pictograms – with arcs, straight lines and geometric shapes emphasising that they were the product of an intelligence. In 1990 numbers rose to over five hundred and formed all over Europe, with resultant increased media attention.

Meaden still tried to fit his weather theory into the by now absurd array of patterns. Andrews, Delgado and other rising stars of the circle world were delighted by the pictograms, which to them proved their case.

For most cerealogists the new marks were proof that someone was conveying a message. Fascinated Americans would arrive in Europe each summer and buy fields where they would carve out symbols and await replies in the crop. In 1993 they claim to have got an answer – the sign for a disabled toilet! Another team armed with lasers tried to initiate contact with the circle makers. One UFO group even claimed a success, with aliens who gave – via automatic writing (words transmitted through the mind of a medium directly on to paper using the medium's hand and a pen) – a self-portrait as a kind of invisible dentist's drill!

The ridiculous level to which the phenomenon had descended was shown through smiling faces, whales, dolphins, flowers and so on – clear frauds turning up in many fields. There was even a message in English saying: 'We are not alone.' Randles and Fuller realised that if this was from an alien visitor it should have said '*You* are not alone'!

Paul Fuller issued a warning in a new magazine of hard-hitting investigation, *The Crop Watcher* and in a further book written with Jenny Randles, *Crop Circles: A Mystery Solved*, both of which appeared in 1990. They were slammed by the cerealogists, but their timely words predicted the coming pictograms, emphasised the need to take hoaxing seriously and pointed out 'name games' being played by what were now clearly human tricksters jousting annually with the cerealogists. But the warnings went unheeded. Circles turned up near Fakenham in Suffolk and nobody batted an eyelid!

The fraudsters come forward

The come-uppance was inevitable. In September 1991 two elderly artists, Doug Bower and Dave Chorley, came forward to claim that they had faked hundreds of circles. After the ones at Westbury had been reported, in 1980, they had constantly elaborated their designs to try to egg the researchers on. The pictograms were expressly designed to kill off Meaden's weather theory, which was getting too much serious exposure for their liking. By 1991 thousands of circles had appeared; Doug and Dave professed to have made about 10 per cent of them and to have largely manipulated people's belief in the mystery.

Doug and Dave approached *Today*, a tabloid newspaper, and faked a circle under journalists' supervision. The unwitting Pat Delgado pronounced it genuine; only later was he told the shocking truth. At first he accepted that the game was up, but after talking with Colin Andrews changed his mind. Thousands of cerealogists breathed more easily. Soon afterwards the partnership split and Andrews moved to the USA, where he was in constant demand to lecture.

Doug and Dave were largely ignored by the cerealogists, despite their evidence. They possessed photographs of earlier circles which they had faked and nobody else had filmed. They said they had signed the last few before 'retirement' in 1991 with big letter 'D's. There were indeed many examples that seemed to support this.

A few small circle groups gave up altogether after *Today*'s exposure, but most fought on as if nothing had happened. A bizarre series of stories were published in the specialist literature, intimating that Doug and Dave were pawns in some secret operation by the British government, out to discredit cerealogy and leave Whitehall free to do their

More than 25 groups of crop circle hoaxers have admitted to their escapades in English crop fields between 1976 and 1994. Some hoaxers have odd code names – like 'Bill Barley' and 'Spiderman'.

One of the photographs from *Today*, showing how Doug Bower and Dave Chorley made their circles.

own research. We find this suggestion absurd – although it has helped cerealogy to ride the storm into the 1990s. But the media attention has gone and, indeed, only a fraction of the circles that used to appear every summer are now found.

Some truth in the matter

Crop Watcher magazine quickly accepted Doug and Dave's story after they examined it; this was in fact easy, as they had stressed hoaxing for some time. However, they do believe that a few simple circles are (and always have been) the result of an atmospheric effect which can also trigger UFOs.

There is good evidence for this. Crop circles have been traced back in scientific journals and through other data to long before Doug and Dave were born. There are even folk tales from the Middle Ages which may relate to them. Single circles swirled into crops have appeared all over the world on a sporadic but regular basis.

Ironically, on the day Doug and Dave were telling the world of their

Crop circles came to world attention during the 1980s but they may not be an entirely new phenomenon. Reports of them have been traced back into previous centuries and this woodcut dating from August 1678 seems to suggest that they may have existed in the Middle Ages, where they were interpreted as the work of 'mowing devils'.

spoof Jenny Randles was in the Queensland bush in Australia investigating a reed swamp near Tully. It was a circle which formed here in January 1966 that was, the two admit, the trigger for their trickery. But they did not hoax the original. It formed in a remote area infested with deadly snakes and aboriginal legends tell of strange lights seen here. Many circles have repeatedly formed locally. Other photographs that pre-date the first hoax by Doug and Dave have also been traced.

Randles and Fuller updated their book in 1993, reviewing all of this evidence and including laboratory experiments by physicists in the USA and Japan who were re-creating the circle-making force. It seems, after all, that a real phenomenon may have been behind a few circles amidst the many hoaxes.

27

WHITLEY STRIEBER – A BREACH IN REALITY?

One of the most controversial and acrimonious abduction cases involved best-selling horror novelist Whitley Strieber, who wrote two books on the affair. The first, *Communion*, was published in 1987, followed by *Transformation* a year later. According to the author, the watershed event occurred over Christmas 1985. The Striebers had an apartment in New York and a 'cabin' in the woods in an isolated part of the state, which was where the main events occurred.

Christmas visitors

On 26 December Whitley and his wife, Anne, went to bed at ten o'clock; their six-year-old son had gone much earlier. In the middle of the night Strieber was woken by a whooshing, whirling noise coming from downstairs. There seemed to be several people moving about. He checked the burglar alarm panel beside the bed, but no door or window had been breached. A short time later the bedroom door opened and a figure entered the room.

The creature was wearing a sort of breastplate and a skirt which came down to its knees. As the being rushed towards him, Strieber blacked out. He then remembers being carried, or floating, naked through the woods. After a further loss of consciousness he found himself sitting in a depression, paralysed, with his eyesight not functioning properly. Opposite him was one of the creatures, wearing some sort of face mask, and beside him, doing something to his head, was another. This one seemed feminine in some indefinable way, and wore dark blue overalls. Then the treetops rushed away beneath him and he was on the grey floor of a 'messy' domed room with a 'lens' at its apex.

Medical experiments

Strieber became terrified as several of the small beings moved about him. The terror was well founded. One of them produced a long, thin needle from a box and 'told' him they were about to insert it into his brain, via his nasal cavity. He argued, but they went ahead and did it anyway. Altogether there were four types. The one in his bedroom had seemed robot-like, while the main group were short and stocky, with deep-set glittering eyes and pug noses. Inside the 'room' he had seen some five-foot-tall creatures with large, almond-shaped black eyes, and a smaller one with round button eyes. The last thing he could recollect about the experience was a feeling of anger as they inserted a long triangular object up his rectum.

When he awoke as normal on the 27th, he had a feeling of unease and a bizarre memory of seeing a barn owl staring at him through the window during the night. Of the abduction he remembered nothing. Yet when he looked for claw marks in the snow on the window ledge there was nothing. Strieber was later to come to the conclusion that the owl was a 'screen memory' to hide what really happened.

Author and abductee, Whitley Strieber.

The terrible aftermath

He then went through a downward personality change. As vague, disturbing images pierced the screen memory, and inexplicable physical symptoms emerged, he believed something awful had happened. He turned to a Christmas present from his brother – *Science and the UFOs* by Jenny Randles and Peter Warrington – and found similarities between their description of an archetypal abduction and his own experiences. In fact the similarities were so close that Strieber says he was 'shocked'.

After discovering that a number of UFO sightings had taken place in the area of the cabin Strieber contacted Budd Hopkins, an American ufologist who uses hypnosis extensively to aid recall. Hopkins prompted him to remember vague details of a previous incident in the cabin. That had occurred on 4 October 1985, when the family had entertained Jacques Sandulescu and Annie Gottlieb as weekend guests.

Strieber remembered an intense light surrounding the cabin during the night, which made him think the roof was on fire. A loud 'bang' had woken them all up. A week later Strieber had a 'memory' of a huge crystal hovering over the cabin, glowing with blue light.

After seeing Hopkins, he phoned up his friends and asked them if they remembered the night in the cabin. Jacques vividly remembered the light. His watch had said it was four-thirty, but the trees and bushes had been lit up as if it was ten in the morning. More disturbing were the recollections of his son. He had suffered a 'dream' where a group of 'little doctors' had taken him outside and put him on a bed. When he grew afraid, they repeated over and over in his head: 'We won't hurt you...'

What followed for Strieber were terrible dreams and stress that almost destroyed his marriage. Finally he went to see Dr Donald Klein of the New York State Psychiatric Institute, wondering if he was insane.

Further abduction memories

Next came hypnotic regression which added details to the October and December incidents, but also uncovered another dimension in the process. Apparently the twelve-year-old Whitley, together with his father and sister, had been abducted from a train in 1957! This led him on a trail of investigation into his own past, which uncovered several other anomalous experiences, remembered in part by childhood friends. There were strange memories of seeing wild animals, which he became convinced were camouflage for terrible experiences. The experiences continued beyond the 1985 Christmas watershed.

Whitley Strieber published his account of events up to 1987 in *Communion*, a title allegedly communicated to him by his wife, speaking in a strange voice whilst in a deep sleep. The book had several immediate effects – it became an international bestseller, precipitated a flood of correspondents who thought they too had been assaulted by 'visitors', and attracted a furious backlash by critics from within the UFO community and outside it. Some of the more extreme sceptics were Strieber's former colleagues in the science fiction and horror genres. Strieber is a major horror *fiction* writer. Although he reported this story as horror *non*-fiction, many of his peers were confused and presumed it was another *Amityville* hoax, a nub of truth embellished to make a better story. Strieber flatly denied this charge.

Dr Klein suggested to Strieber that his experiences might be due to an abnormality in the temporal lobe of his brain. Sufferers often exhibit a lack of humour, report strong smells, and experience vivid hallucinatory journeys and unexplained panic. Strieber underwent tests by two different neurologists. According to him, neither could find evidence of brain abnormality. If indeed there are witnesses to parts, or some, of the experiences, then 'hallucinations' was an untenable explanation anyway.

Strieber subjected himself to some painful laboratory tests and reportedly came out with a clean bill of health. Indeed, Donald Klein provided him with a statement for use in *Communion* which said that 'he is not suffering from a psychosis'. But UFO debunker Philip Klass takes issue with this in his book *UFO Abductions – a Dangerous Game*. Klass states that there is some confusion in the dates provided by Strieber of when the tests took place. In Appendix One of *Transformation*, Strieber states that all the medical findings have been turned over to a Dr John Gliedman. He has been given permission to discuss these findings with enquirers who have proper medical and scientific credentials. Klass has tried, however, to obtain Strieber's permission for access to the complete records, but has so far failed. This is perhaps not surprising, as Strieber might fear that Klass would use the material selectively, to bolster his anti-abduction stance.

An illustration from *Communion* as seen by Whitley Strieber.

Beyond *Communion*

Transformation takes us beyond *Communion*, chronologically and in terms of credulity. While researchers in the field are used to dealing with extreme material, to outsiders and critics this must have seemed 'beyond the boggle threshold'. Here the 'visitors' were woven in with dream material and the very worst nightmares of horror writer H.P. Lovecraft. The visitors began to look less like extraterrestrials and more

Communion was later made into a film. Strieber had a hand in its production, and Christopher Walken played the part of the abductee.

like the ghouls and succubi of demonology. This was no longer the straightforward abduction of a human being for experimentation aboard a spacecraft, but a twisted journey through the subterranean dimensions of inner space. More than ever, the edges of the fact/fiction interface were blurring.

Lecturing on the British Empire

One of the strangest events happened on 1 April. Strieber 'woke up' walking along a corridor with a tingling sensation going through his body. He was being led by two small dark blue beings, and he was dressed in a long flowing garment made of paper. The corridor was the colour of flesh. When Strieber commented to the creatures about their colour, one of them replied: 'We used to be like your blacks but we decided this was better.'

The corridor was lined along one wall with drawers. Strieber felt it was a beautiful place, and wondered if in some way it was alive: 'The *place* seemed conscious. Was I actually inside some kind of creature?' He was then led into a room with louvred windows, 'something like a round version of a regimental dining room from the days of the British Raj in India'. The place was filled with translucent white beings who seemed to be in pain. Their leader led Strieber to the centre of the room where he was asked to give a lecture on why the British Empire had collapsed! He complied, but his efforts met with sarcasm and 'cold indifference'.

Out in the corridor again, one of the blue beings pulled open one of the many drawers. It was full of alien bodies wrapped in cellophane. Strieber admits: 'I would be the first to agree that my perceptions may not reflect the objective reality of the experience.'

Dancing inside others

Similar weird experiences are claimed by Strieber later in the book. He remembers a strange journey on an 'aircraft' in 1968. During the turbulent flight, 'a nurse or stewardess' administered some medicine for nausea on his tongue from an eye dropper, and a blonde-haired passenger next to him 'read aloud from a book made of limp cloth'. At his destination he was met off the craft by several of the small entities.

He was in a desert and transported to an oasis. One of the entities showed him a tumbledown building, which was apparently some sort of university. At first a more fearsome alien refused him entry, saying that Strieber 'was not ready yet'. But the being went, and they entered anyway. Once again he was in a corridor, then he was taken into a room where he began to dance. 'When I danced I found myself for moments inside other people and their lives.' Later he met two khaki-uniformed 'Americans', one of whom was using a ciné camera apparently to film Strieber.

In another episode he was transported to a stone room, where a man was shackled on to a stone table and then whipped. This, he was informed, was punishment for failing to get Strieber 'to obey'. As the man was beaten to death, the entity told Strieber: 'It isn't real, Whitty, it isn't real.'

Problems of analysis

Transformation goes much further than *Communion*. If abduction by alien beings aboard a UFO was hard enough for some critics to swallow, then this was sure to stick in the throat. There are other things, too: apocalyptic visions, levitation, out-of-the-body experiences, disembodied voices and other poltergeist activities.

Strieber is a successful and commercially viable writer. However, his experiences seem essentially visionary and do not seem to be literally true, or, for much of the time, objectively true. This is a point that Strieber himself appreciates. If there really is no evidence of mental illness – a problem he confronts again and again – then either the experiences are a product of some higher self, or they really do originate from an outside source.

But there is a problem in this explanation, too. Strieber lists the names of witnesses who have, to a lesser degree, taken part in his experiences. One of the latest incidents took place in his forest cabin, where, allegedly, some journalists were present. Apparently the front door flew open and two of the journalists became paralysed. They watched in horror as several of the small entities came into the room and lifted up a bed containing a third person.

Strieber himself changes his mind a lot regarding the source of his experiences, and concludes that they are both subjective and objective – an objective source that can manifest to the percipient subjectively. Strieber has made some challenging and wonderful remarks. In *Transformation*, he came up with this speculation: 'I think that they must normally exist in some other state of being and that they use bodies to enter our reality as we use scuba gear to penetrate the depths of the sea.'

In a late night discussion programme called *After Dark*, broadcast on Channel 4 early in 1990, he said: 'It's the same experience described by

St Paul, except I was visited by aliens. It is the same net effect – a
mechanism that seeks to control and bring about change ... I have
experienced a breach in reality.'

— 28 —

INCIDENT ON ILKLEY MOOR

In December 1987 a former policeman was apparently abducted by alien entities on the Moor.

The apparent abduction by entities of a former policeman on Ilkley Moor in Yorkshire allegedly occurred on 1 December 1987. It is one of the most contentious abduction cases in Britain – due, oddly, to a photograph which the man took of one of the beings. Documentary evidence should have made the case more acceptable to the UFO community, but the reverse happened. It is ironic that the incident would have been readily embraced into the body of abduction literature if there had been no picture. The case, investigated and examined in depth by the authors, is vastly complex, and there is only room for an outline here.

Two lost hours

The victim, referred to as 'Philip Spencer', left Ilkley just after 7.10am to walk across the moor and visit his father-in-law who lived in a village on the far side. He took with him a compass, for safety reasons, and a camera, which he intended using for taking pictures of Ilkley town from the moor tops.

He passed the White Wells baths, which is now a museum, and made his way along a stand of trees up over a ridge into a small overgrown quarry. A movement caught his attention, and he turned to see a small 'green creature'. It scuttled away, then stopped, and made a dismissive movement with its right hand. It is at this moment that Spencer took the photograph.

The creature disappeared around an outcrop, and Spencer gave chase. When he arrived there, however, the entity had gone, and he was confronted with a hovering silver disc with a box-like object sliding into the domed top. In a split second it rose at a terrific speed and dis-

Enlargement of the 4′ 6″ entity a former police officer claims to have photographed on Ilkley Moor in December 1987.

appeared into cloud. Bewildered, Spencer returned to Ilkley instead of continuing his walk, and there discovered a discrepancy of almost two hours.

The negative was examined by several photographic experts, and computer image enhancement was attempted by Geoffrey Crawley of the *British Journal of Photography*. The shot was slightly under-exposed and blurred due to camera shake. All that Kodak could say with certainty was that the negative had not been interfered with.

Reversed magnetic fields

Spencer discovered a couple of days after the encounter that his compass was reversed. Instead of pointing north, the needle now pointed south. An electromagnetic field had reversed its polarity.

Peter Hough contacted the University of Manchester Institute of Science and Technology (UMIST), where Dr Edward Spooner, head of the Department of Electrical Engineering and Electronics, agreed to carry out some experiments with a similar compass. Hough and investigator Arthur Tomlinson spent the morning in Dr Spooner's laboratory; eventually he did succeed in reversing the compass. In his report, Spooner wrote: 'The intensity required is not great by some standards; in fact we could not produce a field sufficiently low as not to reverse the polarity of the needle. The minimum field we applied had a flux density of about 0.1 Tesla; this is still about 2000 times greater than the Earth's field.'

The tests had two ramifications. Reversal could be brought about using equipment found in the home or garage, but specialist knowledge was required and there was potential danger from electrocution and fire. Strong industrial magnets had no permanent effect on the compass, causing Dr Spooner to speculate that only a pulsed magnetic field would work. At a later date some new, more powerful magnets were obtained from Japan which did bring about a reversal. However, these were not obtainable outside the industry, and not available at all in 1987.

If an electromagnetic phenomenon connected with the flying object was responsible, it would also have left detectable magnetism in the surrounding rocks – assuming the change had been effected on the moors. Later 'evidence' indicated that it had happened 'elsewhere', thus making a magnetic survey of the location unnecessary.

Hough took a scientist from the Radiological Protection Service to the location. The area was tested for radiation and rocks were taken away for examination, but the results were negative.

Revelations under regression

Some months after the abduction, Spencer starting complaining that he was having dreams of a starry sky, and was concerned about the missing one hour and three-quarters. He wondered if hypnosis might help him remember. Journalist Matthew Hill contacted clinical psychologist Jim Singleton, who agreed to help. Singleton was amazed by the story which emerged during the subsequent hypnosis, although the UFO investigators present were not. It was a classic abduction scenario – although it did have one surprise. The much maligned photograph was taken at the *end* of the experience.

Under hypnosis, Spencer described being approached by the creature earlier in his walk, as he drew level with the trees. He became paralysed, then found himself levitated a few inches off the ground, following the being up the rise and over into the small quarry. There he

Ilkley Moor seems to be a hot bed of activity. Amongst other happenings, there is a strong rumour that another police officer suffered a UFO experience on the moor.

saw the hovering disc and an opening appeared in it. At this point everything went black, and he found himself in a white room. A voice told him over and over again not to be afraid.

Next he was 'put' on a table by several of the beings. A brightly lit horizontal tube then moved over the contours of his body and he closed his eyes. In this state he remarked that his 'nose feels uncomfortable'. Then he was allowed off the table and given a conducted tour of the 'craft'.

Through a 'window' he saw the Earth and realised he was in space. Next Spencer was taken into 'a big round room', where he described some sort of gyroscopic apparatus which provided the motive power for the craft. It was here that the compass and his camera, on straps around his neck, were pulled towards the centre of the room. Then he was in another room where he was shown two 'films'. The first depicted pollution flowing into rivers, scenes of mass destruction and people starving. It was communicated to him that the beings were very concerned about how we were treating our planet. Spencer would not discuss the second film, neither under hypnosis nor out of it. It was personal to him, and, as he told Jim Singleton: 'I'm not supposed to tell anybody about the film. It's not for them to know.'

Philip Spencer was then returned to the exact spot by the trees from where he was abducted. Under hypnosis he then related walking up the hill, seeing the creature and photographing it. His surprise at seeing the entity is remarkable, as he had described being in their company only seconds previously. The segment of 'missing' time has clearly defined edges.

While Spencer was still hypnotised Jim Singleton asked for a description of the beings. 'They're quite small, about four foot, with big pointed ears and big eyes. They're quite dark. They haven't got a nose and only a little mouth. Their hands are enormous, and their arms are long. They've got funny feet, like a V-shape, like two big toes. They've got three big fingers, like sausages. Big sausages.' Afterwards, Spencer told Hough that the skin of the creatures was rough-looking, and that he had seen no evidence of genitals.

Genuine or a hoax?

Did the incident really happen, or was it a complex hoax? There can be no grey area – no talk of subjectivity here – because the photograph puts paid to that argument.

On the picture, to the right of the figure, is a square-shaped blob.

Hough noticed this and realised it was in approximately the right place to correspond with the 'box' which disappeared into the roof of the disc. Was this further photographic evidence?

A year after the incident two Yorkshire investigators, Philip Mantle and Andy Roberts, visited the location and took site photographs. On one of them appeared the 'blob'. Although it was not as obvious as on the original, nevertheless there was no doubt that it was in exactly the same place. They told the authors: 'It would seem that the lighting conditions and the moisture content in the ground have to be exactly right for the phenomenon to appear.'

It was on the slope of the far bank. When they walked towards it, the illusion disappeared. This satisfied Andy Roberts that the whole thing was a hoax. In his opinion Spencer had noticed the blob in the picture and incorporated the idea of the box into his story, then waited for someone to notice it. This reasoning certainly makes sense, but what are the indicators that the affair might be genuine?

From the start, Philip Spencer was adamant that his true identity should never be revealed; it would ruin him socially and professionally, he said. Spencer has never sought to make any money from his story, even though it was on offer. The mainstay of hoaxers is to see their names in print and improve their finances in the process. The only scenario which would make sense is if Spencer was a front man for a group out to discredit the investigators at a later date. Six years on, no one has come forward.

Despite the reference by debunkers of 'little green men', there are hardly any cases where entities have been described as such. Does this validate, or invalidate the Ilkley case? It is interesting that the colour of the figure almost camouflages it into the background. Is this accident or design?

Further incidents

But there were two other major incidents that same year up on Ilkley Moor, neither of which had any publicity. One, incredibly, involved another police officer, who may also have experienced an abduction. The other, in the summer of 1987, involved a local couple driving home.

The Cow and Calf rocks are just a quarter of a mile from where Philip Spencer was abducted. This outcrop overhanging the moor has been the location for several sightings of strange lights. Researcher Paul Devereux believes that such phenomena are a natural earth energy connected with seismic stress. On this occasion, the middle-aged couple were on the Addingham road when they became aware of a mass of white lights hovering over the rocks. Mrs Robinson tried to rationalise the sighting and said to her husband: 'I don't remember there being a farmhouse up there?' Mr Robinson, a fireman, confirmed there was nothing near the rocks to account for the lights.

They continued home, and the lights were still apparent. Although they lived just two minutes drive from the location, the couple decided not to investigate, although Mr Robinson afterwards regretted this decision.

Do these additional experiences validate Philip Spencer? Sometimes motivations for hoaxing are far from clear. Critics have said that such a hoax could have been the result of an abnormal state of mind, although that does not accord with Jim Singleton's observations. Singleton stated that he found Philip to be of a sensitive disposition, and went on to say: 'He was certainly recounting the incident as something which had actually happened. He described things typically as someone would recall a past event. He compares very well with other non-UFO subjects.' While accepting that people under hypnosis can modify and vary their recall, he went on to state: 'However, here I think I've helped Philip to recover memories that were hidden more deeply in the mind.'

Jim Singleton was as certain as he could be that Philip Spencer was not faking the hypnosis. There is another detail, too, which in its own small way strengthens the case. Under hypnosis, Spencer described seeing a door in the object, but did not recollect actually going through it. This 'doorway amnesia' is a component of most abductions. Anyone making up a story would automatically describe going into the 'space-ship'. In 1987 the term 'doorway amnesia' was not around, since ufologists had not yet widely recognised this component, so it is highly unlikely that Philip Spencer would have been aware of it either.

The Ilkley incident is potentially one of the most important abduction accounts. Here, for the first time, a victim may have taken a photograph of one of his abductors, proving the physical reality of the UFO phenomenon.

—— 29 ——

HOT AND COLD IN GULF BREEZE

In November and December 1987 UFOs of classic design were captured on film by Ed Walters.

It was the year of the UFO. Whitley Strieber's book was 1987's number one bestseller in the USA and the subject was on every chat show almost every week. In Britain Tim Good was heading the lists with *Above Top Secret*, which claimed a government cover-up of alien contact.

A new big case had to come. It struck the quiet and rather prim coastal town of Gulf Breeze, Florida, across the bridge from Pensacola with its massive naval air station.

Excellent photographic evidence

The story had unique features which assured notoriety. A large number of photographs were taken on Polaroid film during November and December and given to the *Gulf Breeze Sentinel* by local builder Ed Walters. He claimed to do so on behalf of an anonymous witness, which later proved to be himself.

The pictures were colourful and spectacular, certainly more so than the disappointing fare that had reached UFO groups for many years. Indeed some cautious ufologists were concerned about why, with better cameras and film now available to most of the population, the number and quality of UFO photographs submitted to them was falling – and not rising as expectation should decree.

The Gulf Breeze case changed all of that. Silhouetted against an indigo sky were UFOs of classic design. There were no flickering lights in the sky, such as in the images taken at the Hessdalen window area in Norway and so typical of the UFO photographic cases during the 1980s. These shots were of discs with windows and a complex design.

Gulf Breeze, Florida, is the world's most popular UFO skywatch site. UFO watchers gather every day to scan the skies for visitors.

Sometimes there was a single object, sometimes a flotilla. On one a UFO even appeared partially behind tree branches.

The media loved it. Big-name ufologists largely expressed their delight with the case, putting their reputations on the line by endorsing the images. Some wrote sections in a big-budget book about the case (*The Gulf Breeze Sightings*, published by Bantam in 1990). There were dissenters, mostly outside the USA, but they became a repressed minority barely tolerated by most ufologists.

Those who expressed concern were worried by the semi-transparent feel to the photographs, which had an unusually elaborate look about them. Furthermore, the whole history of ufology taught that UFOs never turned up in identical fashion week after week in one place to be filmed by the same man in a variety of poses. If they had done so here, as he claimed, then this case represented a dramatic new direction for the phenomenon.

Eventually, the identity of the photographer was revealed. Walters and his wife professed multiple experiences between autumn 1987 and spring 1988, many of which Walters had captured on his Polaroid camera. In one shot Ed, wrapped in a bath towel, shakes his fist at one of the UFOs, while in another a blue beam is projected down towards the house. The most remarkable of all is the so-called 'Road shot', on which a UFO is seen hovering only feet above a highway, casting a pool of light on to the ground. Walters took it from only a few feet away, crouching by his truck, apparently terrified. It is undoubtedly most impressive, but the angle of the illuminated patch on the road surface seems to some researchers not to match the orientation of the hovering UFO, although other experts have challenged that interpretation. Walters also professed to see aliens (whom he did not photograph) and even to have what appears to have been a near abduction experience.

Testing the evidence

Sceptics were accusing Walters of a double exposure trick – of taking a photograph of a model UFO in an otherwise darkened room and then refilming the background. When such a picture is processed, the two blend together. There were claims (which Walters denied) that he had created hoax photographs of a ghost in the past. Unfortunately a Polaroid camera has no negative, so meaningful analysis was very difficult in this case.

Dr Bruce Maccabee, an optical physicist who worked with the US Navy and has been a renowned investigator of UFO photographs,

GULF BREEZE

Display boards showing UFO photographs taken at Gulf Breeze, Florida, at MUFON UFO Symposium in 1988.

provided Walters with a specially constructed three-dimensional Polaroid camera which enabled him to try to film more UFOs. Simultaneous images would be secured and this would allow hard data about size and distances of the UFOs to be obtained.

Walters did succeed in taking a few pictures this way in March 1988, but not of the same kinds of object as seen before. Measurements indicated smaller dimensions. None the less, Maccabee was satisfied by the evidence that he saw and insisted that Walters really was filming strange objects. Walters also passed a lie detector test sprung upon him by surprise.

After spring 1988 the Walters's experiences ceased and they concentrated on writing their book, for which they were well paid. However,

Ed and Frances Walters followed up their book The Gulf Breeze Sightings *with a 1994 book* UFO Abductions in Gulf Breeze *concentrating on abduction claims in the Florida town.*

they were supported in their claims by other witnesses in the town, who described seeing UFOs like those that the Walters couple had filmed. Another anonymous photographer (whose identity has never been revealed and who simply called himself 'Believer Bill') supplied the local paper with pictures that were very similar to Ed Walters's Polaroids.

This case has been a source of great controversy within the UFO world. Some researchers, particularly the UFO group MUFON, staunchly defend it, while others, notably the J. Allen Hynek Center for UFO Studies, express doubts – although these were moderated after a time.

After the Walters moved home, evidence of the creation of a model UFO was discovered sketched on a piece of paper. A local youth also came forward to claim that he had helped create a hoax. Ed Walters denied all of this and offered some counter-evidence. His supporters contend that the incriminating material was planted there to discredit him – as indeed it could have been.

By 1993 regular skywatches were taking place by the Pensacola Bay bridge. Quite a few sightings have been alleged and Bruce Maccabee filmed something with his camcorder in May 1992, as have several others. However, some ufologists believe that many of these new sightings result from prank balloons, perhaps manufactured by unknown locals, then set alight and then allowed to drift over the bay in the knowledge that they might stimulate UFO sightings. If true, the motive may be to keep Gulf Breeze on the tourist map. At least one film depicts in close focus what appears to be burning debris from such a man-made 'UFO' dribbling down towards the ground as the glowing reddish light drifts gradually across the sky with the wind.

Whatever the full truth about the Gulf Breeze photographs and the Ed Walters saga, this case has already won a guaranteed place in UFO history.

— 30 —

THE MAJESTIC TWELVE

In 1987 copies of an official-looking document, classified top-secret, were sent anonymously to several prominent ufologists.

D isinformation seeded into the UFO community by persons unknown included some official-looking documents from just after
World War II which referred to a secret panel of politicians and
scientists known as the Majestic 12 or MJ12. According to the papers
their job was to act as a think tank on the UFO phenomenon, and to
report directly to President Truman. Copies of the nine-page report,
which was dated 18 September 1947 and classified top secret, were
sent anonymously during 1987 to several prominent ufologists, including Timothy Good. It named the twelve members who supposedly
dealt with general UFO reports and the Roswell case in particular (see
Part Four).

The twelve were all highly credible, and just the sort of specialists
who would be brought together to study the phenomenon. They
included top nuclear scientist Dr Vannevar Bush; Rear-Admiral Ros-
coe Hillenkoetter, a Director of the CIA and a firm believer in the reality
of UFOs; and General Nathan Twining, who, according to other
released documents, cancelled a previous appointment and rushed to
New Mexico on the day of the Roswell saucer crash.

Towards the end of 1986 Peter Hough and Jenny Randles became
embroiled in a strange affair. A man telephoned Jenny and claimed that
his commanding officer in the British Army had given him certain
documents to hand over. There were six reports totalling 600 pages.
During the conversation certain names and codes were mentioned
which later tallied with the MJ12 documents. The papers offered here
supposedly contained data from a scientist who had conducted biological analysis of alien bodies retrieved from UFO crashes. This report
was dated 1948, and another file, from October 1977, was reputedly
entitled 'Elimination of Non-Military Sources'.

John's story

Eventually a meeting was arranged between Randles, Hough and the man, referred to here as John, at a pub near Manchester. Over several hours he gave them a detailed account of the files and how he had come to be in possession of them. His answers to some very hard questioning were detailed and confident.

John had been in the Army until February 1985. His commanding officer had spent time on attachments in America where he had befriended a US Air Force officer at Wright-Patterson Air Force Base. This officer was a computer technician, and claimed he had accidentally accessed some secret UFO files; he copied them, but was arrested. His British friend found where they were hidden and brought them to England. Both officers believed the information should be released into the public domain. The American allegedly died in a car accident, although his friend thought he had been murdered.

Wondering how the files could be released, the officer tested each of his men to ascertain whom he could trust to assist him. It was not until John had left the Army, and returned for reservist weekend training, that his former commanding officer told him the full story. John agreed to help, and was told where the files were hidden and whom to contact.

John did not have the documents on him the day he met the authors. He claimed that fear had driven him to split them up and hide them in several different locations. Now he was wondering whether he should go ahead and just hand them over as originally planned. However, Randles and Hough demanded proof of their existence and a second meeting was arranged at which they would see 'samples'. This was arranged at a country park – but John never turned up. The investigators just wrote the whole thing off as an elaborate hoax.

Eleven days later, however, Jenny Randles received a letter from John in which he apologised for not attending the meeting; at the time he was taking part in an internal investigation. Two days after the meeting, John claimed he was taken to his base where he was interrogated about 'sensitive' documents which were 'the creation of an educated prankster' to which 'no credence could be attributed'.

This turned out to be perhaps more truthful than was apparent at the time. Central to the authenticity of the MJ12 documents was the signature of President Harry Truman. Supporters of the authenticity of the files pointed out that the signature could be genuine because it was identical to Truman's signature on another, non-UFO paper. But sceptics Joe Nickel and John Fischer claimed that the opposite was true

The UFO subject is littered with examples of interference by 'government officials'. Bogus documents, anonymous phone calls and letters seek to reinforce a belief held by many ufologists that we are being visited from outer space. That this should be attempted at all demonstrates the seriousness with which the authorities view the phenomenon. But are they encouraging a belief in extraterrestrials because the truth is even worse?

– the identicalness was proof that the signature was not genuine. They pointed out that no one signs their name exactly the same twice running. Further, they reasoned, if the signature was a forgery then so were all the MJ12 documents.

The real question that should be asked is this. Who forged the documents, and why did they think it necessary to do so?

—31—

UFO GLASNOST

Between 21 September and 28 October 1989, in the Western Park in Voronezh, there were six landings and one sighting, with the appearance of 'walking beings'.

Two of the largest nations on earth – China and the former USSR – were virtually unknown territory where UFOs were concerned for a very long time.

In communist-ruled China that remains true – although there are plenty of rumours of UFO reports of all complexions within the boundaries of this vast landmass.

As for the Soviet Union, we were a little more knowledgeable here thanks to visits paid by computer scientist Jacques Vallée and the testimony of ufologists who had fled to the west. Indeed one, Juri Lina, even set up a fake marriage to a Finnish girl in order to emigrate and escape the attentions of the KGB after private UFO group meetings in Moscow had been raided.

Despite restrictions on civilian ufology there was an intense military interest in the subject. Vallée discovered that there had been over ten thousand cases even by the mid-1960s. Several commissions were set up by the Academy of Sciences in Moscow, and a behavioural science researcher with government clearance spent time seeking Western UFO data from his base at a secret establishment in Novosibirsk during the late 1970s.

In the early 1980s a military investigation team was mounted and cosmonaut Marina Popovich was put in charge. Since democratisation she has attended UFO conferences and filled in many of the gaps.

UFO chases in Soviet air space

In November 1993 Tim Good claimed to have talked with a top official from the Russian defence establishment, who confirmed persistent rumours about Soviet jets sent in pursuit of UFOs they were tracking on radar. According to Good's source, so many have occurred that the authorities issued clear instructions to air bases: at first they were just to observe, and only later to intercept. Good was told that several aircraft had been shot down and that two pilots had died in pursuit of UFOs; although whether this means they were chasing something identifiable or extraterrestrial is another matter.

This information may relate to a startling episode over Gorky in spring 1983. A UFO was tracked on radar as it crossed secret air space and was merely observed; it continued its flight. A few months later, a similar unidentified target was observed on radar over another patch of secret Soviet air space – Sakhalin Island – but now an interceptor was sent. The object failed to respond to radio warnings and was shot from the skies. As the world knows, this 'UFO' was, in fact, tragically a Korean Airlines jumbo jet packed with passengers, who as a result of this mistake all died.

Of course, when flight KAL 007 went down in 1983 there was a global outcry. But it was noticeable that the fury expected from the White House and the Pentagon did not burst forth, and there were few repercussions. Perhaps the Americans secretly knew that UFOs were a complicating factor. If the Soviets had been 'tested' by several UFO overflights shortly before (as at Gorky), and had even lost pilots in jet chases when their electrical power was snuffed out by the phenomenon, it would be more understandable that they would regard as a threat an unknown object flying where it should not be.

Openness at last

Although much about Soviet ufology post-dates glasnost, 9 October 1989 was a turning point because it marked the transition. The Soviet Union, on the verge of dissolution, joined the ranks of UFO-reporting nations in an open fashion.

Indeed, the case that took place at the industrial city of Voronezh was officially reported and confirmed by TASS, the Soviet press agency. Whilst TASS was notorious for its propaganda, the last thing it could be described as being was a source of wild tales about flying saucers. As a consequence, its pronouncements about the Voronezh affair shook the world's media. Responsible newspapers, from the London *Times* to the *Washington Post*, carried the story in sober fashion. TASS were asked if they meant what they said and a spokesperson, looking suitably offended, intoned: 'TASS *never* jokes.' It was said in such a way that nobody would disbelieve him.

Dr Jacques Vallée was the first scientist to appear on Soviet TV to discuss UFOs. Even then, in 1965, tens of thousands of cases were known by the authorities but kept secret.

As a measure of the impact of the case it was the subject of items on serious news magazine programmes. Jenny Randles was interviewed live in an ITN studio as a politician might be on the national news.

What had caused this remarkable change of attitude by the Western media? They reported only a few scattered facts about an incident that was really part of a major wave that had struck this part of Russia that autumn. TASS had simply legitimised one case. That was what made it unique.

The full picture was gathered later, and we thank Dr Henry Silanov from the geophysical laboratory at the University of Voronezh for providing first-hand assistance. He says that

> between 21 September and 28 October 1989, in the Western Park [area] in Voronezh [there were] six landings and one sighting [hovering] ... with the appearance of walking beings ... We have no doubts [that the witnesses] are telling the truth in their accounts, because details of the landings are recounted by [them] ... [that] could otherwise have only come from specialist UFO literature, which is not published in our country.

The main events occurred between 23 and 27 September and involved various similar reports, notably a red sphere surrounded by a misty vapour ('like a bonfire in fog', one witness termed it). Many people saw it come down towards a tree which it forced to bend as it tried to land.

From the object several nine- or ten-feet-tall figures in silvery suits emerged and clambered down the tree. The entities were nothing like the Greys of American UFO lore nor even the Nordics so common in the rest of Europe. In fact they were more akin to beings from Russian folk tales about ogres in the woods. They even had three eyes. This may be very significant. We might predict that, with later exposure to Western UFO literature, the Russians will eventually start to report similar abductions with Greys.

The giants did some very weird things before returning to the sphere, including freezing a boy in mid-step. Another person, walking to a bus stop, was supposedly made to vanish until the UFO had left, when he reappeared and carried on walking as if no time had passed at all.

The other stories also featured similar UFOs and entities. In one case a robot appeared; in another, human-sized figures with wrinkled faces. One object swayed from side to side on descent in the falling-leaf motion so often reported in Western UFO cases but probably unknown to Russian citizens.

The 1989 sightings at Voronozh achieved a unique distinction in Britain. All four terrestrial TV channels treated it as a serious news item. Ufologists such as Jenny Randles (ITN News) and Mike Wootten (BBC Newsnight) were called in to the studio to debate it.

Giants from outer space take robot for walkies in a Russian park

by **DAVID LAWSON**

Extract from the *Today* newspaper, Tuesday 10 October 1989.

THE aliens have landed. A leading Russian scientist says there is no doubt that they stepped out of their spaceship and went for a walk in a park.

Three giant creatures 12 feet tall with tiny heads chose spare ground at Voronezh, 300 miles south east of Moscow, for a very close encounter with the human race.

Their arrival was heralded by a shining ball seen by dozens of Voronezh residents.

The UFO landed and out came the giants, similar to humans and accompanied by a small robot.

"They went for a promenade near their spaceship," said official news agency Tass. "Then they disappeared back inside.

"Onlookers were overwhelmed with a fear that lasted several days."

Respected

The landing was authenticated by staff from the Voronezh Geophysical Laboratory, whose head, Genrikh Silanov, is a respected scientist.

Tass said: "Scientists confirmed that a UFO landed. They also identified the landing site and found traces of aliens."

Silanov's men discovered a 20-yard depression in the park with four deep dents, and two pieces of rock.

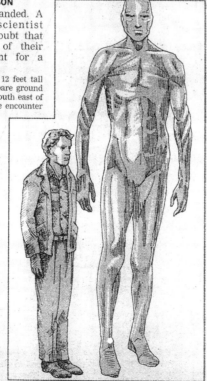

FEARSOME: Alien giant compared with man

259

In 1993 Russians launched AURA-Z, a multi-lingual magazine to discuss serious research into cases.

This was the first real Russian wave which became recognised as it was happening. We know that waves feed upon themselves – the publicity of initial events stimulates others to come forward and creates the appearance of a sequence of events. The USSR was living through the series of reports that had struck France and Britain in autumn 1954 and had demonstrated that the phenomenon was global. Now, in the aptly named Western Park, the mystery was showing itself as no respecter of cultural systems either.

—32—

THE MANHATTAN TRANSFER

In the early hours of 30 November 1989 a woman was seen floating out of her apartment window in Manhattan and entering a UFO.

Despite there being hundreds of alien abduction stories, there was one significant reason why the presence of spacenappers was not accepted by the world. This was the lack of corroborative evidence.

Although there were many apparently sincere reports from seemingly credible people and even a few multiple witness abductions, there was no real hard evidence – such as something provably extraterrestrial that was removed from the spaceship, or a camcorder sequence taken by the witness aboard a UFO. The history of the subject showed that this was not going to happen, which is why the photograph allegedly taken after an abduction on Ilkley Moor (see page 243) was regarded as so sensational by ufologists.

However, what ought not to have been impossible was the existence of uninvolved witnesses who chanced to see the abduction taking place. In the terrible abduction and murder of Liverpool youngster James Bolger police enquiries proceeded quickly because over thirty people had seen the child as he was led away. They did not realise what was happening at the time, but they saw what they saw. The same is true of a bank robbery in the high street, for example. Passers by are simply bound to witness something.

Personal visions?

Yet in the countless examples of alien abduction this was never the case. There were near-misses. In the case of Alan Godfrey's experience at Todmorden in November 1980, several police officers on moors a few miles away spotted a light in the sky. But nobody on Burnley Road in Todmorden itself saw the UFO hovering over the police car or the abduction that followed. Nor, despite subsequent widespread publicity, has anyone come forward who even saw the empty patrol car in the middle of the road.

Indeed, the problem was worse for the reality of spacenapping. In six cases independent observers saw the witness during the period when they felt they were on board the UFO. None of these witnesses had been inside a UFO when testimony suggested they ought to be!

In fact, these people were just where they were before the experience began. In one case, from Brazil, the witness was prone on the ground, seemingly in an altered state of consciousness (in fact presumed drunk by the person walking past). In another example, from Wales, the witness was seen in a near-catatonic state prone on her bed. In an even more extraordinary episode, from Australia, a woman had an encounter with a UFO and entities. Two witnesses who were with her at the time saw her interacting with these beings and then 'enter' the UFO as if abducted by it. However, she never physically went anywhere. She remained in their view seemingly talking to thin air encountering an object that neither of them could see and which, by standard definitions of reality, was not actually there.

This litany of evidence seems to prove that the alien abduction experience, however real it appears to the witness at the time, occurs at an inner level and not in the real world. In other words, it is some form of very strange visionary phenomenon but definitely not physical reality, such as that which underpins some less exotic types of UFO phenomena.

But then, on 30 November 1989, a case occurred that reversed this visionary trend and had a major impact on the UFO world. Like the Ilkley photograph and the Gulf Breeze affair, it instantly overturned a golden rule of ufology and posed a stark choice. Either such anomalous cases are hoaxes, or the phenomenon has undeniably altered its character in a very significant way over the past few years.

Perhaps this new phase of overt activity, concentrating on much fewer but far more individually dramatic cases, was a genuine step forward towards an acclimatisation of the mystery within the human mind.

Floating above Manhattan

The witness to this epic new case was Linda, a young mother who lived in a high-rise apartment in Manhattan. She had already undergone alleged abductions by Greys and been investigated for some time by

Budd Hopkins. So when she called him to talk about another episode, the morning after it had occurred, it appeared to be nothing special and was subjected to the usual follow-through, including hypnosis, but no more.

In brief, Linda claimed that the entities floated her through her shut bedroom window and surrounded her high above the streets of the city. They then transferred her into a UFO hovering over the tower block and did their usual testing before replacing her in bed. She could not recall how, but did describe the terror on noticing that her two young children had been immobilised. She thought the aliens had killed them,

Abductee Linda Napolitano, who has made appearances at UFO conferences to support her story.

Famed psychologist, Dr John Mack, of the Harvard Medical School, received a big pay out to put his Pullitzer Prize winning talents to bear on the abduction mystery. His resultant book, Abduction, was published in the UK in May 1994.

and had to satisfy herself that they were still breathing by holding a mirror to their noses. They were merely deeply unconscious and remembered nothing.

Evidence from the NYPD

This would have been just another 'believe it or not' tale to add to hundreds of others that Hopkins has collected. But in March 1991 Hopkins had a letter from two men claiming to be police officers. Although he had other subsequent correspondence with them (including a tape) they would not meet the ufologist face to face.

These two men claimed to have been parked in a car in the early hours of 30 November 1989 when they had seen a woman floating out of her apartment window in Manhattan and entering a UFO. They saw it fly into the nearby river, submerge and never come out again. The men thought that they had just witnessed a woman being spacenapped by aliens and, for all they knew, murdered. They claimed to feel guilty that they had been unable to do anything about it despite their training, but told Hopkins they could point out the exact apartment involved. Indeed, one of them was in the early throes of a nervous breakdown, having spent weeks parked outside the building trying to summon up the courage to go and knock on the right door and see if the woman existed and knew what they were talking about.

Of course, they apparently had no idea that Hopkins already knew this story and had interviewed the woman herself. As Hopkins tried to check out the story, Linda eventually called him to say that the men had turned up – just as he had warned her they might. They were reputedly stunned by the fact that she was actually expecting them.

Eventually, the two policemen told Hopkins that they were really secret bodyguards for a leading politician. They were ferrying him to the New York heliport when their car stalled, and the incident occurred as if 'stage-managed' for their benefit. This world-renowned statesman had witnessed the entire thing!

A further twist to the tale came when a woman contacted the ufologist to say that she had been driving over the Brooklyn Bridge with some other traffic in the middle of a night two years before when every vehicle's engine stalled, the street lights had gone out, and a group of people witnessed the abduction of Linda from her high-rise apartment. She told essentially the same story to Hopkins as had the two men; although, of course, none of the other affected drivers had gone public with the story in the meantime. Nobody had, as one might expect, even bothered to call the police, and there were no media stories between this dramatic event on the bridge in 1989 and its sudden revelation later.

The most important abduction ever?

Hopkins has considerable faith in this case. He told Jenny Randles when they discussed it at length that he knew the identity of the 'third man', who was of such calibre and integrity that if he chose to tell what had happened to him then the whole world would be convinced about the reality of alien abductions overnight. In August 1993 Hopkins added that he had received a fairly non-committal letter from this man, who has seemingly decided that the time is not right to tell the world. A strong claim published within American ufology is that this man is Javier Perez de Cuellar, the former Secretary General of the United Nations. Hopkins has not endorsed this allegation. Those who have asked de Cuellar to comment have received a flat denial and an insistence that he was not even in New York on the night in question.

An independent team of sceptical ufologists have made their own investigation of the case and presented some disturbing evidence. For example, a newspaper loading bay which is busy all night long is directly opposite the apartment block, but nobody there saw anything. No meetings or helicopter flights were scheduled at the time (although the two bodyguards say this was because it was a top-secret meeting and an unlogged flight). There are a few other nagging questions that are outstanding.

Perhaps more worrying still is that this case fell so conveniently into Budd Hopkins's lap. There is no independent source of contact. All the witnesses came directly to him. He has only their word that they did not know one another beforehand, although there seem no grounds to charge that they did. This is very like the way that 'facts' were so conveniently 'fed out' to Jenny Randles and Brenda Butler after the 1980 Rendlesham Forest case.

Budd Hopkins is very sincere. Linda (Napolitano) has now gone public at UFO conferences and seems genuine. The other witnesses remain anonymous.

With a case of this magnitude it must be proper to express caution. If these witnesses are telling the truth and, especially, if the third man does go public in future, then this may rightly be seen as the most important abduction that has ever occurred. It would confirm our

Author Jim Schnabal claimed in January 1994 that Perez de Cuellor – former Secretary General of the United Nations – has denied being the 'third man' in the Manhatten transfer case.

growing suspicions that the UFO phenomenon has drastically altered its character of late.

Of course, we cannot at present assert any of this. The case remains controversial and will do so until some hard evidence surfaces, perhaps in Hopkins's coming book or the film currently in production. It is intriguing, but sadly not the probative 'case of the century' it has been hailed to be; at least not as it stands.

Part Nine

TOWARDS 2000

33

THE BELGIAN WAVE

The Belgian sightings were at their most dramatic in March 1990.

The remarkable new 'display mode' which UFOs are adopting took a further stride with the saga of the Belgian sightings between 1989 and 1991. These were at their most dramatic in March 1990. But once again controversy surrounds this affair.

It began on the evening of 29 November 1989 – the very night when, three thousand miles away and about twelve hours later, Linda Napolitano would claim to have been abducted from her Manhattan apartment block in the most incredible spacenapping ever. Whether this is relevant can only be a matter for speculation.

The sightings on 29 November 1989 were investigated by the national UFO group SOBEPS (Belgian Society for the Study of Space Phenomena). Useful independent reports were also published by Wim van Utrecht and Paul Vanbrabant.

A vast, triangular object

Over 120 sightings were reported for that first night alone, mostly around Eupen on the eastern border with Germany. The most important came from two police officers, who saw the object from their patrol car and then pulled into the side of the road to watch it drift overhead before pursuing it.

The UFO was like a dark triangle and had bright lights on each corner, with a reddish glow in the centre. It was huge (sizes estimated by witnesses used terms like 'a football pitch'). It also moved very slowly and almost silently: a faint 'buzzing' or 'humming' was heard by some witnesses. All told, the object was visible for well over an hour and possibly longer. It seemed to be parading up and down the skies as if putting on an exhibition for the citizens of Eupen.

Many more reports followed over the coming weeks, spreading to other parts of Belgium. Most were of a triangular object, although other shapes were seen as well. It is important to point out that triangular objects such as these were not new to this wave. In fact, since the late 1970s they had become an important part of the UFO scene – indeed, more common than 'disc' shapes.

Stealth aircraft?

In Britain a cine film was taken in Leicestershire in October 1978 during a series of reports of what came to be called the 'Silent Vulcan' – because the object, whose outline was picked out by lights, resembled a huge Vulcan bomber but made no sound. This early film is similar to that obtained by certain witnesses with camcorders during the Belgian wave a decade later.

When triangular reports continued to occur, British investigators had suspected the flight of stealth aircraft on secret missions. The profile of these slow-moving, quiet and unusual-looking aircraft was reputed to be triangular with smooth edges and a strange lighting configuration. Aviation sources believed that missions flew from RAF Alconbury, close to the focus of the Leicestershire wave.

During the 1980s more sightings occurred in Britain, where the term 'Manta Ray' was often used as witnesses described the smooth, triangular lines of the object they saw. Important cases were recorded from Ashbourne in Derbyshire and then Alvanley in Cheshire on 23 October 1989, where a senior police officer and his wife observed an object very like the ones to be witnessed in Belgium only five weeks later.

Officially, of course, the theory about stealth aircraft overflying Britain was denied. Indeed, the very existence of stealth aircraft was refuted for many years, although it was an open secret in aviation circles. Eventually, in 1988, the Aurora jet was revealed and it did have the characteristics alleged. But aviation sources interviewed by Jenny Randles in the USA in April 1992 told her that prototypes first flew in the 1970s and that new-generation stealth aircraft were constantly being developed in and around the Tonopah Air Force Base and Groom Lake area of Nevada.

This location was where ufologists were alleging that captured alien UFOs were being test-flown. But she was informed that the technology being spotted here was of human design, albeit with some remarkable capabilities, such as nuclear-powered engines under development, easily mistaken for a UFO.

An internal memo from USAF in Europe to Washington regarding the 1990 sightings over Belgium, officially denying the Stealth bomber claims of some sceptics.

```
RUEAMCC/CMC CC WASHINGTON DC
RUEALGX/SAFE
R 301246Z MAR 90
FM ████████████
TO RUEKJCS/DIA WASHDC
INFO RUEKJCS/DIA WASHDC//DAT-7//
RUSNNOA/USCINCEUR VAIHINGEN GE//ECJ2-OC/ECJ2-JIC//
RUFGAID/USEUCOM AIDES VAIHINGEN GE
RHFQAAA/HQUSAFE RAMSTEIN AB GE//INOW/INO//
RHFPAAA/UTAIS RAMSTEIN AB GE//INRMH/INA//
RHDLCNE/CINCUSNAVEUR LONDON UK
RUFHNA/USDELMC BRUSSELS BE
RUFHNA/USMISSION USNATO
RUDOGHA/USNMR SHAPE BE
RUEAIIA/CIA WASHDC
RUFGAID/JICEUR VAIHINGEN GE
RUCBSAA/FICEURLANT NORFOLK VA
RUEKJCS/SECDEF WASHDC
RUEHC/SECSTATE WASHDC
RUEADWW/WHITEHOUSE WASHDC
RUFHBG/AMEMBASSY LUXEMBOURG
RUEATAC/CDRUSAITAC WASHDC
BT
CONTROLS
████████████████████  SECTION 02 OF 02  ████████ 05049


SERIAL:  (U) IIR 6 807 0136 90.

BODY
COUNTRY:  (U) BELGIUM (BE).

SUBJ:  IIR 6 807 0136 90/BELGIUM AND THE UFO ISSUE (U)

MAR TV SHOW.
```

PAGE:0015

```
6.  (U) DEBROUWER NOTED THE LARGE NUMBER OF REPORTED
SIGHTINGS, PARTICULARLY IN NOV 89 IN THE LIEGE AREA AND
THAT THE BAF AND MOD ARE TAKING THE ISSUE SERIOUSLY.  BAF
EXPERTS HAVE NOT BEEN ABLE TO EXPLAIN THE PHENOMENA EITHER.

7.  (U) DEBROUWER SPECIFICALLY ADDRESSED THE POSSIBILITY
OF THE OBJECTS BEING USAF B-2 OR F-117 STEALTH AIRCRAFT
WHICH WOULD NOT APPEAR ON BELGIAN RADAR, BUT MIGHT BE
SIGHTED VISUALLY IF THEY WERE OPERATING AT LOW ALTITUDE IN
THE ARDENNES AREA.  HE MADE IT QUITE CLEAR THAT NO USAF
OVERFLIGHT REQUESTS HAD EVER BEEN RECEIVED FOR THIS TYPE
MISSION AND THAT THE ALLEDGED OBSERVATIONS DID NOT
CORRESPOND IN ANY WAY TO THE OBSERVABLE CHARACTERISTICS OF
EITHER U.S. AIRCRAFT.
```

Of course, test flying such a device in the Nevada desert is one thing, but doing so over Cheshire or Belgium seems rather more difficult to justify. One interesting possibility is that the UFO phenomenon was being deliberately used as a smokescreen for test flights in areas where it was desirable to fly new models but where population density would otherwise preclude it. If the aircraft were seen, it would appear so unusual that it would be reported as a UFO. So new military aircraft could fly with impunity, the authorities knowing that rival military powers would probably not pay too much attention to one more UFO sighting.

Belgian investigators were quick to consider this option for their sudden wave of triangular UFOs. The US Air Force were equally speedy in refuting the claim.

Yet despite these flat denials, such as one in December 1989 that 'the F-117 stealth fighter has never flown in the European theatre', some experts have expressed a different view. Consider, for instance, the comments by former French Minister of Defence Robert Galley (see page 201), and an interesting and seemingly unambiguous comment made on 21 April 1990 by Colonel Tom Tolin, a USAF officer who was speaking in France about the then current Belgian wave. He said that 'F-117s are flying in Europe during night missions, sometimes piloted by United Kingdom RAF pilots, but we are not authorised to tell you where.'

Concerted efforts at investigation

Nevertheless, taking the official denials seriously, the Belgian government set up a remarkable experiment. Not only did they create a system whereby all incoming UFO reports were sent immediately to UFO investigators, but they opened up contacts at radar stations and other facilities to allow the ufologists to do their job. This was a unique joint effort to try to resolve the problem that was clearly vexing the nation.

The outcome was an amazing decision to mount a fully coordinated skywatch over the Easter weekend in March 1990. The public were encouraged to report sightings. The ufologists were allowed to set up a temporary HQ at Bierset airport near Liège. Two military aircraft were put on standby alert – one equipped with sophisticated cameras. On the ground across eastern Belgium the ufologists had teams in contact with with one another via mobile phones and ground-based video-recording systems. Belgium was ready for the UFOs!

During 1991 Eastern Belgium topped a poll of the top 10 most active UFO hot spots in the world, narrowly beating Gulf Breeze (Florida) and Todmorden (West Yorkshire).

During the four-day experiment there were a few sightings but little corroboration. However, a detailed study of one incident led SOBEPS to the conclusion that an important event had taken place.

Between 11pm on 30 March and 2am on the 31st a series of police officers around Wavre, 15 miles south of Brussels and 40 miles west of the base at Bierset airport, spotted lights in the sky. These do not seem to have been as exciting as many of the other reports and resemble stars observed through expectation and unusual atmospheric conditions. However, two F-16 fighters were scrambled in response and just after midnight reported radar lock-ons. The pilots saw nothing visually.

Analysis of the film of the onboard computer radar graphics and that of three ground-based radar systems which also tracked the objects did seem to match up. However, the contacts were sporadic and intermittent rather than continuous, and never lasted longer than about twenty seconds. Various echoes were seen moving about the screen at what might be interpreted as incredible speeds – although that does depend upon whether these are material objects, rather than spurious targets on the radar, differing emissions at different points.

Opposing conclusions about this case have been drawn. Some researchers were convinced that this was vital proof of a strange encounter. Others decided that the lights seen by the police were too close a match to the stars and planets in the sky plotted by computer to show what was visible on that night. A SOBEPS scientific expert given full access to all the radar data also concluded that the night's events did not prove anything extraterrestrial, although he suspected that a rare meteorological and atmospheric effect might have stimulated the sightings. Whatever the case, the bold experiment seemingly failed to snare the mystery triangle.

The triangular form of UFO, as seen during the Belgian wave, has by 1994 become more frequently reported than the traditional UFO categories of 'saucers' and 'cigars'.

Sightings continued into the summer of 1991, but faded to a trickle. Some thirty films and camcorder images were analysed during that time, but all bar three were misperceptions – of ordinary aircraft, for instance. Sadly, nothing spectacular was obtained despite all the attention. One man did film a triangle of lights crossing the Brussels skyline about ninety minutes after the F-16 radar lock-ons, but some ufologists argue that this was a jumbo jet.

A further theory: refuelling aircraft

Theories about the Belgian wave are still split among stealth aircraft, alien objects and a piloted microlite being used to simulate UFOs. A similar theory to this – involving a formation team of night fliers – was used by some ufologists to explain another major wave of triangular lights that were seen in the Hudson Valley, New York area in 1985. So the idea may not be as wild as it appears.

One option not widely considered has been borne out by British investigators and might be very appropriate. On several occasions during the period of the Belgian wave very similar large formations of lights were witnessed over central and eastern England. Staffordshire MP William Cash, even asked questions in the House of Commons about them. Witnesses described a huge dark object speckled by lights moving silently and with unusual slowness on its course; they also used phrases like 'the size of a football pitch'.

Investigation proved what these witnesses had seen, although many have refused to accept that answer. It was a formation of aircraft involved in a series of mid-air refuelling exercises, necessary to mount long-distance bombing raids to the Middle East during the Gulf War without having to land en route and waste time. These were secret operations, relatively tricky and dangerous. They are supposed to occur over the North Sea, between England and Belgium, but witnesses saw the aircraft lining up before refuelling actually began.

In these exercises large tanker aircraft full of fuel are linked by umbilical cords to several smaller fighters that surround the tanker as close as possible and use it as a flying fuel station. Because it is such a difficult exercise, especially at night, the aircraft are covered in an unusual and very bright array of lights. Such refuelling also takes place at a considerable height.

On clear nights witnesses will see this very strange formation drifting over. The aircraft are flying as slowly as possible to retain proximity to each other, and relatively slowly because of their great height. As nobody on the ground is expecting to see many aircraft spread over a huge area of sky in a very odd formation, they always misinterpret the lights as being on one huge, and (because of the flying formation) often triangular, object – that is dark and silent, or perhaps making a faint noise as would a dozen high-flying aircraft engines even if miles up in the sky.

Some of the Belgian sightings may also be explicable in this way.

In December 1993 and January 1994 a repeat run of triangular UFOs provoked a major wave over Lincolnshire. Witnesses included a senior officer at RAF Donna Nook. The MoD investigated but found no explanation for the sightings.

34

MID-AIR CONFLICT

Six British incidents of
mid-air encounters are
on record between 1991
and 1993, others have
almost certainly
occurred.

On 21 April 1991, just after 9pm, an Alitalia MD-80 jet carrying fifty-seven passengers from Milan to London Heathrow was crossing the Kent coast near Lydd. Suddenly Captain Achille Zaghetti spotted a cigar-shaped object above and ahead of him. It flashed past them on a dangerously close path. The object was unlike anything he had seen before, but from its lozenge shape and great speed he feared it might be a missile.

At Heathrow, radar was tracking the aircraft through 22,000 feet on its steady descent. Now they picked up an unidentified object on screen just as the captain reported the frightening incident. The UFO was about ten miles behind the jet and disappearing fast. They had no idea what it was.

This case was effectively hushed up by both the Ministry of Defence and the CAA (Civil Aviation Authority) as they started enquiries, although Zaghetti submitted an official report. He then chose to talk about it back in Italy and the British authorities were forced, perhaps reluctantly, to go public about their investigations.

The CAA confirmed that 'extensive enquiries have failed to indicate what the sighting may have been'. They had ruled out all possibility that it was a rogue missile from a range on the Kent coast. These could not reach the height of this object. The MoD were equally explicit. They said: 'What happened was a mystery. It was yet another UFO.'

A series of near-misses

Indeed so, but it was not *just* another UFO. What these reports fail to reveal is that this near-disaster was merely one of a whole spate of mid-air encounters that have been occurring since the middle of 1991, and which have rapidly turned into something of a dangerous trend. The public are generally unaware of them. Nobody is going out of their way to tell you of the incidents if you choose to fly. But they clearly represent yet another strange step into the limelight by the UFO phenomenon, now demonstrating their amazing manoeuvrability in close proximity to our passenger aircraft.

Reports of these objects have come from all over the world since 1991. The French military helicopter encounter over Brignoles in 1992 is described on page 208. There have been similar encounters over Tasmania, New York, Russia and the California desert. Indeed, in the last case one crew member even took a photograph of the dark cylindrical mass as it shot through the air at a quite remarkable speed.

However, we have paid particular attention to gathering cases from Britain. Six incidents are on record between 1991 and 1993 – although these seem merely to be the ones that have been traceable, and others almost certainly have occurred and remain unknown. Pilots are notoriously reluctant to report UFOs because of the problems that can result. Airlines are also not particularly keen in case it should have an adverse effect on passenger bookings in the cut-throat economic climate.

Yet no airline seems to have been singled out for a close encounter. Over a two-year period we have reports involving Aeroflot, US Air, Qantas and, in Britain, Dan Air, Britannia and British Airways. It seems likely that most airlines have had a close encounter at some stage. Two of the British incidents are particularly important because they again involve radar trackings.

In July 1993 it emerged that a British Airways Boeing 767 on an internal flight from Edinburgh to London had observed a similar object when passing over north-west England at about 30,000 feet. The air traffic control centre based at Manchester Airport had apparently tracked the object briefly, but no further information on this matter has been made available as it was still 'under investigation'.

On 15 July 1991 a Britannia Airways Boeing 737 was descending through 15,000 feet on its way into London Gatwick with a group of holidaymakers returning from Crete. It was passing the Sussex coast at the time on a sunny afternoon. The co-pilot observed, yet again, a dark, lozenge-shaped object on what seemed to be a collision course with the jet. He yelled out. The pilot looked up to see the object sweep past the wing at an estimated distance of only a few hundred feet. In aviation terms that is about as close to a disaster as you can get. The object was thought to be quite small.

In December 1978 the Kaikoura area of New Zealand generated UFOs that were seen by regular cargo air flights. Later they took an Australian TV film crew up who captured some of the most famous video images of UFOs ever recorded.

The most frightening aerial encounter was in 1986 when a Japanese Airlines jumbo had a lengthy term contact with a giant object over the North Pole during a long-haul flight.

The crew reported the matter immediately and London radar had the UFO on screen. It resembled a small aircraft but was not giving out a transponder signal, the electronic code used by all traffic to indicate a known aircraft type. The UFOs speed was just over 100 mph, refuting later speculation that it might have been a balloon. London control was sufficiently concerned to order another incoming aircraft to change course, as the UFO was heading out to sea in its general direction.

In a subsequent investigation the matter was taken very seriously by the CAA and the identity of the object was not established. The risk of collision was rated 'high' by their final report. Thankfully, no collision has ever taken place – these incidents appear to be no more than shots across the bow.

It is early days in the investigation of such cases, but they seem to represent a new and rather worrying pattern. Whatever UFOs turn out to be, the provocative way in which they are interacting with passenger aircraft makes their investigation imperative. We cannot afford to joke about something that is paying such close attention to air traffic above densely populated areas of the world. We owe it to ourselves to take the UFO subject seriously.

Perhaps that is the point of this new phase of aerial activity. The world can readily forget about distant lights in the sky or the claim that someone, somewhere was spacenapped by aliens. But if air traffic is in persistent danger from a near-collision with unknown objects then we ignore that fact at our peril.

—35—

UFOs in Focus

During 1993 there was a noticeable spate of photographic cases.

It is difficult to predict where the UFO mystery will take us next. It now appears to be changing so rapidly that anything can happen. However, during 1993 there was a noticeable spate of photographic cases. The twist was that this new wave of activity was being captured on the new generation of camcorders.

In Britain alone during 1993 no fewer than nine such cases were reported; the same trend is indicated in other parts of the world. Certainly this is partly due to the rapid rise in camcorder ownership, but the similar escalation in the ownership of still cameras was unmatched by any such increase in UFO photographs. So there may be something more behind this dramatic expansion of the evidence.

Venus rising

It is early days to tell whether the pattern will continue, or, indeed, if any of the cases will offer substantial proof of the extraordinary. Most of the objects filmed are lights in the sky, and many have explanations. Venus was a particular source, being unusually bright in the early morning sky for much of 1993. The automatic focus on cameras tried but failed to 'lock on' to this point of light, and as a result produced a fuzzy spaceship-like blob that looks a good deal more mysterious than it ever was.

A case in the Hartcliffe area of Bristol in late June 1993 resulted in a whole street skywatching for UFOs over several days, and a video image of 'the big one' climbing into the dawn sky night after night. This was without doubt the planet Venus – even so, the story got national and some international media coverage and the film was sent for computer enhancement in the USA.

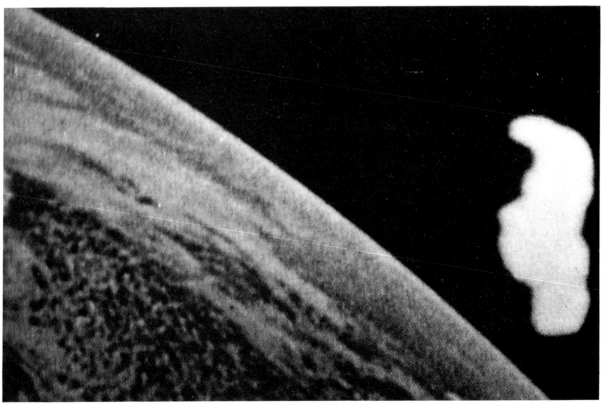

See opposite above

UFO photographs flooded in during the 1950s but little investigation into them was carried out on the misguided premise that a picture was worth a thousand words. This image from Pescara, Italy, taken in September 1957 is typical of those about which we know very little and whose status is now impossible to confirm or deny.

See opposite below

Many UFO-like photographs were taken during the space missions but almost all have explanations – eg as window bolts reflecting the very strong sunlight, junk floating in a nearby space orbit and even waste matter ejected from the capsule and floating in tandem with it. This shot taken by the crew of Apollo 11 in July 1969 does not show an alien entity but some detritus in orbit above the earth.

This image taken at Playa Sangrila, Uruguay on 23 September 1968 shows a common problem with UFO photographs. They often depict nothing but the UFO and surrounding sky. This prevents meaningful analysis by comparison with foreground or background details. However, investigators have learnt to watch for a dark aura that delineates the edges of a UFO image. When present this can demonstrate that it is a small object close to the camera lens rather than a huge disc thousands of feet in the air.

During the 1970s the number of submitted UFO photographs began to fall dramatically. Instead of hundreds of fuzzy black and white shots only a few – often sharp and spectacular and usually colour – images began to reach ufologists. Whether this turnabout increased or decreased the credibility of the evidence was a contentious question. This image was taken by an unknown source over Germany.

Other – perhaps unexplained – things may well have been seen during the Hartcliffe flap, but the camcorder image upon which everybody concentrated their attention was, in fact, easily resolved.

A similar incident occurred in the West Country during August 1993, when a family set off early in the morning for a day trip to London. They saw a light in the sky and filmed it for some minutes. The camcorder recorded the sound as well as the vision, and provided a very useful example of how many other reported UFO sightings must come about.

The witnesses here understandably misinterpreted the light as it grew and then faded through cloud cover. The camera's inability to focus caused it to look bizarre through the viewfinder; as a consequence the witnesses, ranging across three generations, assumed that what they were viewing *was* bizarre. As they talked about the affair, pre-existing social beliefs about UFOs came into play. They presumed the light's origin to be extraterrestrial and feared that aliens might spacenap and operate on them. In the end the object, which was not moving and was certainly Venus, triggered a complex close encounter.

We stress that the family concerned are not to be singled out as wildly gullible or incompetent. What they went through is the process that most human beings experience in these circumstances. Indeed, this has occurred in many close encounter UFO cases in the past. The only difference here is that we have it captured on sound and video and can analyse the genesis of a UFO encounter from the raw material of a distant light in the sky. In many ways that makes this particular cam-corder sequence far more important to ufology than an unexplained flickering light might have been.

Caught on security video

However, there have been a few more puzzling encounters captured on camera. In particular two security camera systems set up at major industrial complexes have provided much food for thought.

At a shopping centre site near Warrington in Cheshire in February 1991 a white 'soap bubble'-like object was recorded moving around an alleyway for several minutes (see page 282). As investigators examined the possibility that a camera fault might be responsible a second camera, looking at a different part of the site, produced a longer sequence of the same object the following April. Various experiments proved that it was glowing with infra-red light.

In September 1993 another security camera at a factory unit in south Lancashire recorded a brilliant white glow moving very slowly towards the north-west over the course of several minutes. This was just after 6am and appears to have been travelling much too slowly to be any obvious aircraft.

The figure on the beach

A few days beforehand a very curious film was submitted to Peter Hough by a family who had been for an August day trip to Rhyl in north Wales. In one sequence the camera panned across the sands and picked up a strange figure standing beside a wooden groyne (see page 283). The figure appeared to glow white – or a semi-transparent silvery hue – and could easily be interpreted as an alien entity. There are some

During the 1990s one of the major new trends within UFO study has been the capturing of objects on video camera. This still is taken from a security camera at a shopping mall in Warrington, Cheshire, on 26 April 1991 and depicts a large object tracked around the complex for 20 minutes before disappearing into the sky. Investigation failed to identify the cause.

similarities with the being photographed by Jim Templeton in Cumbria in 1964 (see page 156).

The witness looked up from the viewfinder and failed to spot the entity with his eyes, causing him to interpret (and report) this experience as a possible ghost. However, evaluation suggests that, as the camera was on a telephoto setting and there was a huge expanse of light sky and beach, his eyes, having just focused through the viewfinder, would find it almost impossible to pick out such a small image easily against a non-contrasting background.

These two cases were considered by scientists at the University of Manchester Institute of Science and Technology, who told investigators Peter Hough and Vic Sleigh that they did not consider them mysterious. The scientists thought the UFO was probably just a slow-moving aircraft, and the entity a man wearing a light mackintosh-type coat whose reflectivity produced an anomalous effect on the film due to

Strange figure on Rhyl beach.

a factor inherent within most home camcorders when shooting light materials and colours.

Ufologists are still waiting

Sadly, as yet there have been no amazing camcorder images, filmed in daylight, of what could only be described as a disc-like object or exotically constructed craft. A lengthy sequence taken in a rural area of Ontario in August 1991 was submitted anonymously to ufologists by a man identifying himself only as 'The Guardian'. It allegedly depicts a rotating lighted disc with army trucks down below, although it is difficult to see too much against the dark background.

Superficially this seems very impressive; an American researcher claims that he has checked out the case and that local people do recall military activity cordoning off the area. 'The Guardian' has allegedly submitted reliable material in the past. However, other sources within ufology are more dubious about this story and say that their enquiries reveal no evidence of a UFO encounter, let alone the capture of an alien vehicle by some military unit at the time.

Some brief images of an 'alien face' were also sent, but these are stills, not camcorder images, and are very hard to interpret. The Ontario film is simply the most visually impressive of the influx of camcorder images in the past few years. It is unlikely to remain the most spectacular for very long, and most ufologists hope that someone, somewhere will

There are several key advantages of camcorder film over still photographs. One of the less obvious is that it provides sound. What the witnesses say during a close encounter can be surprisingly revealing.

shortly secure definitive evidence of the kind of unknown object that will offer no possible doubt.

What they want is a UFO that is not a misperception of some mundane stimulus such as Venus, an airship, laser lights, or so on, as 95 per cent of all UFO sightings prove to be; not a flickering light in the sky, which may be some kind of exotic natural phenomena which evidence strongly suggests do exist; and not the technologically clever but ufologically unconvincing hoax shot of a UFO in the dark, as a few photographic cases these days are wont to be.

What ufologists are waiting for is a clear, unambiguous image of a disc-like craft moving across the daytime sky in such a way that it can only be a large constructed object powered by a method that is far beyond us; or, better still, a close focus image of an alien being – be it a Grey, a Nordic or any other type – moving in such a way that its earthly origin is ruled out.

Whether we shall ever receive such a case depends upon one simple truth. It is a truth which, after fifty years of research into this subject, we still cannot prove one way or the other. We *know* that countless people sincerely observe and report UFOs but that many of these things are not really UFOs at all. We *know* that many of the unexplained cases are UAP (unidentified atmospheric phenomena) – natural energies on the fringes of scientific understanding. But we do *not know* whether any UFOs are alien craft or visitors from another place.

If they are, then with our modern technology in the very near future someone must inevitably film one in such a way that there can be no doubt. Then the world will know for sure. But if no such case arrives quite soon we may have to face one simple, if stunning, conclusion – that there are IFOs and there are UFOs, but there are no alien craft waiting to be filmed!

—36—

WHO OR WHAT IS BEHIND THE UFO PHENOMENON?

The arguments will carry on, but one thing is certain – the UFO subject is NOT history.

We are not concerned here with the 90–95 per cent of UFO reports which probably turn out to have mundane explanations, such as bright stars or planets, aircraft landing lights, weather balloons, airships and hoaxes. Rather, we are examining the hard core of cases which resist down-to-earth solutions – the 5–10 per cent that cause such heated debate between sceptics and ufologists and even amongst the ranks of ufologists themselves.

There is absolutely no doubt of the objective reality of UFOs *per se*. Convincing eye-witness reports have been received for decades – centuries, some argue. More than this, the public denial of major governments to charges that they have been secretly investigating the phenomenon were shown, by the release of official documents in the early 1980s to be disinformation. We have demonstrated the truth of this beyond reasonable doubt. British military reports declassified under the thirty-year-rule unambiguously describe the scrambling of RAF jet interceptors chasing 'silver discs'.

All this shows that the argument of whether 'they' do or do not exist is long past. Sceptics should now accept this fact, and address the possible exotic explanations. To do otherwise is tiresome and time-wasting.

The extraterrestrial hypothesis

This is the natural explanation for UFO reports, and a favourite with the media who are unable to grasp the subtleties that permeate the phenomenon: UFOs represent visits by extraterrestrials. They are here to study us, to help mankind, or to 'borrow' human specimens for the extraction of genetic material to manufacture hybrid beings.

Many ufologists, particularly those in America, doubt that there

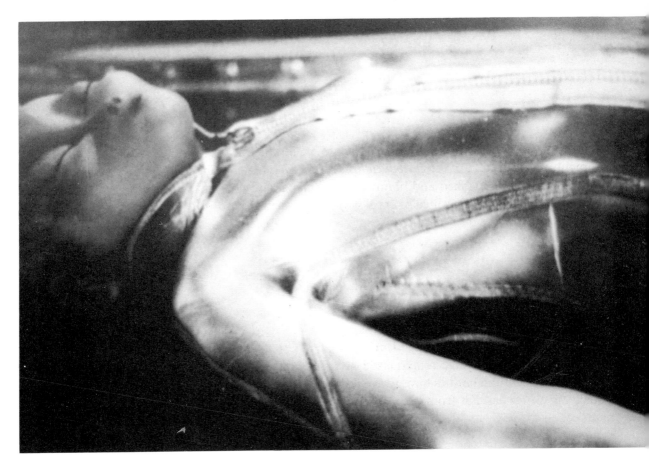

The current debate in ufology rages around the alleged capture of bodies retrieved from crashed UFOs by American security patrols and kept under strict secrecy for up to 50 years. When this photograph hit the media, stories circulated that the final proof had arrived – but this 'alien body' turned out to be a model prepared for an exhibition!

could be any other explanation. The very reason for this belief is also, perhaps, the theory's weakest link. Those in favour of an extraterrestrial explanation cite something obvious in support of their theory: the phenomenon *appears* to be extraterrestrial – it uses all the trappings of 'aliens' and 'spaceships'. Close encounter experiences involve craft which are obviously 'space age', and in contactee and abduction cases the beings inform victims of their extraterrestrial origins. They display star maps, describe their home planets and give terrestrials conducted tours around their flying machines. This must be the answer, if 'they' say so, surely?

The problem with the belief that we are dealing with a culture and technology from another planet is that it is too like us, sometimes to the point of absurdity. 'They' mirror our expectations and our own imaginative excursions into an age where space travel is possible, just as the airship pilots and their craft reflected the expectations of the turn of the last century.

Critics argue that we have anthropomorphised the phenomenon – given it the attributes of our own culture. Genuine extraterrestrials would be so 'alien' they would be beyond comprehension, and not like extras from low-budget SF films. They also point out that the vast distances between star systems would entail journeys lasting centuries – even at just below the speed of light.

Philip J. Klass, an American UFO debunker of many years' standing, makes a point which is perhaps more subtle than he intended. He comments in the Preface of *UFO Abductions: A Dangerous Game*: 'The public has been hoodwinked and brainwashed. I can assure you that there is absolutely no scientifically credible physical evidence to indicate that the Earth is being visited by extraterrestrials – let alone that they are abducting people.'

'The public has been hoodwinked and brainwashed. After having spent more than twenty-two years investigating famous, seemingly mysterious UFO reports, I can assure you there is absolutely no scientifically credible evidence that the Earth is being visited by extraterrestrials – let alone that they are abducting people.' Philip J. Klass – American aviation journalist.

Other dimensions

The phenomenon could *appear* extraterrestrial because the real visitors want us to believe it is. There are many cases in which UFOs and entities have behaved more like apparitions than solid flesh and blood creatures. Flying craft have materialised and dematerialised before startled witnesses, and entities have walked through walls and become visually insubstantial. Far from being located in outer space, the ufo-nauts seems to arrive and depart from another dimension. They could be sharing this planet with us, but are not on the same plane. This would explain their concern with our potential for destroying the Earth. Major changes to the environment could affect them too. The visitors would lie about their true origins to cover their tracks should we develop interdimensional travel. Who could blame them?

Some speculate that the visitors are time travellers, hiding behind the guise of 'aliens'. The subterfuge could be part of a sociological experiment to observe our behaviour. Under this scenario, UFO abductions could be a reality.

Humans are 'trapped' much in the way that we take animals from the wild. The fuzziness and blackouts experienced at this stage could reflect the administration of drugs or mind control. Once in the 'laboratory' abductees are psychologically tested and medically examined for diseases, the effects of pollution or something introduced into the environment. Finally, after being 'tagged', victims are released back into the wild. This enables them to be picked up again at a later date for re-examination. Of course this could also apply if extraterrestrials were involved.

However, the other-dimension theory would also account for the phenomenon's cultural tracking – its apparent ability to change its cosmetic appearance to suit the times. Victorians had little concept of outer space, but they could grasp the idea of giant airships.

The paranormal option

Some argue that UFOs are not 'nuts and bolts' machines manufactured by flesh and blood beings, but transient paranormal phenomena able to replicate solid objects and entities on a temporary basis. That would explain why UFO encounter scenarios read like third-rate science fiction. The phenomenon would be drawing on information stored in mankind's collective unconscious – a databank containing every human being's thought, first suggested by the Swiss psychologist Carl Jung.

UFO encounters could be a response to wishful thinking, projected fears and hopes – a distorted reflection of man's psyche. If there is an intelligence, it could be attempting to communicate information using metaphors to aid us in our individual and global problems. Intelligence is not even necessary for this theory. The response could be an auto-matic mechanism, an extension of our own consciousness, capable of physical materialisation for a limited period.

Physical mediums were allegedly capable of bringing spirits into a temporary physical form through the use of a psychic substance called ectoplasm – supposedly an amorphous misty material. Many UFOs have been observed bathed in mist and UFO entities, as we have already noted, often behave like apparitions.

The idea of 'thought-forms' is not new. Tibetan monks apparently had the ability to create entities from their own minds. These beings could eventually take on a life of their own and could be observed by people other than their creators. French traveller and explorer Alex-andra David-Neel spent fourteen years in Tibet and called up her own *tulpa*, as they are called. Using meditation and Tibetan rituals she sought to develop the image of a short, fat, jolly monk. This took several months, after which she was rewarded by the materialisation of the monk. But the entity became alarmingly independent and it took several more months to dissolve – during which time others saw it too.

Are all these phenomena interconnected? Researchers, including the authors, have noted some similarities between UFO abductions and near death experiences. Both sets of percipients describe out-of-body states, white lights and encounters with entities. Dr Kenneth Ring, a psychologist from the University of Connecticut, had been doing some comparisons between NDEs and UFO abductions. Ring told Jenny Randles that both sets of experients were 'highly comparable psychologically'. He also noted that, in general, both had an enhanced awareness of psychic phenomena from childhood; this is something that the authors have been aware of in connection with UFO percipients for many years. Dr Ring concludes that they 'may have a common underlying source'.

In his book *The Omega Project*, Ring postulates that both types of experiences are symptoms of the evolution of human consciousness – tools to hone into shape a more advanced form of thinking and awareness. They are driving us towards a state of 'omega'.

The psycho-social theory

This is a reductionist theory that seeks to explain the phenomenon purely in psychological and cultural terms. Carl Jung referred to UFOs as 'a modern myth' and a 'rumour' in his book *Flying Saucers*, published in 1959. He saw the circular shape of some UFOs as having great psychological significance. The *mandala*, Jung noted, is a deep-seated symbol common in dreams and rooted in the unconscious. No doubt, too, if Sigmund Freud had been around to address the issue, he would have interpreted the descriptions of disc- and cigar-shaped objects as a subconscious obsession with the female and male genitalia.

But even Jung was not entirely convinced by his own theory and comments in *Flying Saucers*:

> Unfortunately, however, there are good reasons why UFOs cannot be disposed of in this simple manner. So far as I know it remains an established fact, supported by numerous observations, that UFOs have not only been seen visually but have also been picked up on radar screen and have left traces on the photographic plate. It boils down to nothing less than this: that either psychic projections throw back a radar echo, or else the appearance of real objects affords an opportunity for mythological projections.

Despite Jung's misgivings, there are no lack of supporters for a psychological interpretation of UFO reports and experiences. Advocates believe that individual and group social pressures are exteriorised in a convincing delusion of 'saviours' or 'fiends', which arrive in spacecraft to benefit or abuse human civilisation. The experiences are a

'My own opinions, which developed in the early years of my interest, conform to the psychic hypothesis. Probing the psychiatric and psychic dimensions to UFOs, the UFO-dynamics, promises to give a more comprehensive picture.'
Berthold E. Schwarz, M.D. – UFO investigator.

psychological response to the fears and hopes of individuals in society. They are subjective, internal experiences.

Eddie Bullard is an American folklorist who has studied UFO experiences and compared them with traditional folk tales to determine if they are one and the same. In the February 1988 *MUFON UFO Journal* Bullard writes: 'Abduction reports as a body show far more similarities than accident, random hoaxes or pure fantasies can explain. The consistencies in form and content down to numerous minute details demonstrate that abductions make up a coherent phenomenon, whatever its ultimate nature.'

In his study, Bullard concludes:

> If abductions are stories then the accounts should branch off into a different national version for each geographical area, but they do not. If abductions are stories the investigator should be able to impose an individual style on them ... If abductions are stories they should change according to an expected pattern over time, but their history is steady instead, even to the point of opposing external influences.

In June 1992 Boston's Massachusetts Institute of Technology (MIT) played host to a gathering of UFO researchers, among them Jenny Randles. The delegates also included psychologists and social workers who reported on their studies of the abduction phenomenon. Paper after paper on the results of the psychological testing of abductees was presented: they established that abductees were ordinary citizens, sincere, with no detectable psychopathic disorders.

Australian researcher Keith Basterfield had long been a supporter of the 'fantasy-prone hypothesis'. This suggests that abductees are part of a small group of humanity (not more than 5 percent) who have such rich inner fantasy lives that they cannot separate imaginative experiences from reality. After the results of three different tests had been read out, Basterfield withdrew the theory from further discussion.

Mind-bending earth lights

In 1982 a book was published which was to have repercussions around the UFO community. *Earth Lights*, written by Paul Devereux with the collaboration of geochemist Paul McCartney, postulated a natural energy which could manifest as balls of light and interact with the mind. Devereux drew on an experience of his own when he was a college student in Bromley, Kent. In May 1967, a curious rectangular orange light appeared outside. As he watched, the phenomenon seemed to change and structure itself into a figure with arms outstretched. This was also seen by other students, although the identity of the figure varied depending on the belief system of each observer.

Although there had been a previous work, *Space-Time Transients and Unusual Events* by Canadian researchers Michael Persinger and Gyslaine Lafrenière, Devereux's book was the first to draw together all the pieces of the mystery and present new regional studies. He has since produced several more publications.

Light phenomena appear all over the planet. Earthquake lights were reported – and ignored – for years, and it was not until 1910 that scientists started to take an interest. The phenomenon manifests as balls or aurora-like displays of light in the air prior to or just after an earthquake. Many lights reported as UFOs may be connected with earthquake lights.

Researchers discovered that anomalous lights occurred over heavily faulted lines in the Earth's crust – typical sites of earthquake activity. The Pennines in the north of England, and the Chinati Mountains near Marfa in Texas, are two good examples where hundreds of sightings have been recorded, photographed and even filmed.

The main explanation for earth lights is the 'piezo-electric effect'. Laboratory experiments were carried out where crystal was put under tremendous pressure, and at a certain point electrical discharges were created. It is deduced from this that crystal-bearing rocks put under pressure through subterranean stress would similarly produce electrically charged plasma in the atmosphere. A witness could misperceive the lights as UFOs.

Paul Devereux took the theory a step further, and concluded that witnesses close to the phenomenon would be directly effected. The electrical field of the light form would interact with the observer's brain, and the result would be an empathy between them. The witness, already thinking 'UFO' and bringing forth the appropriate imagery from the subconscious, would have that idea tapped by the plasma which would obligingly structure itself to represent the thought visually.

Michael Persinger, while believing that light phenomena are responsible for close encounter experiences, does not go as far as Devereux. He postulates that electromagnetic fields emanating from the phenomenon would affect the temporal lobe areas of the brain. This could trigger off 'temporal lobe epilepsy'. During a seizure of this kind,

'Of course the flying saucers are real – and they are interplanetary.' Air Chief Marshall Lord Dowding, head of the RAF during World War II, August 1954.

sufferers report hearing disembodied voices, experiencing out-of-body states and observing exotic figures.

Earth light research has generated some fascinating arguments which should be taken into account by ufologists. However, beyond the sensible assumption that exotic luminosities might be mistaken for 'spaceships', the rest is speculation, founded though it is on detailed research.

Certainly there seems more to this phenomenon than Persinger would admit. Earth lights appear to exhibit an intelligence in their movements, and seem to react to witnesses. Some UFO researchers have postulated the idea that UFOs are life-forms that inhabit the upper atmosphere. Kenneth Arnold came to this conclusion towards the end of his life.

Final thoughts

The source of UFO sightings and experiences could be one of the above, a combination, or none of them at all. Voices in some quarters say that UFO sightings and UFO abductions are entirely separate phenomena. It has been suggested that UFO organisations should concentrate on sightings and leave the abduction cases to the psychologists. Some groups concur with this suggestion, while others feel the phenomenon is paranormal and have expanded their interests accordingly. Ufology is coming to a crossroads.

Even psychologists cannot make up their minds. Peter Hough, who has worked with several clinical psychologists, has come up against this dilemma. One concluded that the case he was working on was based on objective reality, while the other thought that his case was internal and a reflection of childhood abuse. Both were abduction experiences.

The dilemma here is that on the one hand we seem to be dealing with hardware that is seen, reflects the sun and can be recorded on radar, and on the other encounters with entities who exhibit nothing new at all. Quite the contrary, they are an amalgam of every fantasy we have read and every science fiction film we have seen. This is fact. We must face it. Nevertheless, the encounters could still be objectively 'real'.

The phenomenon could be so 'alien' it is beyond comprehension. Cultural tracking, first brought to our notice by Jacques Vallée in his 1970 classic *Passport to Magonia*, demonstrates the similarities between the abduction of human beings by fairies, who were taken to 'fairyland', and modern kidnappings by extraterrestrials. Is it a coincidence that toadstools, supposedly the domain of fairies, resemble modern saucer-shape craft? This seems at odds with Thomas Bullard's study, but it is true all the same.

One answer is that witnesses in previous times described extraterrestrials and their flying machines in terms of fairies and toadstools because they had no concept of outer space. Another is this: when the mind is suddenly confronted with an anomaly it struggles to identify it in terms of previous experience and information stored in the subconscious. That is why witnesses initially seek to identify UFOs as terrestrial aircraft or astronomical bodies. But when this fails the mind draws on more exotic possibilities. When an anomaly is utterly alien, beyond anything previously experienced or imagined, the mind will have to impose on it whatever is available – images from science fiction scenarios.

Perhaps this is mankind's saving grace. Such interpretations foisted

Were the fairies and toadstools of bygone ages really extraterrestrials and their flying machines?

on the conscious mind by the subconscious could be protecting us from a horror that would psychologically destroy us if we could perceive it in its true form.

The arguments will carry on, but one thing is certain – the UFO subject is not history. While you, the reader, mull over the contents of this book, and the investigators and researchers argue over who is right, UFOs continue to be chased by Air Force jets, recorded on radar, filmed and photographed. Ordinary men, women and children, from all walks of life, continue to suffer 'missing time' followed by fear and incomprehension as 'memory' returns of being in a white room, undergoing an examination by some abomination better left in the pages of a Stephen King novel.

SOURCES

ALDISS, Brian W., *Billion Year Spree*, Weidenfeld & Nicolson, 1973

ANDREWS, Colin and DELGADO, Pat, *Circular Evidence*, Bloomsbury, 1989

ARNOLD, Kenneth and PALMER, Ray, *The Coming of the Saucers*, Amherst Press, 1952

BARRY, Bill, *Ultimate Encounter*, Corgi, 1981

BASTERFIELD, Keith, *UFOs: The Image Hypothesis*, Reed, 1980

BOWEN, Charles (ed.), *The Humanoids*, Futura, 1977

BROWNELL, Winfield S., *UFOS: Key to Earth's Destiny!*, Legion of Light Publications, 1980

CAMPBELL, Stewart, *The UFO Mystery Solved*, Explicit Books, 1994

CLARKE, David and ROBERTS, Andy, *Phantoms of the Sky*, Hale, 1990

CONDON, Edward (ed.), *Scientific Study of UFOs*, Bantam, 1969

CUFOS, *Plains of San Agustin Controversy*, 1992

DEVEREUX, Paul, *Earth Lights Revelation*, Blandford, 1990

EVANS, Hilary, *The Evidence for UFOs*, Aquarian, 1983

EVANS, Hilary, *Visions, Apparitions, Alien Visitors*, Aquarian, 1986

EVANS, Hilary and SPENCER, John (eds), *UFOS 1947–1987*, Fortean Tomes, 1987

FAWCETT, Larry and GREENWOOD, Barry, *Clear Intent*, Prentice-Hall, 1984

FLAMMONDE, Paris, *UFOs Exist!*, Ballantine, 1977

FREWIN, Anthony, *One Hundred Years of Science Fiction Illustrations*, Jupiter, 1974

FULLER, John G., *The Interrupted Journey*, Souvenir, 1980

GOOD, Timothy, *George Adamski, the Untold Story*, CETI, 1983

GOOD, Timothy, *Above Top Secret*, Sidgwick & Jackson, 1987

HARBINSON, W.A., *Genesis*, Corgi, 1980

HIND, Cynthia, *UFOs African Encounters*, Gemini, 1982

HOBANA, Ion and WEVERBURGH, Julien, *UFOs from behind the Iron Curtain*, Corgi, 1975

HOLDSTOCK, Robert (consultant ed.), *Encyclopedia of Science Fiction*, Octopus, 1978

HOPKINS, Budd, *Missing Time*, Merak, 1982

HOPKINS, Budd, *Intruders*, Random House, 1987

HOUGH, Peter and RANDLES, Jenny, *Looking for the Aliens*, Blandford, 1992

HYNEK, J. Allen, *The UFO Experience*, Regnery, 1972

JACOBS, David, *UFO Controversy in America*, IUP, 1975

KEEL, John A., 'Mystery Aeroplanes of the 1930s', in *Flying Saucer Review*, Vol.16, Nos 3 and 4

KEEL, John A., *UFOs: Operation Trojan Horse*, Putnam, 1970

KEYHOE, Donald, *Flying Saucers Are Real*, Fawcett, 1950

KLASS, Philip J., *UFOs: The Public Deceived*, Prometheus, 1983

KLASS, Philip J., *UFO Abductions: A Dangerous Game*, Prometheus, 1989

MACK, Dr John, *Abduction*, Simon & Schuster, 1994

MONDEY, David and TAYLOR, Michael J.H., *The Guinness Book of Aircraft*, Guinness, 1988

MOORE, William and BAERLITZ, Charles, *The Roswell Incident*, Grafton, 1980

MOULTON HOWE, Linda, 'Animal Mutilation Up-Date', in *Enigmas*, May/June 1993

PAGE, Thornton and SAGAN, Carl (eds), *UFOs: A Scientific Debate*, Cornell, 1972

RANDLE, Kevin and SCHMITT, Don, *UFO Crash at Roswell*, Avon, 1992

RANDLES, Jenny, *Alien Abduction*, Inner Light, 1989

RANDLES, Jenny, *Aliens: The Real Story*, Hale, 1993

RANDLES, Jenny, *From Out of the Blue*, Berkeley, 1993

RANDLES, Jenny and FULLER, Paul, *Crop Circles: A Mystery Solved*, Hale, 1990 (updated 1993)

RANDLES, Jenny and HOUGH, Peter, *Death by Supernatural Causes?*, Grafton, 1988

RANDLES, Jenny and HOUGH, Peter, *Scary Stories*, Futura, 1991

RANDLES, Jenny and HOUGH, Peter, *Encyclopedia of the Unexplained*, Michael O'Mara, 1994

RING, Kenneth, *The Omega Project*, Morrow, 1992

ROBERTS, Anthony and GILBERTSON, Geoff, *The Dark Gods*, Rider, 1980

RUPPELT, Edward, *The Report on UFOs*, Ace, 1956

SACHS, Margaret, *The UFO Encyclopedia*, Corgi, 1981

SAUNDERS, David and HARKINS, Roger, *UFOs? Yes!*, World, 1968

SCHNABEL, Jim, *Round in Circles*, Hutchinson, 1993 and *Dark White*, Hamish Hamilton, 1994

STEIGER, Brad (ed.), *Project Blue Book*, Bantam, 1978

STRIEBER, Whitley, *Communion*, Moraw, 1987

STORY, Ronald D. (ed.), *The Encyclopedia of UFOs*, New English Library, 1980

VALLÉE, Jacques, *Anatomy of a Phenomenon*, Regnery, 1965

VALLÉE, Jacques, *Passport to Magonia*, Neville Spearman, 1970

WALTERS, Ed and Frances, *The Gulf Breeze Sightings*, Bantam, 1990

Recommended publications and research groups

AFU, Box 11027 600, 11 Norrkoping, 11 Sweden

Association for the Scientific Study of Anomalous Phenomena (ASSAP), Hugh Pincott, ASSAP Secretary, 20 Paul Street, Frome, Somerset BA11 1DX

Aura-Z, PO Box 224, Moscow 117463, Russia

Bulletin of Anomalous Experience, 2 St Clair Ave West, Suite 607, Toronto, Canada M4V 1L5

Crop Watcher, 3 Selborne Court, Tavistock Close, Romsey, SO51 7TY

J. Allen Hynek Center for UFO Studies, 2457 West Peterson Ave, Chicago, Illinois 60659, USA

Enigmas (Scotland), 41 The Braes, Tullibody, Clackmannanshire, FK10 2TT

Fate, PO Box 1940, 170 Future Way, Marion, Ohio 43305, USA

Flying Saucer Review, Snodland, Kent ME6 5HJ

Northern UFO News, 37 Heathbank Road, Stockport, Cheshire, SK3 0UP

OVNI Presence, BP 324, Aix-en-Provence, Cedex 1, France

UFO Afrinews, PO Box MP 49, Mount Pleasant, Harare, Zimbabwe

UFO Research Australia, PO Box 2435, Cairns, QLD 4970, Australia

UFO Call is a news and information service provided by British Telecom and BUFORA. Available in Britain only, at information line rates, it is presently written and recorded weekly by Jenny Randles and available on 0891-121886

In June 1994 a group of British ufologists combined to produce a pioneering high quality journal, *The New Ufologist*. Unique in the UFO world this is independent of all groups and non-profit making. It will put any money raised back into a newly created research fund and at regular open gatherings will invite proposals from anyone with an important case needing scientific study or an interesting research scheme waiting to be carried out. A majority vote of those present will distribute funding to any proposals thought to contribute new knowledge to the subject.

The New Ufologist, 71 Knight Avenue, Canterbury, Kent CT2 8PY

Readers who wish to report any UFO encounter (in confidence if preferred) can contact the authors. They will, upon request, put the witness in touch with a reliable local investigator. Write to: 37 Heathbank Road, Stockport, Cheshire SK3 0UP

Please include SAEs or International Reply Coupons when writing to any of the above addresses.

INDEX